GEO

Buddy BOOKS
Prehistoric Animals

Giant Ground Sloth

ABDO
Publishing Company

A Buddy Book
by
Michael P. Goecke

VISIT US AT

www.abdopub.com

Published by Buddy Books, an imprint of ABDO Publishing Company, 4940 Viking Drive, Edina, Minnesota 55435. Copyright © 2003 by Abdo Consulting Group, Inc. International copyrights reserved in all countries. No part of this book may be reproduced in any form without written permission from the publisher.

Printed in the United States.

Edited by: Christy DeVillier
Contributing Editor: Matt Ray
Graphic Design: Deborah Coldiron
Image Research: Deborah Coldiron
Illustrations: Deborah Coldiron, Denise Esner
Photographs: Digital Stock, Eyewire Inc., Fotosearch, Getty Images, Hulton Archives, Steve McHugh

Library of Congress Cataloging-in-Publication Data

Goecke, Michael P., 1968-
    Giant ground sloth / Michael P. Goecke.
       p. cm. — (Prehistoric animals Set I)
    Includes index.
    Contents: Prehistoric animals — Giant sloth — What did it look like? — Giant claws — Armor — When did it live and where? — Tree sloth — Jefferson sloth — How did it disappear?
    ISBN 1-57765-968-6
    1. Megatherium—Juvenile literature. [1. Megatherium. 2. Sloths, Fossil. 3. Ground sloths. 4. Prehistoric animals. 5. Paleontology.] I. Title.

QE882.E2 G64 2003
569'.31—dc21

                                                          2002028198

Table of Contents

Prehistoric Animals

Scientists called paleontologists study fossils. Fossils help them understand what prehistoric animals were like. Prehistoric animals lived more than 5,500 years ago. Some of them were dinosaurs, saber-toothed cats, and short-faced bears.

Prehistoric Animals

5

The Giant Ground Sloth

Megatherium
(meg-uh-THEER-ree-um)

The *Megatherium* was a prehistoric ground sloth. Paleontologists believe it was the biggest sloth that ever lived. "*Megatherium*" means giant beast.

The first *Megatherium* fossil was found in Brazil in 1789. Scientist Richard Owen named the *Megatherium* in 1856. Another name for the *Megatherium* is giant ground sloth.

Sir Richard Owen

What It Looked Like

Giant ground sloths grew to become as big as elephants. Adults grew as long as 20 feet (6 m). They weighed about 7,000 pounds (3,175 kg).

The Giant Ground Sloth's Size

Giant Ground Sloth

Elephant

The giant ground sloth was a big animal.

The giant ground sloth looked a bit like a bear. It had dark brown, shaggy hair. It had a big tail and thick back legs. Its front legs were smaller.

9

The giant ground sloth had three curved claws on each foot. The front claws could grow as long as 12 inches (30 cm).

A fossil of the giant ground sloth's claw.

Tree Sloths

Today's tree sloths are related to the giant ground sloth. But tree sloths are much smaller. They live in trees and eat leaves. They move slowly and sleep a lot. Tree sloths live in Brazil, Peru, and Argentina.

This tree sloth is related to the giant ground sloth.

How It Lived

Unlike tree sloths, the giant ground sloth lived on the ground. It ate leaves, fruits, and roots. It could pull down tree leaves with its big claws.

Some scientists believe the giant ground sloth ate meat, too. It may have been a scavenger. Scavengers eat dead animals that they did not kill.

Today's vultures (top) and hyenas (bottom) are scavengers.

13

Paleontologists know how giant ground sloths walked from studying their footprints. These footprints are fossils. These fossils show that giant ground sloths mostly walked on their back feet. But they did not walk with their feet flat on the ground. They walked on the sides of their back feet.

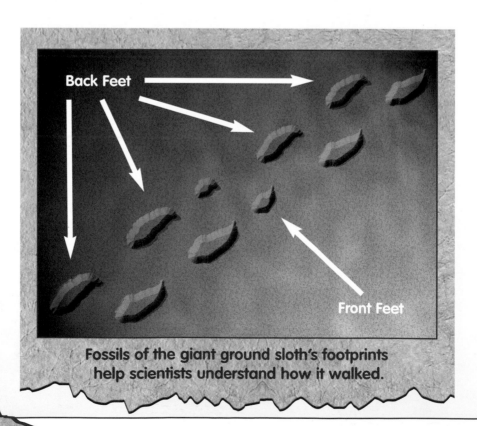

Fossils of the giant ground sloth's footprints help scientists understand how it walked.

Giant ground sloths mostly walked on the sides
of their back feet.

15

Meat-eating predators lived among the giant ground sloths. There were saber-toothed cats and short-faced bears. The giant ground sloth could fight these predators with its big claws.

The giant ground sloth had big claws to fight off predators.

Saber-toothed cats were deadly predators.

Dermal ossicles also helped the giant ground sloth against predators. They were pebble-like bones under the giant ground sloth's skin. Dermal ossicles made it hard for animals to hurt the giant ground sloth.

Today's starfish (top) and tortoises (bottom) have dermal ossicles.

Giant Ground Sloth's World

The giant ground sloths lived in North America and South America. They were around for millions of years.

A Geologic Timeline
248 Million Years Ago – Today

Triassic 248 – 213 Million Years Ago	Jurassic 213 – 145 Million Years Ago	Cretaceous 145 – 65 Million Years Ago	Paleocene 65 – 56 Million Years Ago	Eocene 56 – 34 Million Years Ago	Oligocene 34 – 24 Million Years Ago	Miocene 24 – 5 Million Years Ago	Pliocene 5 – 2 Million Years Ago	Pleistocene 2 Million – 11,500 Years Ago	Holocene 11,500 Years Ago – Today

Age Of Dinosaurs
248 – 65 Million Years Ago

Age Of Mammals
65 Million Years Ago – Today

Giant ground sloths lived between 30 million and 8,000 years ago.

The giant ground sloths lived during the last Ice Age. The Ice Age happened during a period of time called the Pleistocene. The Pleistocene began about two million years ago. It ended about 11,500 years ago.

During the Ice Age, the world cooled. Giant sheets of ice covered many lands.

The Pleistocene Ice Age

Ice covered parts of the world during the Ice Age.

Giant apes (left) and woolly mammoths (right) lived during the Pleistocene Ice Age.

Many other big animals lived during the Ice Age. There were giant armadillos, apes, bears, mammoths, and deer. Many of them died out around the end of the Ice Age. No one is sure why this happened.

Maybe illness killed the giant ground sloth and other Ice Age animals. Maybe they died from a great climate change. Did early humans have something to do with it? Paleontologists are working to uncover this great mystery.

There are many unanswered questions about the prehistoric world and its exciting animals.

Important Words

climate the weather of a place over time.

fossil remains of very old animals and plants commonly found in the ground. A fossil can be a bone, a footprint, or any trace of life.

Ice Age a period in Earth's history when ice covered parts of the world. The last Ice Age ended about 11,500 years ago.

paleontologist a scientist that studies prehistoric plants and animals. Paleontologists often study fossils.

predator an animal that hunts and eats other animals.

prehistoric describes anything that was around more than 5,500 years ago.

Web Sites

To learn more about the giant ground sloth, visit ABDO Publishing Company on the World Wide Web. Web sites about the giant ground sloth are featured on our Book Links page. These links are routinely monitored and updated to provide the most current information available.

www.abdopub.com

23

Index

Ronald A. Anderson · 4th Edition

Professor of Law and Government
    Drexel University
Member of the Pennsylvania and Philadelphia Bars
Coauthor of Business Law
Author of Anderson on the Uniform Commercial Code
        Business Law Principles and Cases
        Government and Business
        Social Forces and the Law
        Anderson's Pennsylvania Civil Practice
        Purdon's Pennsylvania Forms
        Couch's Cyclopedia of Insurance Law
        Insurer's Tort Law
        Hotelman's Basic Law
        Running a Professional Corporation
Consulting Editor of the Pennsylvania Law Encyclopedia

GOVERNMENT AND BUSINESS

Published by

H57   **SOUTH-WESTERN PUBLISHING CO.**

CINCINNATI   WEST CHICAGO, ILL.   DALLAS   PELHAM MANOR, N.Y.   PALO ALTO, CALIF.

Library of Congress Catalog Card Number: 79-67672

ISBN: 0-538-08570-3

2 3 4 5 6 7 D 6 5 4 3 2 1

Printed in the United States of America

PREFACE

A little more than two centuries ago, a shot was fired that the poet says was heard round the world. That shot was to bring us, the American people, political independence and democracy. Democracy today and in the approaching century faces problems unheard of in 1776 which have arisen because we, the people, are today a large industrialized nation. What is the role of government in modern democratic America? For almost a century the answer of the people has been that government must increasingly take part in the economic life of the country by regulating business.

There is every indication that this trend will continue. An understanding of government regulation of business is therefore of lasting importance. Government regulation of business will affect our America and our future the rest of our lives.

This fourth edition has been written not only to update the third edition and add recent cases but also to place greater emphasis on the patterns or currents which are not readily apparent to the beginning student. There are so many trees, it is very difficult to see the forest. Yet the forest is that which endures and which the students must perceive in order to play an intelligent part as citizens, business people, and leaders in a democracy.

Since the subject of government regulation of business raises the question of "which government" as well as "what business," the first part of the book is devoted to a summary of the distribution of powers within our multi-unit system of government. The second part of the book deals with constitutional limitations that restrict government in regulating business. The third part then treats specifically the different powers of the governments and the regulations that have been imposed under their authority. The fourth part of the book deals with the actual problems of administration. The success or the failure of government regulation of business may depend to a very large degree on the powers and the abilities of the administrators who make or apply the regulations.

Both the textbook method and the casebook method of presentation have been employed, the nature of the material determining in each instance which method would be followed. Source materials have been liberally edited and correlated so as to stress the fundamental principles and problems.

A number of significant decisions have been rendered by the United States Supreme Court since the appearance of the third edition. This growth of the law accounts for the addition of 22 opinions of that court.

As to physical arrangement, each chapter of the book is divided into numbered sections. These sections are themselves subdivided under lettered headings calling attention to the particular topic and opinion which are there set forth.

The table of contents for the entire book includes the full titles of all sections, as well as the chapter titles. The table of cases includes not only the opinions set forth in the book but also the more important cases cited in the text or footnotes.

Because of its great importance, a new Chapter 7 on the constitutional protection of the rights of the person has been added. In the interest of simplifying the subject for the student, formerly separate chapters on the taxing, borrowing, spending, and currency powers have been combined into Chapter 16, The Financial Powers. With the same objective, the chapters on limitations on review of administrative action and the scope of review of such action have been combined into a new Chapter 23.

The questions at the end of each chapter are arranged in order of ascending difficulty. It will be noted that to give a complete answer to the questions of one chapter, it may be necessary to apply principles learned in an earlier chapter. This is intentionally designed to impress upon the student the continuity of principles and to increase the appreciation for what may be called the great common denominators that run through many of the problems of government.

It will also be noted that while some questions may be answered directly from the text and cases, other questions have no answer. They are truly questions for discussion. It is the hope that such questions will challenge the minds of the students to face and solve the many problems of government for which society has not yet found any satisfactory answer.

As one reads the book, the political platforms of many parties both past and present come to mind. This resemblance is not purely accidental, for the greater part of the regulations and the problems discussed either were or still are matters of political controversy. This book, however, has not been written with the view or hope of persuading the reader. Its only goal has been an understandable presentation of the problems that confront society when government regulates business.

Ronald A. Anderson

CONTENTS

PART I   THE FEDERAL SYSTEM

PART II   CONSTITUTIONAL LIMITATIONS

PART IV   ADMINISTRATION

INDEX OF CASES

Government in some form is as old as the history of the human race. The Constitution of the United States establishes what is known as a federal system by which power is divided between a national government and the governments of the states.

1

The New Constitution and the Division of Power

§ 1:1. THE NEW CONSTITUTION

The historians tell us that there was a revolution in 1776 and that the Constitution of the United States was adopted in 1789. This is only partly correct for, without the firing of a single shot, another revolution took place in the middle third of this century. To give it a date, we can say 1937. And out of that revolution there emerged a new Constitution. Structurally it was still the original Constitution of 1789, but decisions of the Supreme Court have interpreted that 1789 Constitution in such a way that it is more accurate to say that we now have a new Constitution.

In reading this comment, it is not to be thought that the Supreme Court in effect single-handedly changed "the good old Constitution." For the most part, the changes made by the Supreme Court merely reflected the will of "We, the people."[1] Thus it can be said that the Supreme Court merely saved the country the time and expense of going through the formal constitution-amending processes by making amendments which the country would have undoubtedly made.

How and why did all this happen? It was merely the social and economic pressure of the times. No foreign ideology captured the minds of the American people. No foreign soldier landed on our shores. Merely the endless pounding

---

[1]The preamble of the Constitution declares that it is adopted by "We, the people of the United States."

of new social demands led to Constitutional changes. The people wanted more from the government and gradually those demands changed the Constitution. For the convenience of study, we view separately history, economics, political science, constitutional law, and all the other disciplines. But when we finish our studies, we must recognize that all these disciplines are but one. They are merely the many faces of the same thing. They are the many faces of life. In the realism of life, each discipline is intertwined with and interacts with the others. It was this combined interaction which produced the demand and the pressure for change—first in 1776, and then again in 1932.

Painting the scene with broad strokes, we start in 1776 with some 3.5 million people in 13 basically agrarian and highly self-sufficient colonies, soon to be states, straggling along the Atlantic seaboard. In the course of the next century, these people are to move westward to the Pacific. In 1912, Arizona and New Mexico are admitted to the United States as the last states of continental America. Modern machine industrialization had already begun, but the new era really dates from the development of the Ford assembly line in the middle of the second decade of this century. From that time on, problems of industrialization and population growth faced society and caused popular views and attitudes to change. "We the people" of 1937 and of today are not the same "people" as of 1789. We are now over 220 million. Moreover, World War I, the depression of the 30's, World War II, problems of world leadership, Korea, and Vietnam have all made a deep imprint upon our political and economic concepts and objectives.

Just as a navigator must bear in mind the winds and the currents, we, in studying the Constitution, must bear in mind the changing winds and currents in our political and economic beliefs. These changes have taken the letter of the Constitution of 1789 and changed that Constitution into what is basically a new Constitution. It is this new Constitution under which we live. It is important that we see and understand this living Constitution of today.

§ 1:2. CHARACTERISTICS OF THE NEW CONSTITUTION

The new Constitution of today is a radical change from the Constitution of 1789 in many ways. In the following chapters we will see the following significant aspects of the new Constitution:

(a) *Strong government.* The characteristic feature of the new Constitution is strong government. The concept of Adam Smith, of *laissez faire,* of a "hands off" policy of government, has been largely forgotten. While freedom of the individual as a human being has expanded, as will be noted under subheading (d), business enterprises can be regulated and the economy controlled.

(b) *Eclipse of the states.* Under the new Constitution, all governments have powers which they never possessed before, but the center of gravity has shifted from the states to the nation. When the Constitution was adopted in 1789, the federal government was to have only the very limited powers specified in Article I, Sec. 8, of the Constitution. What regulation of business was permissible was to be imposed by the states. Today, the great bulk of the regulation of business is adopted by the federal government through the Congress or its administrative agencies. As the American economy moved from the local community stage to the nationwide stage, the individual states were obviously unable to regulate, so that it was inevitable that regulation would be drawn to the central government. Consequently, when we speak of government regulation of business, we ordinarily mean the national government, not the state or local governments.

(c) *Administrative agencies.* These were virtually unheard of in 1789 and no mention is made of them in the Constitution of 1789. The vast powers of the new Constitution are exercised to a very large degree by administrative agencies. They are in effect a fourth branch of the government not provided for in the written Constitution. More importantly, for the vast majority of people it is the administrative agencies which come in contact with the business person and the citizen. The agencies are the "government" for most people.

In other words, the vast power of government to regulate business is not exercised directly by the branches of government that are most familiar to us; namely, the legislatures, the courts, and the executive officers. But rather, this power is exercised by persons or agencies known as administrators. They are not elected by the voters and their decisions are to a large degree not subject to effective review or reversal by the courts.

(d) *Human rights.* The scope of human rights protected from governments has dramatically broadened. These rights are protected not merely from invasion by the federal government, but by any government. Most significant of all, "unwritten" rights are protected although not guaranteed by any express constitutional provision.

It is important to everyone to understand what has happened and what is likely to happen in the future. With respect to the future, as long as science brings forth ever-continuing technological changes, and socioeconomic problems continue to rise, the only conclusion which appears reasonable is that in the minds of the voters the need for governmental action will continue to increase, and that, correspondingly, the powers of government, and above all, those of the federal government, will continue to expand and government will increasingly regulate business.

The study of the past evolution of the Constitution will serve us as a guide to understand the present and to foresee, even if dimly, the future, and to appreciate the problems that are involved. As people working in a business world, it is essential that we have this understanding. As citizens living and voting in an organized democratic society, it is our duty to ourselves and our nation to understand these problems so that we can take an intelligent part in their solution.

With this general survey of the rise of the new Constitution, we will turn to a consideration of the document we know as the Constitution of 1789 with particular reference to government regulation of business.

§ 1:3. THE NATIONAL POWERS

(a) The problem

Regulation of business in the United States always raises a legal or a constitutional question. Because our American governmental system is based upon written constitutions, every government, whether national, state, or local, finds that its power to regulate business, as well as to take any other action, is restricted in some way by either the national constitution or a state constitution, or by both.

This problem does not arise in an unlimited monarchy in which there is no restraint on governmental power. In such a monarchy the power to regulate business exists without any limitation, and the only question that faces the sovereign is whether there should be such regulation and how it should be enforced. The ruler is concerned only with questions of policy and plan.

In contrast with this, the regulation of business in the United States raises the preliminary question of whether the governing body has the authority, under the applicable constitutional provisions, to make the regulation at all. It is therefore a threefold problem of power, policy, and plan. It is to the questions of power and of plan that the present book is directed. The question of policy is only incidentally raised, as such a question involves underlying problems of economics, sociology, and political expediency.

(b) The historical background

Turning to consideration of the question of power, its analysis in the United States is made more complicated by the fact that power is divided among different governments. Even the statement that power is divided is not strictly accurate, for some powers are shared by different governmental bodies. Examination of the historical development of our governmental system will explain this.

The states that formed the United States in 1789 had come into being as colonies of England. By the long war of the Revolution, they obtained their independence; but, even before the formal declaration of that war, the colonies regarded themselves as independent. Pursuant to the call of the Continental Congress of May 15, 1776, the colonies drew up state constitutions, many of which were merely adaptations of their colonial charters.

These revolutionary state constitutions must be kept in mind because they and the succeeding state constitutions remained in the picture of governmental power from those days on. The effect or the purpose of a state constitution was to prescribe the structure and the power of the state government and to set forth the limitations of that power. In addition, such state constitutions, or later state constitutions adopted in their place, set forth the powers of the political subdivisions of states (towns, cities, boroughs, and counties) or merely authorized the legislatures to pass laws to specify the powers and the structure of such political subdivisions. On top of this pattern of state constitutions and state laws, all prescribing the powers and the structure of state and local governments, is added the national constitution.

The first national written constitution was the Articles of Confederation, which came into effect in 1781 and remained until displaced by the present Constitution of the United States in 1789. The central government under the Confederation was in substance a league or group to which the ex-colonies belonged but by which they could not be controlled. Differences between the states led to clashes on questions of boundaries and commerce. These became so numerous that finally a series of meetings was called to endeavor to remedy this evil.

The third of these meetings was the Philadelphia Convention, which, although officially called "to take into consideration the situation of the United States, to devise such further powers as shall appear to them necessary to render the Constitution of the federal government adequate to the exigencies of the union," soon turned its attention to drafting an entirely new constitution. This new constitution, which is the one by which we are now governed, specifies the structure and the power of the national government and contains limitations on the powers of both national, state, and local governments.

The effect of the adoption of the national constitution was to take certain powers away from the states and to give them to the national government. Thus the power to wage war was exclusively given to the national government. Other powers given to the national government could be exercised concurrently by the states. For instance, the power to tax granted to the federal government did not destroy the state power to tax, even though both governments were to tax the same subject or base. In addition, some powers may be exercised by the states only so long as they are not exercised by the national government. Thus state safety appliance laws may apply until a federal law on the subject is adopted. Other powers are denied to all governments, such as the passage of ex post facto laws making criminal an act already committed that was not criminal when committed or increasing the penalty for an act already committed above the penalty in force at the time it was committed.

(c) Delegation of powers

Speaking generally, we are concerned with three types of government: the government of the United States, the government of the states, and the government of the political subdivisions of the states. By the term "political subdivision" is meant any county, city, borough, township, or district that is created by a state. The national government may exercise only those powers expressly enumerated in the Constitution as being delegated to it and such powers as may be construed as reasonably necessary and proper to carry into execution the expressly granted powers. The power of the national government is based upon the power of the President and the Senate to execute treaties, of the executive to conduct foreign relations generally, and of Congress to exercise the following powers expressly enumerated in Article 1, Section 8, of the Constitution:

The Congress shall have Power To lay and collect Taxes, Duties, Imposts and Excises, to pay the Debts and provide for the common Defence and general Welfare of the United States; but all Duties, Imposts and Excises shall be uniform throughout the United States;

To borrow money on the credit of the United States;

To regulate Commerce with foreign Nations, and among the several States, and with the Indian Tribes;

To establish an uniform Rule of Naturalization, and uniform Laws on the subject of Bankruptcies throughout the United States;

To coin Money, regulate the Value thereof, and of foreign Coin, and fix the Standard of Weights and Measures;

To provide for the Punishment of counterfeiting the Securities and current Coin of the United States;

To establish Post Offices and post Roads;

To promote the Progress of Science and useful Arts, by securing for limited Times to Authors and Inventors the exclusive Right to their respective Writings and Discoveries;

To constitute Tribunals inferior to the supreme Court;

To define and punish Piracies and Felonies committed on the high Seas, and Offenses against the Law of Nations;

To declare War, grant Letters of Marque and Reprisal, and make Rules concerning Captures on Land and Water;

To raise and support Armies, but no Appropriation of Money to that Use shall be for a longer Term than two Years;

To provide and maintain a Navy;

To make Rules for the Government and Regulation of the land and naval Forces;

To provide for calling forth the Militia to execute the Laws of the Union, suppress Insurrections and repel Invasions;

To provide for organizing, arming, and disciplining the Militia, and for governing such Part of them as may be employed in the Service of the United States, reserving to the States respectively, the Appointment of the Officers, and the Authority of training the Militia according to the discipline prescribed by Congress;

To exercise exclusive Legislation in all Cases whatsoever, over such District (not exceeding ten Miles square) as may, by Cession of particular States, and the acceptance of Congress, become the Seat of the Government of the United States, and to exercise like Authority over all Places purchased by the Consent of the Legislature of the State in which the Same shall be, for the Erection of Forts, Magazines, Arsenals, dock-Yards, and other needful Buildings;—And

To make all Laws which shall be necessary and proper for carrying into Execution the foregoing Powers, and all other Powers vested by this Constitution in the Government of the United States, or in any Department or Officer thereof.

In reading this list of powers, one is inevitably impressed by the absence of any provision respecting many matters that are today the subject of federal regulation. To a large extent this book is the story of the expansion of Article 1, Section 8, into the Constitution of today.

§ 1:4. STATE POWERS

For the moment, we will look at the reserved powers of the states which were protected by the Constitution of 1789. At the same time we must not forget that this balance of power has been modified as the new Constitution evolved.

All powers not delegated to the Congress of the United States nor prohibited are expressly reserved to the states by the Tenth Amendment. This provision merely confirmed the fact that the states had only surrendered to the national government those powers expressly delegated by the Constitution. Among the powers thus retained by the states is the police power, the power to tax, the power to take private property by eminent domain, and the power to own and operate businesses. Of these four powers, the police power confers the broadest ability to control business. The police power is in a general sense the power or right to govern. It is defined as the power of a state to enact laws for the public health, safety, morals, and general welfare.

§ 1:5. FEDERAL LIMITATIONS ON STATE POWERS

Because the American system is a federal system in which powers are distributed to and shared by the different governments, there are certain limitations which bar or prohibit the states from exercising a power which a state would ordinarily possess.

(a) Constitutional prohibitions

The Constitution contains a number of express prohibitions which bar a state from acting. For example, a state may not issue currency, make treaties, or wage war. In addition to the express prohibitions in the Constitution, additional prohibitions designed to protect people have been read into the Constitution by the Supreme Court as discussed in Chapter 7.

(b) Federal supremacy

Some powers of governing may be exercised by either the state or the federal government. When the federal government acts, such action excludes action by a state. To illustrate, both the state and national governments can regulate the labels on goods purchased by consumers. If the federal government requires that the label state the net weight in both the English and the metric systems, a state law could not contradict this command and declare that a label is not required to state the metric weight.

This supremacy of the federal Constitution over the state provision is expressly directed by what is known as the Supremacy Clause of the Constitution. This is Article VI, Cl. 2, and declares:

> This Constitution, and the Laws of the United States which shall be made in Pursuance thereof; and all Treaties made, or which shall be made, under the Authority of the United States, shall be the supreme Law of the Land; and the Judges in every State shall be bound thereby, any Thing in the Constitution or Laws of any State to the Contrary notwithstanding.

(c) Federal preemption

Under the concept of federal supremacy, it has just been seen that when there is a direct conflict between state and federal law, the state law must give way. What conclusion is reached when there is no direct conflict? For example, assume a federal law stating that goods shall bear labels that show the net weight. If the federal law stops there, can a state then proceed further and specify that the weight may be stated only in the English system?

This raises the question of (1) whether the federal government intended to leave the door open for such supplementing state legislation, or (2) whether once the federal law required "labels," Congress intended that neither the federal law nor the state law should add any additional requirements. If the latter alternative is adopted, it is said that the federal law has *preempted* the field. In ordinary words, once the federal government moves in, a "keep out" sign goes up against state action.

This concept of preemption has great importance in the federal-state relationship because there is no such thing as a last word in drafting a statute. Something more may always be added or new situations may arise which suggest additions. If the federal law preempts the field, the states cannot supply the missing provisions. If the federal law has not preempted the field, the states can supplement the federal law and correct the situation.

(d) Silence of Congress

When a power may be exercised by both state and federal governments, does the failure of the Congress to adopt a law permit the states to proceed to exercise their power? In some instances, the silence of Congress is regarded as permission for the states to proceed to exercise their powers as they choose. In other situations, the silence of Congress is regarded as showing the intent of Congress that neither it nor anyone else should regulate the subject. In such cases the silence of Congress bars the states from exercising their powers, just as though Congress had adopted a policy declaration stating: "No laws shall be passed on the following subject." The silence of Congress concept will be discussed at greater length in Chapter 9 of this book, relating to the effect of the commerce power upon states.

(e) What constitutes federal law

In the foregoing, reference is made to "federal law" as contrasted to state law. The term "federal law" is a broad term and embraces anything which governs conduct by virtue of federal authority. It is therefore not limited to statutes adopted by Congress but includes treaties of the United States, executive proclamations issued by the President of the United States, and regulations of the many federal administrative agencies. In a situation in which the federal law is supreme, everything resting on state authority must give way. For example, a provision in a state constitution which regulated transportation was invalidated by a regulation of the Federal Interstate Commerce Commission which conflicted with the terms of the state constitution.

§ 1:6. FEDERAL PREEMPTION AS TO PHYSICAL MATTERS

The concept of federal preemption is easier to apply when the matters which are regulated are physical things, processes, or machines.

BURBANK v LOCKHEED AIR TERMINAL, INC.

411 US 624 (1973)

The City of Burbank, California, adopted an ordinance prohibiting the nighttime takeoffs of jet aircraft between 10 P.M. and 7 A.M. Lockheed Air Terminal owned and operated the Hollywood-Burbank Airport. It sued Burbank to prevent the enforcement of the ordinance.

OPINION BY DOUGLAS, J.

. . . The Federal Aviation Act of 1958, as amended by the Noise Control Act . . . and the regulations under it, . . . provides in part, "The United States of America is declared to possess and exercise complete and exclusive national sovereignty in the airspace of the United States . . ." By § 1348 the Administrator of the Federal Aeronautics Act (FAA) has been given broad authority to regulate the use of the navigable airspace, "in order to insure the safety of aircraft and the efficient utilization of such airspace. . . ." and for the protection of persons and property on the ground. . ."

. . . The District Court found: "The imposition of curfew ordinances on a nationwide basis would result in a bunching of flights in those hours immediately preceding the curfew. This bunching of flights during these hours would have the twofold effect of increasing an already serious congestion problem and actually increasing, rather than relieving, the noise problem by increasing flights in the period of greatest annoyance to surrounding communities. Such a result is totally inconsistent with the objectives of the federal statutory and regulatory scheme." It also found "the imposition of curfew ordinances on a nationwide basis would cause a serious loss of efficiency in the use of the navigable air-space." . . .

The Noise Control Act of 1972, . . . amending § 611 of the Federal Aviation Act, also involves the Environmental Protection Agency (EPA) in the comprehensive scheme of federal control of the aircraft noise problem. Under the amended § 611(b)(1) the FAA, after consulting with EPA, shall provide "for the control and abatement of aircraft noise and sonic boom, including the application of such standards and regulations in the issuance, amendment, modification, suspension or revocation of any certificate authorized by this title." Section 611(b)(2) as amended provides that future certificates for aircraft operations shall not issue unless the new aircraft noise requirements are met. . . .

. . . The pervasive nature of the scheme of federal regulation of aircraft noise . . . leads us to conclude that there is pre-emption. . . . "Federal control is intensive and exclusive. Planes do not wander about in the sky like vagrant clouds. They move only by federal permission, subject to federal inspection, in the hands of federally certified personnel and under an intricate system of federal command. The moment a ship taxis onto a runway it is caught up in an elaborate and detailed system of controls." . . .

. . . Control of noise is of course deepseated in the police power of the States. Yet the pervasive control vested in EPA and in FAA under the 1972 Act seems to us to leave no room for local curfews or other local controls. . . . The ultimate remedy for aircraft noise which plagues many communities and tens of thousands of people is not known. The procedures under the 1972 Act are under way. In addition, the Administrator has imposed a variety of regulations relating to takeoff and landing procedures and runway preferences. The Federal Aviation Act requires a delicate balance between safety and efficiency . . . and the protection of persons on the ground. . . . Any regulations adopted by the Administrator to control noise pollution must be consistent with the "highest degree of safety." . . . The interdependence of these factors requires a uniform and exclusive system of federal regulation if the congressional objectives underlying the Federal Aviation Act are to be fulfilled.

If we were to uphold the Burbank ordinance and a significant number of municipalities followed suit, it is obvious that fractionalized control of the timing of take-offs and landings would severely limit the flexibility of the FAA in controlling air traffic flow. The difficulties of scheduling flights to avoid congestion and the concomitant decrease in safety would be compounded. In 1960 the FAA rejected a proposed restriction on jet operations at the Los Angeles airport between 10 P.M. and 7 A.M. because such restrictions could "create critically serious problems to all air transportation patterns." . . . The complete FAA statement said: "The proposed restriction on the use of the airport by jet aircraft between the hours of 10 P.M. and 7 A.M. under certain surface wind conditions has also been reevaluated and this provision has been omitted from the rule. The practice of prohibiting the use of various airports during certain specific hours could create critically serious problems to all air transportation patterns. The network of airports throughout the United States and the constant availability of these airports are essential to the maintenance of a sound air transportation system. The continuing growth of public acceptance of aviation as a major force in passenger transportation and the increasingly significant role of commercial aviation in the nation's economy are accomplishments which cannot be inhibited if the best interest of the public is to be served. It was concluded therefore that the extent of relief from the noise problem which this provision must have achieved would not have compensated the degree of restriction it would have imposed on domestic and foreign Air Commerce."

This decision, announced in 1960, remains peculiarly within the competence of the FAA, supplemented now by the input of the EPA. We are not at liberty to diffuse the powers given by Congress to FAA and EPA by letting the States or municipalities in on the planning. If that change is to be made, Congress alone must do it.

[Enforcement of ordinance enjoined]

---

§ 1:7. FEDERAL PREEMPTION AS TO ECONOMIC MATTERS

There are no limits to the doctrine of federal preemption in terms of the subject matter. Consequently, when the federal government has adopted a particular policy for the purpose of advancing the social or economic welfare, state action is excluded by the federal preemption of the field.

MACHINISTS v WISCONSIN EMPLOYMENT RELATIONS COMMISSION

427 US 132 (1976)

The federal law requires that an employer bargain collectively with the representatives of employees in negotiating terms of employment. The federal law makes no provision as to how the parties should conduct themselves while the collective bargaining is going on. The employees of Kearney & Trecker Corp. were members of Local 76 of the Machinists Union. While the union and employer were negotiating a new contract, the employees refused to work any overtime. The employer obtained an order from the Wisconsin Employment Relations Commission directing the employees to stop refusing to work overtime. This was affirmed by the state courts on the ground that the refusal to work overtime was intended as coercion and was therefore an unfair labor practice under the state law. The union petitioned for review by the United States Supreme Court.

OPINION BY BRENNAN, J.

The question to be decided in this case is whether federal labor policy preempts the authority of a state labor relations board to grant an employer covered by the National Labor Relations Act an order enjoining a union and its members from continuing to refuse to work overtime pursuant to a union policy to put economic pressure on the employer in negotiations for renewal of an expired collective-bargaining agreement. . . .

The national . . . Act . . . leaves much to the states, though Congress has refrained from telling us how much. We must spell out from conflicting indications of congressional will the area in which state action is still permissible. . . . Federal labor policy as reflected in the National Labor Relations Act, as amended, has been construed not to preclude the States from regulating aspects of labor relations that involve "conduct touch[ing] interests so deeply rooted in local feeling and responsibility that . . . we could not infer that Congress had deprived the States of the power to act." Policing of actual or threatened violence to persons or destruction of property has been held most clearly a matter for the States. . . .

. . . A . . . line of preemption analysis has been developed in cases focusing upon the crucial inquiry whether Congress intended that the conduct involved be unregulated because left "to be controlled by the free play of economic forces." . . .

Insurance Agents, [*NLRB v Insurance Agents International Union,* 361 US 477 (1960)], involved a charge of a refusal by the union to bargain in good faith in violation of § 8(b)(3) of the Act. The charge was based on union activities that occurred during good-faith bargaining over the terms of a collective-bargaining agreement. During the negotiations, the union directed concerted on-the-job activities by its members of a harassing nature designed to interfere with the conduct of the employer's business, for the avowed purpose of putting economic pressure on the employer to accede to the union's bargaining demands. The harassing activities [were] all peaceful. . . . We held that such tactics would not support a finding by the NLRB that the union had failed to bargain in good faith as required by § 8(b)(3) and rejected the per se rule applied by the Board that use of "economically harassing activities" alone sufficed to prove a violation of that section. . . . We noted further that "Congress has been rather specific when it has come to outlaw particular economic weapons on the part of unions" and "the activities here involved have never been specifically outlawed by Congress." . . . Accordingly, the Board's claim "to power . . . to distinguish among various economic pressure tactics and brand [some as] inconsistent with good-faith collective bargaining," . . . was simply inconsistent with the design of the federal scheme in which "the use of economic pressure by the parties to a labor dispute is . . . part and parcel of the process of collective bargaining." . . .

The Court had earlier recognized in preemption cases that Congress meant to leave some activities unregulated and to be controlled by the free play of economic forces. . . .

There is simply no question that the Act's processes would be frustrated in the instant case were the State's ruling permitted to stand. The employer in this case invoked the Wisconsin law because it was unable to overcome the union tactic with its own economic self-help means. Although it did employ economic weapons putting pressure on the union when it terminated the previous agreement, it apparently lacked sufficient economic strength to secure its bargaining demands under "the balance of power between labor and management expressed in our national labor policy." . . . It is clear beyond question that Wisconsin "[entered] into the substantive aspects of the bargaining process to an extent Congress has not countenanced." . . .

Our decisions hold that Congress meant that these activities, whether of employer or employees, were not to be regulable by States any more than by the NLRB, for neither States nor the Board is "afforded flexibility in picking and choosing which economic devices of labor and management shall be branded as unlawful." . . . Rather, both are without authority to attempt to "introduce some standard of properly 'balanced' bargaining power," . . . or to define "what economic sanctions might be permitted negotiating parties in an 'ideal' or 'balanced' state of collective bargaining." . . . To sanction state regulation of such economic pressure deemed by the federal Act "desirabl[y] . . . left for the free play of contending economic forces, . . . is not merely [to fill] a gap [by] outlaw[ing] what federal law fails to outlaw; it is denying one party to an economic contest a weapon that Congress meant him to have available." . . . Such regulation by the State is impermissible because it "stands as an obstacle to the accomplishment and execution of the full purposes and objectives of Congress."

[Judgment reversed]

---

§ 1:8. LOCAL POWERS

The police power of the state may also be exercised to some extent by the political subdivisions of the state, subject to the constitutional or public law limitations of each particular state in addition to those imposed by the federal Constitution on the states. The term "police power" embraces the area of laws designed to protect the public health, welfare, safety, and morals.

§ 1:9. COMPARISON OF NATIONAL, STATE, AND LOCAL POWERS

The power of the states to regulate business differs from that of the national government. In the case of a state regulation, the court begins with the assumption that the law is within the power of the state to enact. If the power of the state is to be successfully challenged, it is necessary to show that the law in question cannot be adopted because of some constitutional limitation or the surrender or prohibition of the power to adopt the law.

By contrast, in order to sustain a federal law it must be shown at the outset that the law comes within the type of law expressly covered by one of the powers delegated to the national government. If it is not within such express grant of power and cannot be reasonably implied from an express grant, then the federal law is unconstitutional, as it goes beyond the power of the federal government.

As respects the states, the political subdivisions occupy a position similar to that of the national government. Like the national government, the political subdivisions can only exercise such powers as have been delegated to them. In the case of the political subdivisions, it will be found that the state constitution or a law passed by the state legislature has created the subdivision in question and defined what powers it can exercise. Generally, these powers are more limited in scope than the powers of the state and are ordinarily confined in operation to the geographic area over which the subdivision is given control; that is, a city would be given power to run affairs within the city, but ordinarily would not have any power to regulate matters extending outside the city limits. As a practical matter also, the authority generally given a subdivision is more likely to be confined to minor details or matters directly affecting the actual physical health and safety of the people.

Because of these three classes of governments in the United States, a law calling for the regulation of business raises the question as to which of the three governments, if any, has the power to adopt the particular law. The situation is also complicated by the fact that business problems are no respecters of geography. City problems in many areas have ceased to become merely citywide in scope and have become metropolitan, reaching out beyond the city limits into neighboring suburbs and territories. Many socioeconomic problems that formerly were merely local or state problems have risen to national significance. Big business has become national and international in scope. The history of the regulation of business has been that of a constant drive towards national legislation to keep pace with the nationalization of the economy.

Questions for Discussion

1. Do the powers of a city have anything in common with the powers of the federal government or a state government?

2. Can the states exercise any power they choose?

3. What are the characteristics of the Constitution as it is today?

4. The Federal Trade Commission adopts a regulation covering advertising. A state law is adopted which is inconsistent with the regulation. The attorney general of the state claims that the state law is controlling because the regulation of the Federal Trade Commission is merely the act of an administrative agency and is not a federal law, and therefore the supremacy clause of the Constitution does not make the Trade Commission regulation superior to the state law. Is the attorney general correct?

5. The state pollution control board ordered the Jones Corporation to reduce smoke pollution. Jones claims that the order is invalid because there is nothing in the state constitution which gives the state legislature the power to create the pollution control board or to give the board the authority to make orders. Is this defense valid?

6. Except as modified by express amendments, the federal Constitution means today exactly what it meant in 1789. Appraise this statement.

7. What provision of the Constitution declares the doctrine of preemption?

8. Compare federal supremacy and federal preemption.

9. How would the decision in the *Burbank* case have been affected if the takeoff time had been extended so that the curfew began two hours later and ended two hours sooner?

10. Louise claims that the *Machinists* case should be classified as illustrating the supremacy of federal law. Henry claims that it applies the silence of Congress rule. Who is correct?

11. Perez was sued for damages arising from an automobile collision. A judgment was entered against Perez. He then filed a petition in bankruptcy. In due course, he was given a discharge in bankruptcy which discharged him from all debts, including the judgment. The state of Arizona then suspended Perez's automobile registration and operator's license pursuant to a state statute providing for such suspension whenever a judgment remained unpaid for 60 days, even though the judgment had been discharged in bankruptcy. Perez claimed that the state statute was unconstitutional and that the suspension of his licenses was therefore improper. Was he correct? [*Perez v Campbell*, 402 US 637 (1971)]

12. The California Labor Code prohibits an employer from knowingly employing an alien who is not entitled to lawful residence in the United States if this would deprive a lawful resident of a job. An employer charged with violating this statute claimed that it was unconstitutional because it related to immigration and naturalization and any state law on those subjects was displaced because the federal Immigration and Nationality Act preempted the field; and the state law, in any case, was invalidated because of the supremacy clause of the Constitution. Was the California law valid? [*Canas v Bica*, 424 US 351 (1976)]

2

The Courts as the Guardians
of the Constitution

§ 2:1. SUPREMACY OF THE CONSTITUTION

Because the powers of American governments are either conferred or limited by constitutions, the question is always present whether a particular statute comes within the constitutional authority. In the case of a federal law, it must conform to the federal Constitution. In the case of a state law, the law must conform both to the state constitution and to the federal Constitution. As between the federal Constitution and the state constitutions, the federal Constitution is supreme. In the case of an ordinance or a regulation adopted by a political subdivision, it must conform to the charter or the statute giving the political subdivision authority and also to both the federal and a state constitution. Who is to determine whether a law or an ordinance conforms to the constitutional requirements?

§ 2:2. THE SUPREME COURT AS THE FINAL INTERPRETER OF THE CONSTITUTION

During the early years of our national existence, there was strong controversy over whether there was any umpire or referee to decide whether the rules of the constitutional game were being observed. Viewed abstractly, a constitution could provide that (1) one particular branch of the government should be the final interpreter of the constitution; or (2) each officer or official of the government could decide the question when the need arose; or (3) every citizen could determine whether a law should or should not be obeyed. Nothing is contained in our federal Constitution which expressly states which, if any, of these three alternatives is to be followed.

As a matter of practical necessity, alternative (3) is readily eliminated. If alternative (3) were adopted, it would give everyone freedom to ignore the law. It is obvious that no law could ever be enforced if every person affected thereby could choose to ignore the law by claiming it was unconstitutional.

For the same reason of practical expediency, it can be concluded that only one branch of the government should determine the question of constitutionality. This eliminates alternative (2) and only alternative (1) remains. That is, one branch and only one branch is to determine the question of the validity of laws and the meaning of the Constitution. This, however, does not finally decide the matter, for it merely opens the door to the question of "which branch?"

In 1803, Chief Justice Marshall established that only one branch of the government could determine whether laws were constitutional and that that branch was the judicial branch. He reasoned that (1) the Constitution was the bedrock on which government rested,[1] (2) judges were sworn to uphold the Constitution, and (3) any statute which was inconsistent with the Constitution necessarily was void and had to be ignored by the judges.

This concept has been challenged at various times in our national history but is now firmly established. Moreover, the concept has expanded so that not only the Supreme Court of the United States, but every court of any rank, whether state or federal, has the power to declare a law unconstitutional, as is discussed in the next section.

§ 2:3. EXTENT OF JUDICIAL REVIEW

The right of the Supreme Court to invalidate all laws conflicting with the federal Constitution was firmly established by subsequent decisions, which held that the Court could declare unconstitutional a state law that conflicted with the Constitution and could hear appeals from state supreme courts in order to determine such questions.

It should be noted that the Supreme Court enforces only the federal Constitution, although it may enforce it against national law, or state constitution or law, or local ordinance or regulation. The picture of *judicial review,* as this process of examining the constitutionality of a law is called, is not complete, however, without noting that, in addition to the right of the Supreme Court to make such decisions, any lower federal court may make such decisions subject to review by the Supreme Court of the United States. In addition, any state court may declare a state law or local ordinance unconstitutional because it violates the federal or the state constitution. With respect to a violation of the state constitution, the supreme court of the state is the final arbiter; but, with respect to a violation of the federal Constitution, the final decision is made by the Supreme

---

[1]See § 3:2 of this book.

Court of the United States. Any state court may also declare a federal law unconstitutional because it is in violation of the federal Constitution, although in this instance the Supreme Court of the United States will have the final word in the matter.

§ 2:4. CRITICISM OF JUDICIAL REVIEW

Numerous attacks have been made from the first on the power of judicial review. Andrew Jackson stated that every branch of the government was bound to recognize the federal Constitution as supreme and therefore must follow its own conviction as to what the Constitution meant, rather than be bound to accept what the Supreme Court said it meant. Objection was repeatedly made that the American system of government was based on a division of executive, judicial, and legislative functions into coordinate branches and that this system was destroyed if judicial review raised the Court above the other two branches. The fact that the power of judicial review was not expressly conferred, that decisions could be rendered by a one-person majority, and that, until comparatively recent times, the general attitude of the Court was conservative, also brought the doctrine under general attack.

As a practical matter, the doctrine of judicial review is now so firmly entrenched that a direct attack on that doctrine seems futile. As a question of political science or the art of government, the power of judicial review must be lodged in someone or in some branch of the government. Just as a game cannot be played without an umpire or a referee, a government of limited powers cannot be run without some arbiter to determine whether its limitations are being observed. This problem does not arise in an unlimited monarchy, for there is no requirement in such a state that the government stay within any boundaries. We must therefore conclude that, if we wish to retain a constitutionally limited government, we must accept the fact that there must be an umpire and that, when a decision is against the interest of the particular group or class to which we belong, we should not condemn the authority of the umpire to make the decision.

§ 2:5. PROPOSALS FOR CHANGE

It has been suggested that in place of judicial review by the courts, the public should be allowed to express its wishes at the polls. This suggestion is based on the thought that, since the judges of the Supreme Court of the United States are not elected by the people of the United States, it is in conflict with the principle of government through popularly elected representatives to permit the Court to nullify a law enacted by the representatives of the people in Congress. Such a proposal is open to the theoretical, but nevertheless real, objection that the limitations contained in the constitutions would cease to be legal barriers and could be ignored when the will of a sufficient number of voters so desired. The proposal thus converts a legal problem into a political issue. Another very practical objection to such a plan is that modern legislation relates to matters of such complexity that it is unreasonable to expect the great mass of voters to have acquired sufficient knowledge of the subject matter and of the relative merits and demerits of the law in question to enable them to cast an intelligent vote.

§ 2:6. INHERENT DIFFICULTIES OF THE PROBLEM

The problem of government under constitutional limitations is further complicated by the fact that the constitution, or book of rules, which the court, or umpire, applies is, in the case of the federal Constitution and of most state constitutions, a very vague guide. While a number of state constitutions are unusually long and detailed, they remain basically vague in many points. It will be noted in the discussion of the "due process" clause in Chapter 4 that, when interpreting and applying such general, vague provisions to our modern life, the umpire's decision will inevitably be colored by individual concepts of what is socially, morally, and economically proper.

The only way to avoid the personal factor in interpretation is by the adoption of a specific, detailed constitution that would cover every possible situation that would arise. The impossibility of drafting such a constitution and securing its adoption, the inability to foresee the future and to provide for it in such a constitution, and the inability of such a constitution to change with the arrival of new eras indicate that such an alternative, while theoretically a solution, is not practical.

The need for an umpire cannot be avoided. The solution for what are termed "bad" decisions is a constant demand by the public that competent and sincere judges be appointed. It is obvious that the better the courts, the better the decisions. In a democracy the ultimate responsibility for securing good judges rests upon "we, the people."

But having good judges does not mean that we or society will approve the decisions that will be made. Much depends on the attitude of the judges toward the Constitution, for almost every question that arises under the Constitution can be answered either way. That is, the decision could be for the government or could be against the government. Which it will be is ordinarily the result of whether the Constitution is viewed as the bedrock on which government rests or as a living document. These two conflicting views will be discussed in the next chapter.

Questions for Discussion

1. A state statute is constitutional as long as it satisfies the requirements of the federal Constitution. Appraise this statement.

2. Ellen claims that the supremacy clause of the Constitution gives the Supreme Court power to declare laws unconstitutional. Is she correct?

3. What court can declare a city ordinance invalid because it violates the federal Constitution?

4. Is judicial review inevitable?

5. Can the United States Supreme Court declare a state law void if it conflicts with the state constitution?

6. The power of the Supreme Court to declare laws void because they are contrary to the Constitution has been attacked as creating a one-person tyranny. Explain.

7. What plan could be adopted in place of judicial review by the Supreme Court?

8. A federal law provides that an appeal may be taken from the highest court of any state to the United States Supreme Court when a federal question is involved. X is convicted in a state court for doing a particular act. He claims that he is authorized to do the act by virtue of federal law. The state supreme court denies that the federal law gives him the authority to do the act, affirms the conviction, and then refuses to permit the case to go on appeal to the Supreme Court of the United States. Can the United States Supreme Court compel the state supreme court to allow the appeal?

9. Z is required to pay a tax imposed by a state statute. She claims that the statute is contrary to the state constitution because a quorum as required by the state constitution was not present in the state legislature when the tax law was adopted. The state supreme court holds that there was a quorum within the meaning of the state constitution and that the state law is constitutional. Z appeals to the United States Supreme Court and asks the Court to review the decision of the state court. What decision will the Supreme Court make?

10. How would you answer Andrew Jackson's argument against the doctrine of judicial review?

11. Which of the following provides the greatest protection against arbitrary or tyrannical government: (a) Division of powers into several branches, as executive, legislative, and judicial. (b) Popular elections. (c) Judicial review.

12. Which of the following systems is preferable and why: (a) Judicial review by the courts. (b) A referendum system under which a law that is declared unconstitutional may be passed over the Court's decision if three fourths of the voters approve the law at a later election. (c) No power of judicial review, but power given to the voters to call a special election to repeal any law that is unsatisfactory to them.

3

Interpreting and Amending the Constitution

§ 3:1. INTERPRETATION OF THE CONSTITUTION

Once the Constitution of 1789 was adopted, it might be thought that the great debate over the powers of the federal government had ended. This was not so, for almost immediately there arose the question of whether the written words of the Constitution should be interpreted strictly, so as to give the federal government the least power possible, or broadly, so as to give the federal government the greatest power that the words would permit. These two views can be given the names of (a) the bedrock view and (b) the living document view.

By the bedrock view, the purpose of a constitution is to state certain fundamental principles for all time. By the living document view, a constitution is merely a statement of goals and objectives and a constitution is intended to grow and change with the times.

Whether the Constitution is to be liberally interpreted, under the living document view, or narrowly interpreted, under the bedrock view, has a direct effect upon the living constitution. In general terms, the Court over a period of years has followed the living document concept, which has resulted in strengthening the power of the federal government, permitting the rise of administrative agencies, and expanding the protection of human rights. If the Constitution had been strictly interpreted according to the bedrock theory, the central or federal government would have relatively little power today, administrative agencies would not be allowed, and many human rights would not be protected from governmental invasion. The living document view has given us the new Constitution described in § 1:2 of this book.

Can we decide that we should adopt the bedrock view or the living document view? We cannot select one view to the exclusion of the other for the simple reason that we want both. Contradictory as this sounds, it is obvious that we want our Constitution to be durable. We do not want a set of New Year's Resolutions that will be forgotten shortly. At the same time, we know that the world changes and therefore we do not want a constitution that will hold us tied in a straightjacket of the past.

In terms of social forces that make the law, we are torn between our desire for stability and our desire for flexibility. We want a constitution which is stable. At the same time, we want one which is flexible. There is probably no one living today who believes that the Constitution should be 100 percent stable nor, on the other hand, who believes that it should be 100 percent flexible. Everyone wants both qualities and the problem is how to reach a compromise. This is where the conflict arises: where do we draw the line between the extremes of never changing and of always changing? Some people will favor more change than others. That is why we have conflict.

It is essential that we recognize that our Constitution is in a sense torn between the conflicting desires of change and no change. To look only at the Constitution as it was written in 1789 and to ignore the stresses and strains of the "change-no change" conflict is misleading. If we do not see the conflict, we do not see the Constitution as it really is today. Even more important, we lack the understanding needed to meet the problems of tomorrow.

§ 3:2. THE BEDROCK VIEW

The bedrock view regards a written constitution as the bedrock on which government rests. By this view, a written constitution must remain constant, unchanging, unalterable, even as the laws of the Medes and Persians. In everyday speech, this view regards the U.S. Constitution as the basic rules and holds that neither the players nor the umpire can change the rules.

This concept was clearly stated by Chief Justice Marshall as early as 1803 in holding that a federal statute which conflicted with a provision of the Constitution was void and that the Supreme Court was obligated to so declare.

(a) Judicial review

In a broad sense, every time that a court acts on a matter decided by a lower court or an administrator, there is a judicial review. The term, however, has become confined to a review by a court to determine whether a statute, ordinance, or regulation is constitutional. That is, instead of being any review by a court, it is a review by a court on the narrow question of constitutionality. No express provision is made in the United States Constitution either authorizing or prohibiting such judicial review.

MARBURY v MADISON

1 Cranch 137 (1803)

Marbury was appointed a justice of the peace for the District of Columbia, but the commission by which his appointment would become effective was not delivered to him. He brought an action to compel the Secretary of State, Madison, to deliver the commission. This action was brought in the Supreme Court, which had been given authority to hear such cases by the Judiciary Act of 1789. The Constitution did not permit the bringing of actions of this nature in the Supreme Court. The Supreme Court therefore had to consider whether the Constitution or the statute was the superior authority.

OPINION BY MARSHALL, C. J.

That the people have an original right to establish, for their future government, such principles as, in their opinion, shall most conduce to their own happiness, is the basis on which the whole American fabric has been erected. . . .

This original and supreme will organizes the government, and assigns to different departments their respective powers. It may either stop here, or establish certain limits not to be transcended by those departments.

The government of the United States is of the latter description. The powers of the legislature are defined and limited; and that those limits may not be mistaken, or forgotten, the Constitution is written. To what purpose are powers limited, and to what purpose is that limitation committed to writing, if these limits may, at any time, be passed by those intended to be restrained? The distinction between a government with limited and unlimited powers is abolished, if those limits do not confine the persons on whom they are imposed, and if acts prohibited and acts allowed are of equal obligation. It is a proposition too plain to be contested, that the Constitution controls any legislative act repugnant to it; or, that the legislature may alter the Constitution by an ordinary act.

Between these alternatives there is no middle ground. The Constitution is either a superior paramount law, unchangeable by ordinary means, or it is on a level with ordinary legislative acts, and, like other acts, is alterable when the legislature shall please to alter it.

If the former part of the alternative be true, then a legislative act contrary to the Constitution is not law; if the latter part be true, then written constitutions are absurd attempts, on the part of the people, to limit a power in its own nature illimitable.

Certainly all those who have framed written constitutions contemplate them as forming the fundamental and paramount law of the nation, and, consequently, the theory of every such government must be, that an act of the legislature, repugnant to the constitution, is void. . . .

If an act of the legislature, repugnant to the Constitution, is void, does it, notwithstanding its invalidity, bind the courts, and oblige them to give it effect?

Or, in other words, though it be not law, does it constitute a rule as operative as if it was a law? . . .

It is emphatically the province and duty of the judicial department to say what the law is. . . . If two laws conflict with each other, the courts must decide on the operation of each.

So if a law be in opposition to the Constitution; if both the law and the Constitution apply to a particular case, so that the court must either decide that case conformably to the law, disregarding the Constitution, or conformably to the Constitution, disregarding the law, the court must determine which of these conflicting rules governs the case. This is of the very essence of judicial duty.

If, then, . . . the Constitution is superior to any ordinary act of the legislature, the Constitution, and not such ordinary act, must govern the case to which they both apply. . . .

Why does a judge swear to discharge his duties agreeably to the Constitution of the United States, if that Constitution forms no rule for his government?
. . .

It is also not entirely unworthy of observation, that in declaring what shall be the supreme law of the land, the Constitution itself is first mentioned; and not the laws of the United States generally, but those only which shall be made in pursuance of the Constitution, have that rank.

Thus, the particular phraseology of the Constitution of the United States confirms and strengthens the principle, supposed to be essential to all written constitutions, that a law repugnant to the Constitution is void; and that courts, as well as other departments, are bound by that instrument. . . .

[Judgment against Marbury because the statute which authorized him to sue in the Supreme Court was unconstitutional]

---

§ 3:3. THE LIVING DOCUMENT VIEW

The view that the Constitution is to be liberally interpreted as a living document in order to adjust to current needs was stated as early as 1819.[1]

(a) Incorporation of a national bank

McCULLOCH v MARYLAND

4 Wheat 316 (1819)

The first bank of the United States was chartered for 20 years in 1791 and again in 1816. Hostile state legislation attempted to drive it out of existence. In 1818, Maryland adopted a law imposing a tax on bank notes issued by any bank not chartered by the state legislature. McCulloch, the cashier of the Baltimore

---

[1]Its classic application was made in that year in sustaining the constitutionality of the United States Bank.

branch of the National Bank, issued bank notes on which this tax had not been paid. Suit was brought by the State of Maryland against him to recover the statutory penalties imposed for violation of the statute.

OPINION BY MARSHALL, C. J.

The first question . . . is, has Congress power to incorporate a bank? . . .

This government of the Union . . . is acknowledged by all to be one of enumerated powers. . . .

Among the enumerated powers, we do not find that of establishing a bank or creating a corporation. . . . A constitution, to contain an accurate detail of all the subdivisions of which its great powers will admit, and of all the means by which they may be carried into execution, would partake of the prolixity of a legal code, and could scarcely be embraced by the human mind. It would probably never be understood by the public. Its nature, therefore, requires, that only its great outlines should be marked, its important objects designated, and the minor ingredients which compose those objects be deduced from the nature of the objects themselves. . . .

Although, among the enumerated powers of government, we do not find the word "bank" or "incorporation," we find the great powers to lay and collect taxes; to borrow money; to regulate commerce; to declare and conduct a war; and to raise and support armies and navies. The sword and the purse, all the external relations, and no inconsiderable portion of the industry of the nation, are intrusted to its government . . . A government, intrusted with such ample powers, on the due execution of which the happiness and prosperity of the nation so vitally depends, must also be intrusted with ample means for their execution. The power being given, it is the interest of the nation to facilitate its execution. It can never be their interest, and cannot be presumed to have been their intention, to clog and embarrass its execution by withholding the most appropriate means. Throughout this vast republic, . . . revenue is to be collected and expended, armies are to be marched and supported. The exigencies of the nation may require that the treasure raised in the North should be transported to the South, that raised in the East conveyed to the West, or that this order should be reversed. Is that construction of the Constitution to be preferred which would render these operations difficult, hazardous, and expensive? Can we adopt that construction (unless the words imperiously require it) which would impute to the framers of that instrument, when granting these powers for the public good, the intention of impeding their exercise by withholding a choice of means? If, indeed, such be the mandate of the Constitution, we have only to obey; but that instrument does not profess to enumerate the means by which the powers it confers may be executed; nor does it prohibit the creation of a corporation, if the existence of such a being be essential to the beneficial exercise of those powers. It is, then, the subject of fair inquiry, how far such means may be employed. . . .

The government which has a right to do an act, and has imposed on it the duty of performing that act, must, according to the dictates of reason, be allowed to select the means; and those who contend that it may not select any appropriate means, that one particular mode of effecting the object is excepted, take upon themselves the burden of establishing that exception. . . .

But the Constitution of the United States has not left the right of Congress to employ the necessary means, for the execution of the powers conferred on the government, to general reasoning. To its enumeration of powers is added that of making "all laws which shall be necessary and proper, for carrying into execution the foregoing powers, and all other powers vested by this Constitution, in the government of the United States, or in any department thereof."

. . . This provision is made in a constitution intended to endure for ages to come, and, consequently, to be adapted to the various crises of human affairs. To have prescribed the means by which government should, in all future time, execute its powers, would have been to change, entirely, the character of the instrument, and give it the properties of a legal code. It would have been an unwise attempt to provide, by immutable rules, for exigencies which, if foreseen at all, must have been seen dimly, and which can be best provided for as they occur. [The Court rejected the contention that "necessary" means "absolutely necessary."] . . . Sound construction of the Constitution must allow to the national legislature that discretion, with respect to the means by which the powers it confers are to be carried into execution, which will enable that body to perform the high duties assigned to it, in the manner most beneficial to the people. Let the end be legitimate, let it be within the scope of the Constitution, and all means which are appropriate, which are plainly adapted to that end, which are not prohibited, but consist with the letter and spirit of the Constitution, are constitutional.

. . . It can scarcely be necessary to say, that the existence of state banks can have no possible influence on the question. No trace is to be found in the Constitution of an intention to create a dependence of the government of the Union on those of the states, for the execution of the great powers assigned to it. . . . The choice of means implies a right to choose a national bank in preference to state banks, and Congress alone can make the election.

[Judgment against Maryland on the basis that, as Congress had authority to create a bank, a state law designed to harm that bank was unconstitutional, and therefore Maryland could not recover the penalty authorized by that state statute]

§ 3:4. AMENDMENT OF THE CONSTITUTION

The framers of the Constitution saw the need for making changes to it. However, they intended that these changes should be made by the adoption of amendments to the Constitution. Article V of the Constitution provides the machinery for adopting such amendments:

The Congress, whenever two-thirds of both Houses shall deem it necessary, shall propose Amendments to this Constitution, or, on the Application of the Legislatures of two-thirds of the several States, shall call a Convention for proposing Amendments, which, in either Case, shall be valid to all Intents and Purposes, as part of this Constitution, when ratified by the Legislatures of three-fourths of the several States, or by Conventions in three-fourths thereof, as the one or the other Mode of Ratification may be proposed by the Congress; Provided that no Amendment which may be made prior to the Year One thousand eight hundred and eight shall in any Manner affect the first and fourth Clauses in the Ninth Section of the first Article; and that no State, without its Consent, shall be deprived of its equal Suffrage in the Senate.

Are there any limits today on the nature of amendments that can be adopted? No limitation is specified by the Constitution other than the prohibition against destroying the equality of the states in voting in the Senate. Is there a spirit or a plan behind the Constitution that places an unwritten limitation on amendments? The Eighteenth, or Prohibition, Amendment was attacked on the ground that it was unconstitutional because it regulated local consumption, which was a matter reserved to the states. The Nineteenth, or Women's Suffrage, Amendment was attacked because it made a fundamental change in the body of voters within each state and was therefore unconstitutional. The Supreme Court held that both amendments were constitutional because adopted in the manner prescribed by the Constitution and that there was no unwritten spirit in the Constitution that restricted the kind of amendments that could be adopted.

The amending power therefore confers the right to make any change in the structure or powers of the national government if the amendment is adopted according to the prescribed procedure. It is immaterial how far-sweeping the economical, political, or social effects of the amendment may be or how novel or radical its purpose. The fact that the Constitution may be amended to provide anything that a sufficient majority of the public desires emphasizes the importance of an intelligent and active electorate.

Amendment of the Constitution by formal change under Article V is a slow and difficult process, as evidenced by the small number of amendments that have been adopted when compared with the number of years of our national life under the Constitution or the number of amendments proposed during that time.

§ 3:5. AMENDMENT BY JUDICIAL INTERPRETATION

The greatest change to the Constitution has been made by judicial interpretation. This is one of the realities of legal life, although it is in conflict with the theory that judges merely declare and do not make the law. According to the classical school of thought, a judge merely declares what the law is and does not make the law, because to do the latter would usurp the function of the legislative branch. By this theory, a decision of the court cannot be regarded as amending the Constitution. It is true that, in a great many cases, judges merely apply a recognized or accepted rule of law to a set of facts. In such a case, the judge is merely declaring the law. When, however, the court is faced with a set of facts that do not come within the scope of any previously recognized or established rule of law, there is no law for the judge to declare.

To illustrate, consider the problem presented when the first suit was brought to recover damages against an airline for the death of a passenger in an airplane crash. The court was faced with the problem of deciding how the liability of an air carrier should be determined. Since this was, by hypothesis, the first case of its kind, there would be nothing in the lawbooks or decisions determining or stating what the rule of law was. The judge was nevertheless required to decide the case, and in so doing made new law because before that time there was no law applicable to those facts. If it is contended that the judge did not make the law, but merely declared preexisting law, difficult questions arise. How did the judge find out the preexisting law, if such a case had never been decided before? If the judge was merely declaring the law, when did it come into existence? Did it spring into being the minute the Wright Brothers defied the law of gravity for 12 fateful seconds in 1903, or did the principle of the liability of air carriers come down to the courts before the air carrier was invented? If so, how long before? The concept of principles of law floating about in some rarefied atmosphere until, in some later century, a judge, faced with a new factual situation, draws the principle from the clouds in the manner of a judicial Franklin is not one that appeals to common sense.

The fact must be accepted that a judge, when faced with a new situation, makes new law, just as though a legislature or the Congress had adopted a new statute. To be sure, the new law may draw on past law for support or analogy, and the court will desire to make it conform to the prior law or the policy of the prior law as far as is practical and reasonable. Nevertheless, when a rule of law results from a decision where there was no rule of law before, it is obvious that the court has made law.

The Supreme Court of the United States has been a very powerful factor in the making of law and the decisional amendment of the Constitution of the United States, an effect that will become apparent in the subsequent chapters of this book.

The state courts have also, but to a lesser degree, been active in revising their constitutions through decisional interpretation. To a large extent, the action of the state supreme courts has been merely to follow the federal decisions in construing similar provisions of their own state constitutions.

Questions for Discussion

1. What provision does the Constitution of the United States make for amendment? Compare it with the provision for amending the constitution of your own state.

2. Would an amendment to the United States Constitution be valid that deleted the present Article V and in its place provided that an amendment could be adopted by a majority of those voting at a presidential election?

3. (a) Does the amending process established by the federal Constitution encourage or discourage amendments to the Constitution? (b) Should the process be made easier or more difficult?

4. What effect do decisions of the Supreme Court have on the growth of the Constitution?

5. One judge in the Supreme Court can change the course of national events for years. Is this correct?

6. Does a judge declare the law or does a judge make the law?

7. Does a judge violate the oath of office to maintain the Constitution when the judge changes the meaning of the Constitution by a decision?

8. What objection is there to having judges make the law? Does the process of judge-made law conflict with the principle of responsibility to the people?

9. Can a judge be impeached for openly disregarding the Constitution? For interpreting it so that its meaning is changed?

10. Does *Marbury v Madison* illustrate the bedrock or the living document view of the Constitution? Explain your answer.

11. Does the case of *McCulloch v Maryland* represent the bedrock or the living document view of interpreting the Constitution? Explain your answer.

12. What are the greatest obstacles to adopting 100 percent the bedrock view of interpreting the Constitution?

In this part, four limitations imposed on government by the federal Constitution will be examined. There are other limitations, but these four have been selected because of the striking contrast between them in terms of source, development, and scope.

4

Due Process of Law

In this chapter, one of the constitutional limitations on government is discussed. From its very nature, "due process of law" is obviously vague; therefore, it is not surprising to find that the Supreme Court has put into that phrase more meaning than is obvious from a mere reading of the words.

§ 4:1. GUARANTEES OF INDIVIDUAL RIGHT

During the period of the American Revolution, emphasis was placed upon the rights of the individual as opposed to the rights of the government. When the Constitution was drafted, comparatively little attention was given to the rights of individuals, even though many of the framers of the Constitution had been leaders in the Revolution.

It is true that some restrictions can be found in the Constitution apart from its amendments, such as the limitations on the exercise of the express powers given to the federal government as stated in Article 1, Section 9, the prohibition against outlawing the slave trade before 1808, and prohibitions imposed upon states because of their new position within a federal system, Article 1, Section 10. There were likewise prohibitions of ex post facto laws and bills of attainder. The significant emphasis upon private or individual rights, however, did not come until the first ten amendments and the Civil War amendments were added to the Constitution. It has already been noted that demand for the Bill of Rights of the Constitution was so great that the ratification of the federal Constitution could not be secured until it was agreed by the Federalists that, if the Constitution was ratified, a bill of rights would be adopted. This was done by the First Congress under the new Constitution in 1790, and in 1791 the first ten amendments of the new Constitution became effective.

In addition to the guarantees contained in the federal Constitution, the constitution of each state contains various guarantees, frequently employing the same wording as the federal Constitution. As a starting point, the United States Supreme Court is the final interpreter of the meaning of the guarantees contained in the federal Constitution, and the supreme court of each state is the final judge of the guarantees contained in its constitution. There is a natural tendency, however, for a state supreme court to follow a decision of the federal Supreme Court in interpreting a provision that is the same as, or similar to, a provision of the federal Constitution.

§ 4:2. THE EVOLUTION OF DUE PROCESS

The Fifth and Fourteenth Amendments of the Constitution declare that neither Congress nor any state may deprive any person of "life, liberty or property without due process of law." In the following sections you will learn of the changing meanings given to the phrase "due process of law." You will see it go through the following phases:

(a) A guarantee of historical procedure.

(b) A guarantee of reasonable procedure.

(c) No guarantee of substance.

(d) A guarantee of freedom of contract.

(e) A guarantee of nonarbitrary substance.

(f) A guarantee of equal protection.

(g) A protection of significant interests.

At present the due process clause is in phases (b), (e), (f), and (g). That is, it is a guarantee of reasonable procedure, nonarbitrary substance, and equal protection; and it is a protection of significant interests, as well as life, liberty and property.

Why this evolution? Did you ever buy a car or move into a new house and, after the excitement of new ownership had passed, gradually become aware that it was not everything you expected? You then do what you can to remedy this. The same evolution takes place with society. It strives for a particular goal, thinking that the attainment of that goal will solve all its problems. When it attains that goal, it finds that there are additional problems and that the goal must be restated.

It is the restating of goals which causes the shifting statement of the constitutional guarantees. This will be noted as the particular stages of due process are discussed in the following sections.

§ 4:3. DUE PROCESS AS A GUARANTEE OF HISTORICAL PROCEDURE

During the centuries, from the earliest recorded days, the prime object of society was to make the king govern according to established rules. For centuries, arbitrary kings ignored the rules that had developed. This was the thought which inspired the nobles when, in 1215, they compelled King John at Runnymede to sign the Magna Charta, in which he agreed that he would respect their feudal rights and would not take any action against them except by the "law of the land." Later kings were required to sign similar charters and gradually the phrase "due process of law" took the place of "law of the land."

Words change their meaning across the centuries and we can better understand what was meant by this phrase if we think of "due" as money which is owed to someone. It is money which is "owing" or "due." Likewise, we may think of "process" as "processing" or "proceeding," so that "process of law" is the way the law proceeds or does things. We can now see that "due process of law" means doing things the way that the law says that they should be done. For centuries, "due process" meant doing things the way they were always done before. By this historical test, the due process clauses of the federal Constitution guaranteed doing things the way they had been done in the past.

§ 4:4. DUE PROCESS AS A GUARANTEE OF REASONABLE PROCEDURE

As long as the danger facing the people was an arbitrary ruler who ignored established rules, it seemed that the logical objective was to make the ruler follow the established rules. When democracy replaced monarchy, the people became the rulers. Did the people want to tie themselves forever to the old rules? If the answer is yes, the result would be that reform and improvement would be impossible. If the people were always tied to the old rules, endless centuries could pass but everything still would have to be run the way it was when the colonies were founded.

Society was not happy with this conclusion. Society wanted to adopt new procedures and, as long as the new procedures were "reasonable," it seemed that there was no reason why society should not be allowed to change the way things had been done.

This, of course, begs the question because if we believe in the historical test, the only procedure which is reasonable is that which was followed when the colonies were founded. This standard fits in with the bedrock view of the Constitution, which maintains that the Constitution established principles and procedures once and for all.

If we follow the living document view of the Constitution, we will say that the Constitution established a bedrock requirement of reasonableness but that the definition and applications of reasonableness are to be determined by the living document view, according to the attitudes of society and the century when the question arises.

During the latter quarter of the 19th century, the Supreme Court followed the living document approach to the interpretation of the due process clause. That is, instead of requiring the exact procedure of the colonization era, new procedures could be adopted as long as they satisfied the basic fairness standards of the old procedures. By the turn of the century the Court could state in *Twining v New Jersey,* 211 US 78 (1908): "... It does not follow, however, that a procedure settled in English law at the time of the emigration, and brought to this country and practiced by our ancestors, is an essential element of due process of law. If that were so the procedure of the first half of the seventeenth century would be fastened upon the American jurisprudence like a straight-jacket, only to be unloosed by constitutional amendment. . . ."

The existence of authority to sustain a new procedure on the ground that it was basically fair and just, and, conversely, the power to declare a procedure invalid if it was not, opened the door to a great expansion of the power of the courts. From that time on, instead of merely playing the part of the historian, the court could interpose its independent judgment as to whether a new procedure was basically fair. Thus the new view removed the question from the area of demonstrable facts—what the procedure was in the colonial day—to an area of nondemonstrable beliefs—what the court felt was fair and just. This substitution of the judge's personal view on what is right in effect casts the judge in the role of philosopher and subjects decisions to attack by all who hold a different philosophy, as well as those who would go further, and those who would not go as far as the judge.

(a) Prosecution on information

HURTADO v CALIFORNIA
110 US 516 (1884)

At the common law a person could not be tried for a felony unless there had been an accusation or indictment by a grand jury. Under the Fifth Amendment to the Federal Constitution a grand jury indictment or presentment is required in the case of every "capital, or otherwise infamous crime." The State of California adopted a law which provided that whenever the prosecuting attorney believed that a person had committed certain types of crimes, the prosecuting attorney could bring the offender to trial by filing a complaint or information with a local magistrate. Hurtado was brought to trial for a crime in this manner and claimed that the procedure denied him due process in depriving him of the protection of a grand jury. The Supreme Court considered whether a state was bound by the concept of due process or any other provision to provide for a grand jury indictment in all cases.

OPINION BY MATTHEWS, J.

. . . There is nothing in *Magna Charta,* rightly construed as a broad charter of public right and law, which ought to exclude the best ideas of all systems and of every age; and as it was the characteristic principle of the common law to draw its inspiration from every fountain of justice, we are not to assume that the sources of its supply have been exhausted. On the contrary, we should expect that the new and various experiences of our own situation and system will mould and shape it into new and not less useful forms. . . .

It follows that any legal proceeding enforced by public authority, whether sanctioned by age and custom, or newly devised in the discretion of the legislative power, in furtherance of the general public good, which regards and preserves . . . principles of liberty and justice, must be held to be due process of law. . . .

[The procedure was valid because it was reasonable, even though it departed from the common-law pattern]

(b) Burden of disproving disqualification

SPEISER v RANDALL

357 US 513 (1958)

The constitution of California prohibits allowing a tax exemption to anyone advocating the unlawful overthrow of the government of the United States or of any state. A California tax statute provided that any taxpayer claiming an exemption must sign a declaration stating that such prohibited activity had not been engaged in. If the tax assessor did not believe that the claimant was entitled to an exemption, the assessor could disallow the exemption and the burden was then upon the taxpayer to prove entitlement to the exemption. Speiser and Prince were honorably discharged veterans, who applied for the state veterans' tax exemption. When they were refused the exemption because the assessor believed that they advocated the unlawful overthrow of the government, they appealed from his decision and finally to the United States Supreme Court on the ground that the statute deprived them of due process of law.

OPINION BY BRENNAN, J.

. . . The question remains whether California has chosen a fair method for determining when a claimant is a member of that class to which the California court has said the constitutional and statutory provisions extend. . . .

To experienced lawyers it is commonplace that the outcome of a lawsuit— and hence the vindication of legal rights—depends more often on how the factfinder appraises the facts than on a disputed construction of a statute or interpretation of a line of precedents. Thus the procedures by which the facts of the case are determined assume an importance fully as great as the validity of the substantive rule of law to be applied. And the more important the rights at stake, the more important must be the procedural safeguards surrounding those rights. . . . When the State undertakes to restrain unlawful advocacy it must provide procedures which are adequate to safeguard against infringement of constitutionally protected rights—rights which we value most highly and which are essential to the workings of a free society. . . .

The principal feature of the California procedure . . . is that the appellants, "as taxpayers under state law, have the affirmative burden of proof, in Court as well as before the Assessor. . . . It is their burden to show that they are proper persons to qualify under the self-executing constitutional provision for the tax exemption in question—i.e., that they are not persons who advocate the over-throw of the government of the United States or the State by force or violence or other unlawful means or who advocate the support of a foreign government against the United States in the event of hostilities." . . .

It is of course within the power of the State to regulate procedures under which its laws are carried out, including the burden of producing evidence and the burden of persuasion, "unless in so doing it offends some principle of justice so rooted in the traditions and conscience of our people as to be ranked as fundamental." . . . "Of course the legislature may go a good way in raising . . . [presumptions] or in changing the burden of proof, but there are limits. . . . It is not within the province of a legislature to declare an individual guilty or presumptively guilty of a crime." . . . The legislature cannot "place upon all defendants in criminal cases the burden of going forward with the evidence. . . . [It cannot] validly command that the finding of an indictment, or mere proof of the identity of the accused, should create a presumption of the existence of all the facts essential to guilt. This is not permissible. . . ."

In civil cases too this Court has struck down state statutes unfairly shifting the burden of proof.

It is true that due process may not always compel the full formalities of a criminal prosecution before criminal advocacy can be suppressed or deterred, but it is clear that the State which attempts to do so must provide procedures amply adequate to safeguard against invasion of speech which the Constitution protects. . . . It is, of course, familiar practice in the administration of a tax program for the taxpayer to carry the burden of introducing evidence to rebut the determination of the collector. . . . But while the fairness of placing the burden of proof on the taxpayer in most circumstances is recognized, this Court has not hesitated to declare a summary tax-collection procedure a violation of due process when the purported tax was shown to be in reality a penalty for a crime. . . . The underlying rationale of these cases is that where a person is to suffer a penalty for a crime he is entitled to greater procedural safeguards than when only the amount of his tax liability is in issue. Similarly it does not follow that because only a tax liability is here involved, the ordinary tax assessment procedures are adequate when applied to penalize speech. . . .

Due process commands that no man shall lose his liberty unless the Govern-ment has borne the burden of producing the evidence and convincing the factfinder of his guilt. . . . Where the transcendent value of speech is involved, due process certainly requires in the circumstances of this case that the State bear the burden of persuasion to show that the appellants engaged in criminal speech. . . .

The vice of the present procedure is that, where particular speech falls close to the line separating the lawful and the unlawful, the possibility of mistaken factfinding—inherent in all litigation—will create the danger that the legitimate utterance will be penalized. The man who knows that he must bring forth proof and persuade another of the lawfulness of his conduct necessarily must steer far wider of the unlawful zone than if the State must bear these burdens. . . . How can a claimant whose declaration is rejected possibly sustain the burden of proving the negative of these complex factual elements? In practical operation, therefore, this procedural device must necessarily produce a result which the State could not command directly. It can only result in a deterrence of speech which the Constitution makes free. . . .

We hold that when the constitutional right to speak is sought to be deterred by a State's general taxing program due process demands that the speech be unencumbered until the State comes forward with sufficient proof to justify its inhibition. The State clearly has no such compelling interest at stake as to justify a short-cut procedure which must inevitably result in suppressing protected speech. . . .

[Judgment for Speiser and Prince because the state statute was unconstitutional]

---

§ 4:5. DUE PROCESS AS INAPPLICABLE TO SUBSTANCE

While the judicial development noted above was proceeding, an economic change was taking place that was soon to compel a further extension of the due process clause. Spurred by the Civil War and the expansion of transportation, the industrial revolution began to appear in earnest in the United States. In the wake of this change came numerous social and economic problems that gave rise to legislation regulating wages and hours of labor, establishing workers' compensation, prohibiting food and drug adulteration, prohibiting conspiracies in restraint of commerce, and regulating rates of carriers and trade practices.

To the spirit of free enterprise of the last century, such interference with the natural operation of the laws of economics was unreasonable, contrary to nature, and therefore deemed unlawful. But, to declare a statute unconstitutional, it is necessary to point to some provision of the Constitution and say that the statute conflicts with it. Which provision of the federal Constitution could be summoned forth to support the claim that an "uneconomic" law was unconstitutional? No express provision was available, for the Constitution, drafted in an era long before the rise of the new economy, naturally contained no reference to the various regulatory statutes now coming into existence. Efforts were made to induce the Court to hold that such economically unsound or unfair laws must violate due process. These efforts at first failed, as the Supreme Court refused to extend this clause beyond a guarantee of procedure.[1]

---

[1]*Davidson v New Orleans*, 96 US 97 (1877).

§ 4:6. DUE PROCESS AS GUARANTEE OF FREEDOM OF CONTRACT

Gradually, however, the Supreme Court adopted the view that the guarantee of a fair procedure is a meaningless gesture if the legislature or Congress is permitted, as long as it follows the proper procedure, to adopt a law the substance of which is unfair, capricious, or unsound. Accordingly, the guarantee of due process was expanded to guarantee not merely procedural fairness, but also that the substance of the statutes themselves be fair and reasonable.

But who is to judge what is reasonable and fair? It should be obvious that these are not fixed, immutable values but flexible concepts that change in the light of the personal history and philosophy of each individual.

For many years, the same conservative spirit that brought forth the concept of due process as a weapon against the new regulatory legislation held, in effect, that free enterprise was the criterion of reasonableness and fairness.

As an application of this view, it was held by the Supreme Court in *Adkins v Children's Hospital,* 261 US 525 (1923), that minimum wage laws violated the guarantee of due process because they interfered with the freedom of adult persons to make any contracts they saw fit. The Court said:

> . . . The statute in question . . . forbids two parties having lawful capacity —under penalties as to the employer—to freely contract with one another in respect of the price for which one shall render service to the other in a purely private employment where both are willing, perhaps anxious, to agree, even though the consequences may be to oblige one to surrender a desirable engagement and the other to dispense with the services of a desirable employee. . . .
>
> It has been said that legislation of the kind now under review is required in the interest of social justice, for whose ends freedom of contract may lawfully be subjected to restraint. The liberty of the individual to do as he pleases, even in innocent matters, is not absolute. It must frequently yield to the common good. . . . But, nevertheless, there are limits to the power, and when these have been passed, it becomes the plain duty of the courts in the proper exercise of their authority to so declare. To sustain the individual freedom of action contemplated by the Constitution is not to strike down the common good but to exalt it; for surely the good of society as a whole cannot be better served than by the preservation against arbitrary restraint of the liberties of its constituent members. . . .

(a) Criticism of the view

That such cases were decided on the basis of economic belief rather than a rule of law is evident from a study of the cases involving government regulation of business. This criticism was very well stated in the dissenting opinions in *Lochner v New York,* 198 US 45 (1905). The State of New York had enacted a law limiting the hours of employment for men in bakeries. This was held unconstitutional on the ground that it was unreasonable to limit the freedom of employers and employees in a nonhazardous business to contract as they chose respecting hours of employment.

The conservative judicial attitude of the Court in regarding itself as the protector of society against the encroachments of radical and evil-minded legislatures is seen from the following statement in that case:

> . . . It is impossible for us to shut our eyes to the fact that many of the laws of this character, while passed under what is claimed to be the police power for the purpose of protecting the public health or welfare, are, in reality, passed from other motives. We are justified in saying so when, from the character of the law and the subject upon which it legislates, it is apparent that the public health or welfare bears but the most remote relation to the law. The purpose of a statute must be determined from the natural and legal effect of the language employed; and whether it is or is not repugnant to the Constitution of the United States must be determined from the natural effect of such statutes when put into operation, and not from their proclaimed purpose. . . .

These views were not shared by Justice Harlan who, in a dissenting opinion, recognized the basic conflict between the individual and public interests, stating:

> . . . I find it impossible, in view of common experience, to say that there is here no real or substantial relation between the means employed by the State and the end sought to be accomplished by its legislation.
>
> We judicially know that the question of the number of hours during which a workman should continuously labor has been, for a long period, and is yet, a subject of serious consideration among civilized peoples, and by those having special knowledge of the laws of health. . . . What is the true ground for the State to take between legitimate protection, by legislation, of the public health and liberty of contract is not a question easily solved, nor one in respect of which there is or can be absolute certainty. . . .
>
> . . . It is enough for the determination of this case, and it is enough for this court to know, that the question is one about which there is room for debate and for an honest difference of opinion. There are many reasons of a weighty, substantial character, based upon the experience of mankind, in support of the theory that, all things considered, more than ten hours steady work each day, from week to week, in a bakery or confectionary establishment, may endanger the health and shorten the lives of the workmen, thereby diminishing their physical and mental capacity to serve the State and to provide for those dependent upon them.

If such reasons exist that ought to be the end of this case, for the State is not amenable to the judiciary, in respect of its legislative enactments, unless such enactments are plainly, palpably, beyond all question, inconsistent with the Constitution of the United States. . . .

Two other justices joined in this dissent, and another dissenting opinion was filed by Justice Holmes in which he directly charged:

This case is decided upon an economic theory which a large part of the country does not entertain. If it were a question whether I agreed with that theory, I should desire to study it further and long before making up my mind. But I do not conceive that to be my duty, because I strongly believe that my agreement or disagreement has nothing to do with the right of a majority to embody their opinions in law. . . .

The Fourteenth Amendment does not enact Mr. Herbert Spencer's Social Statics. . . . A constitution is not intended to embody a particular economic theory, whether of paternalism and the organic relation of the citizen to the State or of laissez faire. It is made for people of fundamentally differing views, and the accident of our finding certain opinions natural and familiar or novel and even shocking ought not to conclude our judgment upon the question whether statutes embodying them conflict with the Constitution. . . .

. . . I think that the word "liberty" in the Fourteenth Amendment is perverted when it is held to prevent the natural outcome of a dominant opinion, unless it can be said that a rational and fair man necessarily would admit that the statute proposed would infringe fundamental principles as they have been understood by the traditions of our people and our law. It does not need research to show that no such sweeping condemnation can be passed upon the statute before us. A reasonable man might think it a proper measure on the score of health. Men whom I certainly could not pronounce unreasonable would uphold it as a first installment of a general regulation of the hours of work.

The same view was expressed by Justice Stone in his dissenting opinion in the minimum wage case of *Moorehead v New York ex rel Tipaldo,* 298 US 587 (1936):

In the years that have intervened since the *Adkins* case we have had opportunity to learn that a wage is not always the resultant of free bargaining between employers and employees. . . .

It is not for the courts to resolve doubts whether the remedy by wage regulation is as efficacious as many believe, or is better than some other, or is better even than the blind operation of uncontrolled economic forces. The legislature must be free to choose unless government is to be rendered impotent. The Fourteenth Amendment has no more embedded in the Constitution our preference for some particular set of economic beliefs than it has adopted, in the name of liberty, the system of theology which we may happen to approve.

In speaking of the then prevailing view that a minimum wage law violated the freedom of contract guaranteed by the due process clause, Justice Stone observed: ". . . There is grim irony in speaking of the freedom of contract of those who, because of their economic necessities, give their services for less than is needful to keep body and soul together. . . ."

§ 4:7. DUE PROCESS AS A GUARANTEE OF NONARBITRARY SUBSTANCE

As the result of continuous and growing pressure by the labor class, the farmers, and the social reformers, and the changing philosophy encouraged by international war and depression, a new view of freedom and of due process came to be adopted. Instead of considering every individual as a legal being fully the equal of every other, with the same power to make contracts as everyone else, the courts departed from the concept of Adam Smith to a new conscious-ness of society's stake in the making of what were formerly considered private contracts, of the possible need of protecting one of the parties to such contracts from exploitation by the other and of protecting society from the effect of such exploitation.

The right of the lawmaker to seek economic and social salvation was no longer to be restrained because the court did not share the lawmaker's social and economic views. Even before the so-called "New Deal revolution" appeared in the Supreme Court, that body had adopted the new social philosophy. In *Nebbia v New York,* 291 US 502 (1934), the Court sustained a minimum resale price law for milk. Against the argument that price-fixing limited freedom of contract and thus violated the due process clause, the Court stated:

> . . . The due process clause makes no mention of sales or of prices any more than it speaks of business or contracts or buildings or other incidents of property. The thought seems nevertheless to have persisted that there is something peculiarly sacrosanct about the price one may charge for what he makes or sells, and that, however able to regulate other elements of manufacture or trade, with inci-dental effect upon price, the state is incapable of directly controlling the price itself. This view was negatived many years ago. *Munn v Illinois,* 94 US 113.

This new view was permanently established by the decision in the *West Coast Hotel* case in which the Court considered a state law imposing minimum wages for women and children.

(a) Minimum wage laws

WEST COAST HOTEL CO. v PARRISH

300 US 379 (1937)

The State of Washington adopted a law requiring employers to pay wages not lower than the statutory minimum. The West Coast Hotel paid its women employees less than the statutory minimum. A proceeding was brought against the hotel because of such noncompliance with the statutory rate. The West Coast Hotel claimed that the statute was unconstitutional as a deprivation of property without due process of law.

OPINION BY HUGHES, C. J.

. . . The Constitution does not speak of freedom of contract. It speaks of liberty and prohibits the deprivation of liberty without due process of law. In prohibiting that deprivation the Constitution does not recognize an absolute and uncontrollable liberty. . . . But the liberty safeguarded is liberty in a social organization which requires the protection of law against the evils which menace the health, safety, morals and welfare of the people. Liberty under the Constitution is thus necessarily subject to the restraints of due process, and regulation which is reasonable in relation to its subject and is adopted in the interests of the community is due process. . . .

This power under the Constitution to restrict freedom of contract has had many illustrations. That it may be exercised in the public interest with respect to contracts between employer and employee is undeniable. . . .

We think that the . . . decision in the *Adkins* case was a departure from the true application of the principles governing the regulation by the State of the relation of employer and employed. . . .

. . . What can be closer to the public interest than the health of women and their protection from unscrupulous and overreaching employers? And if the protection of women is a legitimate end of the exercise of state power, how can it be said that the requirement of the payment of a minimum wage fairly fixed in order to meet the very necessities of existence is not a permissible means to that end? The legislature of the State was clearly entitled to consider the situation of women in employment, the fact that they are in the class receiving the least pay, that their bargaining power is relatively weak, and that they are the ready victims of those who would take advantage of their necessitous circumstances. The legislature was entitled to adopt measures to reduce the evils of the "sweating system," the exploiting of workers at wages so low as to be insufficient to meet the bare cost of living, thus making their very helplessness the occasion of a most injurious competition. The legislature had the right to consider that its minimum wage requirements would be an important aid in carrying out its policy of protection. The adoption of similar requirements by many States evidences a deep-seated conviction both as to the presence of the evil and as to the means adapted to check it. Legislative response to that conviction cannot be regarded as arbitrary or capricious, and that is all we have to decide. Even if the wisdom of the policy be regarded as debatable and its effects uncertain, still the legislature is entitled to its judgment.

There is an additional and compelling consideration which recent economic experience has brought into strong light. The exploitation of a class of workers who are in an unequal position with respect to bargaining power and are thus relatively defenseless against the denial of a living wage is not only detrimental to their health and well being but casts a direct burden for their support upon the community. What these workers lose in wages the taxpayers are called upon to pay. The bare cost of living must be met. We may take judicial notice of the unparalleled demands for relief which arose during the recent period of depression and still continue to an alarming extent despite the degree of economic recovery which has been achieved. . . . The community is not bound to provide what is in effect a subsidy for unconscionable employers. The community may direct its law-making power to correct the abuse which springs from their selfish disregard of the public interest. . . .

Our conclusion is that the case of *Adkins v Children's Hospital, supra,* should be, and is, overruled. . . .

[The hotel was required to pay the minimum wage specified in the statute because the statute was constitutional and did not deprive the hotel of its property without due process of law]

(b) Confirmation of due process as a guarantee of nonarbitrary substance

The new view has also been stated by Justice Frankfurter in *Osborn v Ozlin,* 310 US 53 (1940):

It is equally immaterial that such state action may run counter to the economic wisdom either of Adam Smith or of J. Maynard Keynes, or may be ultimately mischievous even from the point of view of avowed state policy. . . .

The same justice has also stated this view at greater length in his concurring opinion in *A. F. of L. v American Sash & Door Co.,* 335 US 538 (1949):

. . . [In the 19th century] Adam Smith was treated as though his generalizations had been imparted to him on Sinai and not as a thinker who addressed himself to the elimination of restrictions which had become fetters upon initiative and enterprise in his day. Basic human rights expressed by the constitutional conception of liberty were equated with theories of laissez faire. The result was that economic views of confined validity were treated by lawyers and judges as though the framers had enshrined them in the constitution. . . .

The attitude which regarded any legislative encroachment upon the existing economic order as infected with unconstitutionality led to disrespect for legislative attempts to strengthen the wage-earner's bargaining power. . . . But when the tide turned, it was not merely because circumstances had changed and there had arisen a new order with new claims to divine origin. . . . [It was because] of increased deference to the legislative judgment . . . [on the part of the Supreme Court].

The rationale of the . . . legislation . . . is founded on a . . . resolution of conflicting interests. Unless we are to treat as unconstitutional what goes against the grain because it offends what we may strongly believe to be socially desirable, that resolution must be given respect. . . .

Even where the social undesirability of a law may be convincingly urged, invalidation of the law by a court debilitates popular democratic government. Most laws dealing with economic and social problems are matters of trial and error. . . .

But there is reason for judicial restraint in matters of policy deeper than the value of experiment: it is founded on the recognition of the gulf of difference between sustaining and nullifying legislation. . . . As history amply proves, the judiciary is prone to misconceive the public good by confounding private notions with constitutional requirements, and such misconceptions are not subject to legitimate displacement by the will of the people except at too slow a pace. . . . Matters of policy . . . are by definition matters which demand the resolution of conflicts of value, and the elements of conflicting values are largely imponderable. Assessment of their competing worth involves differences of feeling; it is also an exercise in prophecy. Obviously the proper forum for mediating a clash of feelings and rendering a prophetic judgment is the body chosen for those purposes by the people. Its functions can be assumed by this court only in disregard of the historic limits of the Constitution.

In *Williamson v Lee Optical of Oklahoma,* 348 US 483 (1955), the Court declared:

The day is gone when this Court uses the Due Process Clause of the Fourteenth Amendment to strike down state laws, regulatory of business and industrial conditions, because they may be unwise, improvident, or out of harmony with a particular school of thought. . . . "For protection against abuses by legislatures the people must resort to the polls, not to the court."

§ 4:8. DUE PROCESS AS A GUARANTEE OF EQUAL PROTECTION

There is nothing in the federal Constitution which requires the federal government to act uniformly or equally with respect to all persons similarly situated. That is, there is no guarantee that the federal government extend to every person the equal protection of the law.

In contrast, the Fourteenth Amendment expressly imposes that obligation on the states. This gives us a significant insight into history. In 1789 and 1791, people were not concerned with equal protection but were afraid of the central government. Contrastingly, they were not afraid of their own state governments. In 1868, the people were afraid that the victory won on the battlefields of the Civil War would be nullified by states making racial discriminations. Therefore, "We the people" in 1868 prohibited the states from denying equal protection, but still no thought was given to prohibiting such conduct by the federal government. In 1954, the Supreme Court read into the due process clause of the Fifth Amendment which binds the federal government an obligation to provide equal protection to all persons. Consequently, due process today is a guarantee not merely of reasonable procedure and nonarbitrary substance, but also of equal protection with respect to conduct of the federal government.

§ 4:9. DUE PROCESS AS PROTECTION OF SIGNIFICANT INTERESTS

As government widens the scope of services, benefits, and privileges made available to the public, the scope of the due process clause expands to protect these new interests. Although literally neither life, liberty, nor property is involved, the interests involved are important. The living document view therefore expands the Constitution to protect these new significant interests.

For example, an automobile driver's license is a protected interest. Similarly, although there is no "right" to receive public welfare, a state cannot exclude a person from receiving welfare without following reasonable procedures that satisfy due process. When the state law provides for the parole of persons convicted of crime, it cannot revoke a parole once granted without following a procedure satisfying the fair-play elements of due process.

(a) School suspension

GOSS v LOPEZ

419 US 565 (1975)

Lopez and other public high school students were suspended for misconduct for periods up to ten days. A state statute authorized the principal of a public school to suspend a student for periods up to ten days without any hearing. A suit was brought by Lopez and others claiming that the statute was unconstitutional because it deprived them of due process by not giving them notice and a hearing to determine whether a suspension was justified. The lower court held the statute unconstitutional, and Goss and other school officials appealed.

OPINION BY WHITE, J.

. . . Appellants contend that because there is no constitutional right to an education at public expense, the Due Process Clause does not protect against expulsions from the public school system. This position misconceives the nature of the issue. . . .

Having chosen to extend the right to an education to people of appellees' class generally, Ohio may not withdraw that right on grounds of misconduct, absent fundamentally fair procedures to determine whether the misconduct has occurred. . . .

The Due Process Clause . . . forbids arbitrary deprivations of liberty. "Where a person's good name, reputation, honor, or integrity is at stake because of what the government is doing to him," the minimal requirements of the Clause must be satisfied. . . . School authorities here suspended appellees from school for periods of up to 10 days based on charges of misconduct. If sustained and recorded, those charges could seriously damage the students' standing with their fellow pupils and their teachers as well as interfere with later opportunities for higher education and employment. It is apparent that the claimed right of the State to determine unilaterally and without process whether that misconduct has occurred immediately collides with the requirements of the Constitution.

Appellants proceed to argue that even if there is a right to a public education protected by the Due Process Clause generally, the Clause comes into play only when the State subjects a student to a "severe detriment or grievous loss." The loss of 10 days, it is said, is neither severe nor grievous. . . . A 10-day suspension from school is not [trivial] in our view and may not be imposed in complete disregard of the Due Process Clause.

A short suspension is, of course, a far milder deprivation than expulsion. But, "education is perhaps the most important function of state and local governments," . . . and the total exclusion from the educational process for more than a trivial period, and certainly if the suspension is for 10 days, is a serious event in the life of the suspended child. Neither the property interest in educational benefits temporarily denied nor the liberty interest in reputation, which is also implicated, is so insubstantial that suspensions may constitutionally be imposed by any procedure the school chooses, no matter how arbitrary.

"Once it is determined that due process applies, the question remains what process is due." . . . We turn to that question, fully realizing as our cases regularly do that the interpretation and application of the Due Process Clause are intensely practical matters and that "the very nature of due process negates any concept of inflexible procedures universally applicable to every imaginable situation." . . . "Many controversies have raged about the cryptic and abstract words of the Due Process Clause but there can be no doubt that at a minimum they require that deprivation of life, liberty or property by adjudication be preceded by notice and opportunity for hearing appropriate to the nature of the case." . . . At the very minimum, therefore, students facing suspension and the consequent interference with a protected property interest must be given some kind of notice and afforded some kind of hearing. "Parties whose rights are to be affected are entitled to be heard; and in order that they may enjoy that right they must first be notified." . . .

The timing and content of the notice and the nature of the hearing will depend on appropriate accommodation of the competing interests involved. . . . The student's interest is to avoid unfair or mistaken exclusion from the educational process, with all of its unfortunate consequences. The Due Process Clause will not shield him from suspensions properly imposed, but it disserves both his interest and the interest of the State if his suspension is in fact unwarranted. . . . The risk of error is not at all trivial, and it should be guarded against if that may be done without prohibitive cost or interference with the educational process. . . .

We do not believe that school authorities must be totally free from notice and hearing requirements if their schools are to operate with acceptable efficiency. Students facing temporary suspension have interests qualifying for protection of the Due Process Clause, and due process requires, in connection with a suspension of 10 days or less, that the student be given oral or written notice of the charges against him and, if he denies them, an explanation of the evidence the authorities have and an opportunity to present his side of the story. . . .

There need be no delay between the time "notice" is given and the time of the hearing. In the great majority of cases the disciplinarian may informally discuss the alleged misconduct with the student minutes after it has occurred. We hold only that, in being given an opportunity to explain his version of the facts at this discussion, the student first be told what he is accused of doing and what the basis of the accusation is. . . . Since the hearing may occur almost immediately following the misconduct, it follows that as a general rule notice and hearing should precede removal of the student from school. We agree with the District Court, however, that there are recurring situations in which prior notice and hearing cannot be insisted upon. Students whose presence poses a continuing danger to persons or property or an ongoing threat of disrupting the academic process may be immediately removed from school. In such cases, the necessary notice and rudimentary hearing should follow as soon as practicable. . . .

We stop short of construing the Due Process Clause to require, countrywide, that hearings in connection with short suspensions must afford the student the opportunity to secure counsel, to confront and cross-examine witnesses supporting the charge, or to call his own witnesses to verify his version of the incident. Brief disciplinary suspensions are almost countless. To impose in each case even truncated trial-type procedures might well overwhelm administrative faculties in many places and, by diverting resources, cost more than it would save in educational effectiveness. Moreover, further formalizing the suspension process and escalating its formality and adversary nature may not only make it too costly as a regular disciplinary tool but also destroy its effectiveness as part of the teaching process.

On the other hand, requiring effective notice and informal hearing permitting the student to give his version of the events will provide a meaningful hedge against erroneous action. At least the disciplinarian will be alerted to the existence of disputes about facts and arguments about cause and effect. He may then determine himself to summon the accuser, permit cross-examination, and allow the student to present his own witnesses. In more difficult cases, he may permit counsel. In any event, his discretion will be more informed and we think the risk of error substantially reduced. . . .

We should also make it clear that we have addressed ourselves solely to the short suspension, not exceeding 10 days. Longer suspensions or expulsions for the remainder of the school term, or permanently, may require more formal procedures. Nor do we put aside the possibility that in unusual situations, although involving only a short suspension, something more than the rudimentary procedures will be required. . . .

[Judgment affirmed]

§ 4:10. LIMITATION ON DUE PROCESS PROTECTION

Through judicial construction, due process of law affords the individual a wide protection. The guarantee, however, affords no protection when the matter is reasonably debatable. In view of this conclusion, due process of law does not bar the regulation of business, for any regulation that would have sufficient support to pass a legislature or the Congress would have at least sufficient claim to validity as to be debatable. The fact that many persons would deem the law unsound, unwise, hazardous, or un-American does not in itself make the law invalid under the due process clause.

As the due process concept is a limitation upon governmental action, it does not apply to transactions between private persons, to private employment or other nonpublic situations. In some cases, however, statutes, such as the federal Civil Rights Act and consumer protection laws, apply due process concepts to private transactions.

Questions for Discussion

1. Who is the final interpreter of the meaning of the due process clause?

2. What was the reason for the rise of the present-day meaning of due process of law?

3. (a) What economic school of thought was adopted by the United States Constitution?   (b) What school of thought existed when the Constitution was adopted?

4. Does the due process clause prevent the adoption of a law regulating the hours of employment or wages of adult males in nondangerous occupations?

5. (a) Does a minimum wage law violate due process?   (b) Is the nature of the employment material? Is it material whether the workers whose wages are regulated are men, women, or children?

6. (a) How are the worker, the industry, and society affected by the payment of unreasonably low wages?   (b) What is the test of the "reasonableness" of a wage?

7. (a) What is the constitutional basis for adopting a minimum wage law? (b) Does it make any difference if it is a federal or a state law?

8. Does a law violate the due process clause if the Supreme Court believes that the law is socially undesirable or economically unwise?

9. What is the test to determine whether a regulatory law satisfies the requirements of due process?

10. What provision of the Constitution guarantees freedom of contract?

11. A law provides that, when 5 percent of the voters so request, a special election may be held to determine whether a change should be made in the tax law. If a majority of the voters voting at the election approve the tax proposal, it becomes effective as a law. Assume that such a referendum law has been adopted. A tax law is then adopted under this referendum. A taxpayer objects that the law was not adopted according to due process. Is the taxpayer's objection correct?

12. One of the Western states provides that a person may be convicted on a verdict rendered by two thirds or more of the jury and that a unanimous verdict is not required. *X* is tried for stealing and is found guilty by 10 of the 12 jurors. He is convicted under the statute described above. He then claims that the law is unconstitutional as he is denied due process of law if the protection is removed of requiring that a unanimous verdict be rendered in order to sustain conviction. Is he correct?

13. What decision would have been made in the *Goss* case if the court applied the test that due process guarantees historical procedure whenever life, liberty, or property is involved?

14. Was Goss deprived of life, liberty, or property?

15. Why is it important whether or not a particular party has the burden of proof in litigation?

16. Discuss the present-day meaning of due process of law. Does it mark a retreat of the doctrine of judicial review?

17. Gladys Boddie lived on welfare in Connecticut. She wanted to obtain a divorce but she did not have the $60 required to commence a divorce action. She claimed that the state requirement of the prepayment of such fees deprived her of her constitutional rights and that the statute was therefore invalid. Was she correct? [*Boddie v Connecticut,* 401 US 371 (1971)]

18. An Oregon statute provides that a defendant may be convicted of a noncapital offense by a verdict of 10 out of 12 jurors. Apodaca was convicted of assault with a deadly weapon, a noncapital offense, on a verdict of 11 to 1 in favor of guilt. He appealed from the conviction on the ground that the due process clause required that the verdict of a jury be unanimous. Was he correct? [*Apodaca v Oregon,* 406 US 404 (1972)]

19. The home of the Crafts was supplied with gas by the city gas company. Because of some misunderstanding, the gas company believed that the Crafts were delinquent in paying their gas bill. The gas company had an informal complaint procedure for discussing such matters, but the Crafts had never been informed that such procedure was available. The gas company notified the Crafts that they were delinquent and that the company was shutting off the gas. The Crafts brought an action to enjoin the gas company from so doing on the theory that a termination without any hearing was a denial of due process. The lower courts held that the interest of the Crafts in receiving gas was not a property interest protected by the due process clause and that the procedures which the gas company followed satisfied the requirements of due process. The Crafts appealed. Were they correct in contending that they had been denied due process of law? [*Memphis Light, Gas and Water Division v Craft,* 436 US 1 (1978)]

20. Under New York law a person on trial for murder will be held guilty of only manslaughter if the killing was committed under "extreme emotional disturbance." The New York law imposes upon the defendant the burden of proving by a preponderance of the evidence that such a mental state existed. Patterson was tried for murder. He claimed that he acted under extreme emotional disturbance but failed to convince the jury of that fact. He was convicted of murder. He then appealed claiming that he was deprived of due process by being required to prove the existence of the emotional disturbance. He claimed that the burden was on the state to prove every element of the crime of murder and that one element which it was required to prove was the absence of such extreme emotional disturbance as would reduce the offense to manslaughter. Was he correct? [*Patterson v New York,* 432 US 197 (1977)]

5

Obligation of Contracts

§ 5:1. THE GUARANTEE

The federal Constitution prohibits the states from impairing the obligation of contracts. We now study this guarantee because it is very clear just what the framers meant. In studying the due process clause, one was not surprised to find the Supreme Court could read different meanings into those words because those words were so vague as to invite "interpretation." In contrast, one would think that the no impairment clause is so precise that no "interpretation" was possible. Yet it will be seen in this chapter that the no impairment clause has been "interpreted" with just as free a hand as the due process clause. This leads to the conclusion that whether a constitutional provision is vague or specific has nothing to do with its durability. As soon as the socioeconomic pressure is sufficiently great, the constitutional provision will give way regardless of what the Constitution says. In other words, no provision of a constitution can withstand the force of the moving pattern of life. If you doubt this, read the Second Amendment to the federal Constitution: ". . . the right of the people to keep and bear arms shall not be infringed." Now walk past the police station with a copy of the Constitution under one arm and a submachine gun under the other. What can we say? Times change. And with them, even constitutions.

What did the no impairment clause mean to the framers of the Constitution? They were familiar with state laws passed to prevent the collection of debts. These debtor relief and stay laws were regarded as inconsistent with sound business. The framers of the Constitution, concerned with the advancement of commerce and business, therefore sought to protect contracts that formed the basis for commerce from being set aside by state laws.

Accordingly, it was provided by Article 1, § 10, Clause 1, that no state could impair the obligation of contracts. Curiously enough, no such prohibition was placed upon the national Congress. This omission has, however, been corrected by the Supreme Court, which has read the obligation of contract clause into the guarantee of due process.

A history of the interpretation of the anticontract impairment clause clearly shows the force of the socioeconomic background, even to the point of inducing the court to fly in the face of both the express letter and the history of the constitutional provision.

§ 5:2. THE CONTRACTS PROTECTED

All contracts between private individuals are protected. This was the class of contracts that the framers had in mind. In addition, the protection of the contract clause has been extended by decision to grants and charters given by a state to a corporation or a person. If the state has granted a charter or made a land grant, it is an impairment of the obligation of contracts for the state to revoke such grant. But if the grant is not by its terms an exclusive grant, the contract clause does not prohibit the state from giving to another corporation or person a similar grant, even though the competition from the second grant will impair the first grant or even make it worthless.

(a) State bonds

UNITED STATES TRUST CO. v NEW JERSEY

431 US 1 (1977)

The Port Authority of New York and New Jersey was created by those states to coordinate the facilities of the New York harbor area. The Port Authority was authorized to issue bonds. In order to make the bonds more attractive to investors, the legislatures of New York and New Jersey limited the amount of the Authority funds that could be used to develop and maintain rail passenger service. In 1974, the legislatures of the two states passed laws abolishing this restriction or covenant with respect to passenger service. The legislatures did this to enable the Authority to invest more money in the development of mass transportation. The United States Trust Company, as trustee for and as a holder of Port Authority bonds, brought a suit to declare the repeal of the covenant invalid. From a decision sustaining the repeal, the Trust Company appealed.

OPINION BY BLACKMUN, J.

. . . It long has been established that the Contract Clause limits the power of the States to modify their own contracts as well as to regulate those between

private parties. . . . As a preliminary matter, appellant's claim requires a determination that the repeal has the effect of impairing a contractual obligation.

In this case the obligation was itself created by a statute, the 1962 legislative
covenant. It is unnecessary, however, to dwell on the criteria for determining
whether state legislation gives rise to a contractual obligation. . . .

The 1962 covenant constituted a contract between the two States and the
holders of the Consolidated Bonds issued between 1962 and the 1973 prospective repeal. . . .

The parties sharply disagree about the value of the 1962 covenant to the
bondholders. . . .

The question of valuation need not be resolved in the instant case because
the State has made no effort to compensate the bondholders for any loss.
. . .

The trial court recognized that there was an impairment in this case: "To the
extent that the repeal of the covenant authorizes the Authority to assume greater
deficits for such purposes, it permits a diminution of the pledged revenues and
reserves and may be said to constitute an impairment of the states' contract with
the bondholders." . . .

Having thus established that the repeal impaired a contractual obligation of
the States, we turn to the question whether that impairment violated the Contract Clause. . . .

[A] subsequent modification . . . may be constitutional if it is reasonable and
necessary to serve an important public purpose. In applying this standard, however, complete deference to a legislative assessment of reasonableness and necessity is not appropriate because the State's self-interest is at stake. A governmental entity can always find a use for extra money, especially when taxes do
not have to be raised. . . .

Mass transportation, energy conservation, and environmental protection are
goals that are important and of legitimate public concern. Appellees contend
that these goals are so important that any harm to bondholders from repeal of
the 1962 covenant is greatly outweighed by the public benefit. We do not accept
this invitation to engage in a utilitarian comparison of public benefit and private
loss. . . . A State cannot refuse to meet its legitimate financial obligations simply
because it would prefer to spend the money to promote the public good rather
than the private welfare of its creditors. . . .

The more specific justification offered for the repeal of the 1962 covenant
was the States' plan for encouraging users of private automobiles to shift to
public transportation. The States intended to discourage private automobile use
by raising bridge and tunnel tolls and to use the extra revenue from those tolls
to subsidize improved commuter rail service. Appellees contend that repeal of
the 1962 covenant was necessary to implement this plan because the new mass
transit facilities could not possibly be self-supporting and the covenant's "permitted deficits" level had already been exceeded. We reject this justification.
. . .

The determination of necessity can be considered on two levels. First, it
cannot be said that total repeal of the covenant was essential; a less drastic
modification would have permitted the contemplated plan without entirely

removing the covenant's limitations on the use of Port Authority revenues and reserves to subsidize commuter railroads. Second, without modifying the covenant at all, the States could have adopted alternative means of achieving their twin goals of discouraging automobile use and improving mass transit. Appellees contend, however, that choosing among these alternatives is a matter for legislative discretion. But a State is not completely free to consider impairing the obligations of its own contracts on a par with other policy alternatives. . . .

In the instant case the need for mass transportation in the New York metropolitan area was not a new development, and the likelihood that publicly owned commuter railroads would produce substantial deficits was well known. As early as 1922, over a half century ago, there were pressures to involve the Port Authority in mass transit. It was with full knowledge of these concerns that the 1962 covenant was adopted. Indeed, the covenant was specifically intended to protect the pledged revenues and reserves against the possibility that such concerns would lead the Port Authority into greater involvement in deficit mass transit.

During the 12-year period between adoption of the covenant and its repeal, public perception of the importance of mass transit undoubtedly grew because of increased general concern with environmental protection and energy conservation. But these concerns were not unknown in 1962, and the subsequent changes were of degree and not of kind. We cannot say that these changes caused the covenant to have a substantially different impact in 1974 than when it was adopted in 1962. And we cannot conclude that the repeal was reasonable in the light of changed circumstances.

We therefore hold that the Contract Clause of the United States Constitution prohibits the retroactive repeal of the 1962 covenant. . . .

[Judgment reversed]

(b) Reservation of right to change

The inviolability of state grants has been offset to a large degree by the recognition of a right of the state to include in the charter or the grant the reservation of a power to make future changes in its terms. When this has been done, a later modification, in most instances, is not regarded as an impairment of the contract.

A reservation of the right to change may also be included or exist in the general corporation law under the terms of which the particular corporation has been incorporated. In such cases, the corporation receives its charter subject to the provisions of the corporation law, and therefore the state has the same right to change its provisions as stated above.

§ 5:3. THE POLICE POWER

Independently of the existence of a reservation of the right to change, the effectiveness of the contract clause has been gradually and increasingly restricted as to both private and corporate contracts by giving the police power greater latitude in restricting contracts in the interest of the common good. This latter doctrine has seen its greatest application in the host of debtor relief laws inspired by the depression following 1929. Efforts at voluntary debt reduction or forbearance had met with but slight success. The legislatures and the Congress therefore came to the aid of the debtors in much the same manner as the colonial and early state legislatures had adopted stay laws for the protection of the farmer and debtor classes. In order to protect both homeowners and farmers from virtual economic destruction by mortgage foreclosure, numerous laws were passed either prohibiting the foreclosure of mortgages for a stated period, limiting the rights of the mortgagee in some manner, or restricting the amount of the deficiency judgment that could be entered against the debtor. The validity of these limiting laws raised a question of social policy in conflict with the letter of the Constitution. There could be no question of the propriety and validity of the mortgages; the law recognized them as lawful, and they were contracts protected by the constitutional guarantee. On the other hand, there were the personal, humanitarian, and community economic arguments that it was no time in which to stand on legal rights and that mortgagees must forbear the assertion of their legal rights or else general disaster would come upon both the individual mortgagors and the community, including the mortgagees as members of the community.

The Supreme Court solved the dilemma by applying the test of reasonableness. The Supreme Court held that, when the rights of the creditor were too seriously impaired, the law was void as a violation of the contract clause in the case of a state law or a violation of the due process clause in the case of a federal law. On the other hand, wherever the law merely delayed the creditor for a reasonable time and gave just compensation for any loss or merely prevented the creditor from obtaining an unreasonable profit at the expense of the debtor, the law was constitutional.

(a) State mortgage moratorium

HOME BUILDING & LOAN ASSN. v BLAISDELL

290 US 398 (1934)

OPINION BY HUGHES, C. J.

Appellant contests the validity of . . . the Minnesota Mortgage Moratorium Law, as being repugnant to the contract clause. . . . [which limits state legislative action].

The Act provides that, during the emergency declared to exist, relief may be had through authorized judicial proceedings with respect to foreclosures of mortgages, and execution sales, of real estate; that sales may be postponed and periods of redemption may be extended. . . .

[A state cannot] . . . adopt as its policy the repudiation of debts or the destruction of contracts or the denial of means to enforce them. But it does not follow that conditions may not arise in which a temporary restraint of enforcement may be consistent with the spirit and purpose of the constitutional provision and thus be found to be within the range of the reserved power of the State to protect the vital interests of the community. It cannot be maintained that the constitutional provision should be so construed as to prevent limited and temporary interpositions with respect to the enforcement of contracts if made necessary by a great public calamity such as fire, flood, or earthquake. . . . The reservation of state power appropriate to such extraordinary conditions may be deemed to be as much a part of all contracts, as is the reservation of state power to protect the public interest in the other situations to which we have referred. And if state power exists to give temporary relief from the enforcement of contracts in the presence of disasters due to physical causes such as fire, flood, or earthquake, that power cannot be said to be nonexistent when the urgent public need demanding such relief is produced by other and economic causes. . . .

It is manifest . . . that there has been a growing appreciation of public needs and of the necessity of finding ground for a rational compromise between individual rights and public welfare. The settlement and consequent contraction of the public domain, the pressure of a constantly increasing density of population, the interrelation of the activities of our people and the complexity of our economic interests, have inevitably led to an increased use of the organization of society in order to protect the very bases of individual opportunity. Where, in earlier days, it was thought that only the concerns of individuals or of classes were involved, and that those of the State itself were touched only remotely, it has later been found that the fundamental interests of the State are directly affected; and that the question is no longer merely that of one party to a contract as against another, but of the use of reasonable means to safeguard the economic structure upon which the good of all depends.

It is no answer to say that this public need was not apprehended a century ago, or to insist that what the provision of the Constitution meant to the vision of that day it must mean to the vision of our time. . . . We must never forget it is *a constitution* we are expounding. . . ., a constitution intended to endure. . . .

[The state law was held constitutional]

DISSENTING OPINION BY SUTHERLAND, J.

The present exigency is nothing new. From the beginning of our existence as a nation, periods of depression, of industrial failure, of financial distress, of unpaid and unpayable indebtedness, have alternated with years of plenty . . . and the attempt by legislative devices to shift the misfortune of the debtor to the shoulders of the creditor without coming into conflict with the contract impairment clause has been persistent and oft-repeated.

The defense of the Minnesota law is made upon grounds which were discountenanced by the makers of the Constitution and have many times been rejected by this court. That defense should not now succeed, because it constitutes an effort to overthrow the constitutional provision by an appeal to facts and circumstances identical with those which brought it into existence. . . .

A statute which materially delays enforcement of the mortgagee's contractual right of ownership and possession does not modify the remedy merely; it destroys, for the period of delay, *all* remedy so far as the enforcement of that right is concerned. The phrase, "obligation of a contract," in the constitutional sense imports a legal duty to perform the specified obligation of *that* contract, not to substitute and perform, against the will of one of the parties, a different, . . . obligation. . . .

(b) Mortgage deficiency judgments

GELFERT v NATIONAL CITY BANK

313 US 221 (1941)

A mortgagee foreclosed his mortgage and purchased the property at the foreclosure sale. At the time when the mortgage had been executed, the law of the state provided that a mortgagee was entitled to a deficiency judgment against the mortgagor for the balance of the mortgage debt remaining unsatisfied after the mortgagor was credited with the net proceeds of the foreclosure sale. At the time when the mortgage was foreclosed, the state law provided that the court in fixing the amount of the deficiency judgment should "determine, upon affidavit or otherwise as it shall direct, the fair and reasonable market value of the mortgaged premises" and should deduct from the amount of the debt the "market value as determined by the court or the sale price of the property whichever shall be higher. . . ." The mortgagee objected to the application of this statute in determining the amount of his deficiency judgment on the ground that it impaired the obligation of the mortgage contract.

OPINION BY DOUGLAS, J.

. . . We are concerned here solely with the application of this statute to a situation where the mortgagee purchases the property at foreclosure sale. We intimate no opinion of its constitutionality as applied to the case where the mortgagee is not the purchaser. . . .

The formula which a legislature may adopt for determining the amount of a deficiency judgment is not fixed and invariable. That which exists at the date of the execution of the mortgage does not become so imbedded in the contract between the parties that it cannot be constitutionally altered. . . . "Not only are existing laws written into contracts in order to fix obligations as between the parties, but the reservation of essential attributes of sovereignty is also read into contracts. . . ." . . .

[It is realized] that the price which property commands at a forced sale may be hardly even a rough measure of its value. The paralysis of real estate markets during periods of depression, the wide discrepancy between the money value of property to the mortgagee and the cash price [received at such a] sale . . . reflect the considerations which have motivated departures from the theory that competitive bidding in this field amply protects the debtor.

Mortgagees are constitutionally entitled to no more than payment in full. . . . They cannot be heard to complain on constitutional grounds if the legislature takes steps to see to it that they get no more than that. . . . There is no constitutional reason why in lieu of the more restricted control by a court of equity the legislature cannot substitute a uniform comprehensive rule designed to reduce or to avoid in the run of cases the chance that the mortgagee will be paid more than once. . . . Certainly under this statute it cannot be said that more than that was attempted. The "fair and reasonable market value" of the property has an obvious and direct relevancy to a determination of the amount of the mortgagee's prospective loss. . . . The fact that men will differ in opinion as to the adequacy of any particular yardstick of value emphasizes that the appropriateness of any one formula is peculiarly a matter for legislative determination. . . . The fact that an emergency was not declared to exist when this statute was passed does not bring [the mortgage] within the protective scope of the contract clause. . . .

Respondent points out that earlier decisions of this court have struck down under the contract clause, as respect contracts previously made, a state statute requiring judicial sale to bring two thirds of the amount of the appraised value of the property. . . . We cannot permit the broad language which those early decisions employed to force legislatures to be blind to the lessons which another century has taught.

[The deficiency owed by the mortgagor was to be calculated in the manner specified by the statute, as the statute was constitutional]

---

§ 5:4. THE EFFECT OF A CHRONIC EMERGENCY

A significant extension of this power to impair the obligation of contracts was recognized in *East New York Savings Bank v Hahn,* 326 US 230 (1945), in which the Supreme Court sustained a debtor relief law in 1944, although it had originally been designed to correct evils existing in 1933, on the basis that the repeal or the invalidation of that law in 1944 would cause a revival of the conditions that gave rise to the law in 1933. The full implication of this decision may be that an emergency law can be sustained indefinitely if the repeal of the law would cause the emergency to revive.

(a) Continuing temporary impairment

EAST NEW YORK SAVINGS BANK v HAHN
326 US 230 (1945)

OPINION BY FRANKFURTER, J.

This was an action begun in 1944 to foreclose a mortgage on real property in the City of New York for nonpayment of principal that had become due in 1924. The trial court held that the foreclosure proceeding was barred by the applicable New York Moratorium Law. . . . This Law, Chapter 93 of the Laws of New York of 1943, extended for another year legislation first enacted in 1933, whereby the right of foreclosure for default in the payment of principal was suspended for a year as to mortgages executed prior to July 1, 1932. Year by year (except in 1941 when an extension for two years was made) the 1933 statute was renewed for another year. . . .

Since *Home Bldg. & L. Ass'n v Blaisdell,* . . . there are left hardly any open spaces of controversy concerning the constitutional restrictions of the Contract Clause upon moratory legislation referable to the depression. . . . The *Blaisdell* case and decisions rendered since . . . yield this governing constitutional principle: when a widely diffused public interest has become enmeshed in a network of multitudinous private arrangements, the authority of the State "to safeguard the vital interests of its people" . . . is not to be gainsaid by abstracting one such arrangement from its public context and treating it as though it were an isolated private contract constitutionally immune from impairment.

. . . This "protective power of the state" . . . may be treated as an implied condition of every contract and, as such, as much part of the contract as though it were written into it, whereby the State's exercise of its power enforces, and does not impair, a contract. A more candid statement is to recognize . . . that the power "which, in its various ramifications, is known as the police power, is an exercise of the sovereign right of the government to protect the . . . general welfare of the people, and is paramount to any rights under contracts between individuals. . . ."

Applying these considerations to the immediate situation brings us to a quick conclusion. In 1933, New York began a series of moratory enactments to counteract the virulent effects of the depression upon New York realty which have been spread too often upon the records of this Court to require even a summary. Chapter 793 of the Laws of 1933 gave a year's grace against foreclosures of mortgages, but it obligated the mortgagor to pay taxes, insurance, and interest. The validity of the statute was sustained. . . . The moratorium has been extended from year to year. . . . [The Court reviewed the careful studies made prior to each extension.]

Appellant asks us to reject the judgment of the joint legislative committee, of the Governor, and of the Legislature, that the public welfare, in the circumstances of New York conditions, requires the suspension of mortgage foreclosures for another year. . . . We are invited to assess not only the range and incidence of what are claimed to be determining economic conditions insofar as they affect the mortgage market—bank deposits and war savings bonds; increased payrolls and store sales; available mortgage money and rise in real estate values—but also to resolve controversy as to the causes and continuity of such improvements, namely the effect of the war and of its termination, and similar matters. Merely to enumerate the elements that have to be considered shows that the place for determining their weight and their significance is the legislature not the judiciary. . . . here there was no "studied indifference to the interests of the mortgagee or to his appropriate protection." Here the Legislature was not even acting merely upon the pooled general knowledge of its members. The whole course of the New York moratorium legislation shows the empiric process of legislation at its fairest: frequent reconsideration, intensive study of the consequences of what has been done, readjustment to changing conditions, and safeguarding the future on the basis of responsible forecasts. The New York Legislature was advised by those having special responsibility to inform it that "the sudden termination of the legislation which has dammed up normal liquidation of these mortgages for more than eight years might well result in an emergency more acute than that which the original legislation was intended to alleviate." . . . It would indeed be strange if there were anything in the Constitution of the United States which denied the State the power to safeguard its people against such dangers. There is nothing. Justification for the 1943 enactment is not negatived because the factors that induced and constitutionally supported its enactment were different from those which included and supported the moratorium statute of 1933. . . .

[Judgment for Hahn. The state mortgage moratorium law was valid]

Questions for Discussion

1. Which governments are bound by the obligation of contract clause?

2. What contracts are protected by the obligation of contract clause?

3. Can a state change the terms of a charter that has already been given to a corporation?

4. (a) What kind of debtor relief laws were adopted during the 1929 depression? (b) Were the laws similar to those adopted during the Confederation period? (c) What was the attitude of the framers of the Constitution with respect to such laws?

5. (a) What is a mortgage moratorium law? (b) Why is it so called? (c) Is such a law constitutional?

6. In *Home B. & L. Assn. v Blaisdell,* the Court reasons that the right to give temporary relief from the enforcement of contracts during a period of disaster due to physical causes includes the right to give such relief when disaster is due to "other and economic causes." (a) Were there in fact any causes other than economic present in this case? (b) Does the majority opinion dispose of the objection raised by the dissenting opinion?

7. "The decision in *Home B. & L. Association v Blaisdell* is bad law but good statesmanship." Do you agree with this statement in whole or in part? Explain.

8. In considering the validity of a mortgage deficiency judgment act, does the Supreme Court determine whether the standard for determining the value of the property that is set off against the mortgage debt is a fair standard? Does it accept the decision of the lawmaker as to what is the fair method of determining value? Does it substitute its own judgment for that of the lawmaker?

9. In determining the legal effect of operation of a mortgage stay law, should the Court consider the overall picture of a stay law annually extended or merely the current extension and dispose of the validity of the law on the basis of its staying enforcement for one year?

10. In *East New York Savings Bank v Hahn,* the Court stresses the study made by the legislature prior to the adoption of the law in question. Does this have any bearing on the question of the legality or the constitutionality of the law as apart from its social necessity?

11. Does *East New York Savings Bank v Hahn* meet the objection raised by the dissenting opinion in *Home B. & L. Assn. v Blaisdell?*

12. What was the extent of the impairment of the contract in the *United States Trust Company* case?

13. Were the contracts in the *United States Trust Company* case private or public contracts?

14. What limitations on the powers of the state are recognized in *Home B. & L. Assn. v Blaisdell?*

15. A state granted a company a charter to operate a toll bridge across a particular river. Thereafter the state granted a similar charter to another corporation. The second corporation built a bridge several hundred feet away from the first. Because of the competition of the second bridge, the profits of the first corporation were materially reduced. The first corporation brought an action to prohibit the second corporation from operating within the area of the first bridge. Decide. [*Charles River Bridge v Warren Bridge,* 11 Peters 420 (1837)]

16. The federal Congress adopted an act in 1934 which provided in part that a farmer could delay the foreclosure of a mortgage for a period of five years, during which time the farmer could remain in possession of the mortgaged farm and pay a reasonable rental that would be distributed among all of the creditors of the farmer, whether their claims were secured or unsecured. A mortgagee claimed that this statute was unconstitutional because it deprived the mortgagee of the right to collect the mortgage debt by foreclosing and diverted the rent to persons not entitled to it. The mortgagee claimed that this was an unconstitutional impairment of the obligation of the mortgage contract. The answer was made that a federal statute was involved and that there was no prohibition in the Constitution against impairment of contracts by the federal government. Was the statute valid? [*Louisville Joint Stock Land Bank v Radford,* 295 US 555 (1935)]

6

Equal Protection of the Law

§ 6:1. THE GUARANTEE

On July 4, 1776, the colonies proclaimed:

> We hold these truths to be self-evident, that all men are created equal, that they are endowed by their Creator with certain unalienable Rights, that among these are Life, Liberty, and the pursuit of Happiness. That to secure these rights, Governments are instituted among Men, . . .

What did the people of the United States say about equality in 1789 in the Constitution? Nothing. There is nothing in the Constitution as adopted in 1789 which guarantees equality. Neither was anything said about equality in the first ten amendments which were so carefully imposed on the new federal government in 1791 to prevent the revival of tyranny.

How do we explain the absence of any guarantee of equality in this basic document that was to be the bedrock on which the new government would rest? It is easy to explain why the original Constitution contained no guarantee. We know from the Federalist opposition to the adoption of the first ten amendments that the Federalists believed a bill of rights was unnecessary because the federal government did not have any power given to it to violate rights. This was a good legal argument, but we know that it did not satisfy the people so the first ten amendments, or the "Bill of Rights," were added to the Constitution to make doubly sure. Why did the Bill of Rights contain no guarantee of equal protection? There is no explanation; we can only guess that even the most cautious felt that equality was so undisputed that it was taken for granted and no one thought it necessary to say anything about it in the Constitution. That is, no one thought so until 1868 when the desire to prevent a cancellation of the civil liberties won by the Civil War led to the adoption of the Fourteenth Amendment, one provision of which prohibits the states from denying any person the equal protection of the law.

But note that nothing was said to protect equality from federal action. As of 1868, equality is protected from violation by state action. As of that year, the Fourteenth Amendment to the federal Constitution declares that "no state shall . . . deny to any person within its jurisdiction the equal protection of the laws." But nothing is said to protect equality from federal action—not until the modern expansion of the due process clause led, in 1954, to the reading of a guarantee of equal protection into the Fifth Amendment's due process guarantee, binding on the federal government.[1]

At last, in 1954, equality became protected from all governments: (1) from the states by the express terms of the Fourteenth Amendment and (2) from the federal government by the interpretation of the Fifth Amendment's due process clause. Thus we can see that the Constitution of today protects equality from invasion by any government.

The guarantee of the equal protection of the laws may be invoked on behalf of anyone, whether a natural person or a corporation, a citizen or an alien. As in the case of other constitutional guarantees, the limitation can only be invoked against governmental action. It must be shown that the discrimination complained of is made by or under the authority of a law or an ordinance of a state, a political subdivision, or an agency, board, or court acting under governmental authority. The guarantee does not protect an individual from discrimination by other private individuals, groups, or clubs. "Civil rights" laws have been adopted by the federal government and by a number of states to protect individuals from discrimination by private persons. Such laws are held constitutional although they restrain the individual's liberty.

§ 6:2. CLASSIFICATION

The equal protection clause does not require that all persons be protected or treated equally, and a law is valid even though it does not apply to everyone or everything. Whether a classification is reasonable depends on whether the nature of the classification made bears a reasonable relation to the evil to be remedied or to the object to be attained by the law. In determining this, the courts have been guided generally by considerations of historical treatment in the past and by the logic of the situation. The trend is to permit the classification to stand unless it is clear that the lawmaking body has been arbitrary or capricious.

---

[1]§ 4:8.

Although classification is by definition the opposite of equality of treatment, since those within the class are treated differently than those outside of the class, many laws would be absurd or oppressive if applied equally. For example, complete equality would permit any person, whether aged 10 or 100, to obtain a license to drive an automobile; would require that the steel beam manufacturer and the baker conform to the same standards with respect to the packaging of their products; and would require that an employer in a downtown office install the same safety devices as every other employer, whether a factory operator or a coal mine owner. Manifestly, "equality" should not prevent the recognition of reasonable distinctions and "natural" classifications, and this is the view of the law.

(a) Tax law exemption

STEWARD MACHINE CO. v DAVIS

301 US 548 (1937)

The Federal Social Security law imposes taxes upon employers and employees in order to create a fund from which to pay the social security benefits. Certain classes of employers were exempted from this tax as is set forth in the portion of the opinion that follows. It was claimed that this exemption made the law unconstitutional.

OPINION BY CARDOZO, J.

. . . The excise is not invalid under the provisions of the Fifth Amendment by force of its exemptions.

The statute does not apply, as we have seen, to employers of less than eight. It does not apply to agricultural labor, or domestic service in a private home or to some other classes of less importance. Petitioner contends that the effect of these restrictions is an arbitrary discrimination vitiating the tax.

The Fifth Amendment unlike the Fourteenth has no equal protection clause. . . . But even the states, though subject to such a clause, are not confined to a formula of rigid uniformity in framing measures of taxation. . . . They may tax some kinds of property at one rate, and others at another, and exempt others altogether. . . . They may lay an excise on the operations of a particular kind of business, and exempt some other kind of business closely akin thereto. . . . If this latitude of judgment is lawful for the states, it is lawful, a fortiori, in legislation by the Congress. . . .

The classifications and exemptions directed by the statute now in controversy have support in considerations of policy and practical convenience that cannot be condemned as arbitrary. The classifications and exemptions would therefore be upheld if they had been adopted by a state and the provisions of the Fourteenth Amendment were invoked to annul them. . . .

[The Social Security Act was held constitutional]

(b) Traffic regulation exemption

RAILWAY EXPRESS AGENCY, INC. v NEW YORK

336 US 106 (1949)

A traffic regulation of New York City prohibited the operation on any street of "an advertising vehicle; provided that nothing . . . shall prevent the putting of business notices upon business delivery vehicles, so long as such vehicles are engaged in the usual business or regular work of the owner and not used merely or mainly for advertising." The Railway Express Agency was a nationwide express business, operating about 1,900 trucks in New York City. It sold the space on the exterior sides of the trucks for advertising unconnected with its own business. It was fined for violating the traffic regulation against advertising vehicles, and it appealed.

OPINION BY DOUGLAS, J.

. . . The Court of Special Sessions concluded that advertising on vehicles using the streets of New York City constitutes a distraction to vehicle drivers and to pedestrians alike and therefore affects the safety of the public in the use of the streets. We do not sit to weigh evidence on the due process issue in order to determine whether the regulation is sound or appropriate; nor is it our function to pass judgment on its wisdom. . . . We would be trespassing on one of the most intensely local and specialized of all municipal problems if we held that this regulation had no relation to the traffic problem of New York City. It is the judgment of the local authorities that it does have such a relation. And nothing has been advanced which shows that to be palpably false.

The question of equal protection of the laws is pressed more strenuously on us. It is pointed out that the regulation draws the line between advertisements of products sold by the owner of the truck and general advertisements. It is argued that unequal treatment on the basis of such a distinction is not justified by the aim and purpose of the regulation. It is said, for example, that one of appellant's trucks carrying the advertisement of a commercial house would not cause any greater distraction of pedestrians and vehicle drivers than if the commercial house carried the same advertisement on its own truck. Yet the regulation allows the latter to do what the former is forbidden from doing. It is therefore contended that the classification which the regulation makes has no relation to the traffic problem since a violation turns not on what kind of advertisements are carried on trucks but on whose trucks they are carried.

That, however, is a superficial way of analyzing the problem, even if we assume that it is premised on the correct construction of the regulation. The local authorities may well have concluded that those who advertise their own wares on their trucks do not present the same traffic problem in view of the nature or extent of the advertising which they use. It would take a degree of omniscience which we lack to say that such is not the case. If that judgment is correct, the advertising displays that are exempt have less incidence on traffic than those of appellants.

We cannot say that that judgment is not an allowable one. Yet if it is, the classification has relation to the purpose for which it is made and does not contain the kind of discrimination against which the Equal Protection Clause affords protection. It is by such practical considerations based on experience rather than by theoretical inconsistencies that the question of equal protection is to be answered. . . . And the fact that New York City sees fit to eliminate from traffic this kind of distraction but does not touch what may be even greater ones in a different category, such as the vivid displays on Times Square, is immaterial. It is no requirement of equal protection that all evils of the same genus be eradicated or none at all. . . .

[Judgment for New York, sustaining the regulation]

§ 6:3. IMPROPER CLASSIFICATION

Laws that make distinctions in the regulation of business, the right to work, and the right to use or enjoy property in terms of race, alienage, or religion are generally invalid.[2] A law prohibiting the ownership of land by aliens has been traditionally regarded as an exception to this rule, as the danger of large alien holdings of land is considered such a social evil as to justify legislation directly prohibiting such holding, although it appears that in course of time this discrimination may be declared invalid.[3]

(a) Moral standards and culture patterns

The lawmaker may not discriminate on the basis of moral standards and culture patterns. Persons cannot be deprived of the same treatment given to other persons because they do not have the same moral standards or culture patterns as the lawmaker. Lawmakers cannot penalize people because they do not live, think, and dress the same as the lawmakers.

UNITED STATES DEPARTMENT OF AGRICULTURE v MORENO

413 US 528 (1973)

The Federal Food Stamp Act provided for the distribution of food stamps to needy "households." In 1971, § 3(e) of the statute was amended to define "households" as limited to groups whose members were all related to each other. This was done because of Congressional dislike for the lifestyles of unrelated "hippies" who were living together in "hippie communes." Moreno and others applied for food stamps but were refused them

---

[2]*Kotch v Board of River Port Pilot Commissioners,* 330 US 552 (1947).
[3]The alien land laws have been held unconstitutional by the supreme courts of California, Montana, and Oregon, as violating the Fourteenth Amendment of the United States Constitution.

because the "relationship" requirement was not satisfied. An action was brought to have the "relationship" requirement declared unconstitutional. The lower court held the statute unconstitutional and the Department of Agriculture appealed.

OPINION BY BRENNAN, J.

Appellees [the applicants for the food stamps] . . . consist of several groups of individuals who allege that, although they satisfy the income eligibility requirements for federal food assistance, they have nevertheless been excluded from the program solely because the persons in each group are not "all related to each other." Appellee Jacinta Moreno, for example, is a 56-year-old diabetic who lives with Ermina Sanchez and the latter's three children. They share common living expenses, and Mrs. Sanchez helps to care for appellee. Appellee's monthly income, derived from public assistance, is $75; Mrs. Sanchez receives $133 per month from public assistance. The household pays $135 per month for rent, gas, and electricity, of which appellee pays $50. Appellee spends $10 per month for transportation to a hospital for regular visits, and $5 per month for laundry. That leaves her $10 per month for food and other necessities. Despite her poverty, appellee has been denied federal food assistance solely because she is unrelated to the other members of her household. Moreover, although Mrs. Sanchez and her three children were permitted to purchase $108 worth of food stamps per month for $18, their participation in the program will be terminated if appellee Moreno continues to live with them.

Appellee Sheilah Hejny is married and has three children. Although the Hejnys are indigent, they took in a 20-year-old girl, who is unrelated to them, because "we felt she had emotional problems." The Hejnys receive $144 worth of food stamps each month for $14. If they allow the 20-year-old girl to continue to live with them, they will be denied food stamps by reason of § 3(e).

Appellee Victoria Keppler has a daughter with an acute hearing deficiency. The daughter requires special instruction in a school for the deaf. The school is located in an area in which the appellee could not ordinarily afford to live. Thus, in order to make the most of her limited resources, appellee agreed to share an apartment near the school with a woman who, like appellee, is on public assistance. Since appellee is not related to the woman, appellee's food stamps will be cut off if they continue to live together. . . .

In essence, appellees contend, and the District Court held, that the "unrelated person" provison of § 3(e) creates an irrational classification in violation of the equal protection component of the Due Process Clause of the Fifth Amendment. We agree.

Under traditional equal protection analysis, a legislative classification must be sustained if the classification itself is rationally related to a legitimate governmental interest. . . . The purposes of the Food Stamp Act were expressly set forth in the congressional "declaration of policy":

It is hereby declared to be the policy of Congress . . . to safeguard the health and well-being of the Nation's population and raise levels of nutrition among low-income households. The Congress hereby finds that the limited food purchasing power of low-income households contributes to hunger and malnutrition among members of such households. The Congress further finds that increased utilization of food in establishing and maintaining adequate national levels of nutrition will promote the distribution in a beneficial manner of our agricultural abundances and will strengthen our agricultural economy, as well as result in more orderly marketing and distribution of food. To alleviate such hunger and malnutrition, a food stamp program is herein authorized which will permit low-income households to purchase a nutritionally adequate diet through normal channels of trade. The challenged statutory classification (households of related persons versus households containing one or more unrelated persons) is clearly irrelevant to the stated purposes of the Act. As the District Court recognized, "the relationships among persons constituting one economic unit and sharing cooking facilities have nothing to do with their ability to stimulate the agricultural economy by purchasing farm surpluses, or with their personal nutritional requirements." . . .

Thus, if it is to be sustained, the challenged classification must rationally further some legitimate governmental interest other than those specifically stated in the congressional "declaration of policy." Regrettably, there is little legislative history to illuminate the purposes of the 1971 amendment of § 3(e). The legislative history that does exist, however, indicates that that amendment was intended to prevent so-called "hippies" and "hippie communes" from participating in the food stamp program. . . . The challenged classification clearly cannot be sustained by reference to this congressional purpose. For if the constitutional conception of "equal protection of the laws" means anything, it must at the very least mean that a bare congressional desire to harm a politically unpopular group cannot constitute a *legitimate* governmental interest. As a result, "a purpose to discriminate against hippies cannot, in and of itself and without reference to [some independent] considerations in the public interest, justify the 1971 amendment." . . .

The Government maintains that the challenged classification should nevertheless be upheld as rationally related to the clearly legitimate governmental interest in minimizing the fraud in the administration of the food stamp program. . . .

In practical effect, the challenged classification simply does not operate so as rationally to further the prevention of fraud. . . . Two *unrelated* persons living together . . . would constitute a single household ineligible for assistance. If financially feasible, however, these same two individuals can legally avoid the "unrelated person" exclusion simply by altering their living arrangements [by living apart]. . . . By so doing, they effectively create two separate "households," both of which are eligible for assistance. . . .

Thus, in practical operation, the 1971 amendment excludes from participation in the food stamp program, *not* those persons who are "likely to abuse the program" but, rather, *only* those persons who are so desperately in need of aid that they cannot even afford to alter their living arrangements so as to retain their eligibility. Traditional equal protection analysis does not require that every classification be drawn with precise " 'mathematical nicety:' " . . . But the classification here in issue is not only "imprecise," it is wholly without any rational basis. The judgment of the District Court holding the "unrelated person" provision invalid under the Due Process Clause of the Fifth Amendment is therefore affirmed.

[Judgment affirmed]

(b) Discriminatory violation of constitutional rights

The denial of equal protection of the laws is constitutionally wrong. The denial of constitutional rights is obviously wrong. When some people are deprived of their constitutional rights, while others are not, there is what might be called a double wrong.

POLICE DEPARTMENT OF CHICAGO v MOSLEY

408 US 92 (1972)

A Chicago ordinance prohibited all picketing within 150 feet of a school while classes were in session but expressly exempted peaceful picketing in connection with a labor dispute in which the school was involved. Mosley had for seven months picketed the Jones Commercial High School with a sign protesting the school's racially discriminatory practices. His conduct was peaceful and orderly. He was arrested for violating the ordinance. He claimed that the ordinance was unconstitutional. The District Court sustained the ordinance, but this was reversed by the Court of Appeals which held the ordinance invalid. The Chicago Chief of Police petitioned the Supreme Court to review the case.

OPINION BY MARSHALL, J.

. . . Because Chicago treats some picketing differently from others, we analyze this ordinance in terms of the Equal Protection Clause of the Fourteenth Amendment. . . . As in all equal protection cases, however, the crucial question is whether there is an appropriate governmental interest suitably furthered by the differential treatment. . . .

The central problem with Chicago's ordinance is that it describes permissible picketing in terms of its subject matter. Peaceful picketing on the subject of a school's labor-management dispute is permitted, but all other peaceful picketing is prohibited. The operative distinction is the message on a picket sign. But, above all else, the First Amendment means that government has no power to restrict expression because of its message, its ideas, its subject matter, or its content. . . . To permit the continued building of our politics and our culture, and to assure self-fulfillment for each individual, our people are guaranteed the right to express any thought, free from government censorship. The essence of this forbidden censorship is content control. Any restriction on expressive activity because of its content would completely undercut the "profound national commitment to the principle that debate on public issues should be uninhibited, robust, and wide-open." . . .

Necessarily, then, under the Equal Protection Clause, not to mention the First Amendment itself, government may not grant the use of a forum to people whose views it finds acceptable, but deny use to those wishing to express less favored or more controversial views. And it may not select which issues are worth discussing or debating in public facilities. There is an "equality of status in the field of ideas," and government must afford all points of view an equal opportunity to be heard. Once a forum is opened up to assembly or speaking by some groups, government may not prohibit others from assembling or speaking on the basis of what they intend to say. Selective exclusions from a public forum may not be based on content alone, and may not be justified by reference to content alone.

Guided by these principles, we have frequently condemned such discrimination among different users of the same medium for expression. In *Niemotko v Maryland,* 340 US 268 (1951), a group of Jehovah's Witnesses were denied a permit to use a city park for Bible talks, although other political and religious groups had been allowed to put the park to analogous uses. Concluding that the permit was denied because of the city's "dislike for or disagreement with the Witnesses or their views," this Court held that the permit refusal violated "the right to equal protection of the laws, in the exercise of those freedoms of speech and religion protected by the First and Fourteenth Amendments." . . .

This is not to say that all picketing must always be allowed. We have continually recognized that reasonable "time, place, and manner" regulations of picketing may be necessary to further significant governmental interests. . . . Similarly, under an equal protection analysis, there may be sufficient regulatory interests justifying selective exclusions or distinctions among pickets. Conflicting demands on the same place may compel the State to make choices among potential users and uses. And the State may have a legitimate interest in prohibiting some picketing to protect public order. But these justifications for selective exclusions from a public forum must be carefully scrutinized. Because picketing plainly involves expressive conduct within the protection of the First Amendment, . . . discriminations among pickets must be tailored to serve a substantial governmental interest. . . .

In this case, the ordinance itself describes impermissible picketing not in terms of time, place, and manner, but in terms of subject matter. The regulation "thus slip[s] from the neutrality of time, place, and circumstance into a concern about content." This is never permitted. In spite of this, Chicago urges that the ordinance is not improper content censorship, but rather a device for preventing disruption of the school. Cities certainly have a substantial interest in stopping picketing which disrupts a school. . . .

Although preventing school disruption is a city's legitimate concern, Chicago itself has determined that peaceful labor picketing during school hours is not an undue interference with school. Therefore, under the Equal Protection Clause, Chicago may not maintain that other picketing disrupts the school unless that picketing is clearly more disruptive than the picketing Chicago already permits. . . .

The Equal Protection Clause requires that statutes affecting First Amendment interests be narrowly tailored to their legitimate objectives. . . . Chicago may not vindicate its interest in preventing disruption by the wholesale exclusion of picketing on all but one preferred subject. Given what Chicago tolerates from labor picketing, the excesses of some nonlabor picketing may not be controlled by a broad ordinance prohibiting both peaceful and violent picketing. . . . Far from being tailored to a substantial governmental interest, the discrimination among pickets is based on the content of their expression. Therefore, under the Equal Protection Clause, it may not stand.

[Judgment affirmed]

---

§ 6:4. DISCRIMINATION BY COURT ACTION

The act of a state court in enforcing a discriminatory agreement or awarding money damages for its breach is regarded as state action within the prohibition of the equal protection clause.[4] The state courts are therefore subject to the same limitation as the state legislatures. Neither by court order nor by legislative mandate may equal protection be denied.

(a) Racial restrictive covenants

SHELLEY v KRAEMER

334 US 1 (1948)

OPINION BY VINSON, C. J.

These cases present for our consideration questions relating to the validity of court enforcement of private agreements, generally described as restrictive covenants, which have as their purpose the exclusion of persons of designated race or color from the ownership or occupancy of real property.

. . . It cannot be doubted that among the civil rights intended to be protected from discriminatory state action by the Fourteenth Amendment are the rights to acquire, enjoy, own and dispose of property.

. . . It is . . . clear that restrictions on the right of occupancy of the sort sought to be created by the private agreements in these cases could not be squared with the requirements of the Fourteenth Amendment if imposed by state statute or local ordinance.

---

[4]*Barrows v Jackson,* 346 US 249 (1953).

. . . The principle has become firmly embedded in our constitutional law that the action inhibited by the first section of the Fourteenth Amendment is only such action as may fairly be said to be that of the States. That Amendment erects no shield against merely private conduct, however discriminatory or wrongful.

We conclude, therefore, that the restrictive agreements standing alone cannot be regarded as a violation of any rights guaranteed to petitioners by the Fourteenth Amendment. So long as the purposes of those agreements are effectuated by voluntary adherence to their terms, it would appear clear that there has been no action by the State and the provisions of the Amendment have not been violated.

. . . But here there was more. These are cases in which the purposes of the agreements were secured only by judicial enforcement by state courts of the restrictive terms of the agreements.

. . . That the action of state courts and of judicial officers in their official capacities is to be regarded as action of the State within the meaning of the Fourteenth Amendment, is a proposition which has long been established by decisions of this Court.

. . . We hold that in granting judicial enforcement of the restrictive agreements in these cases, the States have denied petitioners the equal protection of the laws and that, therefore, the action of the state courts cannot stand. We have noted that freedom from discrimination by the States in the enjoyment of property rights was among the basic objectives sought to be effectuated by the framers of the Fourteenth Amendment. That such discrimination has occurred in these cases is clear. Because of the race or color of these petitioners they have been denied rights of ownership or occupancy enjoyed as a matter of course by other citizens of different race or color.

[Decision of state court sustaining racially restrictive covenant reversed]

§6:5. DISCRIMINATION BY ADMINISTRATIVE ACTION

While a government under a constitution has often been extolled as guaranteeing a government of laws and not of people, it must be remembered that laws have no effect until they are enforced, that is, until people apply them to other people. If the administrative officials or officers charged with the enforcement of the laws are so minded, it is often possible for them to discriminate against certain individuals or to grant favors to others. Thus a law that is fair and nondiscriminatory on its face may in actual application be applied unfairly and unequally. This raises the problem of whether the guarantee that the law be on its face equal in application, subject to reasonable classification, is to be defeated by the discriminatory practices of the administrators. The Supreme Court has held that it will look beyond the surface or the face of the law to determine what the actual application has been and will hold unconstitutional state action denying an equal treatment, although the state law is itself a fair or proper law.

For practical purposes, however, it would seem that this doctrine will be decreasing in importance as the trend continues for government regulation to become increasingly discretionary in character. Under much of modern-day regulation, it is difficult, if not impossible, to determine whether there is a right or a wrong, so that it cannot be determined whether the official has in fact abused discretion for the purpose of making a discriminatory decision.

§6:6. SUMMARY

The equal protection clause with respect to the states and the due process clause with respect to the federal government require that any statutory classification be reasonable. Neither, however, requires that there be absolute equality of treatment for everyone, since classification by definition means some are treated differently than others. These guarantees do not in any way prevent the regulation of business.

The equal protection clause may, in some instances, be operative to prevent intentional inequalities in the administration of a law that on its face is valid.

Questions for Discussion

1. Must a state statute afford equal protection of the laws? Must a federal statute?

2. (a) Does equal protection prevent classification? (b) When is classification proper?

3. A state statute prohibits an employer from discriminating in the employment of persons on the ground of color, race, or creed. A railroad refuses to employ an alien and claims that the law is unconstitutional. (a) Is the railroad's claim correct? (b) Does it affect your answer if the alien is a naturalized citizen of the United States?

4. Why was the classification sustained in *Steward Machine Co. v Davis?*

5. What is the difference between classification and discrimination, and how is it involved in the *Moreno* case?

6. Did the applicants for the food stamps in the *Moreno* case have the right to receive government assistance?

7. In the *Mosley* case would it have made any difference if picketing had not been involved?

8. What similarity is there between the *Moreno* and the *Mosley* cases?

9. The Illinois Community Currency Exchange Act required that anyone providing a check-cashing service or selling or issuing money orders must obtain a state license and be subject to state regulation. In the case of money orders, the statute did not apply to the United States Post Office, the American Express Company, the Postal Telegraph Company, or the Western Union Telegraph Company. Doud and his partner sold money orders in Illinois through the proprietors of drug and grocery stores who acted as their agents. The American Express Company, organized in 1868, conducted a worldwide business that included the sale of money orders. In Illinois, American Express also sold money orders locally in the same manner as Doud and his partner. Doud and his partner sought an injunction to prevent Morey, a state official, from enforcing the Illinois statute against them by requiring that they obtain a license, pay the fee, and comply with regulations under the statute. They claimed that the Illinois statute was unconstitutional because it exempted the American Express Company but applied to the competitors of that company. Was the statute valid? [*Morey v Doud,* 354 US 457 (1957)]

10. An Idaho statute provided that a person attending night school could obtain unemployment compensation but that a daytime student could not. It was claimed that this distinction between the day and night students violated the equal protection clause of the Fourteenth Amendment. Is the statute constitutional? [*Idaho Department of Employment v Smith,* [434 US 100 (1977)]

11. The New York Civil Service law provided that only United States citizens could hold permanent civil service positions. Dougall was an alien who had lawfully entered and was lawfully residing in the United States. He held a job with the City of New York but was fired because of the state statute. He claimed that the statute was unconstitutional. Was he correct? [*Sugarman v Dougall,* 413 US 634 (1973)]

12. An Illinois statute provided that if a woman died without a will, her children, both legitimate and illegitimate, would share her estate. The same statute provided that if a man died without a will, only his legitimate children could share in his estate. An Illinois court determined that Gordon was the father of an illegitimate child and ordered him to contribute to her support. He died sometime thereafter without leaving any will. The child claimed the right to share in Gordon's estate but was excluded because of the statute. The child claimed that the statute was unconstitutional. Was the child correct? [*Trimble v Gordon,* 430 US 762 (1977)]

7

Protection of the Person

§7:1. PERSPECTIVE

No study of the federal Constitution is now complete without recognition of the "unwritten" protection given by the Constitution to personal or human rights. Prior to 1937 a person had only the rights that were expressly guaranteed by the federal Constitution. As of 1936, the federal Constitution protected certain rights from violation by the federal government. Some of these rights and other additional rights were protected from state violation. But there was no general protection of human rights. There was no guarantee of the "inalienable rights of 1776."

It would appear that the people of 1791 who secured the adoption of the Bill of Rights recognized that the written Constitution, even with its Bill of Rights, did not protect all their rights. In what became the Ninth Amendment to the Constitution, they expressly declared "the enumeration in the Constitution of certain rights, shall not be construed to deny or disparage others retained by the people." This suggests that the preceding eight amendments had not declared every right that was protected. Had they done so, there would be no other rights to protect and this Ninth Amendment would be meaningless. That is, the Ninth Amendment would have no meaning unless there was some pool of unwritten, inalienable rights.[1]

---

[1]The term "inalienable right" is employed in preference to "natural right," "fundamental right," or "basic right." Apart from the question of scope or coverage, the adjective "inalienable" emphasizes the fact that the right is still possessed by the people, as opposed to the contention that

The problem here considered has often been obscured by the blunder of calling the first ten amendments to the Constitution a "Bill of Rights," instead of by the accurate title of "Bill of limitations upon the exercise of governmental powers." If the first ten amendments to the Constitution were literally a bill of rights, it would necessarily follow that people, as far as the federal Constitution was concerned, had only those rights which were enumerated therein and that anything which was not protected by those amendments was not protected at all and therefore could be destroyed by government as it chose.

The significance of the difference between a true bill of rights and a bill of limitations can be seen by considering the right to select a spouse. If the federal Constitution is the exclusive source of people's rights, the answer must be that there is no right to select one's spouse because the Constitution does not confer any such right. Yet the American society and the Supreme Court recognize that there is a basic, or fundamental, right to select one's spouse, even though not written in the Constitution, and that no government can interfere with that right.[2]

Following the Civil War, "We the people" added the Thirteenth, Fourteenth and Fifteenth Amendments to the Constitution. Of these, the Fourteenth, added in 1868, has the greatest current importance.

But as the years went by society again found itself not satisfied with the extent to which the Constitution protected human rights, and ultimately the Supreme Court began to interpret the Constitution to find in it a protection of rights not stated there. Starting with the express guarantees of the Constitution as a base, the Supreme Court gradually moved beyond the written Constitution to find new protection for new rights.

At times the judicial process has been obscured by the fact that the Court stated its decision in terms of equal protection of the law. The decision process, however, involved more than the technical defining of the guarantee of equal protection. As will be seen in § 7:4 to § 7:6 of this chapter, the Supreme Court has refused to sustain classifications which in prior years were regarded as proper. In prior years, equal protection allowed classifying on the basis of nonresidence and alienage, poverty, and sex. Today it does not, and today such classifications are ordinarily held to violate the guarantee of equal protection. What has happened to outlaw these time-honored classifications? Respect for the individual human being has grown. The human being is too important to be downgraded because of nonresidence or alienage, poverty, or sex. Classifications based on those criteria are therefore no longer proper. If the human being were not so important, the old classifications would still be held valid and the making of such classifications would not be a denial of equal protection. We therefore do not know whether equal protection is improperly denied until we

---

people have surrendered or subordinated such rights to the will of society. The word "alien" is the term of the old common law for transferring title or ownership. Today we would say transfer and, instead of saying inalienable rights, would say nontransferable rights. Inalienable rights of the people were therefore those which not only were possessed by the people, but which they could not give up, even if they wanted to. Therefore they are still owned by everyone.

[2]*Loving v Virginia,* 388 US 1 (1967).

first decide whether we approve where the dividing line has been drawn. If we approve, it is a reasonable classification; if we do not approve, it is a denial of equal protection. The labels remain constant, but the dividing line moves.

The Supreme Court was slow to recognize that it was "writing" an unwritten Constitution when it gave to human rights a protection not given by the express letter of the federal Constitution. Gradually the Court came to the open recognition that it was protecting unwritten rights; that people have certain rights because they are alive; and that no government, national, state, or local, can interfere unreasonably or unnecessarily with those rights, whether or not there is an express constitutional prohibition of such interference. Otherwise stated, it was recognized that the guarantees of the Constitution are not the sum total of the protection of the individual. The constitutional guarantees are merely specific illustrations of certain rights; the negative implication is not to be made that there is no right if there is no express constitutional guarantee.

More specifically, the above evolution occurred as follows. Beginning in 1937, the fundamental guarantees of the first eight amendments, which were binding on Congress, were expanded so as to limit state action. The Supreme Court held that the fundamental guarantees, such as free speech, were to be "incorporated" into the due process clause of the Fourteenth Amendment so as to be binding on the states.

The next big step was taken in 1954 when the Supreme Court read into the Fifth Amendment, binding the federal government, the equal protection guarantee of the Fourteenth Amendment, which was binding on the states.

The net result of these two techniques was to fuse together virtually all the rights protected by all the amendments to the Constitution and to declare that no government, whether federal or state, could violate the rights protected by those amendments. The underlying rationale for these changes was that our American society had outlived the fears of earlier years and the Supreme Court in effect acted as a constitutional convention to amend the Constitution to bring it in harmony with the current temper of "We the people of the United States." In 1791, the people feared only a federal invasion of free speech. Today we want free speech protected from all governments. In 1791, only the federal government was not to be allowed to interfere with our religious freedom. Today, no government is to be allowed to interfere with our religious freedom. The Constitution, however, does not say what we the people of the United States today desire.

Society today desires that certain rights be protected from all governments. The protection of certain rights from the federal government only, which satisfied the society of 1791, is not sufficient today. The protection of certain rights from violation by state governments, which satisfied the society of 1868, does not satisfy the society of today. As of today, society wants not only the rights of 1791 and 1868 protected but wants them protected from violation by any government, whether federal or state; and in addition, wants certain rights protected which were never protected before.

The Supreme Court, by applying the living document concept, has in effect amended or rewritten the Constitution to say what we want it to say. This evolution is of obvious importance to us because, as people, we are concerned about our rights. Those who will run businesses and governments must understand and respect the rights of employees and citizens. We are all involved.

§ 7:2. PROTECTION OF PRIVACY

There is nothing in the written Constitution which guarantees privacy. Yet protection of privacy is probably one of the strongest objectives of our modern American society. Those of you who have left your parents' home have felt the drive of "I want to lead my own life." Deep in the hearts of we the people of today is the feeling of "leave me alone."

To repeat, the Constitution gave no express protection to the privacy of being left alone. The Fourth Amendment, by limiting the use of search warrants, provided a protection of privacy from invasion by police and government. Beyond this, the Constitution did not go.

The recent judicial recognition of privacy, however, bars the Congress and the state legislatures from specifying who you may marry, defining what books you may have in your home, or refusing you food stamps or other public assistance because you live in a group whose members are not related by blood or marriage. Persons cannot be refused statutory benefits because they are not married or not legitimate. Zoning laws may not exclude families with children.

The protection given to privacy by the unwritten Constitution may be regarded as stemming from the expansion of the First Amendment's guarantee of freedom of speech. The freedom to speak without restraint, however, is merely an aspect of a freedom to act, to think, to live, without restraint. In its interpretation of the First Amendment, the Supreme Court had already declared, in *West Virginia Board of Education v Barnette,* that: if there is any fixed star in our constitutional constellation, it is that no official, high or petty, can prescribe what shall be orthodox in politics, nationalism, religion, or other matters of opinion or force citizens to confess by word or act their faith therein.[3]

Viewed in the light of the decisions of the decades which followed the *Barnette* case, we see that the Barnette star not only illuminated a narrow definition of the First Amendment, but lit the way to a return to the basic principles of 1776. The fundamental, unalterable, and inalienable rights of the human being must be protected.

(a) Marriage

Nothing in the Constitution gives you the freedom to choose the person you will marry. States may impose licensing restrictions on marriage for the purpose of enforcing health standards. But a state cannot tell A to marry B instead of C. This choice is regarded as a private matter which, though not guaranteed by the Constitution, is as fully protected as though the Constitution expressly declared such right.

---

[3]319 US 624, 642 (1943).

LOVING v VIRGINIA

388 US 1 (1967)

Virginia statutes made it a crime for any white person to marry someone of another race. Richard Loving, white, made an interracial marriage. He and his wife were prosecuted under the Virginia statutes. They claimed the statutes were unconstitutional. The state court held that the statutes were constitutional and convicted the Lovings. They appealed to the United States Supreme Court.

OPINION BY WARREN C. J.

[The state court]. . . reasoned that marriage has traditionally been subject to state regulation without federal intervention, and, consequently, the regulation of marriage should be left to exclusive state control by the Tenth Amendment.

While the state court is no doubt correct in asserting that marriage is a social relation subject to the State's police power, the State does not contend in its argument before this Court that its powers to regulate marriage are unlimited notwithstanding the commands of the Fourteenth Amendment. Nor could it do so in light of *Meyer v Nebraska,* 262 US 390 (1923), and *Skinner v Oklahoma,* 316 US 535 (1942). Instead, the State argues that the meaning of the Equal Protection Clause, as illuminated by the statements of the Framers, is only that state penal laws containing an interracial element as part of the definition of the offense must apply equally to whites and Negroes in the sense that members of each race are punished to the same degree. Thus, the State contends that, because its miscegenation statutes punish equally both the white and the Negro participants in an interracial marriage, these statutes, despite their reliance on racial classifications, do not constitute an invidious discrimination based upon race. . . .

We reject the notion that the mere "equal application" of a statute containing racial classifications is enough to remove the classifications from the Fourteenth Amendment's proscription of all invidious racial discriminations. . . .

The Equal Protection Clause requires the consideration of whether the classifications drawn by any statute constitute an arbitrary and invidious discrimination. The clear and central purpose of the Fourteenth Amendment was to eliminate all official state sources of invidious racial discrimination in the States.

. . .

There can be no question but that Virginia's miscegenation statutes rest solely upon distinctions drawn according to race. The statutes proscribe generally accepted conduct if engaged in by members of different races. Over the years, this Court has consistently repudiated "distinctions between citizens solely because of their ancestry" as being "odious to a free people whose institutions are founded upon the doctrine of equality." . . . At the very least, the Equal Protection Clause demands that racial classifications, especially suspect in criminal statutes, be subjected to the "most rigid scrutiny," . . . and, if they are ever to be upheld, they must be shown to be necessary to the accomplishment of some permissible state objective, independent of the racial discrimination which it was the object of the Fourteenth Amendment to eliminate. Indeed, two members of this Court have already stated that they "cannot conceive of a valid legislative purpose . . . which makes the color of a person's skin the test of whether his conduct is a criminal offense." . . .

There is patently no legitimate overriding purpose independent of invidious racial discrimination which justifies this classification. . . . We have consistently denied the constitutionality of measures which restrict the rights of citizens on account of race. There can be no doubt that restricting the freedom to marry solely because of racial classifications violates the central meaning of the Equal Protection Clause.

These statutes also deprive the Lovings of liberty without due process of law in violation of the Due Process Clause of the Fourteenth Amendment. The freedom to marry has long been recognized as one of the vital personal rights essential to the orderly pursuit of happiness by free men.

Marriage is one of the "basic civil rights of man," fundamental to our very existence and survival. . . . To deny this fundamental freedom on so unsupportable a basis as the racial classifications embodied in these statutory classifications so directly subversive of the principle of equality at the heart of the Fourteenth Amendment is surely to deprive all the State's citizens of liberty without due process of law. The Fourteenth Amendment requires that the freedom of choice to marry not be restricted by invidious racial discriminations. Under our Constitution, the freedom to marry, or not marry, a person of another race resides with the individual and cannot be infringed by the State.

[Convictions reversed]

(b) Zoning

MOORE v EAST CLEVELAND

431 US 494 (1977)

Moore lived in East Cleveland with her son and two grandchildren who were first cousins. A zoning ordinance limited occupancy of a dwelling unit to members of a single family. This ordinance was violated by Moore because her grandchildren lived with her. She was prosecuted for violating the ordinance. She claimed it was unconstitutional. The ordinance was sustained and she was fined. She appealed to the United States Supreme Court.

OPINION BY POWELL, J.

. . . Appellant, Mrs. Inez Moore, lives in her East Cleveland home together with her son, Dale Moore, Sr., and her two grandsons, Dale, Jr., and John Moore, Jr. The two boys are first cousins rather than brothers; we are told that John came to live with his grandmother and with the elder and younger Dale Moores after his mother's death. . . .

The city argues that our decision in *Village of Belle Terre v Boraas,* 416 US 1 . . . (1974), requires us to sustain the ordinance attacked here. Belle Terre, like East Cleveland, imposed limits on the types of groups that could occupy a single dwelling unit. Applying the constitutional standard announced in this Court's leading land-use case, *Euclid v Ambler Realty Co.,* 272 US 365 . . . (1926), we sustained the Belle Terre ordinance on the ground that it bore a rational relationship to permissible state objectives.

But one overriding factor sets this case apart from Belle Terre. The ordinance there affected only *unrelated* individuals. It expressly allowed all who were related by "blood, adoption, or marriage" to live together, and in sustaining the ordinance we were careful to note that it promoted "family needs" and "family values." . . . East Cleveland, in contrast, has chosen to regulate the occupancy of its housing by slicing deeply into the family itself. This is no mere incidental result of the ordinance. On its face it selects certain categories of relatives who may live together and declares that others may not. In particular, it makes a crime of a grandmother's choice to live with her grandson in circumstances like those presented here.

When a city undertakes such intrusive regulation of the family, neither Belle Terre nor Euclid governs; the usual judicial deference to the legislature is inappropriate. "This Court has long recognized that freedom of personal choice in matters of marriage and family life is one of the liberties protected by the Due Process Clause of the Fourteenth Amendment." . . . A host of cases . . . have consistently acknowledged a "private realm of family life which the state cannot enter." . . . Of course, the family is not beyond regulation. . . . But when the government intrudes on choices concerning family living arrangements, this Court must examine carefully the importance of the governmental interests advanced and the extent to which they are served by the challenged regulation. . . .

When thus examined, this ordinance cannot survive. The city seeks to justify it as a means of preventing overcrowding, minimizing traffic and parking congestion, and avoiding an undue financial burden on East Cleveland's school system. Although these are legitimate goals, the ordinance before us serves them marginally, at best. For example, the ordinance permits any family consisting only of husband, wife, and unmarried children to live together, even if the family contains a half dozen licensed drivers, each with his or her own car. At the same time it forbids an adult brother and sister to share a household, even if both faithfully use public transportation. The ordinance would permit a grandmother to live with a single dependent son and children, even if his school-age children number a dozen, yet it forces Mrs. Moore to find another dwelling for her grandson John, simply because of the presence of his uncle and cousin in the same household. . . . [The ordinance] has but a tenuous relation to alleviation of the conditions mentioned by the city.

The city . . . suggests that any constitutional right to live together as a family extends only to the nuclear family—essentially a couple and its dependent children.

To be sure, [earlier] cases did not expressly consider the relationship presented here. They were immediately concerned with freedom of choice with respect to childbearing, . . . of parents to the custody and companionship of their own children, . . . or with traditional parental authority in matters of child rearing and education. . . . But unless we close our eyes to the basic reasons why certain rights associated with the family have been accorded shelter under the Fourteenth Amendment's Due Process Clause, we cannot avoid applying the force and rationale of these precedents to the family choice involved in this case.

Understanding those reasons requires careful attention to this Court's function under the Due Process Clause. Mr. Justice Harlan described it eloquently:

> Due process has not been reduced to any formula; its content cannot be determined by reference to any code. The best that can be said is that through the course of this Court's decisions it has represented the balance which our Nation, built upon postulates of respect for the liberty of the individual, has struck between that liberty and the demands of organized society. If the supplying of content to this Constitutional concept has of necessity been a rational process, it certainly has not been one where judges have felt free to roam where unguided speculation might take them. The balance of which I speak is the balance struck by this country, having regard to what history teaches are the traditions from which it developed as well as the traditions from which it broke. That tradition is a living thing. A decision of this Court which radically departs from it could not long survive, while a decision which builds on what has survived is likely to be sound. No formula could serve as a substitute, in this area, for judgment and restraint.
>
> . . . The full scope of the liberty guaranteed by the Due Process Clause cannot be found in or limited by the precise terms of specific guarantees elsewhere provided in the Constitution. This "liberty" is not a series of isolated points pricked out in terms of the taking of property; the freedom of speech, press, and religion; the right to keep and bear arms; the freedom from unreasonable searches and seizures; and so on. It is a rational continuum which, broadly speaking, includes a freedom from all substantial arbitrary impositions and purposeless restraints, . . . and which also recognizes, what a reasonable and sensitive judgment must, that certain interests require particularly careful scrutiny of the state needs asserted to justify their abridgment. *Poe v Ullman,* [367 US 497] (dissenting opinion).

Substantive due process has at times been a treacherous field for this Court. There *are* risks when the judicial branch gives enhanced protection to certain substantive liberties without the guidance of the more specific provisions of the Bill of Rights. . . . There is reason for concern lest the only limits to such judicial intervention become the predilections of those who happen at the time to be Members of the Court. . . . History counsels caution and restraint. But it does not counsel abandonment, nor does it require what the city urges here: cutting off any protection of family rights at the first convenient, if arbitrary boundary —the boundary of the nuclear family.

Appropriate limits on substantive due process come not from drawing arbitrary lines but rather from careful "respect for the teachings of history [and] solid recognition of the basic values that underlie our society." . . . Our decisions establish that the Constitution protects the sanctity of the family precisely because the institution of the family is deeply rooted in this Nation's history and tradition. It is through the family that we inculcate and pass down many of our most cherished values, moral and cultural.

Ours is by no means a tradition limited to respect for the bonds uniting the members of the nuclear family. The tradition of uncles, aunts, cousins, and especially grandparents sharing a household along with parents and children has roots equally venerable and equally deserving of constitutional recognition. Over the years millions of our citizens have grown up in just such an environment, and most, surely, have profited from it. Even if conditions of modern society have brought about a decline in extended family households, they have not erased the accumulated wisdom of civilization, gained over the centuries and honored throughout our history, that supports a larger conception of the family. Out of choice, necessity, or a sense of family responsibility, it has been common for close relatives to draw together and participate in the duties and the satisfactions of a common home. Decisions concerning child rearing . . . recognized as entitled to constitutional protection, long have been shared with grandparents or other relatives who occupy the same household—indeed who may take on major responsibility for the rearing of the children. Especially in times of adversity, such as the death of a spouse or economic need, the broader family has tended to come together for mutual sustenance and to maintain or rebuild a secure home life. This is apparently what happened here.

Whether or not such a household is established because of personal tragedy, the choice of relatives in this degree of kinship to live together may not lightly be denied by the State. *Pierce* [*v Society of Sisters*, 268 US 510 (1925)] struck down an Oregon law requiring all children to attend the State's public schools, holding that the Constitution "excludes any general power of the State to standardize its children by forcing them to accept instruction from public teachers only." By the same token the Constitution prevents East Cleveland from standardizing its children—and its adults—by forcing all to live in certain narrowly defined family patterns.

[Judgment reversed]

§ 7:3. PROTECTION OF PARENTAL CONTROL

The federal Constitution contains no provision guaranteeing parents the right to raise and educate their children in any particular way. As the federal

Constitution has no provision on this matter, a strict or bedrock interpretation of the federal Constitution would mean that the federal Constitution has nothing to say on the matter and that the states are therefore free to regulate the subject as they choose, limited only by an applicable state constitutional provision. The Supreme Court has not followed this construction but, to the contrary, has found that there is a right of parental control which is protected by the federal Constitution, although there is no express provision in the Constitution on the subject.

(a) Education of children

The state can require that children go to grammar school or to a private school but cannot prohibit parents from sending their children to a private school. The states can require school attendance up to an age which takes the child into high school unless such high school attendance is contrary to the sincere religious beliefs of the parents.

WISCONSIN v YODER

406 US 205 (1972)

Children of Yoder and of his neighbor Miller had graduated from grammar school. As the children were under 16 years of age, they were required by state law to go to high school. Yoder and Miller were Amish and objected to sending the children to public high school because they regarded it as too "worldly" and in conflict with their religious beliefs. It was admitted that the religious beliefs of the parents were sincere and that they had been held by Amish communities for nearly three centuries. The parents claimed that the compulsory school attendance statute was unconstitutional. This claim was overruled and the parents were convicted of violating the state law. The Court of Appeals reversed the conviction and the state petitioned the Supreme Court to review the case.

OPINION BY BURGER, C. J.

. . . There is no doubt as to the power of a State, having a high responsibility for education of its citizens, to impose reasonable regulations for the control and duration of basic education. . . .

We turn . . . to the State's broader contention that its interest in its system of compulsory education is so compelling that even the established religious practices of the Amish must give way. . . .

The requirement for compulsory education beyond the eighth grade is a relatively recent development in our history. Less than 60 years ago, the educational requirements of almost all of the States were satisfied by completion of the elementary grades, at least where the child was regularly and lawfully employed. . . .

This case, of course, is not one in which any harm to the physical or mental health of the child or to the public safety, peace, order, or welfare has been demonstrated or may be properly inferred. . . . Our holding today in no degree depends on the assertion of the religious interest of the child as contrasted with that of the parents. It is the parents who are subject to prosecution here for failing to cause their children to attend school, and it is their right of free exercise, not that of their children, that must determine Wisconsin's power to impose criminal penalties on the parent. . . . The children are not parties to this litigation. . . . The State's position from the outset has been that it is empowered to apply its compulsory-attendance law to Amish parents in the same manner as to other parents—that is, without regard to the wishes of the child. That is the claim we reject today. . . .

The State's argument . . . appears to rest on the potential that exemption of Amish parents from the requirements of the compulsory-education law might allow some parents to act contrary to the best interests of their children by foreclosing their opportunity to make an intelligent choice between the Amish way of life and that of the outside world. . . .

Indeed it seems clear that if the State is empowered, as parents patriae, to "save" a child from himself or his Amish parents by requiring an additional two years of compulsory formal high school education, the State will in large measure influence, if not determine, the religious future of the child. . . . This case involves the fundamental interest of parents, as contrasted with that of the State, to guide the religious future and education of their children. The history and culture of Western civilization reflect a strong tradition of parental concern for the nurture and upbringing of their children. This primary role of the parents in the upbringing of their children is now established beyond debate as an enduring American tradition. If not the first, perhaps the most significant statements of the Court in this area are found in *Pierce v Society of Sisters* [268 US 510 (1925)] in which the Court observed:

> Under the doctrine of *Meyer v Nebraska,* 262 US 390, we think it entirely plain that the Act of 1922 [barring private school attendance] unreasonably interferes with the liberty of parents and guardians to direct the upbringing and education of children under their control. As often heretofore pointed out, rights guaranteed by the Constitution may not be abridged by legislation which has no reasonable relation to some purpose within the competency of the State. The fundamental theory of liberty upon which all governments in this Union repose excludes any general power of the State to standardize its children by forcing them to accept instruction from public teachers only. The child is not the mere creature of the State; those who nurture him and direct his destiny have the right, coupled with the high duty, to recognize and prepare him for additional obligations.

The duty to prepare the child for "additional obligations," referred to by the Court, must be read to include the inculcation of moral standards, religious beliefs, and elements of good citizenship. Pierce, of course, recognized that where nothing more than the general interest of the parent in the nurture and education of his children is involved, it is beyond dispute that the State acts "reasonably" and constitutionally in requiring education to age 16 in some public or private school meeting the standards prescribed by the State.

However read, the Court's holding in Pierce stands as a charter of the rights of parents to direct the religious upbringing of their children. . . .

In the face of our consistent emphasis on the central values underlying the Religion Clauses in our constitutional scheme of government, we cannot accept a parens patriae claim of such all-encompassing scope and with such sweeping potential for broad and unforeseeable application as that urged by the State.

[Judgment affirmed]

§ 7:4. PROTECTION OF THE STRANGER FROM DISCRIMINATION

From time immemorial, communities have raised barriers against the stranger. The alien could be refused entrance. If allowed to enter the community, the alien could be disqualified from holding office, owning property, practicing specified professions, and so on.

By judicial decision, virtually all power to discriminate against nonresidents or aliens has been removed. The alien and the nonresident are no longer inferior persons or second class citizens. A state may not discriminate in favor of its local citizens by imposing a residence requirement on welfare and public assistance or requiring one year's residence as a qualification for voting.

(a) Protection of aliens from discrimination

The federal government may discriminate against classes of aliens to the extent of refusing to permit their entry into the United States. Thus all of a particular nationality may be barred admission into the United States or the number of entrants may be limited. If an alien can meet the conditions required for admission, even the federal government cannot exclude the alien. The individual states have no power to exclude an alien who has been admitted by the United States.

With respect to aliens who are already lawfully within the United States, neither the federal administrative agencies nor the states may discriminate on the basis of alienage. Once lawfully admitted, the alien is a "person" and must be treated equally with all other persons.

HAMPTON v MOW SUN WONG

426 US 88 (1976)

The United States Civil Service Commission adopted a regulation which restricted civil service examinations and permanent civil service appointments to United States citizens. Mow Sun Wong and four other aliens who had been

lawfully admitted into the United States claimed that this regulation was unconstitutional. They brought an action in the federal district court to invalidate the
regulation. The district court sustained the regulation. The plaintiff took an
appeal to the Court of Appeals. That court reversed the district court and the
Civil Service Commission then petitioned the Supreme Court to review the case.

OPINION BY STEVENS, J.

. . . During the period of over two years that the appeal was pending in the
Ninth Circuit, we decided two cases that recognize the importance of protecting
the employment opportunities of aliens. In *Sugarman v Dougall,* 413 US 634,
. . . we held that a section of the New York civil service law which provided that
only United States citizens could hold permanent positions in the competitive
class of the State's civil service violated the Equal Protection Clause of the
Fourteenth Amendment; that Clause also provided the basis for our holding in
In re Griffiths, 413 US 717, . . . that Connecticut's exclusion of aliens from the
practice of law was unconstitutional.

In this case, the Court of Appeals recognized that neither Sugarman nor
Griffiths was controlling because the Fourteenth Amendment's restrictions on
state power are not directly applicable to the Federal Government and because
Congress and the President have broad power over immigration and naturalization which the States do not possess. Nevertheless, those decisions provided
the Court of Appeals with persuasive reasons for rejecting the bases asserted
by the defendants in the District Court as justifications for the Civil Service
Commission's policy of discriminating against noncitizens. For we specifically
held that the State's legitimate interest in the undivided loyalty of the civil
servant who participates directly in the formulation and execution of Government policy was inadequate to support a state restriction indiscriminately dis-
qualifying the "sanitation man, class B," the typist, and the office worker,
. . . moreover, we expressly considered, and rejected, New York's contention
that its special interest in the advancement and profit of its own citizens could
justify confinement of the State's civil service to citizens of the United States.
. . .

The Court of Appeals reversed [the district court and held the regulation
invalid]. . .

The petitioners advance alternative arguments to justify the discrimination
as an exercise of the plenary federal power over immigration and naturalization.
First, the petitioners argue that the equal protection aspect of the Due Process
Clause of the Fifth Amendment is wholly inapplicable to the exercise of federal
power over aliens, and therefore no justification for the rule is necessary. Alternatively, the petitioners argue that the Fifth Amendment imposes only a slight
burden of justification on the Federal Government, and that such a burden is
easily met by several factors not considered by the District Court or the Court
of Appeals. Before addressing these arguments, we first discuss certain limitations which the Due Process Clause places on the power of the Federal Government to classify persons subject to its jurisdiction.

The federal sovereign, like the States, must govern impartially. The concept of equal justice under law is served by the Fifth Amendment's guarantee of due process, as well as by the Equal Protection Clause of the Fourteenth Amendment. . . .

In this case we deal with a federal rule having nationwide impact. The petitioners correctly point out that the paramount federal power over immigration and naturalization forecloses a simple extension of the holding in Sugarman as decisive of this case. We agree with the petitioners' position that overriding national interests may provide a justification for a citizenship requirement in the federal service even though an identical requirement may not be enforced by a State.

We do not agree, however, with the petitioners' primary submission that the federal power over aliens is so plenary that any agent of the National Government may arbitrarily subject all resident aliens to different substantive rules from those applied to citizens. . . .

In this case the petitioners have identified several interests which the Congress or the President might deem sufficient to justify the exclusion of noncitizens from the federal service. They argue, for example, that the broad exclusion may facilitate the President's negotiation of treaties with foreign powers by enabling him to offer employment opportunities to citizens of a given foreign country in exchange for reciprocal concessions—an offer he could not make if those aliens were already eligible for federal jobs. Alternatively, the petitioners argue that reserving the federal service for citizens provides an appropriate incentive to aliens to qualify for naturalization and thereby to participate more effectively in our society. They also point out that the citizenship requirement has been imposed in the United States with substantial consistency for over 100 years and accords with international law and the practice of most foreign countries. Finally, they correctly state that the need for undivided loyalty in certain sensitive positions clearly justifies a citizenship requirement in at least some parts of the federal service, and that the broad exclusion serves the valid administrative purpose of avoiding the trouble and expense of classifying those positions which properly belong in executive or sensitive categories. . . .

It is the business of the Civil Service Commission to adopt and enforce regulations which will best promote the efficiency of the federal civil service. That agency has no responsibility for foreign affairs, for treaty negotiations, for establishing immigration quotas or conditions of entry, or for naturalization policies. Indeed, it is not even within the responsibility of the Commission to be concerned with the economic consequences of permitting or prohibiting the participation by aliens in employment opportunities in different parts of the national market. On the contrary, the Commission performs a limited and specific function.

The only concern of the Civil Service Commission is the promotion of an efficient federal service. In general it is fair to assume that its goal would be best served by removing unnecessary restrictions on the eligibility of qualified applicants for employment. . . . [The matters urged by the] Commission . . . in this case are not matters which are properly the business of the Commission. . . . One exception is the administrative desirability of having one simple rule excluding all noncitizens when it is manifest that citizenship is an appropriate and legitimate requirement for some important and sensitive positions. Arguably, therefore, administrative convenience may provide a rational basis for the general rule. . . .

There is nothing in the record before us, or in matter of which we may properly take judicial notice, to indicate that the Commission actually made any considered evaluation of the relative desirability of a simple exclusionary rule on the one hand, or the value to the service of enlarging the pool of eligible employees on the other. . . .

In sum, assuming without deciding that the national interests identified by the petitioners would adequately support an explicit determination by Congress or the President to exclude all noncitizens from the federal service, we conclude that those interests cannot provide an acceptable rationalization for such a determination by the Civil Service Commission. The impact of the rule on the millions of lawfully admitted resident aliens is precisely the same as the aggregate impact of comparable state rules which were invalidated by our decision in Sugarman. By broadly denying this class substantial opportunities for employment, the Civil Service Commission rule deprives its members of an aspect of liberty. Since these residents were admitted as a result of decisions made by the Congress and the President, implemented by the Immigration and Naturalization Service acting under the Attorney General of the United States, due process requires that the decision to impose that deprivation of an important liberty be made either at a comparable level of government or, if it is to be permitted to be made by the Civil Service Commission, that it be justified by reasons which are properly the concern of that agency. We hold that . . . the Civil Service Commission Regulation . . . has deprived these respondents of liberty without due process of law and is therefore invalid.

[Judgment affirmed]

---

§ 7:5. PROTECTION FROM WEALTH AND POVERTY DISCRIMINATION

Nothing in the Constitution prohibits discrimination against a person who does not possess money. Historically such discrimination was recognized and approved by our founding fathers. Ownership of property was a common requirement for eligibility to vote. Not until the Jacksonian era in the 19th century was the right to vote freed in all states from the requirement of owning property. Indirect or economic discrimination against poverty was long permitted by allowing the charging of fees for particular privileges which had the practical effect of prohibiting the poor from obtaining what the rich could afford to buy.

Within the last few decades, the Supreme Court has found another unwritten right of the person to be free from any poverty discrimination. Thus a state may not impose property or money qualifications on the right to vote or to seek a public office. And indigent persons cannot be required to pay a filing fee in order to bring a divorce action when the effect is to bar them from bringing such action because they do not have the filing fee.

(a) Punishment

TATE v SHORT

401 US 395 (1971)

Texas adopted a policy of imposing only fines for motor vehicle traffic violations. Tate was convicted for 9 violations and fined a total of $425. He did not have any money. In accordance with local law, the court ordered him imprisoned for 85 days, with each day of imprisonment counting as a substitute for $5 of the fine. Tate filed a petition for his release, naming Short, the local chief of police, as defendant. Tate claimed that imprisoning him because he did not have the money to pay the fine was unconstitutional. The state court rejected his claim and he appealed to the United States Supreme Court.

OPINION BY BRENNAN, J.

. . . The Illinois statute involved in Williams authorized both a fine and imprisonment. Williams was given the maximum sentence for petty theft of one year's imprisonment and a $500 fine, plus $5 in court costs. The judgment, as permitted by the Illinois statute, provided that if, when the one-year sentence expired, Williams did not pay the fine and court costs, he was to remain in jail a sufficient length of time to satisfy the total amount at the rate of $5 per day. We held that the Illinois statute as applied to Williams worked as an invidious discrimination solely because he was too poor to pay the fine, and therefore violated the Equal Protection Clause.

Although the instant case involves offenses punishable by fines only, petitioner's imprisonment for nonpayment constitutes precisely the same unconstitutional discrimination since, like Williams, petitioner was subjected to imprisonment solely because of his indigency. In *Morris v Schoonfield,* 399 US 508, 509 . . . (1970), four members of the Court anticipated the problem of this case and stated the view, which we now adopt, that "the same constitutional defect condemned in Williams also inheres in jailing an indigent for failing to make immediate payment of any fine, whether or not the fine is accompanied by a jail term and whether or not the jail term of the indigent extends beyond the maximum term that may be imposed on a person willing and able to pay a fine. In each case, the Constitution prohibits the State from imposing a fine as a sentence and then automatically converting it into a jail term solely because the defendant is indigent and cannot forthwith pay the fine in full."

Our opinion in Williams stated the premise of this conclusion in saying that "the Equal Protection Clause of the Fourteenth Amendment requires that the statutory ceiling placed on imprisonment for any substantive offense be the same for all defendants irrespective of their economic status." . . . Since Texas has legislated a "fines only" policy for traffic offenses, that statutory ceiling cannot, consistently with the Equal Protection Clause, limit the punishment to payment of the fine if one is able to pay it, yet convert the fine into a prison term for an indigent defendant without the means to pay his fine. Imprisonment in such a case is not imposed to further any penal objective of the State. It is imposed to augment the State's revenues but obviously does not serve that purpose; the defendant cannot pay because he is indigent and his imprisonment, rather than aiding collection of the revenue, saddles the State with the cost of feeding and housing him for the period of his imprisonment.

There are, however, other alternatives to which the State may constitutionally resort to serve its concededly valid interest in enforcing payment of fines. . . .

Several States have a procedure for paying fines in installments. . . .

This procedure has been widely endorsed as effective not only to collect the fine but also to save the expense of maintaining a prisoner and avoid the necessity of supporting his family under the state welfare program while he is confined.

[Judgment reversed]

§ 7:6. PROTECTION FROM SEX DISCRIMINATION

The founding fathers and the early American society regarded it as proper to treat females as a separate class, on the basis of which some laws would disqualify women from acting or other laws would extend to women a special protection not given to men. The English common law followed the ecclesiastical concept that the wife became one with her husband. On this basis, laws were common which prohibited married women from making contracts.

In the last few decades, all such laws have been declared unconstitutional on the ground that there was no valid reason for treating women differently than men with respect to the particular matters involved and that to treat them differently when there was no basis for such treatment constituted a denial of equal protection. In the case of the states, this was held a violation of the express requirement of equal protection of the Fourteenth Amendment. In the case of the federal government, it was held a violation of the guarantee of equal protection "read" into the Fifth Amendment's guarantee of due process. In consequence of this new constitutionally protected equality, a state may not give a preference to a man when appointing an administrator of a decedent's estate, and a man in the armed forces cannot be given an automatic dependency allowance for his wife when a woman in the armed forces is required to prove the dependency of her husband before she is given a dependency allowance for him.

(a) Alimony and divorce

In prior years, many states allowed a wife to obtain alimony from her husband while a divorce action was pending. After the divorce was ended, the states differed, some allowing post-divorce alimony and others denying alimony after the divorce. No provision was made for the payment of alimony to a husband. To the extent that the wife was allowed alimony and the husband could not obtain alimony, there was a discrimination based on sex.

ORR v ORR

US   , 59 L Ed 2d 306 (1979)

William Orr was divorced from his wife. The Alabama court ordered him to pay her alimony. He failed to do so and was prosecuted for contempt of the court order. He raised the defense that the statute under which the payment of alimony had been ordered was unconstitutional because it only authorized alimony payments to a divorced wife and made no provision for alimony to a divorced husband. The lower court sustained the Alabama statute and Orr petitioned for review by the United States Supreme Court.

OPINION BY BRENNAN, J.

In authorizing the imposition of alimony obligations on husbands, but not on wives, the Alabama statutory scheme "provides that different treatment be accorded . . . on the basis of . . . sex; it thus establishes a classification subject to scrutiny under the Equal Protection Clause. . . ." The fact that the classification expressly discriminates against men rather than women does not protect it from scrutiny. . . ."To withstand scrutiny" under the equal protection clause, "classifications by gender must serve important governmental objectives and must be substantially related to achievement of those objectives." . . . We shall, therefore, examine the three governmental objectives that might arguably be served by Alabama's statutory scheme.

Appellant views the Alabama alimony statutes as effectively announcing the State's preference for an allocation of family responsibilities under which the wife plays a dependent role, and as seeking for their objective the reinforcement of that model among the State's citizens. . . . We agree, as he urges, that prior cases settle that this purpose cannot sustain the statutes. *Stanton v Stanton,* 421 US 7 . . . (1975), held that the "old notion" that "generally it is the man's primary responsibility to provide a home and its essentials," can no longer justify a statute that discriminates on the basis of gender. "No longer is the female destined solely for the home and the rearing of the family, and only the male for the marketplace and the world of ideas," . . . If the statute is to survive constitutional attack, therefore, it must be validated on some other basis.

The opinion of the Alabama Court of Civil Appeals suggests other purposes that the statute may serve. Its opinion states that the Alabama statutes were

"designed" for "the wife of a broken marriage who needs financial assistance.
. . ." This may be read as asserting either of two legislative objectives. One is
a legislative purpose to provide help for needy spouses, using sex as a proxy for
need. The other is a goal of compensating women for past discrimination during
marriage, which assertedly has left them unprepared to fend for themselves in
the working world following divorce. We concede, of course, that assisting
needy spouses is a legitimate and important governmental objective. We have
also recognized "reduction of the disparity in economic condition between men
and women caused by the long history of discrimination against women . . . as
. . . an important governmental objective." . . . It only remains, therefore, to
determine whether the classification at issue here is "substantially related to
achievement of those objectives." . . .

Ordinarily, we would begin the analysis of the "needy spouse" objective by
considering whether sex is a sufficiently "accurate proxy" . . . for dependency
to establish that the gender classification rests "upon some ground of difference
having a fair and substantial relation to the object of the legislation. . . ."
Similarly, we would initially approach the "compensation" rationale by asking
whether women had in fact been significantly discriminated against in the
sphere to which the statute applied a sex-based classification, leaving the sexes
"*not* similarly situated with respect to opportunities" in that sphere. . . .

But in this case, even if sex were a reliable proxy for need, and even if
the institution of marriage did discriminate against women, these factors still
would "not adequately justify the salient features of" Alabama's statutory
scheme. . . . Under the statute, individualized hearings at which the parties'
relative financial circumstances are considered *already* occur. . . . There is no
reason, therefore, to use sex as a proxy for need. Needy males could be
helped along with needy females with little if any additional burden on the
State. In such circumstances, not even an administrative convenience rationale exists to justify operating by generalization or proxy. Similarly, since
individualized hearings can determine which women were in fact discriminated against vis à vis their husbands, as well as which family units
defied the stereotype and left the husband dependent on the wife, Alabama's alleged compensatory purpose may be effectuated without placing
burdens solely on husbands. Progress toward fulfilling such a purpose would
not be hampered, and it would cost the State nothing more, if it were to
treat men and women equally by making alimony burdens independent of
sex. "Thus, the gender-based distinction is gratuitous; without it the statutory scheme would only provide benefits to those men who are in fact similarly situated to the women the statute aids," . . . and the effort to help
those women would not in any way be compromised.

Moreover, use of a gender classification actually produces perverse results
in this case. As compared to a gender-neutral law placing alimony obligations
on the spouse able to pay, the present Alabama statutes give an advantage only
to the financially secure wife whose husband is in need. Although such a wife
might have to pay alimony under a gender-neutral statute, the present statutes
exempt her from that obligation. Thus, "the [wives] who benefit from the

disparate treatment are those who were . . . nondependent on their husbands."
. . . They are precisely those who are not "needy spouses" and who are "least
likely to have been victims of . . . discrimination" by the institution of marriage.
A gender-based classification which, as compared to a gender-neutral one, gen-
erates additional benefits only for those it has no reason to prefer cannot survive
equal protection scrutiny.

Legislative classifications which distribute benefits and burdens on the
basis of gender carry the inherent risk of reinforcing stereotypes about the
"proper place" of women and their need for special protection. . . . Thus,
even statutes purportedly designed to compensate for and ameliorate the
effects of past discrimination must be carefully tailored. Where, as here, the
State's compensatory and ameliorative purposes are as well served by a gender-neutral classification as one that gender-classifies and therefore carries
with it the baggage of sexual stereotypes, the State cannot be permitted to
classify on the basis of sex. And this is doubly so where the choice made by
the State appears to redound—if only indirectly—to the benefit of those
without need for special solicitude.

[Judgment reversed]

§ 7:7. EROSION OF "HUMAN RIGHTS-PROPERTY RIGHTS" CLASSIFICATION

Running through the history of social reform and unrest is the cliché of
"human rights versus property rights." For the purpose of constitutional protection, this distinction has declining importance as it is increasingly recognized
that property rights are themselves "personal rights" because property is owned
by some person.

Recognition of the foregoing does not change the fact, however, that
where people are directly concerned, the law is more likely to extend protection. For example, the earliest and furthest extensions of the right to sue for
harm caused by defective products were made when the plaintiff had been
physically injured, as contrasted with when property had been damaged or
economic loss sustained. Similarly, in the field of constitutional law, an indigent person is entitled to a free court-appointed attorney when prosecuted
for an offense for which conviction could impose a sentence of even one
day's imprisonment. Such protection is not required when the sentence imposed is only a fine.[4] All these variations can be brought into proper focus
when it is recognized that the analysis is quantitative rather than qualitative.
That is, the more the human being is directly and immediately affected, the
more concerned the law and the Constitution are likely to be. When there is
not this direct and immediate effect, as when only property or money loss is

---

[4]*Scott v Illinois,*   US   , 59 L Ed2d 383 (1979).

involved, the law and the Constitution are not likely to be as sympathetic toward the plaintiff.

LYNCH v HOUSEHOLD FINANCE CORP.

405 US 538 (1972)

Lynch owed money to the Household Finance Corporation. She had a savings account in a credit union. Household, acting in accordance with the Connecticut law, garnished the savings account. By this procedure, the credit union was prohibited from allowing Lynch to withdraw any of her money. Lynch claimed that this seizure of her savings account without first giving her a day in court to determine whether any money was owed Household deprived her of due process of law and of equal protection of the law. She brought an action in a federal district court to enjoin the garnishment proceeding, claiming that the court could issue the injunction by virtue of a federal statute, 28 USC § 1343(3), which protected the constitutional and equal rights of citizens and persons. The district court refused to issue the injunction on the theory that this statute only protected "personal" rights and did not protect "property" rights. Lynch appealed to the United States Supreme Court.

OPINION BY STEWART, J.

. . . In dismissing the appellant's complaint, the District Court held that § 1343(3) applies only if "personal" rights, as opposed to "property" rights, are allegedly impaired. . . .

This Court has never adopted the distinction between personal liberties and proprietary rights as a guide to the contours of § 1343(3) jurisdiction. Today we expressly reject that distinction.

Neither the words of § 1343(3) nor the legislative history of that provision distinguishes between personal and property rights. In fact, the Congress that enacted the predecessor of § 1343(3) seems clearly to have intended to provide a federal judicial forum for the redress of wrongful deprivations of property by persons acting under color of state law. . . .

That Act guaranteed "broad and sweeping . . . protection" to basic civil rights. . . . Acquisition, enjoyment, and alienation of property were among those rights. . . .

The Fourteenth Amendment vindicated for all persons the rights established by the Act of 1866. . . . "It cannot be doubted that among the civil rights intended to be protected from discriminatory state action by the Fourteenth Amendment are the rights to acquire, enjoy, own and dispose of property. Equality in the enjoyment of property rights was regarded by the framers of that Amendment as an essential precondition to the realization of other basic civil rights and liberties which the Amendment was intended to guarantee." . . .

The broad concept of civil rights embodied in the 1866 Act and in the Fourteenth Amendment is unmistakably evident in the legislative history of §

1 of the Civil Rights Act of 1871, 17 Stat 13, the direct lineal ancestor of . . .
§ 1343(3). . . . And the rights that Congress sought to protect in the Act of 1871
were described by the chairman of the House Select Committee that drafted the
legislation as "the enjoyment of life and liberty, with the right to acquire and
possess property of every kind, and to pursue and obtain happiness and safety."
. . .

That the protection of property as well as personal rights was intended is
also confirmed by President Grant's message to Congress urging passage of the
legislation, and by the remarks of many members of Congress during the legislative debates. . . .

A final, compelling reason for rejecting a "personal liberties" limitation
upon § 1343(3) is the virtual impossibility of applying it. The federal courts have
been particularly bedeviled by "mixed" cases in which both personal and property rights are implicated, and the line between them has been difficult to draw
with any consistency or principled objectivity. The case before us presents a
good example of the conceptual difficulties created by the test.

Such difficulties indicate that the dichotomy between personal liberties and
property rights is a false one. Property does not have rights. People have rights.
The right to enjoy property without unlawful deprivation, no less than the right
to speak or the right to travel, is in truth a "personal" right, whether the
"property" in question be a welfare check, a home, or a savings account. In fact,
a fundamental interdependence exists between the personal right to liberty and
the personal right in property. Neither could have meaning without the other.
That rights in property are basic civil rights has long been recognized. J. Locke,
Of Civil Government 82–85 (1924); J. Adams, A Defence of the Constitutions
of Government of the United States of America, in F. Coker, Democracy, Liberty, and Property 121–132 (1942); 1 W. Blackstone, Commentaries 138–140.
Congress recognized these rights in 1871 when it enacted the predecessor of
. . . § 1343(3). We do no more than reaffirm the judgment of Congress today.

[Judgment reversed]

---

§ 7:8. SUMMARY

It is important to stop and look back upon the rise of the concept of the
"person" protected from governmental invasion even though there are no express constitutional provisions expressly extending such protection.

From one standpoint, the growth of the concept of protection of the person is the continuation of a graph line of long vintage. Going back thousands
of years, most of us were serfs or slaves. Only a few of us were the pharaoh,
the emperor, the king, the priests, or the nobles. As the current of history that
we describe as Anglo-American wended its way, you and I became promoted
to the level of free subjects of the Crown. But we were still subjects and we
possessed only those rights which a gracious sovereign chose to recognize. On
July 4, 1776, more than a revolution was born. There was a transformation.

We, who by law were subjects, suddenly became human beings, possessed of rights because we were human beings, and these rights could not be impaired by any government.

To the colonials, preoccupied with winning the War of the Revolution, a war which dragged on from 1776 to 1783, little thought was given to the full significance of "rights of human beings." The 19th century with its western expansion further distracted the American society from considering what those rights meant. In a society based on the economic theory of laissez faire or "government hands off" policy, the "person" was rarely hard pressed, and western expansion always provided an open door for escape. That door is closed today and, in addition, society has moved from a negative "do nothing" governmental approach of laissez faire to a positive "do everything" approach. The result is that the individual is becoming more and more regulated and therefore it becomes more and more important to define the rights of the human being and to determine just how far government can go. The labor union movement, the civil rights movement, and the women's liberation movement of this century are merely further gropings to give to the phrase "rights of human beings" a definite meaning.

Just what is the sound line between the human being and government? This is the basic problem which underlies many of the questions that have caused so much ferment in recent years and which are destined to continue to challenge society in the next century.

For the present, it is essential to recognize that, for the most part, the Constitution as adopted in 1789 and its amendments of 1791 and 1868 do not contain the answers. Such answers as we have to date have for the most part been supplied by the judges of the Supreme Court.

The rising tide of protection of human rights has not stopped with the re-interpreting of the Constitution. Many federal and state statutes have been adopted to protect the new rights from violation by private employers, lenders, and merchants. We now live in an era in which human rights are protected by constitutions from governmental invasion and by statutes from private invasion. The shot heard round the world echoes still.

Looking at the evolution of personal rights from another point of view, we perceive that the problem of governing a democratic society is not as simple as was thought in 1776. In that year, the simple solution was "down with the king." We the people believed in 1776 that once the people were in charge, we would have a perfect society. In true democratic spirit, it seemed that once things were run by the will of the majority there would be no governmental trouble.

The experience of two centuries, and particularly the history of the last two decades, tells us that in 1776 we the people over-simplified the problem. People then thought that it was just a matter of classifying the "goodies" and the "baddies," as children do when they watch the late, late show.

What emerges as the American way of life is not a society run by the will of the majority. Instead we find that the American way divides life into two zones. In one zone, the democratic concept is that the majority rules. In the other zone, that of the "person," not even the majority can interfere. To illustrate, the majority can declare by statute that before you marry you must have a health certificate. This is perfectly reasonable for the protection of the general health and welfare. But no one, not the majority, nor even the unanimous action of everyone in the United States, can command you to marry or not marry or choose your mate for you.

Most amazing is the fact that a relatively short time ago the second zone was unheard of and everything was thought to be in the zone which was controlled by the majority unless there was an express prohibition of such action by the Constitution. Even more startling, the emergence of the second zone has taken place for the most part within your lifetime. The expansion of the second zone will have a profound effect on the rest of your life.

Questions for Discussion

1. What section of the Constitution protects the dignity of the human being?

2. Is the difference between the bedrock view and the living document view significant in determining the protection of the person?

3. What provision of the Constitution guarantees freedom of choice in selecting a spouse?

4. In every state it is illegal for near relatives to marry. Is such a statute unconstitutional when it makes such a marriage a crime?

5. Would the *Moore* case ordinance have been valid if it merely said that all persons living in a single residence must be related by blood or marriage?

6. How can it be said that the *Moore* zoning ordinance is unconstitutional if an ordinance prohibiting the residing together of unrelated persons is constitutional?

7. If Yoder's children had been required to go to public high school, would there be any direct violation of his right to religious freedom?

8. Assume that Yoder had objected to the attendance of his children in high school because he did not approve of the curriculum on the ground that he did not think that it trained the child to hold a job and be self-supporting. Would the school attendance law have been held unconstitutional in that case?

9. A civil service regulation is adopted which states that in making appointments to any position, natural born citizens will be given preference over others and naturalized aliens will be given preference over unnaturalized aliens. Is this regulation valid?

10. Why was the *Hampton* case regulation not valid on the ground that the United States could exclude immigrants and therefore could subject them to restrictions after they were admitted?

11. A state wishes to be sure that those who vote for governor and the state legislature will be "stable" citizens who have an interest in the community. It therefore passes a law that no one may vote for governor or for state legislators except persons who own their own homes or who have been living for five years in the same rented residence or apartment. Is this law constitutional?

12. What alternative does the *Tate* case recognize for "$30 or 30 days"?

13. Why did the *Orr* case condemn the statute on the ground of sex discrimination?

14. A state statute declares that the health of children is one of the most important assets of the state and therefore declares that the time lost by an employed mother when she is absent from work taking care of a sick child shall not be deducted in determining the mother's period of employment for purposes of seniority or retirement. Is the statute constitutional?

15. Does the Constitution distinguish between human rights and property rights?

16. Does it make any difference if a right is classified as a human right or a property right?

17. Henry Avaro moved from New Mexico to Arizona. After living in Arizona one month, he was admitted as a charity patient for treatment of his asthma to the Memorial Hospital, a private hospital in Maricopa County. The hospital requested the county to transfer him to the County Hospital and to reimburse the Memorial Hospital for the care it had already given Avaro. The county refused both requests on the ground that an Arizona statute authorized such nonemergency medical care for indigent persons only if they had been living in the county for the 12 months preceding the request for treatment. The Memorial Hospital claimed that the statute was unconstitutional. Was the Memorial Hospital correct? [*Memorial Hospital v Maricopa County,* 415 US 250 (1974)]

18. For a person to register to vote in a state election, a Tennessee statute required that the person be a resident of the state for one year and of the county for three months. Blumstein moved into the state. He could not satisfy the residency requirements and therefore could not register to vote. He claimed that this deprived him of his constitutional right to vote and that therefore the residency requirements were invalid. The state claimed that the residency requirements were designed to insure that voters would be familiar with the issues involved in the elections and to give the voting officials time in which to verify any disputed claim to having a local residence. Were the residency requirements constitutional? [*Dunn v Blumstein,* 405 US 330 (1972)]

19. In order to shorten the election ballots, California required that a candidate for public office must pay a filing fee in order to be listed on the ballot for the primary election. Lubin applied for listing as a candidate but was refused because he could not pay the filing fee. He claimed that he was indigent and that the requirement of a filing fee excluded him from being a candidate and therefore was a denial of equal protection. Was he correct? [*Lubin v Panish*, 415 US 709 (1974)]

20. In order to combat the illegal sale of narcotics, New York adopted a statute requiring that doctors send to the state Department of Health the name and address of any patient for whom a narcotic was prescribed. This information was maintained confidentially in a computer-controlled data storage center. A lawsuit was brought claiming that the statute was unconstitutional as an invasion of privacy. Was the statute valid? [*Whalen v Roe*, 429 US 589 (1977)]

In this part, attention is directed to the use of the powers of government to regulate business.

8

Regulation of Commerce

§ 8:1. PERSPECTIVE

The desire to protect commerce from restrictions and barriers set up by the individual states was the prime factor leading to the adoption of the Constitution of 1789. To protect commerce, the new Congress was given, by Article I, § 8, Clause 3, the power "to regulate Commerce with foreign Nations, and among the several States, and with the Indian Tribes."

Difficulty soon arose as to just what "interstate commerce" was. Until 1937, interstate commerce was interpreted as the crossing of a state line of persons, goods, or communications. Thus people moving from one state to another, merchandise being sent into another state, and radio and telephone communication between the states were all interstate commerce. It was the element of something crossing the state line which made the activity "interstate." The fact that there was no business element of buying and selling in a particular case was immaterial. Hence it was immaterial that the people were traveling for pleasure, that the goods sent were a present, or that a telegram or phone conversation was purely personal.

Beginning in 1937, the Supreme Court began expanding the concept of interstate commerce, so that by 1946 the power to regulate interstate commerce had become the power to regulate the general welfare of the nation. By that year, the power had expanded to the point that the authority given to Congress to adopt regulatory laws was held "as broad as the economic needs of the nation."[1]

In terms of the earlier comparison of the bedrock and living document views,[2] the Supreme Court in 1937 shifted to interpreting the commerce clause by the living document point of view. We the people of the United States, the majority of Congress, the President of the United States, and finally the majority of the Supreme Court believed that in order to keep the Constitution alive and make it keep step with the problems facing the nation, it was necessary to amend the Constitution to give the Congress the power to adopt general welfare laws. But the needs of the nation and the American people were too pressing to permit the delay of adopting amendments. The Supreme Court therefore took the shortcut of amending the Constitution by decision.

What were the needs of the nation that were so pressing? The country was struggling through the Depression following the stock market crash of 1929. This had been followed by a period of bank failures and closings of building and loan associations. Savings were wiped out. Unemployment rose to unprecedented heights. Welfare relief expanded to a point far beyond the financial ability of states and local governmental units, such as cities and counties, to carry. Something had to be done on a national scale and done quickly or to many it seemed that the country would be ruined. After a decade of financial misery, the American people, who had been such firm advocates of free enterprise, were both willing and eager to turn their backs on the policy of "government hands off" and were calling loudly and strongly for the national government to step in and regulate the economy. The true believer in Adam Smith would have advocated that government do nothing, on the theory that finally the Depression would pass and the nation would again rise from the ruins of the past. The advocates of the opposing program[3] won out, and by 1937 the Supreme Court had converted the commerce power into what soon became a general welfare power.

From one point of view, one could say that the pre-1937 cases may now be ignored, as they are no longer the law. The realist would say, "Why waste time and attention on something that no longer is the law?" The answer to this is that the newness of the new is underscored by comparison with the contrary old. Most important of all, we come face to face with a dynamic of society that is often ignored. It is that when change is desired, change will take place and no words on paper can prevent that change. Just as King Canute could not stop the ocean from rolling, we cannot stop the forces of societal movement from changing the status quo. Whether it be a New Year's resolution, a treaty, or a constitution, it is all the same; the rolling tide of social events is a force that nothing can resist.

---

[1]*American Power & Light Co. v Securities and Exchange Commission,* 329 US 90 (1946).

[2]§§ 3:2, 3.

[3]This opposing program was called the "New Deal." Franklin Delano Roosevelt was elected President of the United States in 1932 on the platform that he would bring a "new deal" to the American people.

§ 8:2. INTERSTATE COMMERCE AS CROSSING A STATE LINE

In its first phase, interstate commerce was the crossing of a state line by persons, goods, or communications, whether for profit or not. The fact that the particular method of transportation or communication had not yet been invented when the Constitution was adopted in 1789 was immaterial;[4] if there was any crossing of a state line, there was interstate commerce within the scope of the federal power. If there was no crossing of a state line, there was no interstate commerce. After 1937, this latter statement is not correct, as will be seen in § 8:3. However, even after 1937, if in fact there is a crossing of a state line, there is interstate commerce. The crossing of a state line test will ordinarily still be applied in applying federal criminal laws that prohibit transporting specified articles in interstate commerce.

(a) Manufacturing

Is manufacturing interstate commerce? If the crossing of a state line test is followed, the answer is necessarily no. Does it make any difference if the normal pattern of distribution for the manufactured goods is that they are sent out of the state for use or sale in other states? Prior to 1937, the answer to this question was still most emphatically no. In 1937 the answer became yes.

UNITED STATES v E. C. KNIGHT CO.

156 US 1 (1895)

OPINION BY FULLER, C.J.

By the purchase of the stock of the four Philadelphia refineries, with shares of its own stock, the American Sugar Refining Company acquired nearly complete control of the manufacture of refined sugar within the United States. . . .

The fundamental question is, whether . . . that monopoly can be directly suppressed under the [Sherman Antitrust Act]. . . .

"No distinction is more popular to the common mind, or more clearly expressed in economic and political literature, than that between manufacture and commerce. Manufacture is transformation—the fashioning of raw materials into a change of form for use. . . . If it be held that the term [commerce] includes the regulation of all such manufactures as are intended to be the subject of commercial transactions in the future, it is impossible to deny that it would also include all productive industries that contemplate the same thing. The result would be that Congress would be invested, to the exclusion of the States, with the power to regulate, not only manufactures, but also agriculture, horticulture, stock raising, domestic fisheries, mining—in short, every branch of human

---

[4]*Pensacola Telegraph Co. v Western Union Telegraph Co.,* 96 US 1 (1877).

industry. For is there one of them that does not contemplate, more or less clearly, an interstate or foreign market? . . ."

Contracts, combinations, or conspiracies to control domestic enterprise in manufacture, agriculture, mining, production in all its forms, or to raise or lower prices or wages, might unquestionably tend to restrain external as well as domestic trade, but the restraint would be an indirect result, however inevitable and whatever its extent. . . .

There was nothing in the proofs to indicate any intention to put a restraint upon trade or commerce, and the fact, as we have seen, that trade or commerce might be indirectly affected was not enough to entitle complainants to a decree. . . .

[Judgment against the United States because manufacturing was not interstate commerce and therefore the Sherman Act could not apply]

(b) Codes of competition for industry

A.L.A. SCHECHTER POULTRY CORP. v UNITED STATES

295 US 495 (1935)

The National Industrial Recovery Act authorized representatives of the various industries in the United States to draw up individual codes of fair competition by which each industry was to be governed. It was hoped that by these codes unemployment would be reduced, the volume of business increased, working conditions improved, and child labor and unfair trade practices eliminated. United States officials cooperated in the preparation of these codes, which became effective when approved by the President of the United States. In the event that an industry could not agree to a code by which it was to be governed, the President was authorized to impose a code upon it. Once adopted, a code had the force of law and all members of the industry had to observe the code subject to civil and criminal liability for violation. Schechter claimed that the NIRA was unconstitutional.

OPINION BY HUGHES, C.J.

The question of the application of the provisions of the Live Poultry Code to intrastate transactions . . . presents the question whether the particular provisions of the Live Poultry Code, which the defendants were convicted of violating and for having conspired to violate, were within the regulating power of Congress.

These provisions relate to the hours and wages of those employed by defendants in their slaughterhouses in Brooklyn and to the sales there made to retail dealers and butchers. . . . The interstate transactions in relation to that poultry then ended. . . .

The undisputed facts thus afford no warrant for the argument that the poultry handled by defendants at their slaughterhouse markets was in a "current" or "flow" of interstate commerce and was thus subject to congressional regulation. The mere fact that there may be a constant flow of commodities into a State does not mean that the flow continues after the property has arrived and has become commingled with the mass of property within the State and is there held solely for local disposition and use. So far as the poultry here in question is concerned, the flow in interstate commerce had ceased.

Did the defendants' transactions directly "affect" interstate commerce so as to be subject to federal regulation? The power of Congress extends not only to the regulation of transactions which are part of interstate commerce, but to the protection of that commerce from injury. . . .

In determining how far the federal government may go in controlling intrastate transactions upon the ground that they "affect" interstate commerce, there is a necessary and well-established distinction between direct and indirect effects. The precise line can be drawn only as individual cases arise, but the distinction is clear in principle. Direct effects are illustrated by the railroad cases . . . as e.g., the effect of failure to use prescribed safety appliances on railroads which are the highways of both interstate and intrastate commerce, injury to an employee engaged in interstate transportation by the negligence of an employee engaged in an intrastate movement, the fixing of rates for intrastate transportation which unjustly discriminate against interstate commerce. But where the effect of intrastate transactions upon interstate commerce is merely indirect, such transactions remain within the domain of state power. . . .

The question of chief importance relates to the provisions of the Code as to the hours and wages of those employed in defendants' slaughterhouse markets. It is plain that these requirements are imposed in order to govern the details of defendants' management of their local business. The persons employed in slaughtering and selling in local trade are not employed in interstate commerce. Their hours and wages have no direct relation to interstate commerce. The question of how many hours these employees should work and what they should be paid differs in no essential respect from similar questions in other local businesses which handle commodities brought into a State and there dealt in as a part of its internal commerce. . . . The argument of the Government proves too much. If the federal government may determine the wages and hours of employees in the internal commerce of a State, because of their relation to cost and prices and their indirect effect upon interstate commerce, it would seem that a similar control might be exercised over other elements of cost, also affecting prices, such as the number of employees, rents, advertising, methods of doing business, etc. All the processes of production and distribution that enter into cost could likewise be controlled. If the cost of doing an intrastate business is in itself the permitted object of federal control, the extent of the regulation of the cost would be a question of discretion and not of power.

The Government also makes the point that efforts to enact state legislation establishing high labor standards have been impeded by the belief that unless similar action is taken generally, commerce will be diverted from the States adopting such standards, and that this fear of diversion has led to demands for federal legislation on the subject of wages and hours. The apparent implication is that the federal authority under the commerce clause should be deemed to extend to the establishment of rules to govern wages and hours in intrastate trade and industry generally throughout the country, thus overriding the authority of the States to deal with domestic problems arising from labor conditions in their internal commerce.

It is not the province of the Court to consider the economic advantages or disadvantages of such a centralized system. It is sufficient to say that the Federal Constitution does not provide for it. . . . The authority of the federal government may not be pushed to such an extreme as to destroy the distinction, which the commerce clause itself establishes, between "commerce among the several States" and the internal concerns of a State. The same answer must be made to the contention that is based upon the serious economic situation which led to the passage of the Recovery Act,—the fall in prices, the decline in wages and employment, and the curtailment of the market for commodities. Stress is laid upon the great importance of maintaining wage distributions which would provide the necessary stimulus in starting "the cumulative forces making for expanding commercial activity." Without in any way disparaging this motive, it is enough to say that the recuperative efforts of the federal government must be made in a manner consistent with the authority granted by the Constitution. . . .

[The NIRA was unconstitutional because Congress could only regulate interstate commerce and the intrastate enterprise of Schechter was not interstate commerce]

(c) Code of competition for bituminous coal industry

CARTER v CARTER COAL CO.

298 US 238 (1936)

Congress adopted a law providing for a code for the bituminous coal industry similar to the NRA codes. The Court considered whether the Act was unconstitutional on the ground that working conditions, wages, and hours in mines could not be regulated by Congress under the commerce power.

OPINION BY SUTHERLAND, J.

We have seen that the word "commerce" is the equivalent of the phrase "intercourse for the purposes of trade." Plainly, the incidents leading up to and culminating in the mining of coal do not constitute such intercourse. The employment of men, the fixing of their wages, hours of labor and working conditions, the bargaining in respect of these things—whether carried on separately or collectively—each and all constitute intercourse for the purposes of production, not of trade. The latter is a thing apart from the relation of employer and employee, which in all producing occupations is purely local in character. Extraction of coal from the mine is the aim and the completed result of local activities. Commerce in the coal mined is not brought into being by force of these activities, but by negotiations, agreements and circumstances entirely apart from production. Mining brings the subject matter of commerce into existence. Commerce disposes of it. . . . Everything which moves in interstate commerce has had a local origin. Without local production somewhere, interstate commerce, as now carried on, would practically disappear. Nevertheless, the local character of mining, of manufacturing and of crop growing is a fact, and remains a fact, whatever may be done with the products. . . .

That the production of every commodity intended for interstate sale and transportation has some effect upon interstate commerce may be, if it has not already been, freely granted; and we are brought to the final and decisive inquiry, whether here that effect is direct, as the preamble [of the Act] recites, or indirect. The distinction is not formal, but substantial in the highest degree, as we pointed out in the *Schechter* case. . . .

Whether the effect of a given activity or condition is direct or indirect is not always easy to determine. . . . The distinction between a direct and an indirect effect turns, not upon the magnitude of either the cause or the effect, but entirely upon the manner in which the effect has been brought about. If the production by one man of a single ton of coal intended for interstate sale and shipment, and actually so sold and shipped, affects interstate commerce indirectly, the effect does not become direct by multiplying the tonnage, or increasing the number of men employed, or adding to the expense or complexities of the business, or by all combined. . . .

Much stress is put upon the evils which come from the struggle between employers and employees over the matter of wages, working conditions, the right of collective bargaining, etc., and the resulting strikes, curtailment and irregularity of production and effect on prices; and it is insisted that interstate commerce is greatly affected thereby. But, in addition to what has just been said, the conclusive answer is that the evils are all local evils over which the federal government has no legislative control. The relation of employer and employees is a local relation. At common law, it is one of the domestic relations. The wages are paid for the doing of local work. Working conditions are obviously local conditions. The employees are not engaged in or about commerce, but exclusively in producing a commodity. And the controversies and evils, which it is the object of the act to regulate and minimize, are local controversies and evils affecting local work undertaken to accomplish that local result. Such effect as they may have upon commerce, however extensive it may be, is secondary and indirect. An increase in the greatness of the effect adds to its importance. It does not alter its character. . . .

[The federal statute authorizing the coal industry code was unconstitutional because mining is not interstate commerce]

§ 8:3. THE COMMERCE POWER AND THE GENERAL WELFARE

The pre-1937 cases impress the reader by their total acceptance of the pre-1937 view of interstate commerce. By those decisions, it was an open and shut case that the interstate commerce power gave Congress only power to act when something crossed a state line or directly affected that which did cross a state line. Conversely, it was perfectly clear that the commerce power did not give any power to regulate the general welfare and that an amendment to the Constitution would be required if the American people wanted it to do so. The incredible thing is that, almost overnight, a general welfare power is given to Congress by judicial reinterpretation of the Constitution and not by formal amendment.

To repeat, until 1937, the Supreme Court adhered to the concept that interstate commerce required interstate movement and that the mere fact that it was intended to ship goods in interstate commerce in the future did not place the production of those goods within the reach of the interstate commerce power. During this period, federal control was limited to the regulation of the facilities of interstate commerce and matters that were regarded as directly affecting the facilities or the interstate transit of goods, persons, or communications. Under this view of the commerce power, it is held that laws requiring safety devices on trains or limiting the hours of employment of trainmen on interstate trains are valid. A slightly less direct regulation of commerce, but still clearly within the general area of regulation, is the Federal Employers' Liability Act, which regulates the liability of employers engaged in interstate commerce when sued by employees for damages for industrial accidents arising out of their employment in interstate commerce.

With the decision of *National Labor Relations Board v Jones & Laughlin Steel Corp.,* [5] the Supreme Court abandoned the limitation of the early cases and gradually expanded the concept of interstate commerce until now the power to regulate interstate commerce is held to confer upon the federal government the power to regulate any activity that has an effect on the national economic welfare. Instead of determining whether there is a crossing of a state line or any activity that directly affects persons or goods going across a state line, the Supreme Court now looks at the overall national picture to see if the activity in question has an effect upon, or is part of, the national economic welfare or a segment thereof. Under this view, the power conferred by the interstate commerce power is now as broad as the economic needs of the nation.[6]

The social significance of the *Jones & Laughlin Steel Corp.* case cannot be overestimated. It represents a revolution in constitutional law and was to open the door to a new "commerce" power of far greater scope than could ever have been added to the Constitution by an express amendment. That a different era had begun is further seen from the fact that the *Jones & Laughlin* court was still a

---

[5] 301 US 1 (1937).
[6] *American Power & Light Co. v SEC,* 329 US 90 (1946).

Republican court. It was not a New Deal or Roosevelt court. The first appointment of a Justice of the Supreme Court by Roosevelt was Justice Black, who was appointed on August 12 and confirmed on August 17, 1937. The *Jones & Laughlin* case was decided April 12, 1937. Note also that the *West Coast Hotel Co. v Parrish* case, which changed the concept of due process and sustained a minimum wage law, was decided on March 29, 1937.

(a) Labor relations

NLRB v JONES & LAUGHLIN STEEL CORP.

301 US 1 (1937)

OPINION BY HUGHES, C.J.

The scheme of the National Labor Relations Act . . . may be briefly stated. The first section sets forth findings with respect to the injury to commerce resulting from the denial by employers of the right of employees to organize and from the refusal of employers to accept the procedure of collective bargaining. There follows a declaration that it is the policy of the United States to eliminate these causes of obstruction to the free flow of commerce. The Act then defines the terms it uses, including the terms "commerce" and "affecting commerce." § 2. It creates the National Labor Relations Board and prescribes its organization. §§ 3–6. It sets forth the right of employees to self-organization and to bargain collectively through representatives of their own choosing. § 7. It defines "unfair labor practices." § 8. It lays down rules as to the representation of employees for the purpose of collective bargaining. § 9. The Board is empowered to prevent the described unfair labor practices affecting commerce and the Act prescribes the procedure to that end. . . .

. . . The respondent argues (1) that the Act is in reality a regulation of labor relations and not of interstate commerce; . . .

The facts as to the nature and scope of the business of the Jones & Laughlin Steel Corporation have been found by the Labor Board.

[The Court discussed in detail the interstate organization of the employer with various plants in different states.]

Summarizing these operations, the Labor Board concluded that the works in Pittsburgh and Aliquippa "might be likened to the heart of a self-contained, highly integrated body. They draw in the raw materials from Michigan, Minnesota, West Virginia, Pennsylvania in part through arteries and by means controlled by the respondent; they transform the materials and then pump them out to all parts of the nation through the vast mechanism which the respondent has elaborated."

To carry on the activities of the entire steel industry, 33,000 men mine ore, 44,000 men mine coal, 4,000 men quarry limestone, 16,000 men manufacture coke, 343,000 men manufacture steel, and 83,000 men transport its product.

Respondent has about 10,000 employees in its Aliquippa plant, which is located in a community of about 30,000 persons. . . .

Practically all the factual evidence in the case, except that which dealt with the nature of respondent's business, concerned its relations with the employees in the Aliquippa plant whose discharge was the subject of the complaint. These employees were active leaders in the labor union. . . .

First. The Scope of the Act.—The Act is challenged in its entirety as an attempt to regulate all industry, thus invading the reserved powers of the States over their local concerns. . . .

. . . The grant of authority to the Board does not purport to extend to the relationship between all industrial employees and employers. Its terms do not impose collective bargaining upon all industry regardless of effects upon interstate or foreign commerce. It purports to reach only what may be deemed to burden or obstruct that commerce and, thus qualified, it must be construed as contemplating the exercise of control within constitutional bounds. It is a familiar principle that acts which directly burden or obstruct interstate or foreign commerce, or its free flow, are within the reach of the congressional power. Acts having that effect are not rendered immune because they grow out of labor disputes. . . . It is the effect upon commerce, not the source of the injury, which is the criterion. . . . Whether or not particular action does affect commerce in such a close and intimate fashion as to be subject to federal control, and hence to lie within the authority conferred upon the Board, is left by the statute to be determined as individual cases arise. . . .

We do not find it necessary to determine whether these features of defendant's business dispose of the asserted analogy to the "stream of commerce" cases. . . . The congressional authority to protect interstate commerce from burdens and obstructions is not limited to transactions which can be deemed to be an essential part of a "flow" of interstate or foreign commerce. Burdens and obstructions may be due to injurious action springing from other sources. The fundamental principle is that the power to regulate commerce is the power to enact "all appropriate legislation" for "its protection and advancement." . . . That power is plenary and may be exerted to protect interstate commerce "no matter what the source of the dangers which threaten it." . . . Although activities may be intrastate in character when separately considered, if they have such a close and substantial relation to interstate commerce that their control is essential or appropriate to protect that commerce from burdens and obstructions, Congress cannot be denied the power to exercise that control. *Schechter Corp. v United States.* . . .

It is thus apparent that the fact that the employees here concerned were engaged in production is not determinative. The question remains as to the effect upon interstate commerce of the labor practice involved. In the *Schechter* case, . . . we found that the effect there was so remote as to be beyond the federal power. To find "immediacy or directness" there was to find it "almost everywhere," a result inconsistent with the maintenance of our federal system. In the *Carter* case [298 US 238], the Court was of the opinion that the provisions of the statute relating to production were invalid upon several grounds: that there was improper delegation of legislative power, and that the requirements not only went beyond any sustainable measure of protection of interstate commerce but were also inconsistent with due process. These cases are not controlling here.

. . . The stoppage of [respondent's] operations by industrial strife would have a most serious effect upon interstate commerce. In view of respondent's far-flung activities, it is idle to say that the effect would be indirect or remote. It is obvious that it would be immediate and might be catastrophic. We are asked to shut our eyes to the plainest facts of our national life and to deal with the question of direct and indirect effects in an intellectual vacuum. Because there may be but indirect and remote effects upon interstate commerce in connection with a host of local enterprises throughout the country, it does not follow that other industrial activities do not have such a close and intimate relation to interstate commerce as to make the presence of industrial strife a matter of the most urgent national concern. When industries organize themselves on a national scale, making their relation to interstate commerce the dominant factor in their activities, how can it be maintained that their industrial labor relations constitute a forbidden field into which Congress may not enter when it is necessary to protect interstate commerce from the paralyzing consequences of industrial war? We have often said that interstate commerce itself is a practical conception. It is equally true that interferences with that commerce must be appraised by a judgment that does not ignore actual experience.

Experience has abundantly demonstrated that the recognition of the right of employees to self-organization and to have representatives of their own choosing for the purpose of collective bargaining is often an essential condition of industrial peace. Refusal to confer and negotiate has been one of the most prolific causes of strife. This is such an outstanding fact in the history of labor disturbances that it is a proper subject of judicial notice and requires no citation of instances. The opinion in the case of *Virginia Railway Co. v System Federation No. 40, . . .* points out that, in the case of carriers, experience has shown that before the amendment, of 1934, of the Railway Labor Act "when there was no dispute as to the organizations authorized to represent the employees and when there was a willingness of the employer to meet such representative for a discussion of their grievances, amicable adjustment of differences had generally followed and strikes had been avoided." That, on the other hand, "a prolific source of dispute had been the maintenance by the railroad of company unions and the denial by railway management of the authority of representatives chosen by their employees." The opinion in that case also points to the large measure of success of the labor policy embodied in the Railway Labor Act. But with respect to the appropriateness of the recognition of self-organization and representation in the promotion of peace, the question is not essentially different in the case of employees in industries of such a character that interstate commerce is put in jeopardy from the case of employees of transportation companies. And of what avail is it to protect the facility of transportation, if interstate commerce is throttled with respect to the commodities to be transported!

These questions have frequently engaged the attention of Congress and have been the subject of many inquiries. The steel industry is one of the great basic industries of the United States, with ramifying activities affecting interstate commerce at every point. The Government aptly refers to the steel strike of 1919–20 with its far-reaching consequences. The fact that there appears to have been no major disturbance in that industry in the more recent period did not dispose of the possibilities of future and like dangers to interstate commerce which Congress was entitled to foresee and to exercise its protective power to forestall. It is not necessary again to detail the facts as to respondent's enterprise. Instead of being beyond the pale, we think that it presents in a most striking way the close and intimate relation which [an] industry may have to interstate commerce, and we have no doubt that Congress had constitutional authority. . . .

[The National Labor Relations Act was constitutional as applied to the respondent steel company and was within the scope of the power of Congress over interstate commerce]

(b) Credit practices

By virtue of the new interpretation of the commerce power as authorizing legislation designed to meet the economic needs of the nation, Congress may prohibit extortionate credit practices.

PEREZ v UNITED STATES

402 US 146 (1971)

The federal Consumer Credit Protection Act makes it a crime to use extortionate means to collect a debt. Perez loaned money to a butcher to open a shop. Several times, Perez increased the weekly installments that the borrower was required to pay back. When the borrower objected to the size of the payments, Perez threatened personal violence against the borrower and the borrower's family. Perez was prosecuted under the federal statute. He claimed that the statute was unconstitutional because the loan transaction with the butcher was purely intrastate. The statute was sustained as coming within the federal interstate commerce power, and Perez was convicted. He appealed to the United States Supreme Court.

OPINION BY DOUGLAS, J.

. . . Petitioner is one of the species commonly known as "loan sharks" which Congress found are in large part under the control of "organized crime." "Extortionate credit transactions" are defined as those characterized by the use or threat of the use of "violence or other criminal means" in enforcement. . . .

The House debates include a long article from the New York Times Magazine for January 28, 1968, on the connection between the "loan shark" and organized crime. . . . "The loan shark, then, is the indispensable 'money mover' of the underworld. He takes 'black' money tainted by its derivation from the gambling or narcotics rackets and turns it 'white' by funneling it into channels of legitimate trade. In so doing, he exacts usurious interst that doubles the black-white money in no time; and, by his special decrees, by his imposition of impossible penalties, he greases the way for the underworld takeover of entire businesses." . . .

There were objections on constitutional grounds. Congressman Eckhardt of Texas said: "Should it become law, [it] would take a long stride by the Federal Government toward occupying the field of general criminal law and toward exercising a general Federal police power; and it would permit prosecution in Federal as well as State courts of a typically State offense." . . .

Senator Proxmire presented to the Senate the Conference Report approving essentially the "loan shark" provision . . . , saying: "Once again these provisions raised serious questions of Federal-State responsibilities. Nonetheless, because of the importance of the problem, the Senate conferees agreed to the House provision. Organized crime operates on a national scale. One of the principal sources of revenue of organized crime comes from loan sharking. If we are to win the battle against organized crime we must strike at their source of revenue and give the Justice Department additional tools to deal with the problem. The problem simply cannot be solved by the States alone. We must bring into play the full resources of the Federal Government." . . .

The Commerce Clause reaches, in the main, three categories of problems. First, the use of channels of interstate or foreign commerce which Congress deems are being misused, as, for example, the shipment of stolen goods . . . or of persons who have been kidnaped. . . . Second, protection of the instrumentalities of interstate commerce, as, for example, the destruction of an aircraft . . . or persons or things in commerce, as, for example, thefts from interstate shipments. . . . Third, those activities affecting commerce. It is with this last category that we are here concerned. . . .

Extortionate credit transactions, though purely intrastate, may in the judgment of Congress affect interstate commerce . . .

The Congress also knew about New York's Report, An Investigation of the Loan Shark Racket (1965). See 114 Cong Rec 1428–1431. That report shows the loan shark racket is controlled by organized criminal syndicates, either directly or in partnership with independent operators; that in most instances the racket is organized into three echelons, with the top underworld "bosses" providing the money to their principal "lieutenants," who in turn distribute the money to the "operators" who make the actual individual loans; that loan sharks serve as a source of funds to bookmakers, narcotics dealers, and other racketeers; that victims of the racket include all classes, rich and poor, businessmen and laborers; that the victims are often coerced into the commission of criminal acts in order to repay their loans; that through loan sharking the organized underworld has obtained control of legitimate businesses, including securities brokerages and banks which are then exploited; and that "even where extortionate credit transactions are purely intrastate in character, they nevertheless directly affect interstate and foreign commerce." . . .

The essence of all these reports and hearings was summarized and embodied in formal congressional findings. They supplied Congress with the knowledge that the loan shark racket provides organized crime with its second most lucrative source of revenue, exacts millions from the pockets of people, coerces its victims into the commission of crimes against property, and causes the takeover by racketeers of legitimate businesses. . . .

We have mentioned in detail the economic, financial, and social setting of the problem as revealed to Congress . . . to answer the impassioned plea of petitioner that all that is involved in loan sharking is a traditionally local activity. It appears, instead, that loan sharking in its national setting is one way organized interstate crime holds its guns to the heads of the poor and the rich alike and syphons funds from numerous localities to finance its national operations.

[Judgment affirmed]

§ 8:4. PRESENT FEDERAL POWER OVER PRODUCTION

The doctrine of the *Jones & Laughlin* case at the time of its adoption was regarded as a liberal or radical view, and the conservatives of that day had hopes that a later Court would repudiate this doctrine. This wish was disappointed, for the Court followed this view in other decisions, extended this view to agriculture and insurance, and applied it to warrant national price control in peacetime.

In the course of time, the view was accepted as an established fact by the conservatives, who then sought to use this doctrine to further their own objectives. The conservative group was thus found advocating the adoption of the Taft-Hartley Amendment, now known as the Federal Labor Management Relations Act of 1947, in order to restrict the activity of labor unions. The right to adopt such a restrictive statute is predicated upon the power of Congress under the commerce clause to regulate labor relations in industries manufacturing for interstate business. Both liberals and conservatives had come to agree that the Congressional power extended to regulating labor relations in that production field. The ground of dispute had shifted from the existence of the power to regulate to the manner in which that power should be exercised.

The picture of the present federal power over production is not complete without adding to the new commerce power a reference to the broad powers that stem from the authority to wage war.

By virtue of the war power, Congress can impose any regulation on production. When the war power can be invoked, it is immaterial whether or not the production that is regulated would come within the scope of the commerce power. The war power is all-pervasive and reaches all economic activity if Congress deems it necessary for the proper prosecution of the war. The only limitation is that the regulation be reasonably related to preparation for, prosecution of, or recovery from war.

When the power to regulate production exists, it is immaterial what type of regulation is made. To date, the forms of regulation have followed certain definite patterns. For the most part, regulations of production have been in terms of regulating working conditions, hours and wages of labor, and collective bargaining. Two newcomers in the field of regulation are the regulation of price and the regulation of quantity produced.

To date, government has not attempted to specify what articles should be produced by manufacturers, although at different times in our history bounty or subsidy plans have been adopted to encourage production along certain lines. Some effort has been made along the line of standardizing production so that all manufacturers making the same article would follow the same pattern. This regulation has been mainly the securing of voluntary cooperation of producers rather than the establishment of standards to which manufacturers must adhere.

§ 8:5. THE POWER TO PROHIBIT INTERSTATE COMMERCE

Does the right to "regulate" include the power to "prohibit"? Can Congress state that a particular article may no longer be sent in interstate channels? The argument was advanced that to regulate an activity required the continued existence of the activity, and that, while the activity might be restricted or qualified, it could not be stopped completely.

The Supreme Court rejected this argument and held that the power to regulate included the power to prohibit, since to regulate was to limit or restrict in some way and prohibition was merely the maximum or utmost limitation or restriction. The Supreme Court accordingly sustained federal statutes prohibiting the interstate shipment of articles that could cause harm if permitted to reach their destination, or where the transportation was an essential step in the furthering of a wrong. The Court sustained federal laws prohibiting the interstate shipment of lottery tickets, impure or misbranded food and drugs, filled milk, obscene literature, women transported for an immoral purpose, stolen automobiles, and kidnapped persons. In adopting these statutes Congress was in effect exercising its commerce power to promote the health, safety, morals, and general welfare of the people. Before 1937, it could not do this directly and openly, for no police power to legislate for such ends is given to the Congress.

In 1916, Congress endeavored to end the evil of child labor by prohibiting the interstate shipment of the products of those factories and mines that had employed child labor at any time during the 30 days prior to the time the goods were offered for shipment. This Act was held unconstitutional in *Hammer v Dagenhart*, (reported under (a) of this section), by five of the nine justices, the Court holding that since the child-labor-made goods were themselves harmless and since the harm of the employment of child labor had already been completed before the goods were delivered for interstate shipment, the statute was not a regulation of commerce but was an attempt to regulate production, which was a matter reserved to the states.

Later, with the changing concept of the interstate commerce power so as to permit the regulation of activities within the production area on the ground that they affected interstate commerce, the *Hammer* decision was definitely undermined. Congress therefore again attempted to regulate production by specifying maximum hours and minimum wages and by prohibiting child labor. The constitutionality of this Fair Labor Standards Act came before the Court in *United States v Darby*, reported under (b) of this section. Not only is this case significant in itself, but it is interesting to contrast it with the *Hammer* decision above, noting the way in which the dissenting minority view of the earlier case became the majority view, and also the ease with which the doctrine of the *Hammer* case is rejected as erroneous in spite of the ring of finality and confidence in its correctness found in the *Hammer* opinion.

(a) Embargo on child-labor-made goods

HAMMER v DAGENHART

247 US 251 (1918)

Congress prohibited the interstate shipment of goods produced in plants that had employed children within 30 days prior to shipment.

OPINION BY DAY, J.

The power essential to the passage of this act, the Government contends, is found in the commerce clause of the Constitution. . . . The thing intended to be accomplished by this statute is the denial of the facilities of interstate commerce to those manufacturers in the states who employ children within the prohibited ages. The act in its effect does not regulate transportation among the states, but aims to standardize the ages at which children may be employed in mining and manufacturing within the states. The goods shipped are of themselves harmless. The act permits them to be freely shipped after thirty days from the time of their removal from the factory. When offered for shipment, and before transportation begins, the labor of their production is over, and the mere fact that they were intended for interstate commerce transportation does not make their production subject to federal control under the commerce power. . . . The making of goods and the mining of coal are not commerce, nor does the fact that these things are to be afterwards shipped, or used in interstate commerce, make their production a part thereof. . . . The production of articles intended for interstate commerce is a matter of local regulation. . . . This principle has been recognized often in this court. . . . If it were otherwise, all manufacture intended for interstate shipment would be brought under federal control to the practical exclusion of the authority of the States,—a result certainly not contemplated by the framers of the Constitution when they vested in Congress the authority to regulate commerce among the states. . . .

It is further contended that the authority of Congress may be exerted to control interstate commerce in the shipment of child-made goods because of the effect of the circulation of such goods in other states where the evil of this class of labor has been recognized by local legislation, and the right to thus employ child labor has been more rigorously restrained than in the state of production. In other words, that the unfair competition thus engendered may be controlled by closing the channels of interstate commerce to manufactures in those states where the local laws do not meet what Congress deems to be the more just standard of other states.

There is no power vested in Congress to require the states to exercise their police power so as to prevent possible unfair competition. Many causes may cooperate to give one state, by reason of local laws or conditions, an economic advantage over others. The commerce clause was not intended to give to Congress a general authority to equalize such conditions. In some of the states laws have been passed fixing minimum wages for women; in others the local law regulates the hours of labor of women in various employments. Business done in such states may be at an economic disadvantage when compared with states which have no such regulations; surely, this fact does not give Congress the power to deny transportation in interstate commerce to those who carry on business where the hours of labor and the rate of compensation for women have not been fixed by a standard in use in other states and approved by Congress. . . .

[The statute was unconstitutional because it was not a regulation of interstate commerce but was an indirect attempt to regulate production]

DISSENTING OPINION BY HOLMES, J.

. . . Congress is given power to regulate such commerce in unqualified terms. It would not be argued today that the power to regulate does not include the power to prohibit. . . .

The question, then, is narrowed to whether the exercise of its otherwise constitutional power by Congress can be pronounced unconstitutional because of its possible reaction upon the conduct of the States in a matter upon which I have admitted that they are free from direct control. . . . I should have thought that the most conspicuous decisions of this court had made it clear that the power to regulate commerce and other constitutional powers could not be cut down or qualified by the fact that it might interfere with the carrying out of the domestic policy of any State. . . . The States may regulate their internal affairs and their domestic commerce as they like. But when they seek to send their products across the state line they are no longer within their rights. If there were no Constitution and no Congress their power to cross the line would depend upon their neighbors. Under the Constitution such commerce belongs not to the

States, but to Congress to regulate. It may carry out its views of public policy whatever indirect effect they may have upon the activities of the States. Instead of being encountered by a prohibitive tariff at her boundaries, the State encounters the public policy of the United States which it is for Congress to express. The public policy of the United States is shaped with a view to the benefit of the nation as a whole.... The national welfare as understood by Congress may require a different attitude within its sphere from that of some self-seeking State. It seems to me entirely constitutional for Congress to enforce its understanding by all the means at its command.

(b) Fair Labor Standards Act

UNITED STATES v DARBY

312 US 100 (1941)

OPINION BY STONE, J.

The Fair Labor Standards Act set up a comprehensive legislative scheme for preventing the shipment in interstate commerce of certain products and commodities produced in the United States under labor conditions as respects wages and hours which fail to conform to standards set up by the Act. Its purpose ... is to exclude from interstate commerce goods produced for the commerce and to prevent their production for interstate commerce, under conditions detrimental to the maintenance of the minimum standards of living necessary for health and general well-being; and to prevent the use of interstate commerce as the means of competition in the distribution of goods so produced, and as the means of spreading and perpetuating such substandard labor conditions among the workers of the several states....

While manufacture is not of itself interstate commerce, the shipment of manufactured goods interstate is such commerce and the prohibition of such shipment by Congress is indubitably a regulation of the commerce. The power to regulate commerce is the power "to prescribe the rule by which commerce is governed."... It extends not only to those regulations which aid, foster and protect the commerce, but embraces those which prohibit it.... It is conceded that the power of Congress to prohibit transportation in interstate commerce includes noxious articles ... stolen articles ... kidnapped persons ... and articles such as intoxicating liquor or convict-made goods, traffic in which is forbidden or restricted by the laws of the state of destination....

But it is said that the present prohibition falls within the scope of none of these categories; that while the prohibition is nominally a regulation of the commerce its motive or purpose is regulation of wages and hours of persons engaged in manufacture, the control of which has been reserved to the states and upon which Georgia and some of the states of destination have placed no restriction; that the effect of the present statute is not to exclude the proscribed articles from interstate commerce in aid of state regulation . . . but instead, under the guise of a regulation of interstate commerce, it undertakes to regulate wages and hours within the state contrary to the policy of the state which has elected to leave them unregulated.

. . . Congress, following its own conception of public policy concerning the restrictions which may appropriately be imposed on interstate commerce, is free to exclude from the commerce articles whose use in the states for which they are destined it may conceive to be injurious to the public health, morals or welfare, even though the state has not sought to regulate their use. . . .

The motive and purpose of the present regulation are plainly to make effective the Congressional conception of public policy that interstate commerce should not be made the instrument of competition in the distribution of goods produced under substandard labor conditions, which competition is injurious to the commerce and to the states from and to which the commerce flows. The motive and purpose of a regulation of interstate commerce are matters for the legislative judgment upon the exercise of which the Constitution places no restriction and over which the courts are given no control. . . . Whatever their motive and purpose, regulations of commerce which do not infringe some constitutional prohibition are within the plenary power conferred on Congress by the Commerce Clause. Subject only to that limitation, . . . we conclude that the prohibition of the shipment interstate of goods produced under the forbidden substandard labor conditions is within the constitutional authority of Congress.

In the more than a century which has elapsed since the decision of *Gibbons v Ogden,* these principles of constitutional interpretation have been so long and repeatedly recognized by this Court as applicable to the Commerce Clause, that there would be little occasion for repeating them now were it not for the decision of this Court twenty-two years ago in *Hammer v Dagenhart,* 247 US 251. In that case it was held by a bare majority of the Court over the powerful and now classic dissent of Mr. Justice Holmes setting forth the fundamental issues involved, that Congress was without power to exclude the products of child labor from interstate commerce. The reasoning and conclusion of the Court's opinion there cannot be reconciled with the conclusion which we have reached, that the power of Congress under the Commerce Clause is plenary to exclude any article from interstate commerce subject only to the specific prohibitions of the Constitution.

Hammer v Dagenhart has not been followed. The distinction on which the decision was rested, that Congressional power to prohibit interstate commerce is limited to articles which in themselves have some harmful or deleterious property—a distinction which was novel when made and unsupported by any provision of the Constitution—has long since been abandoned. . . . The thesis of the opinion that the motive of the prohibition or its effect to control in some measure the use or production within the states of the article thus excluded from the commerce can operate to deprive the regulation of its constitutional authority has long since ceased to have force. . . .

The conclusion is inescapable that *Hammer v Dagenhart* was a departure from the principles which have prevailed in the interpretation of the Commerce Clause both before and since the decision and that such vitality, as a precedent, as it then had, has long since been exhausted. It should be and now is overruled. . . .

[The Fair Labor Standards Act was within the federal commerce power and was constitutional]

Questions for Discussion

1. A federal law is adopted providing that no one may operate a television station without a federal license. Is the statute constitutional?

2. A federal law provides that all aircraft must be licensed under the federal law. The owner and operator of a jet-propelled plane refuses to obtain a federal license on the ground that such planes were unknown when the Constitution was framed and that the Constitution does not delegate to Congress the power to regulate such planes. (a) Is the objection valid? (b) How does the Tenth Amendment affect your answer?

3. The object of the framers of the Constitution in conferring the commerce power upon the national government was to protect that commerce from being throttled at the hands of the states. The power to regulate must therefore be construed to mean the power to foster and to protect, but not to include the power to prohibit the interstate shipment of any article not harmful in itself to those things surrounding it. Is this statement correct? Explain.

4. Name two cases in this chapter in which the Court was guided by: (a) A belief that the spirit of the Constitution required that state control be preserved in "local" matters. (b) A fear that, if federal power were to be recognized in the case before it, it would be impossible to find any limitations upon the federal power in any other case.

5. In the *Jones & Laughlin Steel Corporation* case the Court states that it is the effect upon commerce, not the source of the injury, that determines whether a matter may be regulated so as to prevent its harming interstate commerce. What is the test of whether an activity has an effect upon interstate commerce?

6. Did the Court in the *Schechter* case regard the payment of substandard wages as an unfair practice that was furthered by the use of the channels of interstate commerce? Compare with *United States v Darby*.

7. In determining whether an activity may be regulated under the commerce power, does the Court consider whether the activity either (a) is interstate commerce or (b) "directly affects" interstate commerce?

8. A federal law prohibits interstate commerce in intoxicating liquor. A person buys a bottle of intoxicating liquor in Kentucky, puts it in his pocket, and then gets in a trolley car to ride from Kentucky to West Virginia. He is indicted for violating the federal statute prohibiting interstate commerce in intoxicating liquor. Is he guilty? [*United States v Simpson,* 252 US 465 (1920)]

9. A federal law prohibited exporting in foreign commerce munitions of war to countries where domestic violence existed. Such conditions existed in Mexico. Chavez carried 200 rounds of rifle ammunition from El Paso, Texas, to Mexico. He was prosecuted for violating the Act. He claimed that the Act was not applicable since he was carrying the property on his person. Was his defense good? [*United States v Chavez,* 228 US 525 (1913)]

10. The goods of a manufacturer had been taken from the factory loading platform and placed in the manufacturer's truck for delivery to another state. The truck after being loaded was sealed, the bill of lading was made out, and the truck was moved about two blocks from the loading platform and parked in a public street. The driver then removed the keys and took them to the garage where they were to be picked up by the drivers who were to take the truck on its interstate run. Before the two drivers reached the truck, the truck was broken open by the defendants and the contents were stolen. The defendants were prosecuted under a federal statute making it a crime to steal from any carrier or truck goods "moving as or which are part of an interstate shipment of freight." The defendants claimed that the shipment was not within the statute. Decide. [*United States v Gollin,* (CCA3 Pa) 176 F2d 889 (1949)]

11. A national law prohibits the shipment of deceptive, fraudulent, or harmful foods and drugs in interstate commerce. A shipment of eggs was sent by the Hippolite Egg Company to a bakery in another state. The shipment was seized by the federal authorities on the ground that it violated this law. The Hippolite Egg Company claimed that the federal authorities could not touch this shipment as it had already reached the person to whom it was sent and had thus left the channels of interstate commerce. Was this a good defense? [*Hippolite Egg Company v United States,* 220 US 45 (1911)]

12. Does the *Jones & Laughlin Steel Corporation* case make the extension of the commerce power to a manufacturer dependent upon whether the bulk of raw materials is brought in from another state and the bulk of finished products is exported to other states?

13. In the *Jones & Laughlin Steel Corporation* case the Court states: "and of what avail is it to protect the facility of transportation, if interstate commerce is throttled with respect to the commodities to be transported!" What is the value of this statement as a legal argument?

14. What was the test of interstate commerce which the Court applied in the *Perez* case?

15. The Jones Company made clothing from cloth that it purchased within the state and then resold within the state to distributors. It had no association or business transactions with anyone outside of the state. A complaint was filed before the National Labor Relations Board claiming that the Jones Company violated the national act. The company defended on the ground that it was not engaged in or producing for interstate commerce. If this defense was true, the Board did not have jurisdiction. Did the Board have jurisdiction over the complaint? [*NLRB v Fainblatt,* 306 US 601 (1939)]

16. What is the difference between the *Hammer* case and the *Darby* case?

17. How would you define the Federal commerce power on the basis of the decisions in the: (a) *Schechter* case.   (b) *Jones & Laughlin Steel Corporation* case.   (c) *American Power & Light Company v SEC* case, § 11:2(c).

18. In the *Hammer* case the Court states: "This Act in a double sense is repugnant to the Constitution. It not only transcends the authority delegated to Congress over commerce, but also exerts a power as to a local matter to which the federal authority does not extend." Is this interpretation of the scope of the federal powers correct?

19. Name five instances in which the federal commerce power has been used to advance health, welfare, morals, or safety. Why was it necessary to have a federal law on the subject?

20. Does it make any difference in the application of the *Jones & Laughlin Steel Corporation* case whether the title to the goods is owned by the manufacturer, by a consignee, or by an agent of the manufacturer?

9

The Commerce Power
and the States

§ 9:1. THE FEDERAL POWER AS PROHIBITING STATE REGULATION

By the Tenth Amendment, those powers not delegated to the federal government nor prohibited to the states are reserved to the states and the people thereof. This provision emphasized the concept of a division of power between federal and state governments under which a power would be held either by the national government or the state governments, but not concurrently by both. Under a literal interpretation of this Amendment, the granting of the power to regulate interstate commerce to the Congress would mean that no power exists in the states to regulate that commerce.

This interpretation fitted in well with the intent of the framers, who, seeing the evil effects of retaliatory state regulations of interstate commerce, wished to raise this field of commerce above the reach of the states. For the first part of our national life, the authority of the commerce power was invoked, not by the Congress as the basis for adopting a national law, but by the Supreme Court as the basis for declaring invalid a regulation of commerce made by a state, as was done in the following case.

(a) State monopoly of navigation

GIBBONS v OGDEN

9 Wheat 1 (1824)

The state of New York, in order to encourage the development of the steamboat, gave to Livingston and Fulton the exclusive right to operate steam vessels on the waters of the state and prohibited the operation of such vessels by any person not licensed by them. Ogden obtained a license from them to operate a steam vessel on New York waters. Later he sought to enjoin Gibbons from operating on those waters without a license. The latter claimed that he was registered under the Act of Congress of 1793 to engage in the coastal trade and was therefore entitled to operate a steam vessel in the coastal waters of New York state by virtue of the protection of the federal commerce power.

OPINION BY MARSHALL, J.

. . . The words [of the Constitution] are: "Congress shall have power to regulate commerce with foreign nations, and among the several States, and with the Indian tribes." The subject to be regulated is commerce. . . . The counsel for the appellee [Ogden] would limit it to traffic, to buying and selling, or the interchange of commodities, and do not admit that it comprehends navigation. This would restrict a general term, applicable to many objects, to one of its significations. Commerce, undoubtedly, is traffic, but it is something more. . . . It describes the commercial intercourse between nations, and parts of nations, in all its branches, and is regulated by prescribing rules for carrying on that intercourse. The mind can scarcely conceive a system for regulating commerce between nations which shall exclude all laws concerning navigation, which shall be silent on the admission of the vessels of the one nation into the ports of the other, and be confined to prescribing rules for the conduct of individuals, in the actual employment of buying and selling, or of barter.

. . . The sole question is, can a state regulate commerce with foreign nations and among the states while Congress is regulating it?

. . . Steamboats may be enrolled and licensed, in common with vessels using sails. They are, of course, entitled to the same privileges and can no more be restrained from navigating waters and entering ports which are free to such vessels, than if they were wafted on their voyage by the winds, instead of being propelled by the agency of fire. The one element may be as legitimately used as the other, for every commercial purpose authorized by the laws of the Union; and the act of a state inhibiting the use of either to any vessel having a license under the act of Congress, comes, we think, in direct collision with that act. . . .

[The Court refused to enjoin Gibbons from operating without a license under the state law because the state law was unconstitutional as in conflict with the federal commerce power]

(b) Supremacy of federal regulation

LOCAL 24 v OLIVER

358 US 283 (1959)

Members of Local 24 owned their own trucks. They would hire out to drive their trucks as employees of various carriers. Through collective bargaining under the National Labor Management Relations Act, the union and the employing carriers had made an agreement, Article XXXII of which specified the "rental" to be paid by the employing carriers to each truck owner for the owner's services in driving the truck for the carriers. Oliver, one of the truck-owning employees, sued in an Ohio state court to invalidate the rental provision of the agreement on the ground that the Ohio antitrust law made it illegal.

OPINION BY BRENNAN, J.

. . . The point of the Article is obviously not price-fixing but wages. The regulations embody . . . a direct frontal attack upon a problem thought to threaten the maintenance of the basic wage structure established by the collective bargaining contract. The inadequacy of a rental which means that the owner makes up his excess costs from his driver's wages not only clearly bears a close relation to labor's efforts to improve working conditions but is in fact of vital concern to the carrier's employed drivers; an inadequate rental might mean the progressive curtailment of jobs through withdrawal of more and more carrier-owned vehicles from service.

. . . We must decide whether Ohio's antitrust law may be applied to prevent the contracting parties from carrying out their agreement upon a subject matter as to which federal law directs them to bargain. Little extended discussion is necessary to show that Ohio law cannot be so applied. . . . The carriers as employers were under a duty to bargain collectively with the union as to the subject matter of the Article. . . .

The goal of federal labor policy, as expressed in the Wagner and Taft-Hartley Acts, is the promotion of collective bargaining; to encourage the employer and the representative of the employees to establish, through collective negotiation, their own charter for the ordering of industrial relations, and thereby to minimize industrial strife. . . . Within the area in which collective bargaining was required, Congress was not concerned with the substantive terms upon which the parties agreed. . . .

The purposes of the Acts are served by bringing the parties together and establishing conditions under which they are to work out their agreement themselves. To allow the application of the Ohio antitrust law here would wholly defeat the full realization of the congressional purpose. The application would frustrate the parties' solution of a problem which Congress has required them to negotiate in good faith toward solving, and in the solution of which it imposed no limitations relevant here. . . . We believe that there is no room in this scheme for the application here of this state policy limiting the solutions that the parties' agreement can provide to the problems of wages and working conditions. . . . Since the federal law operates here, in an area where its authority is paramount, to leave the parties free, the inconsistent application of state law is necessarily outside the power of the State. . . . Of course, the paramount force of the federal law remains even though it is expressed in the details of a contract federal law empowers the parties to make, rather than in terms of an enactment of Congress. . . . Clearly it is immaterial that the conflict is between federal labor law and the application of what the State characterizes as an antitrust law. ". . . Congress has sufficiently expressed its purpose to . . . exclude state prohibition, even though that with which the federal law is concerned as a matter of labor relations be related by the State to the more inclusive area of restraint of trade." . . .

We have not here a case of a collective bargaining agreement in conflict with a local health or safety regulation; the conflict here is between the federally sanctioned agreement and state policy which seeks specifically to adjust relationships in the world of commerce. If there is to be this sort of limitation on the arrangements that unions and employers may make with regard to these subjects, pursuant to the collective bargaining provisions of the Wagner and Taft-Hartley Acts, it is for Congress, not the States, to provide it.

[Judgment against Oliver because the federal law preempted the field and excluded the state law]

---

§ 9:2. SILENCE OF CONGRESS

Admitting that a law passed by Congress regulating interstate commerce is supreme and prevails over a state law, what happens if Congress does not pass any law on the subject? Is the silence of Congress to be regarded as permission to the states to regulate the commerce or may that silence be an indication that the subject should be unregulated?

The Court finally answered these questions by holding that if the subject matter of the state regulation were of such a nature that local regulation would not have any harmful effect on interstate commerce, the silence of Congress was to be deemed implied permission to the states to regulate in a nondiscriminatory way. Conversely, if the subject matter were such that any regulation should be uniform throughout the country, the silence of Congress was then an indication that it did not desire that there be any regulation.[1]

This doctrine sustains the right of states to make regulations, in the absence of federal legislation, of those local details of interstate commerce that do not require uniformity throughout the nation. A similar state power exists as to foreign commerce.

---

[1]*Cooley v Board of Wardens of the Port of Philadelphia,* 12 How (US) 299 (1852).

(a) Conservation

CITIES SERVICE GAS COMPANY v PEERLESS OIL & GAS COMPANY
340 US 179 (1950)

In order to prevent the wasteful exploitation of natural gas resources, Oklahoma adopted a statute authorizing the state corporation commission to fix the minimum price to be paid for gas at the wellhead. The Commission fixed the price with respect to gas produced at a field from which Cities Service Gas Company ran an interstate line. Cities Service claimed that the fixing of the price by the state commission burdened interstate commerce. This contention was rejected and Cities Service appealed.

OPINION BY CLARK, J.

. . . It is now well settled that a state may regulate matters of local concern over which federal authority has not been exercised, even though the regulation has some impact on interstate commerce. . . . The only requirements consistently recognized have been that the regulation not discriminate against or place an embargo on interstate commerce, that it safeguard an obvious state interest, and that the local interest at stake outweigh whatever national interest there might be in the prevention of state restrictions. Nor should we lightly translate the quiescence of federal power into an affirmation that the national interest lies in complete freedom from regulation. . . .

That a legitimate local interest is at stake in this case is clear. A state is justifiably concerned with preventing rapid and uneconomic dissipation of one of its chief natural resources. The contention urged by appellant that a group of private producers and royalty owners derive substantial gain from the regulations does not contradict the established connection between the orders and a state-wide interest in conservation. . . .

We recognize that there is also a strong national interest in natural gas problems. But it is far from clear that on balance such interest is harmed by the state regulations under attack here. . . . Moreover, the wellhead price of gas is but a fraction of the price paid by domestic consumers at the burner-tip, so that the field price as herein set may have little or no effect on the domestic delivered price. . . . Insofar as conservation is concerned, the national interest and the interest of producing states may well tend to coincide. In any event, in a field of this complexity with such diverse interests involved, we cannot say that there is a clear national interest so harmed that the state price-fixing orders here employed fall within the ban of the Commerce Clause. . . . Nor is it for us to consider whether Oklahoma's unilateral efforts to conserve gas will be fully effective. . . .

We hold that . . . the Oklahoma Corporation Commission issued valid orders, and . . . should be affirmed.

[State regulation held valid]

(b) Advertising

HEAD v NEW MEXICO BOARD OF EXAMINERS
374 US 424 (1963)

Head owned and operated in New Mexico a radio station that served an interstate area, most of which was in Texas. Head's station ran a commercial on the air advertising a Texas optometrist. This was in violation of a New Mexico statute which prohibited commercials on eyeglasses. Head claimed that the New Mexico statute was invalid in that it imposed a burden on interstate commerce. The Supreme Court of New Mexico held the statute constitutional. Head appealed.

OPINION BY STEWART, J.

. . . The purpose of [the New Mexico statute] is to "protect . . . citizens against the evils of price-advertising methods tending to satisfy the need of their pocketbooks rather than the remedial requirements of their eyes." . . . Similar laws have been enacted in many states to assure high standards of professional competence. . . .

The statute here involved is a measure directly addressed to protection of the public health, and the statute thus falls within the most traditional concept of what is compendiously known as the police power. The legitimacy of state legislation in this precise area has been expressly established. . . . A state law may not be struck down on the mere showing that its administration affects interstate commerce in some way. "State regulation, based on the police power, which does not discriminate against interstate commerce or operate to disrupt its required uniformity, may constitutionally stand." . . .

We hold that the New Mexico statute, as applied here to prevent the publication in New Mexico of the proscribed price advertising, does not impose a constitutionally prohibited burden upon interstate commerce.

In dealing with the contention that New Mexico's jurisdiction to regulate radio advertising has been preempted by the Federal Communications Act, we may begin by noting that the validity of this claim cannot be judged by reference to broad statements about the "comprehensive" nature of federal regulation under the Federal Communications Act. "The 'question whether Congress and its commissions acting under it have so far exercised the exclusive jurisdiction that belongs to it as to exclude the State, must be answered by a judgment upon the particular case.' Statements concerning the 'exclusive jurisdiction' of Congress beg the only controversial question: whether Congress intended to make its jurisdiction exclusive." . . . In areas of the law not inherently requiring national uniformity, our decisions are clear in requiring that state statutes, otherwise valid, must be upheld unless there is found "such actual conflict between the two schemes of regulation that both cannot stand in the same area, [or] evidence of a congressional design to preempt the field." . . .

The specific provisions of the federal statute chiefly relied upon . . . are those governing the granting, renewal, and revocation of broadcasting licenses. Under the broad standard of "public interest, convenience, and necessity," the Federal Communications Commission may consider a wide variety of factors in passing upon the fitness of an applicant. It is argued that the content of advertising is one of the factors which may be considered, and there is evidence that the Commission itself has on occasion so interpreted its authority. Further, the United States argues that the Commission has the authority to promulgate general regulations concerning the subject of advertising for the guidance of broadcasters. . . . This grant of federal power, it is argued, is sufficient to oust state regulation of radio advertising.

Assuming this is to be a correct statement of the Commission's authority, we are nevertheless not persuaded that the federal legislation in this field has excluded the application of a state law of the kind here involved. The nature of the regulatory power given to the federal agency convinces us that Congress could not have intended its grant of authority to supplant all the detailed state regulation of professional advertising practices, particularly when the grant of power to the Commission was accompanied by no substantive standard other than the "public interest, convenience, and necessity." The Solicitor General has conceded that the power of license revocation is not a plausible substitute for state law dealing with "traditional" torts or crimes committed through the use of radio. We can find no material difference with respect to the less "traditional" statutory violation here involved. In the absence of positive evidence of legislative intent to the contrary, we cannot believe Congress has ousted the States from an area of such fundamentally local concern.

Finally, there has been no showing of any conflict between this state law and the federal regulatory system, or that the state law stands as an obstacle to the full effectiveness of the federal statute. No specific federal regulations even remotely in conflict with the New Mexico law have been called to our attention. The Commission itself has apparently viewed state regulation of advertising as complementing its regulatory function, rather than in any way conflicting with it. . . . We are satisfied that the state statute "at least so long as any power the [Commission] may have remains 'dormant and unexercised,' will not frustrate any part of the purpose of the federal legislation."

[Judgment affirmed]

§ 9:3. STATE REGULATION AS A BURDEN

Within the area of regulation of local details allowed the states, the state regulation must not impose an unreasonable burden on interstate commerce. If it does, the state law is invalid, even though it imposes that same burden on intrastate as well as interstate commerce, without discrimination. A state statute that required all trains to slow down at grade crossings so that they could stop if necessary was held unconstitutional when applied to an interstate train where this would have required it to slow down at 124 grade crossings in 123 miles, with the result of doubling its running time through the state.

In recent years, less emphasis has been placed on the question of whether the power to regulate interstate commerce is concurrent. The Supreme Court has merely considered whether the state law, considered as a police power or tax law, was or was not an unreasonable burden when extended to interstate commerce. The statute is accordingly held valid if it does not discriminate against or single out interstate commerce alone and if its application to that commerce does not impose an unreasonable burden on it.

Under this doctrine, a state law regulating the payment of wages may be applied to the wages paid to crews of trains moving in interstate commerce where it is a general nondiscriminatory regulation. A quarantine or inspection law may keep out of the state diseased or harmful products or may prohibit their sale within the state even though still in the original package.

(a) Marketability

FLORIDA LIME & AVOCADO GROWERS v PAUL

373 US 132 (1963)

Under the authority of the Federal Agricultural Adjustment Act, a marketing order was made prescribing the maturity test for Southern Florida avocados in terms of picking date, size, and weight. The California Agriculture Code, § 792, prohibited the transportation or sale in California of avocados containing less than 8 percent of oil, by weight, excluding the skin and seed. California officials, acting under this statute, refused to permit the sale in California of avocados from Florida as they had not been certified as to oil content under the California Code, although they had been certified as complying with the federal marketing order. The Florida Lime & Avocado Growers then brought suit to prevent the enforcement of the California statute on the ground that it interfered with interstate commerce.

OPINION BY BRENNAN, J.

. . . Almost all avocados commercially grown in the United States come either from Southern California or South Florida. The California-grown varieties are chiefly of Mexican ancestry, and in most years contain at least 8 percent oil content when mature. The several Florida species, by contrast, are of West Indian and Guatemalan ancestry. . . . [and they] may reach maturity before they attain 8 percent oil content. The District Court concluded, nevertheless, that § 792 did not unreasonably interfere with their marketability since these species "attain or exceed 8 percent oil content while in a prime commercial marketing condition," so that the California test was "scientifically valid as applied to" these varieties. . . .

That the California statute and the federal marketing orders embody different maturity tests is clear. However, this difference poses, rather than disposes of the problem before us. Whether a State may constitutionally reject commodities which a federal authority has certified to be marketable depends upon whether the state regulation "stands as an obstacle to the accomplishment and execution of the full purposes and objectives of Congress." . . . By that test, we hold that § 792 is not such an obstacle; there is neither such actual conflict between the two schemes of regulation that both cannot stand in the same area, nor evidence of a congressional design to preempt the field.

We begin by putting aside two suggestions of the appellants which obscure more than aid in the solution of the problem. First, it is suggested that a federal license or certificate of compliance with minimum federal standards immunizes the licensed commerce from inconsistent or more demanding state regulations. . . . That no State may completely exclude federally licensed commerce is indisputable, but that principle has no application to this case.

Second, it is suggested that the coexistence of federal and state regulatory legislation should depend upon whether the purposes of the two laws are parallel or divergent. . . . The test of whether both federal and state regulations may operate, or the state regulation must give way, is whether both regulations can be enforced without impairing the federal superintendence of the field, not whether they are aimed at similar or different objectives.

The principle to be derived from our decisions is that federal regulation of a field of commerce should not be deemed preemptive of state regulatory power in the absence of persuasive reasons—either that the nature of the regulated subject matter permits no other conclusion, or that the Congress has unmistakably so ordained. . . .

A holding of federal exclusion of state law is inescapable and requires no inquiry into congressional design where compliance with both federal and state regulations is a physical impossibility for one engaged in interstate commerce. . . . That would be the situation here if, for example, the federal orders forbade the picking and marketing of any avocado testing more than 7 percent oil, while the California test excluded from the State any avocado measuring less than 8 percent oil content. No such impossibility of dual compliance is presented on this record, however. As to those Florida avocados of the hybrid and Guatemalan varieties which were actually rejected by the California test, the District Court indicated that the Florida growers might have avoided such rejections by leaving the fruit on the trees beyond the earliest picking date permitted by the federal regulations, and nothing in the record contradicts that suggestion. Nor is there a lack of evidentiary support for the District Court's finding that the Florida varieties marketed in California "attain or exceed 8 percent oil content while in a prime commercial marketing condition," even though they may be "mature enough to be acceptable prior to the time that they reach that content. . . ." . . . Thus the present record demonstrates no inevitable collision between the two schemes of regulation, despite the dissimilarity of the standards.

The issue under the head of the Supremacy Clause is narrowed then to this: Does either the nature of the subject matter, namely the maturity of avocados, or any explicit declaration of congressional design to displace state regulation, require § 792 to yield to the federal marketing orders? The maturity of avocados seems to be an inherently unlikely candidate for exclusive federal regulation.

Certainly it is not a subject by its very nature admitting only of national supervision. . . . Nor is it a subject demanding exclusive federal regulation in order to achieve uniformity vital to national interests. . . .

On the contrary, the maturity of avocados is a subject matter of the kind this Court has traditionally regarded as properly within the scope of state superintendence. Specifically, the supervision of the readying of foodstuffs for market has always been deemed a matter of peculiarly local concern. . . .

Federal regulation by means of minimum standards of the picking, processing, and transportation of agricultural commodities, however comprehensive for those purposes that regulation may be, does not of itself import displacement of state control over the distribution and retail sale of those commodities in the interests of the consumers of the commodities within the State. Thus, while Florida may perhaps not prevent the exportation of federally certified fruit by superimposing a higher maturity standard, nothing in Cloverleaf forbids California to regulate their marketing. Congressional regulation of one end of the stream of commerce does not, ipso facto, oust all state regulation at the other end. Such a displacement may not be inferred automatically from the fact that Congress has regulated production and packing of commodities for the interstate market. We do not mean to suggest that certain local regulations may not unreasonably or arbitrarily burden interstate commerce; we consider that question separately. . . . Here we are concerned only whether partial congressional superintendence of the field (maturity for the purpose of introduction of Florida fruit into the stream of interstate commerce) automatically forecloses regulation of maturity by another State in the interests of that State's consumers of the fruit.

The correctness of the District Court's conclusion that § 792 was a regulation well within the scope of California's police powers is thus clear. While it is conceded that the California statute is not a health measure, neither logic nor precedent invites any distinction between state regulations designed to keep unhealthful or unsafe commodities off the grocer's shelves, and those designed to prevent the deception of consumers. . . . Nothing appearing in the record before us affords any ground for departure in this case from our consistent refusal to draw such a distinction.

Since no irreconcilable conflict with the federal regulation requires a conclusion that § 792 was displaced, we turn to the question whether Congress has nevertheless ordained that the state regulation shall yield. . . .

We turn now to appellants' arguments under the Equal Protection and Commerce Clauses.

It is enough to dispose of the equal protection claim that we express our agreement with the District Court that the state standard does not work an "irrational discrimination as between persons or groups of persons. . . . While it may well be that arguably superior tests of maturity could be devised, we cannot say . . . that this possibility renders the choice made by California either arbitrary or devoid of rational relationship to a legitimate regulatory interest. Whether or not the oil content test is the most reliable indicator of marketability of avocados is not a question for the courts to decide; it is sufficient that on this record we should conclude, as we do, that oil content appears to be an acceptable criterion of avocado maturity. . . .

[California statute held constitutional even though it imposed a higher standard on goods moving in interstate commerce than did the federal law]

DISSENTING OPINION BY WHITE, J., IN WHICH BLACK, DOUGLAS, AND CLARK, JJ., CONCUR

. . . The ultimate question for the Court is whether the California law may validly apply to Florida avocados which the Secretary or his inspector says are mature under the federal scheme. We in the minority believe that it cannot, for in our view the California law "stands as an obstacle to the accomplishment and execution of the full purposes and objectives of Congress."

The central and unavoidable fact is that six out of every 100 Florida avocados certified as mature by federal standards are turned away from the California markets as being immature, and are excluded from that State by the application of a maturity test different from the federal measure. Congress empowered the Secretary to provide for the orderly marketing of avocados and to specify the quality and maturity of avocados to be transported in interstate commerce to any and all markets. Although the Secretary determined that these Florida avocados were mature by federal standards and fit for sale in interstate markets, the State of California determined that they were unfit for sale by applying a test of the type which the Secretary had determined to be unsatisfactory. We think the state law has erected a substantial barrier to the accomplishment of congressional objectives. . . .

Here the Secretary has promulgated a comprehensive and pervasive regulatory scheme for determining the quality and maturity of Florida avocados, pursuant to the statutory mandate to "effectuate orderly marketing of such agricultural commodities." . . . No aspects of avocado maturity are omitted under the federal regulations. Any additional state regulation to "supplement" federal regulation would pro tanto supplant it with another scheme, thereby compromising to some degree the congressional policy expressed in the Act. . . .

The conflict between federal and state law is unmistakable here. The Secretary asserts certain Florida avocados are mature. The state law rejects them as immature. And the conflict is over a matter of central importance to the federal scheme. The elaborate regulatory scheme of the marketing order is focused upon the problem of moving mature avocados into interstate commerce. The maturity regulations are not peripheral aspects of the federal scheme. . . . On the contrary, in the Department of Agriculture order which preceded issuance of the avocado regulations, it was found that the marketing of immature avocados was one of the principal problems, if not the principal problem, faced by the industry and that these regulations should be adopted to solve this problem which was demoralizing the industry. . . .

California nevertheless argues that it should be permitted to apply its oil test cumulatively with the federal test to insure that only mature avocados are offered in its markets. . . .

Even if the California oil test were an acceptable test for the maturity of the Florida avocados, which the Secretary found it was not, the cumulative application of that test solely for the purpose of a second check on the maturity of Florida avocados, solely to catch possible errors in the federal scheme, would prove only that the particular avocados actually tested (and thereby destroyed) were immature, and it would not justify the rejection of whole lots from which these samples came. If Florida avocados are to be subjected to this test, the alternatives are to leave the California market to the California producers (at least, to producers of Mexican varieties) or else, in order to avoid the hazard of rejection, to leave the Florida avocados on the trees past the normal (and federally prescribed) picking date, thereby shortening the post-picking marketing period and thus frustrating the federal scheme aimed at moving avocados mature under federal standards into all interstate markets. A reasonable balancing of the state and federal interests at stake here requires that the former give way as too insubstantial to warrant frustration of the congressional purpose.

We have, then, a case where the federal regulatory scheme is comprehensive, pervasive, and without a hiatus which the state regulations could fill. Both the subject matter and the statute call for uniformity. The conflict is substantial —at least six out of every 100 federally certified avocados are barred for failure to pass the California test—and it is located in a central portion of the federal scheme. The effect of the conflict is to disrupt and burden the flow of commerce and the sale of Florida avocados in distant markets, contrary to the congressional policy underlying the Act. The State may have a legitimate economic interest in the subject matter, but it is adequately served by the federal regulations and this interest would be but slightly impaired, if at all, by the supersession of § 792.

In such circumstances, the state law should give way; it "becomes inoperative and the federal legislation exclusive in its application." . . . The conclusion is inescapable that the California law is an obstacle to the accomplishment and execution of the congressional purposes and objectives, and that the California law and the Agricultural Adjustment Act, as supplemented by the regulations promulgated thereunder, cannot be reconciled and cannot consistently stand together. The Court should not allow avocados certified as mature under the federal marketing order to be embargoed by any State because it thinks that they are immature. We would therefore reverse with instructions to grant the injunction requested.

§ 9:4. FEDERAL CONSENT TO STATE REGULATION

In addition to the power which the states may exercise in the silence of Congress, it has also been held that Congress may consent to the operation of state laws upon what would otherwise be exempt as interstate commerce from state regulation. With respect to commodities, this principle of consent to state regulation has taken the form of waiving the immunity conferred by the original package doctrine. That doctrine found its origin in *Brown v Maryland,* 12 Wheat 419 (1827), in which Chief Justice Marshall held that goods imported from a foreign nation retained their character as imports and immunity from state taxation as long as they remained "the property of the importer, in his warehouse, in the original form of package in which it was imported." While this doctrine has been modified in the field of taxation and does not apply to goods brought into a state to fill a prior order, it has been applied to goods moving in interstate commerce in order to determine when they became subject to regulation by state law.

It has been held that liquor brought from one state into a prohibition state could be sold in the original package in spite of the state prohibition law on the theory that a prohibition of this first sale in the original package would burden interstate commerce by preventing the transaction that was the object of its importation. On the other hand, this protection, when extended to such goods, defeated the state policy of prohibition. In order to permit the state policy to operate, Congress waived the immunity conferred by the original package doctrine by expressly providing that the state law may operate upon the goods even though they are unsold and in the original package. Such waiver has now been made by Congress in the case of both intoxicating liquors and convict-made goods. Congress has even gone farther in these two cases and has made it a federal offense to carry goods through the channels of interstate commerce into a state where the possession or the sale of such goods is illegal under the state law. By this device it is possible for the state, with the permission of Congress, to make effective the state police power, even as to goods that would ordinarily be protected by the immunity based on the federal commerce power. Such federal-state cooperation is a far cry from the federal-state rivalry of our early national life.

Federal consent to state legislation acting upon interstate commerce has not been confined to transactions relating to commodities. For example, by the McCarran-Ferguson Act, the federal government permits state regulations to apply to interstate insurance and insurance companies.

§ 9:5. STATE PRICE CONTROL

During periods of economic distress, it is natural for the states to seek to remedy their difficulties by statutes that place their local interest above that of the neighboring states. Such "beggar-thy-neighbor" statutes had themselves been a reason for the adoption of the federal commerce clause. Statutes of this nature also followed in the wake of the Depression of 1929. Again, the commerce clause was invoked by the Supreme Court as authority for invalidating state laws that harmed interstate commerce although designed to afford local economic relief. A regulatory provision of this character was before the Supreme Court in the following case.

(a) Local price control of imported goods

BALDWIN v SEELIG

294 US 511 (1935)

OPINION BY CARDOZO, J.

The New York Milk Control Act with the aid of regulations made thereunder has set up a system of minimum prices to be paid by dealers to producers. . . . From the farms of New York the inhabitants of the so-called Metropolitan Milk District, comprising the City of New York and certain neighboring communities, derive about 70 percent of the milk requisite for their use. To keep the system unimpaired by competition from afar, the Act has a provision whereby the protective prices are extended to that part of the supply (about 30 percent) which comes from other states. The substance of the provision is that, so far as such a prohibition is permitted by the Constitution, there shall be no sale within the state of milk bought outside unless the price paid to the producers was one that would be lawful upon a like transaction within the state. . . .

Seelig buys its milk from the Creamery in Vermont at prices lower than the minimum payable to producers in New York. The Commissioner of Farms and Markets refuses to license the transaction of its business unless it signs an agreement to conform to the New York statute and regulations in the sale of the imported product. This the applicant declines to do. . . . This suit has been brought to restrain the enforcement of the Act in its application to the complainant. . . .

New York has no power to project its legislation into Vermont by regulating the price to be paid in that state for milk acquired there. So much is not disputed. New York is equally without power to prohibit the introduction within her territory of milk of wholesome quality acquired in Vermont, whether at high prices or at low ones. This again is not disputed. Accepting those postulates, New York asserts her power to outlaw milk so introduced by prohibiting its sale thereafter if the price that has been paid for it to the farmers of Vermont is less than would be owing in like circumstances to farmers in New York. The importer in that view may keep his milk or drink it, but sell it he may not.

Such a power, if exerted, will set a barrier to traffic between one state and another as effective as if custom duties, equal to the price differential, had been laid upon the thing transported. . . . Imposts and duties upon interstate commerce are placed beyond the power of a state. . . . We are reminded in the opinion below that a chief occasion of the commerce clauses was "the mutual jealousies and aggressions of the States, taking form in customs barriers and other economic retaliation." . . . If New York, in order to promote the economic welfare of her farmers, may guard them against competition with the cheaper prices of Vermont, the door has been opened to rivalries and reprisals that were meant to be averted by subjecting commerce between the states to the power of the nation.

The argument is pressed upon us, however, that the end to be served by the Milk Control Act is something more than the economic welfare of the farmers or of any other class or classes. The end to be served is the maintenance of a regular and adequate supply of pure and wholesome milk, the supply being put in jeopardy when the farmers of the state are unable to earn a living income. . . . Price security, we are told, is only a special form of sanitary security; the economic motive is secondary and subordinate; the state intervenes to make its inhabitants healthy, and not to make them rich. On that assumption we are asked to say that intervention will be upheld as a valid exercise by the state of its internal police power, though there is an incidental obstruction to commerce between one state and another. This would be to eat up the rule under the guise of an exception. Economic welfare is always related to health, for there can be no health if men are starving. Let such an exception be admitted, and all that a state will have to do in times of stress and strain is to say that its farmers and merchants and workmen must be protected against competition from without, lest they go upon the poor relief lists or perish altogether. To give entrance to that excuse would be to invite a speedy end of our national solidarity. The Constitution was framed under the dominion of a political philosophy less parochial in range. It was framed upon the theory that the peoples of the several states must sink or swim together, and that in the long run prosperity and salvation are in union and not division.

We have dwelt up to this point upon the argument of the state that economic security for farmers in the milkshed may be a means of assuring to consumers a steady supply of a food of prime necessity. There is, however, another argument which seeks to establish a relation between the well-being of the producer and the quality of the product. We are told that farmers who are underpaid will be tempted to save the expense of sanitary precautions. This temptation will affect the farmers outside New York as well as those within it. For that reason the exclusion of milk paid for in Vermont below the New York minimum will tend, it is said, to impose a higher standard of quality and thereby promote health. We think the argument will not avail to justify impediments to commerce between the states. There is neither evidence nor presumption that the same minimum prices established by order of the board for producers in New York are necessary also for producers in Vermont. But apart from such defects of proof, the evils springing from uncared for cattle must be remedied by measures of repression more direct and certain than the creation of a parity of prices between New York and other states. Appropriate certificates may be exacted from farmers in Vermont and elsewhere . . . ; milk may be excluded if necessary safeguards have been omitted; but commerce between the states is burdened unduly when one state regulates by indirection the prices to be paid to producers in another, in the faith that augmentation of prices will lift up the level of economic welfare, and that this will stimulate the observance of sanitary requirements in the preparation of the product. The next step would be to condition importation upon proof of a satisfactory wage scale in factory or shop, or even upon proof of the profits of the business. Whatever relation there may be between earnings and sanitation is too remote and indirect to justify obstructions to the normal flow of commerce in its movement between states. . . . One state may not put pressure of that sort upon others to reform their economic standards. If farmers or manufacturers in Vermont are abandoning farms or factories, or are failing to maintain them properly, the legislature of Vermont and not that of New York must supply the fitting remedy.

. . . Subject to the paramount power of the Congress, a state may regulate the importation of unhealthy swine or cattle . . . or decayed or noxious food. . . . Things such as these are not proper subjects of commerce, and there is no unreasonable interference when they are inspected and excluded. So a state may protect its inhabitants against the fraudulent substitution, by deceptive coloring or otherwise, of one article for another. . . . None of these statutes . . . approaches in drastic quality the statute here in controversy which would neutralize the economic consequences of free trade among the states.

. . . It is one thing for a state to exact adherence by an importer to fitting standards of sanitation before the products of the farm or factory may be sold in its markets. It is a very different thing to establish a wage scale or a scale of prices for use in other states, and to bar the sale of the products, whether in the original packages or in others, unless the scale has been observed. . . .

[The New York law was invalid with respect to milk brought in from another state]

---

§ 9:6. STATE IMPORT BARRIERS

(a) Reciprocity requirement

GREAT A & P TEA CO. v COTTRELL

424 US 366 (1976)

The Mississippi State Board of Health adopted a regulation, § 11 of which allowed milk brought in from other states to be sold in Mississippi provided that (1) such milk was produced, pasteurized, and labeled under regulations which were substantially similar to the Mississippi standards, and (2) the other states permitted milk from Mississippi to be sold in such other states "on a reciprocal basis." The Great A & P Tea Co. constructed a million-dollar milk-processing plant in Louisiana, intending to supply its 38 outlets in Mississippi from that source. The Mississippi State Board of Health refused to allow the milk to be brought into Mississippi from the Louisiana plant because there was no reciprocity agreement between the two states. Great A & P Tea Co. brought an action to declare the Mississippi regulation unconstitutional as an unreasonable burden on interstate commerce. From a decision in favor of the regulation, A & P appealed.

OPINION BY BRENNAN, J.

. . . Mississippi's answer to appellant's Commerce Clause challenge is that the reciprocity requirement of § 11 is a reasonable exercise of its police power over local affairs, designed to assure the distribution of healthful milk products to the people of its State. We begin our analysis by again emphasizing that . . . at least since *Cooley v Board of Wardens,* 12 How 299, 13 L Ed 996 (1852), it has been clear that "the Commerce Clause was not merely an authorization to Congress to enact laws for the protection and encouragement of commerce among the States, but by its own force created an area of trade free from interference by the States. . . . The Commerce Clause even without implementing legislation by Congress is a limitation upon the power of the States." . . . It is no less true, of course, that under our constitutional scheme the States retain "broad power" to legislate protection for their citizens in matters of local concern such as public health, . . . and that not every exercise of local power is invalid merely because it affects in some way the flow of commerce between the States. . . . Rather, in areas where activities of legitimate local concern overlap with the national interests expressed by the Commerce Clause—where local and national powers are concurrent—the Court in absence of congressional guidance is called upon to make "delicate adjustment of the conflicting state and federal claims," . . . thereby attempting "the necessary accomodation between local needs and the overriding requirement of freedom for the national commerce." . . . In undertaking this task the Court, if it finds that a challenged exercise of local power serves to further a legitimate local interest but simultaneously burdens interstate commerce, is confronted with a problem of balance:

> Although the criteria for determining the validity of state statutes affecting interstate commerce have been variously stated, the general rule that emerges can be phrased as follows: Where the statute regulates even handedly to effectuate a legitimate local public interest, and its effects on interstate commerce are only incidental, it will be upheld unless the burden imposed on such commerce is clearly excessive in relation to the putative local benefits. . . . If a legitimate local purpose is found, then the question becomes one of degree. And the extent of the burden that will be tolerated will of course depend on the nature of the local interest involved, and on whether it could be promoted as well with a lesser impact on interstate activities. . . .

The fallacy in the District Court's reasoning is that it attached insufficient significance to the interference effected by the clause upon the national interest in freedom for the national commerce, and attached too great significance to the state interests purported to be served by the clause. Although not in terms an absolute and universal bar to sales of out-of-state milk, . . . the barrier of the reciprocity clause to sales of out-of-state milk in Mississippi has in this case also "in practical effect excluded from distribution in [Mississippi] wholesome milk produced . . . in [Louisiana]." . . . Only state interests of substantial importance can save § 11 in the face of that devastating effect upon the free flow of interstate milk. . . .

Mississippi next argues that the reciprocity clause somehow enables Mississippi to assure itself that the reciprocating State's (here Louisiana's) health standards are the "substantial equivalent" of Mississippi's. But even if this were true, and the premise may be disputed, there are means adequate to serve this interest that are substantially less burdensome on commerce. . . . The burden of the mandatory reciprocity clause cannot be justified in view of the character of the local interest and these available methods of protecting it. In the absence of adequate assurance that the standards of a sister State, either as constituted or as applied, are substantially equivalent to its own, Mississippi has the obvious alternative of applying its own standards of inspection to shipments of milk from a nonreciprocating State. . . . "Such inspection is readily open to it without hardship for it could charge the actual and reasonable cost of such inspection to the importing producers and processors." . . .

Mississippi argues that apart from the putative health-related interests served by the clause, the reciprocity requirement is in effect a free-trade provision, advancing the identical national interest that is served by the Commerce Clause.

. . . Mississippi argues that the reciprocity requirement serves to help eliminate "hypertechnical" inspection standards that vary between different States. Such hypertechnical standards are said to burden commerce by requiring costly duplicative or out-of-state inspection in instances where, for truly health-related purposes, the standards of the different States are "substantially equivalent." The Court has recognized that mutually beneficial objectives may be promoted by voluntary reciprocity agreements, and that the existence of such an agreement between two or more States is not a per se violation of the Commerce Clause of which citizens of nonreciprocating States who do not receive the benefits conferred by the agreement may complain. . . . But we have not held that acceptance of offered reciprocity is required from other States, . . . or that a State may threaten complete isolation as the alternative to acceptance of its offer of reciprocity. Mississippi may offer reciprocity to States with substantially equivalent health standards, and insist on enforcement of its own, somewhat different, standards as the alternative. But Mississippi may not use the threat of economic isolation as a weapon to force sister States to enter into even a desirable reciprocity agreement. . . .

To allow Mississippi to insist that a sister State either sign a reciprocal agreement acceptable to Mississippi or else be absolutely foreclosed from exporting its products to Mississippi would plainly "invite a multiplication of preferential trade areas destructive of the very purpose of the Commerce Clause." . . .

The mandatory reciprocity provision of § 11, insofar as justified by the State as an economic measure, is "precisely the kind of hindrance to the introduction of milk from other States . . . condemned as an 'unreasonable clog upon the mobility of commerce . . . [It is] hostile in conception as well as burdensome in result.' " . . .

Accordingly, we hold that the mandatory character of the reciprocity requirement of § 11 unduly burdens the free flow of interstate commerce and cannot be justified as a permissible exercise of any state power. . . .

[Judgment reversed]

---

§ 9:7. STATE EXPORT BARRIERS

The converse of the problem of subjecting incoming goods or persons to restrictions or barriers is found in laws that seek to restrict the exportation of goods from a state or to preserve a local monopoly in natural resources. A state law may not prohibit the export of property or of its natural resources or discriminate against foreign business in the regulation or preservation of its natural resources. The fact that a state law is restrictive does not in itself determine its invalidity. If the restriction is reasonably related to the furtherance of public health, safety, morals, or welfare, as distinguished from creating a mere economic preference or barrier, the law is valid until superseded by a federal law regulating the same subject.

(a) Crop standard maintenance

SLIGH v KIRKWOOD
237 US 52 (1915)

OPINION BY DAY, J.

A statute of the state of Florida undertakes to make it unlawful for any one to sell, offer for sale, ship, or deliver for shipment, any citrus fruits which are immature or otherwise unfit for consumption.

. . . Was it within the authority of the state of Florida to make it a criminal offense to deliver for shipment in interstate commerce citrus fruits,—oranges in this case,—then and there immature and unfit for consumption?

It will be observed that the oranges must not only be immature, but they must be in such condition as renders them unfit for consumption; that is, giving the words their ordinary signification, unfit to be used for food. . . .

That Congress has the exclusive power to regulate interstate commerce is beyond question, and when that authority is exerted by the state, even in the just exercise of the police power, it may not interfere with the supreme authority of Congress over the subject; while this is true, this court from the beginning has recognized that there may be legitimate action by the state in the matter of local regulation, which the state may take until Congress exercises its authority upon the subject. . . .

While this proposition seems to be conceded, and the competency of the state to provide local measures in the interest of the safety and welfare of the people is not doubted, although such regulations incidentally and indirectly involve interstate commerce, the contention is that this statute is not a legitimate exercise of the police power, as it has the effect to protect the health of people in other states who may receive the fruits from Florida in a condition unfit for consumption; and however commendable it may be to protect the health of such foreign peoples, such purpose is not within the police power of the state.

The power of the state to prescribe regulations which shall prevent the production within its borders of impure foods, unfit for use, and such articles as would spread disease and pestilence, is well established. Such articles, it has been declared by this court, are not the legitimate subject of trade or commerce, nor within the protection of the commerce clause of the Constitution. "Such articles are not merchantable; they are not legitimate subjects of trade and commerce. They may be rightly outlawed as intrinsically and directly the immediate sources and causes of destruction to human health and life. The self-protecting power of each state, therefore, may be rightfully exerted against their introduction, and such exercises of power cannot be considered regulations of commerce prohibited by the Constitution." . . .

. . . Police power . . . may be none the less efficiently called into play because by doing so interstate commerce may be remotely and indirectly affected. . . .

So it may be taken as established that the mere fact that interstate commerce is indirectly affected will not prevent the state from exercising its police power, at least until Congress, in the exercise of its supreme authority, regulates the subject. Furthermore, this regulation cannot be declared invalid if within the range of the police power, unless it can be said that it has no reasonable relation to a legitimate purpose to be accomplished in its enactment; and whether such regulation is necessary in the public interest is primarily within the determination of the legislature, assuming the subject to be a proper matter of state regulation.

We may take judicial notice of the fact that the raising of citrus fruits is one of the great industries of the state of Florida. It was competent for the legislature to find that it was essential for the success of that industry that its reputation be preserved in other states wherein such fruits find their most extensive market. The shipment of fruits so immature as to be unfit for consumption, and consequently injurious to the health of the purchaser, would not be otherwise than a serious injury to the local trade, and would certainly affect the successful conduct of such business within the state. The protection of the state's reputation in foreign markets, with the consequent beneficial effect upon a great home industry, may have been within the legislative intent, and it certainly could not be said that this legislation has no reasonable relation to the accomplishment of that purpose.

. . . No act of Congress has been called to our attention undertaking to regulate shipments of this character, which would be contravened by the act in question. . . . Therefore until Congress does legislate upon the subject, the state is free to enter the field.

[Florida statute held constitutional]

Questions for Discussion

1. Compare the definition of the commerce power in *Gibbons v Ogden* with the definition in the *Jones & Laughlin Steel Corporation* case, § 8:3(a).

2. Has there been any change in the type of cases involving the commerce clause that have come before the Supreme Court?

3. A federal statute allows the states to regulate the insurance business even when such business is interstate in character. Harold claims that the statute is unconstitutional because only Congress can regulate interstate commerce. Is he correct?

4. In *Local 24 v Oliver,* was there an express federal statutory provision declaring unlawful the agreement that the state law condemned?

5. Does the *Local 24* case illustrate federal preemption or the silence of Congress?

6. Why is the *Cities Service* case classified as illustrating the silence of Congress?

7. Would the *Head* case have been decided differently if the state law required the taking of affirmative action rather than being a negative or prohibitory provision? Assume, for example, that the state law permitted commercials on eyeglasses but required that the commercial statement also include the name and address of the manufacturer of the units of glass from which the glasses were ground on prescription, the chemical content thereof, and an itemization of the various elements of costs involved in making the eyeglasses.

8. Would the *Florida Avocado Growers* case have been decided differently if, instead of avocados, the case had involved radios?

9. Is the opinion of the Court in the *Florida Avocado Growers* case based on the conclusion that the California test was proper because it was the better test?

10. What effect does the *Baldwin* decision have on the effectiveness of the New York state law?

11. (a) Could New York have excluded the milk purchased in other states if it found as a fact that the milk did not meet the New York standards of sanitation? (b) Would it make any difference if the New York standards were higher than those prevailing in other states?

12. In the *Great A & P Tea Company* case, why did not the Court hold that the Mississippi regulation was valid as a nondiscriminatory measure to protect the health of the people in Mississippi?

13. In the *Great A & P Tea Company* case, does the Court hold that reciprocity agreements between the states are invalid?

14. The city of Philadelphia, Pennsylvania, made a contract with owners of land in New Jersey under which the city could dump solid waste on the land of the New Jersey owners. New Jersey adopted a statute prohibiting the depositing in New Jersey of solid waste originating in other states. There was no prohibition against depositing New Jersey solid wastes in New Jersey. Philadelphia and the owners of the New Jersey land claimed that the New Jersey statute was unconstitutional. Was the law unconstitutional? [*Philadelphia v New Jersey*, 437 US 617, (1978)]

15. Oklahoma prohibited shipping out of the state minnows caught in Oklahoma. Hughes was prosecuted for violating the statute. He claimed that the statute was unconstitutional. Was he correct? [*Hughes v Oklahoma*, US   , 60 L Ed 2d 250 (1979)]

16. A Virginia statute prohibited nonresidents from fishing in Chesapeake Bay. Seacoast Products was a foreign corporation. Its vessels were enrolled under the federal statute and were federally licensed to engage in fishing. It claimed the right to fish in Chesapeake Bay. It was refused permission to do so because of the Virginia statute. Seacoast Products claimed that the Virginia statute was unconstitutional. Decide. [*Douglas v Seacoast Products, Inc.*, 431 US 265 (1977)]

17. A North Carolina statute prohibited containers of apples from showing any grade other than the United States grade. An association of Washington apple growers claimed that this statute was unconstitutional because it prevented the Washington growers from sending Washington apples into North Carolina under the Washington grading labels, and that this deprived the apples of the advertising value derived from the fact that they came from the state of Washington because the apple grading standards of the state of Washington were higher than those of the federal government. Was the statute constitutional? [*Hunt v Washington Apple Advertising Commission*, 432 US 333 (1977)]

18. In 1907 Congress adopted a safety law providing that employees working on interstate railways could not be employed for more than 16 continuous hours in one day. The *X* Railroad employed a number of people for 20 consecutive hours each. When prosecuted for violating the law, the *X* Railroad claimed that the first 10 hours in the case of each person was spent on intrastate commerce and therefore the federal law had not been violated. Decide. [*B & ORR v ICC,* 221 US 612 (1911)]

19. The Interstate Commerce Commission granted increases in interstate railroad rates. Wisconsin maintained the former level of rates for intrastate commerce. The effect of this was to require a greater increase for the interstate rates or to cause the railroads to use the proceeds of interstate operations to meet deficits incurred in intrastate operations. The Interstate Commerce Commission requested the Wisconsin State Commission to raise the rates for intrastate transportation. The state commission refused to do so on the ground that the federal authority could not require a change in intrastate rates. Decide. [*Wisconsin v CB & QRR,* 257 US 563 (1922)]

20. A Virginia law was adopted "to prevent the selling of unwholesome meat." To carry out this purpose, the law provided that any meat slaughtered more than 100 miles away from the place of sale must be inspected by a state or local official and an inspection fee of one cent a pound must be paid. This law was attacked as unconstitutional. Decide. [*Brimmer v Rebman,* 128 US 78 (1891)]

10

Regulation of Combinations

§ 10:1. FEDERAL REGULATION

The rise of the modern American antitrust attitude dates from the period following the Civil War when the industrial and territorial expansion of the United States was accompanied by the cutthroat competition of "captains of industry." It is true that an earlier antimonopoly spirit can be seen, but this was opposition to royal monopoly. The special privileges given by the English crown to its favorites or to the famous trading companies did little to make monopolies popular with the general public. This attitude was not altered when England, as punishment for the Boston Tea Party, gave to the famous East India Company a monopoly over tea importation into the colonies. This early spirit of opposition to the royal monopolies can be seen in provisions of some of the state constitutions, such as the provision in the Constitution of Maryland of 1776 that "monopolies are odious, contrary to the spirit of free government and the principles of commerce, and ought not to be suffered." This was a protest against privilege rather than against combinations or concentrations of power.

It was after the Civil War, however, that the private monopoly appeared as a menace to the public welfare. Fortunes were made as industrial empires rose, often by means that were not merely unethical but actually unlawful. So widespread and corrupt were the practices of free enterprise that the adoption of a law to control business became a vital political issue in the 80's.

Finally, in 1890, the Sherman Act was adopted, declaring: "Every contract, combination in the form of trust or otherwise, or conspiracy, in restraint of trade

146

or commerce among the several states, or with foreign nations, is hereby declared to be illegal." (Sec. 1) The Act also made it illegal for any person to "monopolize, or attempt to monopolize, or combine or conspire with any other person or persons, to monopolize any part of the [interstate or foreign] trade or commerce." (Sec. 2)

Later statutes, such as the Clayton Act of 1914 and the Antitrust Improvement Act of 1976, have been adopted to clarify matters not determined by the Sherman Act of 1890.

(a) Punishment and civil remedy

The punishment fixed for the violation of either of the Sherman Act provisions stated above is a fine not exceeding $50,000, or imprisonment not exceeding one year, or both. In addition to this criminal penalty, the law provides for an injunction to stop the unlawful practices and permits suing the wrongdoers for damages. The plaintiff in such civil actions may recover three times the damages sustained (treble damages).

Any person or enterprise harmed may bring a separate action for treble damages. When the effect of an antitrust violation is to raise prices, the attorney general of a state may bring a class action to recover damages on behalf of those who have paid the higher prices. This action is called a *parens patriae* action, on the theory that the state is suing as the "parent" of its people.

(b) Parallel action distinguished

THEATRE ENTERPRISES v PARAMOUNT FILM
DISTRIBUTING COMPANY

346 US 537 (1954)

Theatre Enterprises was a suburban motion picture theatre. It sued the Paramount Film Distributing Corporation and others, claiming that they violated the Sherman Antitrust Law by conspiring to restrict, for unreasonable periods, "first-run" pictures to downtown theatres. Theatre Enterprises proved that the defendants followed common or parallel practices in connection with the distribution of films.

OPINION BY CLARK, J.

. . . Petitioner approached each respondent separately, initially requesting exclusive first-runs, later asking for first-runs on a "day and date" basis. But respondents uniformly rebuffed petitioner's efforts and adhered to an established policy of restricting first-runs in Baltimore to the eight downtown theatres. Admittedly there is no direct evidence of illegal agreement between the respondents. . . . The various respondents advanced much the same reasons for denying petitioner's offers. . . .

The crucial question is whether respondents' conduct toward petitioner stemmed from independent decision or from an agreement, tacit or express. To be sure, business behavior is admissible circumstantial evidence from which the fact finder may infer agreement. . . . But this Court has never held that proof of parallel business behavior conclusively establishes agreement or, phrased differently, that such behavior itself constitutes a Sherman Act offense. Circumstantial evidence of consciously parallel behavior may have made heavy inroads into the traditional judicial attitude toward conspiracy; but "conscious parallelism" has not yet read conspiracy out of the Sherman Act entirely. . . .

[Judgment for Paramount Film Distributing Company]

---

§ 10:2. AREA OF APPLICATION OF THE FEDERAL STATUTES

As the federal statutes against trusts are based upon the power of Congress to regulate interstate commerce, it follows that an activity must be "in interstate commerce" in order to be subject to the federal statutes. The concept of "in interstate commerce" has broadened as the concept of "interstate commerce" has moved from the crossing of a state line to any matter affecting the national economy.

Under subdivision (a) of this section, the original test of crossing a state line is applied in determining the meaning of "in interstate commerce." Under subdivisions (b) and (c), the general welfare or "economic needs" test is applied.

(a) Local transactions relating to transportation

UNITED STATES v YELLOW CAB CO.

332 US 218 (1947)

The Yellow Cab Company was charged with violating the Sherman Act through agreements relating to the transportation of (1) through passengers using taxi service to change from one train to another, and (2) passengers using taxi service between their homes and the railroad station.

OPINION BY MURPHY, J.

. . . It is said that the appellees have agreed that Yellow Cab Sales will not compete with Parmalee for contracts with railroads or railroad terminal associations to transport passengers and their luggage between railroad stations in Chicago. . . . A great majority of the persons making interstate railroad trips which carry them through Chicago must disembark from a train at one railroad station, travel from that station to another some two blocks to two miles distant, and board another train at the latter point. The railroads often contract with the passengers to supply between-station transportation in Chicago. Parmalee then contracts with railroads and the railroad terminal associations to provide this transportation by special cabs carrying seven to ten passengers. Parmalee's contracts are exclusive in nature.

The transportation of such passengers and their luggage between stations in Chicago is clearly a part of the stream of interstate commerce. When persons or goods move from a point of origin in one state to a point of destination in another, the fact that a part of that journey consists of transportation by an independent agency solely within the boundaries of one state does not make that portion of the trip any less interstate in character. . . . That portion must be reviewed in its relation to the entire journey rather than in isolation. So viewed, it is an integral step in the interstate movement.

. . . Any attempt to monopolize or to impose an undue restraint on such a constituent part of interstate commerce brings the Sherman Act into operation. . . . The complaint accordingly states a violation of the Sherman Act in this respect. . . .

Finally, it is said that the appellees have conspired to control the principal taxicab operating companies in Chicago and to exclude others from engaging in transportation of interstate travellers to and from Chicago railroad stations. . . .

. . . Interstate commerce is an intensely practical concept drawn from the normal and accepted course of business. . . . We believe that the common understanding is that a traveller intending to make an interstate rail journey begins his interstate movement when he boards the train at the station and that his journey ends when he disembarks at the station in the city of destination. What happens prior or subsequent to that rail journey, at least in the absence of some special arrangement, is not a constituent part of the interstate movement. The traveler has complete freedom to arrive at or leave the station by [any means]. . . . Taxicab service is thus but one of the many that may be used. . . . From the standpoints of time and continuity, the taxicab trip may be quite distinct and separate from the interstate journey. To the taxicab driver, it is just another local fare. . . .

We do not mean to establish any absolute rule that local taxicab service to and from railroad stations is completely beyond the reach of the federal power or beyond the scope of the Sherman Act. . . .

All that we hold here is that when local taxicabs merely convey interstate train passengers between their homes and the railroad station in the normal course of their independent local service, that service is not an integral part of interstate transportation. And a restraint on or monopoly of that general local service, without more, is not proscribed by the Sherman Act. . . .

[Judgment for United States as to train-to-train taxi service; judgment against United States as to home-to-train taxi service]

(b) Local transactions relating to production

MANDEVILLE ISLAND FARMS v AMERICAN CRYSTAL SUGAR CO.

334 US 219 (1948)

Three California sugar refiners agreed among themselves to pay California sugar-beet farmers a uniform price for their crops. The refined sugar would be sold by the refiners in interstate markets. The petitioners, sugar-beet farmers, sued one of the refiners for treble damages under the Sherman Act on the theory that the agreement between the refiners was an illegal trust in violation of the Act.

OPINION BY RUTLEDGE, J.

. . . Petitioners' farms are located in northern California. . . . The only practical market available to beet farmers in that area was sale to one of three refiners. Respondent was one of these. Each season growers contract with one of the refiners to grow beets and to sell their entire crops to the refiner under standard form contracts drawn by it. Since prior to 1939 petitioners have thus contracted with respondent.

The refiners control the supply of sugar beet seed. Both by virtue of this fact and by the terms of the contracts, the farmers are required to buy seed from the refiner. The seed can be planted only on land specifically covered by the contract. Any excess must be returned to the refiner in good order at the end of the planting season.

. . . Sometime before the 1939 season the three refiners entered into an agreement to pay uniform prices for sugar beets. . . . The refiners adopted identical form contracts and began to compute beet prices on the basis of the average net returns of all three rather than the separate returns of the purchasing refiner.

. . . Since the refiners controlled the seed supply and the only practical market for beets grown in northern California, when the new contracts were offered to the farmers, they had the choice of either signing or abandoning sugar beet farming. . . . Because beet prices were determined for the three seasons with reference to the combined returns of the three refiners, the prices received by petitioners for those seasons were lower than if respondent, the most efficient of the three, had based its prices on its separate returns. . . .

[The respondent claimed that the growing, purchasing, and refining of sugar beets were local activities and not within the reach of the Sherman Act and that no illegal practice occurred in the subsequent interstate distribution of the refined sugar.]

. . . The broad form of respondent's argument cannot be accepted. It is a reversion to conceptions formerly held but no longer effective to restrict either Congress' power . . . or the scope of the Sherman Act's coverage. The artificial and mechanical separation of "production" and "manufacturing" from "commerce," without regard to their economic continuity, the effects of the former two upon the latter, and the varying methods by which the several processes are organized, related and carried on in different industries or indeed within a single industry, no longer suffices to put either production or manufacturing and refining processes beyond reach of Congress' authority or of the statute.

It is true that the first decision under the Sherman Act applied those mechanical distinctions with substantially nullifying effects for coverage both of the power and of the Act. *United States v E. C. Knight Co.,* 156 US 1. That case involved the refining and interstate distribution of sugar. But because the refining was done wholly within a single state, the case was held to be one involving "primarily" only "production" or "manufacturing," although the vast part of the sugar produced was sold and shipped interstate, and this was the main end of the enterprise. The interstate distributing phase however was regarded as being only "incidentally," "indirectly" or "remotely" involved; and to be "incidental," "indirect" or "remote" was to be, under the prevailing climate, beyond Congress' power to regulate, and hence outside the scope of the Sherman Act.

. . . It is clear that the agreement is the sort of combination condemned by the Act, even though the price-fixing was by purchasers, and the persons specially injured under the treble damage claim are sellers, not customers or consumers. And even if it is assumed that the final aim of the conspiracy was control of the local sugar beet market, it does not follow that it is outside the scope of the Sherman Act. For monopolization of local business, when achieved by restraining interstate commerce, is condemned by the Act. . . . And a conspiracy with the ultimate object of fixing local retail prices is within the Act, if the means adopted for its accomplishment reach beyond the boundaries of one state.

. . . The statute does not confine its protection to consumers, or to purchasers, or to competitors, or to sellers. Nor does it immunize the outlawed acts because they are done by any of these. . . . The Act is comprehensive in its terms and coverage, protecting all who are made victims of the forbidden practices by whomever they may be perpetrated.

. . . Nor is the amount of the nation's sugar industry which the California refiners control relevant, so long as control is exercised effectively in the area concerned. . . .

. . . Under the facts characterizing this industry's operation and the tightening of controls in this producing area by the new agreements and understandings, there can be no question that their restrictive consequences were projected substantially into the interstate distribution of the sugar. . . .

Even without the uniform price provision and with full competition among the three refiners, their position is a dominating one. The growers' only competitive outlet is the one which exists when the refiners compete among themselves. There is no other market. The farmers' only alternative to dealing with one of the three refiners is to stop growing beets. They can neither plant nor sell except at the refiners' pleasure and on their terms. The refiners thus effectively control the quantity of beets grown, harvested and marketed, and consequently of sugar sold from the area in interstate commerce, even when they compete with each other. They dominate the entire industry. And their dominant position, together with the obstacles created by the necessity for large capital investment and the time required to make it productive, makes outlet through new competition practically impossible. . . . A tighter or more all-inclusive monopolistic position hardly can be conceived.

. . . Those monopolistic effects not only deprived the beet growers of any competitive opportunity for disposing of their crops by the immediate operation of the uniform price provision; they also tended to increase control over the quantity of sugar sold interstate; and finally by the tie-in provision they interlaced those interstate effects with the price paid for the beets.

These restrictive and monopolistic effects, resulting necessarily from the practices allegedly intended to produce them, fall squarely within the Sherman Act's prohibitions. . . .

[Judgment for Mandeville Island Farms]

(c) Conspiracy to monopolize local markets

The federal statutes are applicable to local markets and prohibit a conspiracy to monopolize a local market by preventing the expansion of a competitor when there is a substantial effect on interstate commerce. The "substantial effect" standard is very vague and is easily satisfied under modern marketing and distribution patterns.

HOSPITAL BUILDING CO. v REX HOSPITAL TRUSTEES

425 US 738 (1976)

Hospital Building Co. operated a hospital, the Mary Elizabeth, in Raleigh, North Carolina. It wanted to relocate and expand. It claimed that the Rex Hospital and others formed a conspiracy to prevent this so that Rex could monopolize the furnishing of hospital services in the city. Hospital Building brought an action against the alleged conspirators claiming a violation of the federal Sherman Antitrust Act. The defendants claimed that the Sherman Act could not apply because any conduct alleged by Hospital Building was purely local and intrastate. The lower court sustained this objection and dismissed the amended complaint filed by Hospital Building. Hospital Building then petitioned to the Supreme Court to review the case.

OPINION BY MARSHALL, J.

. . . Petitioner identifies several areas of interstate commerce in which it is involved. According to the amended complaint, petitioner purchases a substantial proportion—up to 80%—of its medicines and supplies from out-of-state sellers. In 1972, it spent $112,000 on these items. A substantial number of the patients at Mary Elizabeth Hospital, it is alleged, come from out of State. Moreover, petitioner claims that a large proportion of its revenue comes from insurance companies outside of North Carolina or from the Federal Government through the Medicaid and Medicare programs. Petitioner also pays a management service fee based on its gross receipts to its parent company, a Delaware corporation based in Georgia. Finally, petitioner has developed plans to finance a large part of the planned $4 million expansion through out-of-state lenders. All these involvements with interstate commerce, the amended complaint claims, have been and are continuing to be adversely affected by respondents' anticompetitive conduct. . . .

The Sherman Act prohibits every contract, combination, or conspiracy "in restraint of trade or commerce among the several States," . . . and also prohibits monopolizing "any part of the trade or commerce among the several States." . . . It is settled that the Act encompasses far more than restraints on trade that are motivated by a desire to limit interstate commerce or that have their sole impact on interstate commerce. "Wholly local business restraints can produce the effects condemned by the Sherman Act." *United States v Employing Plasterers Assn.,* 347 US 186, 189 . . . (1954). As long as the restraint in question "substantially and adversely affects interstate commerce," . . . the interstate commerce nexus required for Sherman Act coverage is established. "If it is interstate commerce that feels the pinch, it does not matter how local the operation which applies the squeeze." . . .

In this case, the Court of Appeals, while recognizing that Sherman Act coverage requires only that the conduct complained of have a substantial effect on interstate commerce, concluded that the conduct at issue did not meet that standard. We disagree. The complaint, fairly read, alleges that if respondents and their coconspirators were to succeed in blocking petitioner's planned expansion, petitioner's purchases of out-of-state medicines and supplies as well as its revenues from out-of-state insurance companies would be thousands and perhaps hundreds of thousands of dollars less than they would otherwise be. Similarly, the management fees that petitioner pays to its out-of-state parent corporation would be less if the expansion were blocked. Moreover, the multimillion-dollar financing for the expansion, a large portion of which would be from out of State, would simply not take place if the respondents succeeded in their alleged scheme. This combination of factors is certainly sufficient to establish a "substantial effect" on interstate commerce under the Act.

The Court of Appeals found two considerations crucial in its refusal to find that the complaint alleged a substantial effect on interstate commerce. The Court's reliance on neither was warranted. First, the Court observed:

> The effect [on interstate commerce] here seems to us the indirect and fortuitous consequence of the restraint of the intrastate Raleigh area hospital market, rather than the result of activity purposely directed toward interstate commerce.

But the fact that an effect on interstate commerce might be termed "indirect" because the conduct producing it is not "purposely directed" toward interstate

commerce does not lead to a conclusion that the conduct at issue is outside the
scope of the Sherman Act. For instance, in *Burke v Ford,* 389 US 320 . . . (1967),
Oklahoma liquor retailers brought a Sherman Act action against liquor wholesalers in the State, alleging that the wholesalers had restrained commerce by
dividing up the state market into exclusive territories. While the market division
was patently not "purposely directed" toward interstate commerce, we held that
it nevertheless substantially affected interstate commerce because as a matter of
practical economics that division could be expected to reduce significantly the
magnitude of purchases made by the wholesalers from out-of-state distillers.
"The wholesalers' territorial division . . . almost surely resulted in fewer sales
to retailers—hence fewer purchases from out-of-state distillers—than would
have occurred had free competition prevailed among the wholesalers." . . .
Whether the wholesalers intended their restraint to affect interstate commerce
was simply irrelevant to our holding. . . . In the same way, the fact that respondents in the instant case may not have had the purposeful goal of affecting
interstate commerce does not lead us to exempt that conduct from coverage
under the Sherman Act.

The Court of Appeals further justified its holding of "no substantial effect"
by arguing that "no source of supply or insurance company or lending institution can be expected to go under if Mary Elizabeth doesn't expand, and no
market price will be affected." . . . While this may be true, it is not of great
relevance to the issue of whether the "substantial effect" test is satisfied. An
effect can be "substantial" under the Sherman Act even if its impact on interstate commerce falls far short of causing enterprises to fold or affecting market
price. For instance in *United States v Employing Plasterers Assn.* [347 US 186], we
considered a Sherman Act challenge to an alleged conspiracy between a trade
association and union officials to restrain competition among Chicago plastering
contractors. As in the instant case, the District Court dismissed the action on the
pleadings. It did so on the ground that the complaint amounted to no more than
charges of "local restraint and monopoly," . . . not reached by the Sherman Act.
The United States appealed . . . and we reversed. It was sufficient for us that the
allegations in the complaint, if proved, could show that the conspiracy resulted
in *"unreasonable burdens on the free and uninterrupted flow* of plastering materials into
Illinois." . . . (emphasis added). We did not demand allegations, either express
or implied, that the conspiracy threaten the demise of out-of-state businesses
or that the conspiracy affect market price. Thus, since in this case the allegations
fairly claim that the alleged conspiracy, to the extent it is successful, will place
"unreasonable burdens on the free and uninterrupted flow" of interstate commerce, they are wholly adequate to state a claim.

We have held that "a complaint should not be dismissed for failure to state
a claim unless it appears beyond doubt that the plaintiff can prove no set of facts
in support of his claim which would entitle him to relief." . . . And in antitrust
cases, where "the proof is largely in the hands of the alleged conspirators,"
. . . dismissals prior to giving the plaintiff ample opportunity for discovery
should be granted very sparingly. Applying this concededly rigorous standard,
we conclude that the instant case is not one in which dismissal should have been

granted. Petitioner's complaint states a claim upon which relief can be granted under the Sherman Act. . . .

[Judgment reversed]

---

§ 10:3. THE RULE OF REASON

The general approach of the Supreme Court to the trust problem has been that an agreement or a contract is not automatically, or per se, to be condemned as a restraint of interstate commerce merely because it creates a power or a potential to monopolize interstate commerce. It is only when the restraint actually imposed on interstate commerce is unreasonable that the practice is unlawful. In applying this "rule of reason," it is obvious that the court enters into a controversial field. The establishing of the restraint by the parties to the restraining agreement may be regarded by them as an essential step in the stabilization of their industry and as a matter of enlightened self-interest. To the competitors or the general public who might be adversely affected by the application of this restraint, the restraint is unreasonable.

The decision of these points is not one of law, but one of applied economics or the science of governing. It hinges on one's attitude toward large-scale enterprise, free enterprise, the rights of the small producer, the rights of the consumer, and other equally vague and nonmeasurable standards.

(a) Extent of harm

The application of the rule of reason calls for a consideration of the extent of the harm to society caused by the practices in question and an appraisal of whether the harm is so significant that the conduct should be prohibited, or is so inconsequential that it should be ignored.

NATIONAL SOCIETY OF PROFESSIONAL ENGINEERS v UNITED STATES

435 US 679 (1978)

Canon § 11(c) of the Standards of Ethics of the National Society of Professional Engineers in effect prohibited its members from submitting competitive price bids for engineering services by prohibiting an engineer from discussing price with a prospective client. The United States claimed that this suppressed competition as to fees for services and was therefore a violation of the Sherman Act. The Society claimed that the canon was valid and that its purpose was to prevent engineers from entering into price-cutting competition which would produce poor work, which would be harmful to the public. The Society claimed that the rule of reason therefore justified the canon and made it proper to adhere to its pattern of having an owner select an engineer before there was any discussion of fees. The lower courts held the canon invalid and the Society appealed to the Supreme Court of the United States.

OPINION BY STEVENS, J.

. . . The National Society of Professional Engineers (Society) was organized in 1935 to deal with the nontechnical aspects of engineering practice, including the promotion of the professional, social, and economic interests of its members. Its present membership of 69,000 resides throughout the United States and in some foreign countries. Approximately 12,000 members are consulting engineers who offer their services to governmental, industrial, and private clients. Some Society members are principals or chief executive officers of some of the largest engineering firms in the country.

The charges of a consulting engineer may be computed in different ways. He may charge the client a percentage of the cost of the project, may set his fee at his actual cost plus overhead plus a reasonable profit, may charge fixed rates per hour for different types of work, may perform an assignment for a specific sum, or he may combine one or more of these approaches. Suggested fee schedules for particular types of services in certain areas have been promulgated from time to time by various local societies. This case does not, however, involve any claim that the National Society has tried to fix specific fees, or even a specific method of calculating fees. It involves a charge that the members of the Society have unlawfully agreed to refuse to negotiate or even to discuss the question of fees until after a prospective client has selected the engineer for a particular project. . . .

The District Court found that the Society's Board of Ethical Review has uniformly interpreted the "ethical rules against competitive bidding for engineering services as prohibiting the submission of any form of price information to a prospective customer which would enable that customer to make a price comparison on engineering services." If the client requires that such information be provided, then § 11(c) imposes an obligation upon the engineering firm to withdraw from consideration for that job. The Society's Code of Ethics thus "prohibits engineers from both soliciting and submitting such price information," . . . and seeks to preserve the profession's "traditional" method of selecting professional engineers. Under the traditional method, the client initially selects an engineer on the basis of background and reputation, not price. . . .

The Society averred that the standard set out in the Code of Ethics was reasonable because competition among professional engineers was contrary to the public interest. It was averred that it would be cheaper and easier for an engineer "to design and specify inefficient and unnecessarily expensive structures methods of construction." Accordingly, competitive pressure to offer engineering services at the lowest possible price would adversely affect the quality of engineering. Moreover, the practice of awarding engineering contracts to the lowest bidder, regardless of quality, would be dangerous to the public health, safety, and welfare. For these reasons, the Society claimed that its Code of Ethics was not an "unreasonable restraint of interstate trade or commerce." . . .

Petitioner argues that its attempt to preserve the profession's traditional method of setting fees for engineering services is a reasonable method of forestalling the public harm which might be produced by unrestrained competitive bidding. To evaluate this argument it is necessary to identify the contours of the Rule of Reason and to discuss its application to the kind of justification asserted by petitioner.

One problem presented by the language of § 1 of the Sherman Act is that it cannot mean what it says. The statute says that "every" contract that restrains trade is unlawful. But, as Mr. Justice Brandeis perceptively noted, restraint is the very essence of every contract; read literally, § 1 would outlaw the entire body of private contract law. Yet it is that body of law that establishes the enforceability of commercial agreements and enables competitive markets—indeed, a competitive economy—to function effectively.

Congress, however, did not intend the text of the Sherman Act to delineate the full meaning of the statute or its application in concrete situations. The legislative history makes it perfectly clear that it expected the courts to give shape to the statute's broad mandate by drawing on common-law tradition. The Rule of Reason . . . focuses directly on the challenged restraint's impact on competitive conditions. . . .

The . . . cases . . . foreclose the argument that because of the special characteristics of a particular industry, monopolistic arrangements will better promote trade and commerce than competition. . . . That kind of argument is properly addressed to Congress and may justify an exemption from the statute for specific industries, but it is not permitted by the Rule of Reason. . . . "Restraints of trade within the purview of the statute . . . [can] not be taken out of that category by indulging in general reasoning as to the expediency or nonexpediency of having made the contracts or the wisdom or want of wisdom of the statute which prohibited their being made.

The test . . . is whether the challenged contracts or acts "were unreasonably restrictive of competitive conditions." Unreasonableness under that test could be based either (1) on the nature or character of the contracts, or (2) on surrounding circumstances giving rise to the inference or presumption that they were intended to restrain trade and enhance prices. Under either branch of the test, the inquiry is confined to a consideration of impact on competitive conditions.
. . .

The inquiry mandated by the Rule of Reason is whether the challenged agreement is one that promotes competition or one that suppresses competition. "The true test of legality is whether the restraint imposed is such as merely regulates and perhaps thereby promotes competition or whether it is such as may suppress or even destroy competition." . . .

There are, thus, two complementary categories of antitrust analysis. In the first category are agreements whose nature and necessary effect are so plainly anticompetitive that no elaborate study of the industry is needed to establish their illegality—they are "illegal per se"—in the second category are agreements whose competitive effect can only be evaluated by analyzing the facts peculiar to the business, the history of the restraint, and the reasons why it was imposed. In either event, the purpose of the analysis is to form a judgment about the competitive significance of the restraint; it is not to decide whether a policy favoring competition is in the public interest, or in the interest of the members of an industry. Subject to exceptions defined by statute, that policy decision has been made by the Congress. . . .

The Society's affirmative defense confirms rather than refutes the anticompetitive purpose and effect of its agreement. The Society argues that the restraint is justified because bidding on engineering services is inherently imprecise, would lead to deceptively low bids, and would thereby tempt individual engineers to do inferior work with consequent risk to public safety and health. The logic of this argument rests on the assumption that the agreement will tend to maintain the price level; if it had no such effect, it would not serve its intended purpose. The Society nonetheless invokes the Rule of Reason, arguing that its restraint on price competition ultimately inures to the public benefit by preventing the production of inferior work and by insuring ethical behavior. As the preceding discussion of the Rule of Reason reveals, this Court has never accepted such an argument. . . .

The Sherman Act does not require competitive bidding; it prohibits unreasonable restraints on competition. Petitioner's ban on competitive bidding prevents all customers from making price comparisons in the initial selection of an engineer, and imposes the Society's view of the costs and benefits of competition on the entire marketplace. It is this restraint that must be justified under the Rule of Reason, and petitioner's attempt to do so on the basis of the potential threat that competition poses to the public safety and the ethics of its profession is nothing less than a frontal assault on the basic policy of the Sherman Act.

The Sherman Act reflects a legislative judgment that ultimately competition will not only produce lower prices, but also better goods and services. "The heart of our national economic policy long has been faith in the value of competition." . . . The assumption that competition is the best method of allocating resources in a free market recognizes that all elements of a bargain —quality, service, safety, and durability—and not just the immediate cost, are favorably affected by the free opportunity to select among alternative offers. Even assuming occasional exceptions to the presumed consequences of competition, the statutory policy precludes inquiry into the question whether competition is good or bad.

The fact that engineers are often involved in large-scale projects significantly affecting the public safety does not alter our analysis. Exceptions to the Sherman Act for potentially dangerous goods and services would be tantamount to a repeal of the statute. In our complex economy the number of items that may cause serious harm is almost endless—automobiles, drugs, foods, aircraft components, heavy equipment, and countless others, cause serious harm to individuals or to the public at large if defectively made. The judiciary cannot indirectly protect the public against this harm by conferring monopoly privileges on the manufacturers. . . .

In sum, the Rule of Reason does not support a defense based on the assumption that competition itself is unreasonable. . . .

[Canon held invalid]

(b) The relevant market

UNITED STATES v E. I. DU PONT DE NEMOURS & COMPANY

351 US 377 (1956)

The United States sued Du Pont to enjoin it from monopolizing the cellophane market in violation of Section 2 of the Sherman Antitrust Act. Du Pont contended that its domination of cellophane was not the criterion since there were substitutes for cellophane, and that accordingly it did not violate the Act unless it was found to dominate the general market for flexible packaging materials.

OPINION BY REED, J.

. . . If cellophane is the "market" that Du Pont is found to dominate, it may be assumed it does have monopoly power over that "market." Monopoly power is the power to control prices or exclude competition. It seems apparent that Du Pont's power to set the price of cellophane has been limited only by the competition afforded by other flexible packaging materials. Moreover, it may be practically impossible for anyone to commence manufacturing cellophane without full access to Du Pont's technique. However, Du Pont has no power to prevent competition from other wrapping materials. The trial court consequently had to determine whether competition from the other wrappings prevented Du Pont from possessing monopoly power in violation of § 2. . . .

If a large number of buyers and sellers deal freely in a standardized product, such as salt or wheat, we have complete or pure competition. Patents, on the other hand, furnish the most familiar type of classic monopoly. As the producers of a standardized product bring about significant differentiations of quality, design, or packaging in the product that permit differences of use, competition becomes to a greater or less degree incomplete and the producer's power over price and competition greater over his article and its use, according to the differentiation he is able to create and maintain. A retail seller may have in one sense a monopoly on certain trade because of location, as an isolated country store or filling station, or because no one else makes a product of just the quality or attractiveness of his product, as for example in cigarettes. Thus one can theorize that we have monopolistic competition in every nonstandardized commodity with each manufacturer having power over the price and production of his own product. However, this power that, let us say, automobile or soft-drink manufacturers have over their trademarked products is not the power that makes an illegal monopoly. Illegal power must be appraised in terms of the competitive market for the product.

Determination of the competitive market for commodities depends on how different from one another are the offered commodities in character or use, how far buyers will go to substitute one commodity for another. For example, one can think of building materials as in commodity competition but one could hardly say that brick competed with steel or wood or cement or stone in the meaning of Sherman Act litigation; the products are too different. . . . On the other hand, there are certain differences in the formulae for soft drinks but one can hardly say that each one is an illegal monopoly. Whatever the market may be, we hold that control of price or competition establishes the existence of monopoly power under § 2. Section 2 requires the application of a reasonable approach in determining the existence of monopoly power just as surely as did § 1.

. . . Where there are market alternatives that buyers may readily use for their purposes, illegal monopoly does not exist merely because the product said to be monopolized differs from others. If it were not so, only physically identical products would be a part of the market. To accept the government's argument, we would have to conclude that the manufacturers of plain as well as moisture-proof cellophane were monopolists, and so with films such as Pliofilm, foil, glassine, polyethylene, and Saran, for each of these wrapping materials is distinguishable. . . .

The "market" which one must study to determine when a producer has monopoly power will vary with the part of commerce under consideration. The tests are constant. That market is composed of products that have reasonable interchangeability for the purposes for which they are produced—price, use and qualities considered. While the application of the tests remains uncertain, it seems to us that Du Pont should not be found to monopolize cellophane when that product has the competition and interchangeability with other wrappings. . . .

[Judgment for Du Pont, as its control of cellophane did not give it a monopoly of the relevant market of flexible packaging materials]

§ 10:4. THE PER SE VIOLATION CONCEPT

In some situations, the harmful effect upon competition of a particular practice is so obvious that there is no need to examine the facts in detail. In plain words, it is an "open and shut" case of a violation of the Sherman Antitrust Act. In situations which have this characteristic, the rule of reason is not applied. Instead, the particular practice in question is condemned as a *per se* violation of the antitrust law. For example, if there are ten radio dealers in a town and they all enter into an agreement fixing the prices at which they will sell radios, there would be an obvious reduction of competition and the agreement would be a per se violation of the antitrust law.

The significance of applying the per se violation concept lies in the fact that the condemnation of the statute cannot be overcome or erased by contrary evidence. For example, in the illustration of the radio dealers case above given, once the agreement stated is shown, the case is over. The dealers cannot come forth with any evidence that they had made the agreement to stabilize the market or put an end to harmful price cutting. The fact that they made the agreement violates the law and no excuses or explanations can be made.

§ 10:5. STATUTORY AND JUDICIAL EXCEPTIONS

At the same time that the antitrust policy has been extended in certain directions, Congress has made several significant exceptions to its operation. Congress has authorized freight pooling and revenue division agreements between railroad carriers, provided the approval of the Interstate Commerce Commission is obtained. By virtue of statutory exemptions, traffic and freight agreements otherwise prohibited by the antitrust law may be made by ocean carriers, and interstate railroads and telegraph companies may consolidate upon obtaining the approval of the government commission having jurisdiction over them. Marine insurance associations are exempted from the Sherman Act. The Newspaper Preservation Act of 1970 grants an antitrust exemption to operating agreements entered into by newspapers to prevent financial collapse.

By the Webb-Pomerene Act of 1918, authorization was given to exporters to form associations engaged solely in exporting that could make agreements in foreign trade without regard to the antitrust laws, so long as those agreements did not restrain trade within the United States or did not restrain the export trade of any United States exporter. The premise underlying this statute is that foreign trade is subject to such a high degree of monopoly control that it is impossible for American exporters to secure their fair share of the world trade if they are required to deal as individuals and are not permitted to combine to fight monopoly with monopoly insofar as international marketing is concerned.

In 1922 the farmers and dairymen were given authority by the Capper-Volstead Act to form cooperatives for purchasing and selling without regard to the antitrust laws. This statute is not a blanket exemption to farmers and dairymen from the antitrust laws. If their cooperatives combine with other persons not members of the cooperatives to fix prices, they are subject to the antitrust laws. As long as they keep within the normal cooperative functions and do not attempt to fix prices by agreement with third persons, the antitrust laws are not applicable. Here again the exception to the antitrust law is based upon the belief that a policy of free competition is not desirable and that the farmers and dairymen can operate more profitably to themselves and to the community at large if they are permitted to combine, even though the prices at which they sell their goods are thus indirectly controlled or enhanced. In 1965 combinations of financial institutions formed to prevent the drain of dollars from the United States were also exempted from the antitrust laws.

In consequence of the decision of the Supreme Court in *United States v South-Eastern Underwriters' Association*, 322 US 533 (1944), holding that interstate insurance is commerce and subject to the antitrust law, Congress adopted a law which exempts insurance companies from the Sherman Act and federal regulation to the extent that there are state laws that regulate the insurance companies.

In addition to the statutory exemptions from the Sherman Act, it is also to be noted that the Supreme Court has construed statutes that did not expressly exempt labor from the Sherman Act as having that effect as long as labor did not conspire with nonunion groups or persons.

(a) Labor unions

LOS ANGELES LOCAL 626 v UNITED STATES

371 US 94 (1962)

Independent contractors who purchased grease from restaurants and resold it to grease processors joined a union of meat and provision drivers. The union then allocated sales territory to each grease peddler, as the contractors were called, and fixed the prices. The United States brought a suit for an injunction to stop this practice and to require the peddlers to withdraw from the union. From a decision against the peddlers, they appealed.

OPINION BY STEWART, J.

. . . During the period between 1954 and 1959 there were in Los Angeles County eight firms engaged as processors in the production of yellow grease, an inedible grease produced by removing moisture and solid impurities from so-called restaurant grease—waste grease resulting from the preparation of food in restaurants, hotels, and institutions. A substantial part of the yellow grease so produced was sold to overseas purchasers and to purchasers in California for prompt shipment overseas.

The processors procured restaurant grease in two separate ways. They made direct purchases, usually from large restaurants, hotels and other institutions, and in these transactions the processors picked up the restaurant grease from the sellers through employees who were members of the union. Restaurant grease from other sources was usually purchased by the processors from grease peddlers, independent entrepreneurs whose earnings as middlemen consisted of the difference between the price at which they bought the restaurant grease from various sources and the price at which they sold it to the processors, less the cost of operating and maintaining their trucks. There were some 35 to 45 grease peddlers in the Los Angeles area.

In 1954 most of the grease peddlers became members of the appellant union, at the instigation of the appellant business agent, for the purpose of increasing the margin between the prices they paid for grease and the prices at which they sold it to the processors. To accomplish this purpose, fixed purchase and sale prices were agreed upon and enforced by union agents through the exercise or threatened exercise of union economic power in the form of strikes and boycotts against processors who indicated any inclination to deal with grease peddlers who were not union members. The union's business agent allocated accounts and territories for both purchases and sales among the various grease peddlers, who agreed to refrain from buying from or soliciting the customers of other peddlers, and violations of this agreement could result in a grease peddler's suspension from the union, in which event he was, of course, prohibited from carrying on his business.

From 1954 to 1959 this basic plan of price fixing and allocation of business was effectively carried out by elimination of the few peddlers who had not joined the union, and by coercion upon the processors through threats of "union trouble" if they did not comply.

Within the union the grease peddlers were treated as a separate group, distinct from the some 2,400 employee members. The meetings of the grease peddlers were always held apart from regular union meetings, and from 1955 on, the grease peddlers were members of a special "subdivision" of the union —Local 626-B. The affairs of this separate subdivision were administered not by regular union officers, but by the appellant business agent who had originated the scheme, together with a committee of grease peddlers to assist in "policing, enforcing and carrying out the program to suppress and eliminate competition."

There was no showing of any actual or potential wage or job competition, or of any other economic interrelationship, between the grease peddlers and the other members of the union. It was stipulated that no processors had ever substituted peddlers for employee-drivers in acquiring restaurant grease, or had ever threatened to do so. The stipulation made clear that the peddlers and the processors had essentially different sources of supply and different classes of customers. . . .

It is beyond question that a court of equity has power in appropriate circumstances to order the dissolution of an association of businessmen, when the association and its members have conspired among themselves or with others to violate the antitrust laws. . . . And the circumstances stipulated and found in the present case provided ample support, we think, for a decree of dissolution, as a matter of the discreet exercise of equitable power.

It is also beyond question that nothing in the anti-injunction provisions of the Norris-LaGuardia [Antilabor Injunction] Act, nor in the labor exemption provisions of the Clayton Act, insulates a combination in illegal restraint of trade between businessmen and a labor union from the sanctions of the antitrust laws. . . .

The narrow question which emerges in this case, therefore, is whether businessmen who combine in an association, which would otherwise be properly subject to dissolution under the antitrust laws, can immunize themselves from the sanction by the simple expedient of calling themselves "Local 626-B" of a labor union. We think there is nothing in the Norris-LaGuardia Act nor in the Clayton Act, nor in the federal policy which these statutes reflect, to prevent a court from dissolving the ties which bound these businessmen together, and which bound them to the appellant union, in the circumstances of the present case. . . .

This Court's decision in *Columbia River Packers Assn.* v *Hinton,* 315 US 143, . . . is very much in point. That was a private antitrust suit brought by a processor of fish to enjoin an allegedly illegal combination of fishermen, who had joined together in the Pacific Coast Fishermen's Union to regulate the terms under which fish would be sold. The organization was "affiliated with the C. I. O." . . . The defendants claimed that an injunction against them would violate the Norris-LaGuardia Act. The Court held that the controversy was not a "labor dispute" within the meaning of the Norris-LaGuardia Act, pointing out that that statute was "not intended to have application to disputes over the sale of commodities." Here, as in Columbia River Packers Assn., the grease peddlers were sellers of commodities, who became "members" of the union only for the purpose of bringing union power to bear in the successful enforcement of the illegal combination in restraint of the traffic in yellow grease. The District Court was not in error in ordering the complete termination of that illegal combination.

What has been said is not remotely to suggest that a labor organization might not often have a legitimate interest in soliciting self-employed entrepreneurs as members. And both the Norris-LaGuardia Act and the Clayton Act ensure that the antitrust laws cannot be used as a vehicle to stifle legitimate labor union activities. But here the court found upon stipulated facts that there was no job or wage competition or economic interrelationship of any kind between the grease peddlers and other members of the appellant union. If that situation should change in the future, the District Court will have ample power to amend its decree.

[Judgment affirmed, ordering grease peddlers to leave the union]

§ 10:6. SIGNIFICANCE OF EXCEPTIONS

The narrowing down of the scope of the antitrust law, both by court decision and by statutory exceptions, has, in the minds of some, cast serious doubt upon the validity of antitrust legislation. It is claimed that both national and world economy evidence a relentless march toward greater concentration of capital and that increasingly bigger businesses, rather than free competition between small businesses, is the order of the times. By some, this is accepted as an inevitable evil, and the objective of antitrust legislation is approved but its attainment is deemed futile. Others approve of this increasing concentration of economic power on the ground that it would permit a greater stability and a greater realization of the economies of large-scale enterprise. Opposed to these are those who regard the maintenance of the small business and the small enterprise as essential to what has become known as the American way of life. To them, the potential of evil found in large capitalization is not worth the savings that it can bring. To them, small-scale production and free competition are worth preserving at any cost. Others go further and claim that large-scale economy keeps its savings for itself.

The difficulty of scientifically measuring the merit of the arguments advanced, and the realization that much depends upon the applied ethical standards of the persons involved, makes the selection of a steady course most difficult. The solution of the problem is not in any way aided by the fact that certain groups and practices are not subject to the antitrust control to which the remainder of the economy is subject. The advocates of consistency decry this split policy and claim that the exceptions are either the fruit of political pressure or the recognition that the general rule is not workable. In the one case, the exception should be removed; in the other, the general rule should itself be abolished and the exception made the general principle. Those who are not troubled by the need for formal consistency may be able to reconcile the existence of exceptions to the general rule. This, however, is not without its own difficulties, for a clear dividing line cannot be maintained between the excepted areas and those that are not excepted. It is quite possible that exporters who are permitted to combine for export trade purposes may carry over their policies of "cooperation" in some instances into the domestic trade within the United States, contrary to both the spirit and the letter of the antitrust laws.

Questions for Discussion

1. What is the constitutional basis for the Sherman Act?

2. What was the origin of the antimonopoly movement?

3. (a) Can you explain why monopolies are prohibited at the same time that government gives public utilities a monopoly? (b) Can the argument in favor of the public utility monopoly be extended to other basic industries? Would it affect your answer if the nation were at war?

4. Is it unlawful for one manufacturer to fix the prices that that manufacturer charges and for other manufacturers to follow those prices without any prior agreement to do so?

5. Is there any practical difference between the result of parallel action and concerted action?

6. Assume that a traveler through Chicago must go from one station to another in order to catch a connecting train. Is such a person moving in interstate commerce when stopping in a railroad restaurant to have lunch during the delay in connecting train service?

7. Is the Sherman Act limited to agreements between sellers raising the price at which commodities are sold to the public?

8. Does the decision in the *Mandeville* case depend upon the price at which the beet sugar was sold in interstate markets?

9. Assume that the three refiners in the *Mandeville* case were able to show that the prices they paid the beet farmer were still higher than prices paid to such farmers in other states. Would this have affected the decision of the Court?

10. Does the *Mandeville* case give to the Sherman Act the same meaning that it had at the time of its adoption?

11. Did the conspiracy in the *Hospital Building* case relate to intrastate activity?

12. Compare the *Mandeville Island Farm* case with the *Hospital Building* case.

13. Members of a particular trade association make an agreement to refrain from competing with each other. They are then prosecuted for violating the federal antitrust law. They raise the defense that what they have done was reasonable because the effect of their agreement was to eliminate cutthroat competition among the members of the association, competition which in the long run would cause the selling of goods at a below-cost price, which in turn would cause a reduction of quality, which in the long run would be harmful to the general public. The association members claimed that therefore they are protected by the rule of reason. Is their defense valid?

14. A number of railroads and others joined together to promote a publicity campaign against truckers with the purpose of securing regulatory laws that would impose burdens upon the trucking industry and thereby remove a competitor of the railroads. In this campaign, the railroads spread propaganda that was made to appear as though coming from independent groups voicing their spontaneous opinions. The truckers brought a suit against the railroads and the other parties involved claiming that they constituted a conspiracy to restrain trade by eliminating the competition of the truckers. Were the truckers correct? [*Eastern Railroad Presidents Conference v Noerr Motor Freight,* 365 US 127, rehearing denied, 367 US 875 (1961)]

15. The State of Washington adopted a statute prohibiting trusts and monopolies in restraint of commerce. The language of the state statute was almost identical to the federal Sherman Antitrust Act prohibiting similar conduct with respect to foreign and interstate commerce. An action was brought against the Sterling Theatres Co. to enjoin it from violating the state statute. It claimed that the state statute was void because the federal statute preempted the field whenever the persons involved did business in interstate commerce. It was admitted that the distribution of the films involved constituted interstate commerce. Was the state statute valid? [*State v Sterling Theatres Co.,* 64 Wash 2d 748, 394 P2d 226 (1964)]

16. Reiter purchased a hearing aid from the Sonotone Corporation. She claimed that she and other purchasers buying Sonotone and other brands of hearing aids had been overcharged because Sonotone and the other manufacturers had agreed to establish high prices. Reiter brought a suit on behalf of herself and all other consumers to recover treble damages under § 4 of the Clayton Act. That section authorized the recovery of such damages by any person "injured . . . in business or property" by a violation of the antitrust law. The defense was raised that even if higher prices had been charged in violation of the antitrust law, Reiter's property had not been harmed thereby. Was this a valid defense? [*Reiter v Sonotone Corp.,*   US   , 60 L Ed 2d 931 (1979)]

11

Regulation of Enterprise Structure

§ 11:1. BIGNESS

No federal law directly prohibits bigness. That is, there is no ceiling in terms of volume of business or dollar value of assets which limits the size of an enterprise. Some state laws limit property ownership, and federal laws limit the ownership or acquisition of assets in some cases.

§ 11:2. OWNERSHIP OF PROPERTY BY CORPORATIONS

From the early days of corporation law, various limitations have been imposed on corporate ownership and, in more recent times, on corporate structure. All states impose some limitation regulating the formation of corporations and the kinds of stock that may be issued. Limitations may also be imposed on the amount of land that a corporation may own; and foreign corporations may be required to divest themselves of excess holdings within a specified number of years. In view of the modern trend toward commercial as distinguished from subsistence farming, restrictions on the acreage that may be held by a farming corporation are a strong weapon of the small farmer.

Today the ownership of stock in other corporations looms more important than ownership of land. No question of government control ordinarily arises when the ownership of stock is for the purpose of investment only. The investment, however, may be so large as to give a degree of control over the other enterprise. Moreover, the ownership of a stock may be carried to such an extent that the operating company is a wholly owned subsidiary of the owning or holding company.

(a) Purchase by customer of stock of supplier

UNITED STATES v E. I. DU PONT DE NEMOURS & COMPANY

353 US 586 (1957)

From 1917 to 1919, Du Pont acquired 23 percent stock interest in General Motors. During the following years, General Motors bought all its automotive finishes and fabrics from Du Pont. In 1949, the United States claimed the effect of the stock acquisition had been to lessen competition in interstate commerce, on the theory that the sales to General Motors had not been the result of successful competition, but were the result of the stock ownership, and therefore such stock ownership violated the Clayton Act. The United States brought an action against Du Pont, General Motors, and others. From a decision in the companies' favor, the United States appealed.

OPINION BY BRENNAN, J.

. . . The primary issue is whether Du Pont's commanding position as General Motor's supplier of automotive finishes and fabrics was achieved on competitive merit alone, or because its acquisition of the General Motors' stock, and the consequent close intercompany relationship, led to the insulation of most of the General Motors' market from free competition, with the resultant likelihood, at the time of suit, of the creation of a monopoly of a line of commerce [contrary to § 7 of the Clayton Act]. . . .

Section 7 is designed to arrest in its incipiency not only the substantial lessening of competition from the acquisition by one corporation of the whole or any part of the stock of a competing corporation, but also to arrest in their incipiency restraints or monopolies in a relevant market which, as a reasonable probability, appear at the time of suit likely to result from the acquisition by one corporation of all or any part of the stock of any other corporation. The section is violated whether or not actual restraints or monopolies, or the substantial lessening of competition, have occurred or are intended. Acquisitions solely for investment are excepted, but only if, and so long as, the stock is not used by voting or otherwise to bring about, or in attempting to bring about, the substantial lessening of competition. . . .

The first paragraph of § 7 plainly is framed to reach not only the corporate acquisition of stock of a competing corporation, where the effect may be substantially to lessen competition between them, but also the corporate acquisition of stock of any corporation, competitor or not, where the effect may be either (1) to restrain commerce in any section or community, or (2) tend to create a monopoly of any line of commerce. . . .

We hold that any acquisition by one corporation of all or any part of the stock of another corporation, competitor or not, is within the reach of the section whenever the reasonable likelihood appears that the acquisition will result in a restraint of commerce or in the creation of a monopoly of any line of commerce. Thus, although Du Pont and General Motors are not competitors, a violation of the section has occurred if, as a result of the acquisition, there was at the time of suit a reasonable likelihood of a monopoly of any line of commerce. . . .

Appellees argue that there exists no basis for a finding of a probable restraint or monopoly within the meaning of § 7 because the total General Motors market for finishes and fabrics constituted only a negligible percentage of the total market for these materials for all uses, including automotive uses. It is stated in the General Motors brief that in 1947 Du Pont's finish sales to General Motors constituted 3.5 percent of all sales of finishes to industrial users, and that its fabrics sales to General Motors comprised 1.6 percent of the total market for the type of fabric used by the automobile industry.

Determination of the relevant market is a necessary predicate to a finding of a violation of the Clayton Act because the threatened monopoly must be one which will substantially lessen competition "within the area of effective competition." Substantiality can be determined only in terms of the market affected. The record shows that automotive finishes and fabrics have sufficient peculiar characteristics and uses to constitute them products sufficiently distinct from all other finishes and fabrics to make them a "line of commerce" within the meaning of the Clayton Act. . . . Thus, the bounds of the relevant market for the purposes of this case are not coextensive with the total market for finishes and fabrics, but are coextensive with the automobile industry, the relevant market for automotive finishes and fabrics.

The market affected must be substantial. . . . Moreover, in order to establish a violation of § 7 the Government must prove a likelihood that competition may be "foreclosed in a substantial share of . . . [that market]." Both requirements are satisfied in this case. The substantiality of a relevant market comprising the automobile industry is undisputed. The substantiality of General Motors' share of that market is fully established in the evidence.

General Motors . . . accounts annually for upwards of two fifths of the total sales of automotive vehicles in the Nation. . . . Du Pont supplied 67 percent of General Motors' requirements for finishes in 1946 and 68 percent in 1947. In fabrics Du Pont supplied 52.3 percent of requirements in 1946, and 38.5 percent in 1947. Because General Motors accounts for almost one half of the automobile industry's annual sales, its requirements for automotive finishes and fabrics must represent approximately one half of the relevant market for these materials. Because the record clearly shows that quantitatively and percentagewise Du Pont supplies the largest part of General Motors' requirements, we must conclude that Du Pont has a substantial share of the relevant market.

The appellees argue that the Government could not maintain this action in 1949 because § 7 is applicable only to the acquisition of stock and not to the holding or subsequent use of the stock. This argument misconceives the objective toward which § 7 is directed. The Clayton Act was intended to supplement the Sherman Act. Its aim was primarily to arrest apprehended consequences of intercorporate relationships before those relationships could work their evil, which may be at or any time after the acquisition, depending upon the circumstances of the particular case. . . . The Government may proceed at any time that an acquisition may be said with reasonable probability to contain a threat that it may lead to a restraint of commerce or tend to create a monopoly of a line of commerce. . . .

We agree with the trial court that considerations of price, quality, and service were not overlooked by either Du Pont or General Motors. Pride in its products and its high financial stake in General Motors' success would naturally lead Du Pont to try to supply the best. But the wisdom of this business judgment cannot obscure the fact, plainly revealed by the record, that Du Pont purposely employed its stock to pry open the General Motors market to entrench itself as the primary supplier of General Motors' requirements for automotive finishes and fabrics.

Similarly, the fact that all concerned in high executive posts in both companies acted honorably and fairly, each in the honest conviction that his actions were in the best interests of his own company and without any design to overreach anyone, including Du Pont's competitors, does not defeat the Government's right to relief. It is not requisite to the proof of a violation of § 7 to show that restraint or monopoly was intended.

The statutory policy of fostering free competition is obviously furthered when no supplier has an advantage over his competitors from an acquisition of his customer's stock likely to have the effects condemned by the statute. We repeat, that the test of a violation of § 7 is whether, at the time of suit, there is a reasonable probability that the acquisition is likely to result in the condemned restraints. The conclusion upon this record is inescapable that such likelihood was proved as to this acquisition. . . .

[Judgment for United States, ordering divestiture by defendants of General Motors stock]

(b) Purchase by customer of supplier's assets

American manufacturing is to a very large degree the assembling of component parts purchased from other manufacturers. For example, the manufacturer of television sets will ordinarily purchase its transistors from a transistor manufacturer. The manufacturer of the ultimate product, the television set, may decide that it is economically desirable to produce its own transistors, thereby (1) eliminating the profit of its supplier of transistors, and (2) giving the television set manufacturer the potential of selling transistors to other users of transistors.

Nothing in the law prohibits the television set manufacturer from opening its own transistor branch or plant. If, however, the television set manufacturer purchases an existing transistor factory, there is the danger that such acquisition will violate § 7 of the Clayton Act because it may tend to lessen competition.

FORD MOTOR CO. v UNITED STATES

405 US 562 (1972)

The Electric Autolite Company was the second largest manufacturer of spark plugs in the country. The Ford Motor Company purchased spark plugs from Autolite for use in Ford automobiles. Ford purchased the brand name of Autolite, the plant, and most of the assets of Electric Autolite. Autolite then changed its name and continued to produce spark plugs on a small scale under the name of Prestolite. The United States claimed that the acquisition by Ford of the Autolite assets violated § 7 of the Clayton Act. From a decision of the lower court ordering divestiture of the acquisition, Ford appealed to the United States Supreme Court.

OPINION BY DOUGLAS, J.

. . . Ford, the second-leading producer of automobiles, General Motors, and Chrysler together account for 90% of the automobile production in this country. Though Ford makes a substantial portion of its parts, prior to its acquisition of the assets of Autolite it did not make spark plugs or batteries but purchased those parts from independent companies.

The original equipment of new cars, insofar as spark plugs are concerned, is conveniently referred to as the OE tie. The replacement market is referred to as the *aftermarket.* The independents, including Autolite, furnished the auto manufacturers with OE plugs at cost or less, about six cents a plug, and they continued to sell at that price even when their costs increased threefold. The independents sought to recover their losses on OE sales by profitable sales in the *aftermarket* where the requirement of each vehicle during its lifetime is about five replacement plug sets. By custom and practice among mechanics, the *aftermarket* plug is usually the same brand as the OE plug. . . .

Ford was anxious to participate in this *aftermarket* and, after various efforts not relevant to the present case, concluded that its effective participation in the *aftermarket* required "an established distribution system with a recognized brand name, a full line of high volume service parts, engineering experience in replacement designs, low volume production facilities and experience, and the opportunity to capitalize on an established car population."

Ford concluded it could develop such a division of its own but decided that course would take from five to eight years and be more costly than an acquisition. To make a long story short, it acquired certain assets of Autolite in 1961.

General Motors had previously entered the spark plug manufacturing field, making the AC brand. The two other major domestic producers were independents—Autolite and Champion. When Ford acquired Autolite, whose share of the domestic spark plug market was about 15%, only one major independent was left and that was Champion, whose share of the domestic market declined from just under 50% in 1960 to just under 40% in 1964 and to about 33% in 1966. At the time of the acquisition, General Motors' market share was about 30%. There were other small manufacturers of spark plugs but they had no important share of the market. . . .

It is argued, however, that the acquisition had some beneficial effect in making Autolite a more vigorous and effective competitor against Champion and General Motors than Autolite had been as an independent. But . . . a merger is not saved from illegality under § 7, we said, "because, on some ultimate reckoning of social or economic debits and credits, it may be deemed beneficial. A value choice of such magnitude is beyond the ordinary limits of judicial competence, and in any event has been made for us already, by Congress when it enacted the amended § 7. Congress determined to preserve our traditionally competitive economy. It therefore proscribed anticompetitive mergers, the benign and the malignant alike, fully aware, we must assume, that some price might have to be paid." . . .

Ford argues that the acquisition left the marketplace with a greater number of competitors. To be sure, after Autolite sold its New Fostoria plant to Ford, it constructed another in Decatur, Alabama, which by 1964 had 1.6% of the domestic business. Prior to the acquisition, however, there were only two major independent producers and only two significant purchasers of original equipment spark plugs. The acquisition thus aggravated an already oligopolistic market. . . .

"The primary vice of a vertical merger or other arrangement tying a customer to a supplier is that, by foreclosing the competitors of either party from a segment of the market otherwise open to them, the arrangement may act as a 'clog on competition,' *Standard Oil Co. of California v United States,* 337 US 293, 314, . . . which 'deprives . . . rivals of a fair opportunity to compete.' . . . Every extended vertical arrangement by its very nature, for at least a time, denies to competitors of the supplier the opportunity to compete for part or all of the trade of the customer-party to the vertical arrangement."

Moreover, Ford made the acquisition in order to obtain a foothold in the *aftermarket.* Once established, it would have every incentive to perpetuate the OE tie and thus maintain the virtually insurmountable barriers to entry to the *aftermarket.*

The main controversy here has been over the nature and degree of the relief to be afforded. . . .

The relief in an antitrust case must be "effective to redress the violations" and "to restore competition." . . .

Complete divestiture is particularly appropriate where asset or stock acquisitions violate the antitrust laws. . . .

Divestiture is a start toward restoring the pre-acquisition situation. Ford once again will then stand as a large industry customer at the edge of the market with a renewed interest in securing favorable terms for its substantial plug purchases. Since Ford will again be a purchaser, it is expected that the competitive pressures that existed among other spark plug producers to sell to Ford will be re-created. The divestiture should also eliminate the anticompetitive consequences in the *aftermarket* flowing from the second largest automobile manufacturer's entry through acquisition into the spark plug manufacturing business.

The divested plant is given an incentive to provide Ford with terms which will not only satisfy the 50% requirement provided for five years by the decree but which even after that period may keep at least some of Ford's ongoing purchases. The divested plant is awarded at least a foothold in the lucrative *aftermarket* and is provided an incentive to compete aggressively for that market.

As a result of the acquisition of Autolite, the structure of the spark plug industry changed drastically, as already noted. Ford, which before the acquisition was the largest purchaser of spark plugs from the independent manufacturers, became a major manufacturer. The result was to foreclose to the remaining independent spark plug manufacturers the substantial segment of the market previously open to competitive selling and to remove the significant procompetitive effects in the concentrated spark plug market that resulted from Ford's position on the edge of the market as a potential entrant. . . .

The District Court rightly concluded that only divestiture would correct the condition caused by the unlawful acquisition.

[Judgment affirmed]

(c) Dissolution of holding companies

AMERICAN POWER & LIGHT CO. v SECURITIES AND EXCHANGE COMMISSION

329 US 90 (1946)

The Securities and Exchange Act directed the Securities and Exchange Commission as soon as practicable after January 1, 1938,

> to require by order, after notice and opportunity for hearing, that each registered holding company, and each subsidiary company thereof, shall take such steps as the Commission shall find necessary to insure that the corporate structure or continued existence of any company in the holding-company system does not unduly or unnecessarily complicate the structure, or unfairly or inequitably distribute voting power among security holders, of such holding-company system. . . .

Proceedings were begun before the Commission to obtain the dissolution of the Bond and Share holding company system.

OPINION BY MURPHY, J.

. . . The Bond and Share system including American and Electric, possesses an undeniable interstate character . . . this vast system embraces utility properties in no fewer than 32 states . . . as well as in 12 foreign countries. . . . The proper control and functioning of such an extensive multistate network of corporations necessitates continuous and substantial use of the mails and the instrumentalities of interstate commerce. Only in that way can Bond and Share, or its subholding companies or service subsidiary, market and distribute securities, control and influence the various operating companies, negotiate intersystem loans, acquire or exchange property, perform service contracts, or reap the benefits of stock ownership. . . .

Congress, of course, has undoubted power under the commerce clause to impose relevant conditions and requirements on those who use the channels of interstate commerce so that those channels will not be conduits for promoting or perpetuating economic evil. . . . It may compel changes in the voting rights and other privileges of stockholders. It may order the divestment or rearrangement of properties. It may order the reorganization or dissolution of corporations. . . .

Since the mandates of [the statute] are directed solely to public utility holding-company systems that use the channels of interstate commerce, the validity of that section under the commerce clause becomes apparent. It is designed to prevent the use of those channels to propagate and disseminate the evils which had been found to flow from unduly complicated systems and from inequitable distributions of voting power among security holders of the systems. Such evils are so inextricably entwined around the interstate business of the holding-company systems as to present no serious question as to the power of Congress under the commerce clause to eradicate them.

In the extensive studies which preceded the passage of the Public Utility Holding Company Act . . . it had been found that "the most distinctive characteristic, and perhaps the most serious defect of the present holding-company organization is the pyramided structure which is found in all of the important holding-company groups examined." The pyramiding device in its most common form consisted of interposing one or more subholding companies between the holding company and the operating companies and issuing, at each level of the structure, different classes of stock with unequal voting rights. Most of the financing of the various companies in the structure occurred through the sale to the public of bonds and preferred stock having low fixed returns and generally no voice in the managements. Under such circumstances, a relatively small but strategic investment in common stock (with voting privileges) in the high levels of a pyramided structure often resulted in absolute control of underlying operating companies with assets of hundreds of millions of dollars. A tremendous "leverage" in relation to that stock was thus produced; the earnings of a top holding-company were greatly magnified by comparatively small changes in the earnings of the operating companies. The common stock of the top holding company might quickly rise in value and just as quickly fall, making it a natural object for speculation and gambling. In many instances this created financially irresponsible managements and unsound capital structures.

Public investors in such stock found themselves the innocent victims. . . . Those who supplied most of the capital through the purchase of bonds and preferred stock likewise suffered in addition to being largely disfranchised.

Prudent management of the operating companies became a minor consideration, with pressure being placed on them to sustain the excessive capitalization to the detriment of their service to consumers. Reduction of rates was firmly resisted. A conclusion was accordingly reached by those making the studies that the highly pyramided system "is dangerous and has no justification for existence" and "represents the holding-company system at its worst." . . .

[The] pyramided structures and the resulting abuses, like . . . other characteristics [of the holding-company systems], rests squarely upon an extensive use of the mails and instrumentalities of interstate commerce. . . .

To deny that Congress has power to eliminate evils connected with pyramided holding-company systems . . . which have been found to be promoted and transmitted by means of interstate commerce, is to deny that Congress can effectively deal with problems concerning the welfare of the national economy. We cannot deny that power. Rather we reaffirm once more the constitutional authority resident in Congress by virtue of the commerce clause to undertake to solve national problems directly and realistically, giving due recognition to the scope of state power. That follows from the fact that the federal commerce power is as broad as the economic needs of the nation. . . .

[Order of dissolution of holding company system affirmed]

---

§ 11:3. MERGERS

Ordinarily two or more enterprises may combine or merge. Likewise, it is ordinarily immaterial whether they are engaged in the same or related kinds of activity, the combining thus producing what the economist would call horizontal or vertical integration. Also, it is generally immaterial whether they are engaged in unrelated kinds of activities, the combining thus producing what is commonly called a conglomerate.

(a) Effect on competition

When it appears that a merger will adversely affect competition, the present Section 7 of the Clayton Act is violated. That section provides that a merger of corporations doing interstate business is illegal when the effect of the acquisition by one corporation of all or any part of the assets of the other "may be substantially to lessen competition, or to tend to create a monopoly."

(b) Premerger notification

When large enterprises plan to merge, they must give written notice to the Federal Trade Commission and to the attorney in charge of the Antitrust Division of the Department of Justice and then wait a specified time to see if there is any objection to the proposed merger.[1]

---

[1]Antitrust Improvements Act of 1976, PL 94–435, 90 Stat 1383, § 201.

(c) Existence of competition

UNITED STATES v CONTINENTAL CAN CO.

378 US 441 (1964)

Continental Can, the second largest producer of metal containers in the country, acquired all the assets of Hazel-Atlas, the nation's third largest producer of glass containers, by exchanging stock and assuming the latter's liabilities. The United States sought an order to require Continental Can to divest itself of the stock of Hazel-Atlas. The court dismissed the complaint, from which the United States appealed.

OPINION BY WHITE, J.

. . . The industries with which this case is principally concerned are, as found by the trial court, the metal can industry, the glass container industry and the plastic container industry, each producing one basic type of container made of metal, glass, and plastic, respectively. . . .

It is quite true that glass and metal containers have different characteristics which may disqualify one or the other, at least in their present form, from this or that particular use; that the machinery necessary to pack in glass is different from that employed when cans are used; that a particular user of cans or glass may pack in only one or the other container and does not shift back and forth from day to day as price and other factors might make desirable; and that the competition between metal and glass containers is different from the competition between the can companies themselves or between the products of the different glass companies. These are relevant and important considerations but they are not sufficient to obscure the competitive relationships which this record so compellingly reveals. . . .

[The Court surveyed the competition that existed between glass and metal in the packaging of baby foods, soft drinks, and foods generally.]

In the light of this record and these findings, we think the District Court employed an unduly narrow construction of the "competition" protected by § 7 and of "reasonable interchangeability of use or the cross-elasticity of demand" in judging the facts of this case. We reject the opinion below insofar as it holds that these terms . . . were intended to limit the competition protected by § 7 to competition between identical products, to the kind of competition which exists, for example, between the metal containers of one company and those of another, or between the several manufacturers of glass containers. Certainly, that the competition here involved may be called "interindustry competition" and is between products with distinctive characteristics does not automatically remove it from the reach of § 7.

. . . In our view there is and has been a rather general confrontation between metal and glass containers and competition between them for the same end uses which is insistent, continuous, effective and quantitywise very substantial. Metal has replaced glass and glass has replaced metal as the leading container for some important uses; both are used for other purposes; each is trying to expand its share of the market at the expense of the other; and each is attempting to preempt for itself every use for which its product is physically suitable, even though some such uses have traditionally been regarded as the exclusive domain of the competing industry. In differing degrees for different end uses manufacturers in each industry take into consideration the price of the containers of the opposing industry in formulating their own pricing policy. Thus, though the interchangeability of use may not be so complete and the cross-elasticity of demand not so immediate as in the case of most intraindustry mergers, there is over the long run the kind of customer response to innovation and other competitive stimuli that brings the competition between these two industries within § 7's competition-preserving proscriptions. . . .

Based on the evidence thus far revealed by this record we hold that the interindustry competition between glass and metal containers is sufficient to warrant treating as a relevant product market the combined glass and metal container industries and all end uses for which they compete. There may be some end uses for which glass and metal do not and could not compete, but complete interindustry competitive overlap need not be shown. We would not be true to the purpose of the Clayton Act's line of commerce concept as a framework within which to measure the effect of mergers on competition were we to hold that the existence of noncompetitive segments within a proposed market area precludes its being treated as a line of commerce. . . .

Nor are we concerned by the suggestion that if the product market is to be defined in these terms it must include plastic, paper, foil and any other materials competing for the same business. That there may be a broader product market made up of metal, glass and other competing containers does not necessarily negative the existence of submarkets of cans, glass, plastic or cans and glass together, for "within this broad market, well-defined submarkets may exist which, in themselves, constitute product markets for antitrust purposes." . . .

The issue is whether the merger between Continental and Hazel-Atlas will have probable anticompetitive effect within the relevant line of commerce. Market shares are the primary indicia of market power, but a judgment under § 7 is not to be made by any single qualitative or quantitative test. The merger must be viewed functionally in the context of the particular market involved, its structure, history, and probable future. Where a merger is of such a size as to be inherently suspect, elaborate proof of market structure, market behavior and probable anticompetitive effects may be dispensed with in view of § 7's design to prevent undue concentration. Moreover, the competition with which § 7 deals includes not only existing competition but that which is sufficiently probable and imminent. . . .

[The Court discussed the relative positions in the economy of the various companies.]

The evidence so far presented leads us to conclude that the merger between Continental and Hazel-Atlas is in violation of § 7. The product market embracing the combined metal and glass container industries was dominated by six firms having a total of 70.1 percent of the business. Continental, with 21.9

percent of the shipments, ranked second within this product market, and Hazel-Atlas, with 3.1 percent, ranked sixth. Thus, of this vast market—amounting at the time of the merger to almost $3 billion in annual sales—a large percentage already belonged to Continental before the merger. By the acquisition of Hazel-Atlas stock Continental not only increased its own share more than 14 percent from 21.9 percent to 25 percent, but also reduced from five to four the most significant competitors who might have threatened its dominant position. . . . The case falls squarely within the principle that where there has been a "history of tendency toward concentration in the industry" tendencies toward further concentration "are to be curbed in their incipiency." . . . Where "concentration is already great, the importance of preventing even slight increases in concentration and so preserving the possibility of eventual deconcentration is correspondingly great." . . .

Continental insists, however, that whatever the nature of inter-industry competition in general, the types of containers produced by Continental and Hazel-Atlas at the time of the merger were for the most part not in competition with each other and hence the merger could have no effect on competition. This argument ignores several important matters.

First: The District Court found that both Continental and Hazel-Atlas were engaged in interindustry competition characteristic of the glass and metal can industries. . . .

We think it quite clear that Continental and Hazel-Atlas were set off directly against one another in this process and that the merger therefore carries with it the probability of foreclosing actual and potential competition between these two concerns. Hazel-Atlas has been removed as an independent factor in the glass industry and in the line of commerce which includes both metal cans and glass containers. . . .

Continental acquired by the merger the power to guide the development of Hazel-Atlas consistently with Continental's interest in metal containers; contrariwise it may find itself unwilling to push metal containers to the exclusion of glass for those end uses where Hazel-Atlas is strong. It has at the same time acquired the ability, know-how and the capacity to satisfy its customers' demands whether they want metal or glass containers. Continental need no longer lose customers to glass companies solely because consumer preference, perhaps triggered by competitive efforts by the glass container industry, forces the packer to turn from cans to glass. And no longer does a Hazel-Atlas customer who has normally packed in glass have to look elsewhere for metal containers if he discovers that the can rather than the jar will answer some of his pressing problems.

Second: Continental would view these developments as representing an acceptable effort by it to diversify its product lines and to gain the resulting competitive advantages, thereby strengthening competition which it declared the antitrust laws are designed to promote. But we think the answer is otherwise when a dominant firm in a line of commerce in which market power is already concentrated among a few firms makes an acquisition which enhances its market power and the vigor and effectiveness of its own competitive efforts.

Third: A merger between the second and sixth largest competitors in a gigantic line of commerce is significant not only for its intrinsic effect on competition but also for its tendency to endanger a much broader anticompetitive effect by triggering other mergers by companies seeking the same competitive advantages sought by Continental in this case. . . .

Fourth: It is not at all self-evident that the lack of current competition between Continental and Hazel-Atlas for some important end uses of metal and glass containers significantly diminished the adverse effect of the merger on competition. Continental might have concluded that it could effectively insulate itself from competition by acquiring a major firm not presently directing its market acquisition efforts toward the same end uses as Continental, but possessing the potential to do so. Two examples will illustrate. Both soft drinks and baby food are currently packed predominantly in glass, but Continental has engaged in vigorous and imaginative promotional activities attempting to overcome consumer preferences for glass and secure a larger share of these two markets for its tin cans. Hazel-Atlas was not at the time of the merger a significant producer of either of these containers, but with comparatively little difficulty, if it were an independent firm making independent business judgments, it could have developed its soft drink and baby food capacity. The acquisition of Hazel-Atlas by a company engaged in such intense efforts to effect a diversion of business from glass to metal in both of these lines cannot help but diminish the likelihood of Hazel-Atlas realizing its potential as a significant competitor in either line. . . . It would make little sense for one entity within the Continental empire to be busily engaged in persuading the public of metal's superiority over glass for a given end use, while the other is making plans to increase the Nation's total glass container output for that same end use. Thus, the fact that Continental and Hazel-Atlas were not substantial competitors of each other for certain end uses at the time of the merger may actually enhance the long-run tendency of the merger to lessen competition.

We think our holding is consonant with the purpose of § 7 to arrest anticompetitive arrangements, in their incipiency. Some product lines are offered in both metal and glass containers by the same packer. In such areas the interchangeability of use and immediate interindustry sensitivity to price changes would approach that which exists between products of the same industry. In other lines, as where one packer's products move in one type container while his competitor's move in another, there are inherent deterrents to customer diversion of the same type that might occur between brands of cans or bottles. But the possibility of such transfers over the long run acts as a deterrent against attempts by the dominant members of either industry to reap the possible benefits of their position by raising prices above the competitive level or engaging in other comparable practices. And even though certain lines are today regarded as safely within the domain of one or the other of these industries, this pattern may be altered, as it has been in the past. From the point of view not only of the static competitive situation but also the dynamic long-run potential, we think that the Government has discharged its burden of proving prima facie anticompetitive effect. Accordingly the judgment is reversed and the case re-manded for further proceedings consistent with this opinion.

[Judgment reversed]

(d) Potential for harm

Under amended Section 7, the court is only required to determine if there is a probability of harm resulting. Thus, where two competing corporations formed a third corporation in which each owned one half of the stock, it declared that the trial court should

> take into account in assessing the probability of a substantial lessening of competition: the number and power of the competitors in the relevant market; the background of their growth; the power of the joint venturers; the relationship of their lines of commerce; the competition existing between them and the power of each in dealing with the competitors of the other; the setting in which the joint venture was created; the reasons and necessities for its existence; the joint venture's line of commerce and the relationship thereof to that of its parents; the adaptability of its line of commerce to noncompetitive practices; the potential power of the joint venture in the relevant market; an appraisal of what the competition in the relevant market would have been if one of the joint venturers had entered it alone instead of through [the joint corporation]; the effect, in the event of this occurrence, of the other joint venturer's potential competition; and such other factors as might indicate potential risk to competition in the relevant market. In weighing these factors the court should remember that the mandate of the Congress is in terms of the probability of a lessening of substantial competition, not in terms of tangible present restraint.[2]

It is important to note the difference between remedial law and preventive law. In the case of remedial law, the wrongdoer commits the wrong and the victim seeks to recover damages for the harm. In the case of preventive law, the possible victim seeks the aid of the court before the wrongdoer has committed the wrong. But here a further distinction must be made between private law and public law. In the case of private law, the court will not act in the absence of a very good cause for believing that harm is imminent. In the case of public law, where the danger to so many is so great and actual harm to anyone is so difficult to prove, the statute law has substituted the much less certain standards that the conduct "may" lessen competition or "tend to" create a monopoly. "One purpose of § 7 was 'to arrest the tendency toward integration, the *tendency* to monopoly, before consumer's alternatives disappeared through merger.' "[3] "The

---

[2]*United States v Penn-Olin Chemical Co.*, 378 US 158, 177 (1964).
[3]*United States v El Paso Natural Gas Co.*, 376 US 651, 659 (1964).

objective was to prevent accretions of power which 'are individually so minute as to make it difficult to use the Sherman Act test against them.' "[4]

Questions for Discussion

1. Could Congress amend the Sherman Act so as to make mere size illegal?

2. Assume that size or "bigness" is the economic evil to be prevented. Draft a sentence defining what is to be outlawed. Examine your draft to see if it is clear and precise or if it is capable of more than one meaning.

3. What percentage of the market must be represented by each of the merging companies in order to make § 7 of the Clayton Act, as amended, applicable to their merger?

4. The decisions of the Supreme Court with respect to § 7 of the Clayton Act, as amended, relating to merger through the acquisition of assets, illustrate the doctrine of the minimization of error. Explain.

5. How was competition harmed by Ford's acquisition of Autolite?

6. What is the effect of divestiture?

7. (a) To what extent did the Bond and Share holding company engage in interstate commerce?   (b) Was this interstate commerce the primary object of the holding company or merely incidental to its operations? (c) Is it material which it was?

8. How do you define the commerce power after reading the *American Power and Light Company* case? In the opinion, the Court stated: "We reaffirm . . . the constitutional authority resident in Congress . . . to solve national problems . . . giving due recognition to the scope of state power." What importance do you find in the phrase "giving due recognition to the scope of state power"?

9. Company *A* and Company *B* plan to merge. Does it make any difference if the following situation (a) or (b) is involved?   (a) There are approximately 5,000 producers of the same products in the United States, these producers ranging in size from ¼ to 3 times that of Company *A* and Company *B* combined, with the majority of the enterprises being about the same size as that combination.   (b) The relative size of the other producers is the same as stated in (a), but there are only 10,000 other producers, as against 5 years ago when there were 20,000 such producers, and 10 years ago when there were 30,000 such producers.

---

[4]*United States v Aluminum Co. of America*, 337 US 271, 280 (1964).

10. The first and the fourth largest commercial banks in Lexington, Kentucky, planned to merge. This was opposed by the United States on the ground that it violated § 1 of the Sherman Antitrust Act. Decide. [*United States v First National Bank and Trust Co.,* 376 US 665 (1964)]

11. The El Paso Natural Gas Company acquired the stock and assets of the Pacific Northwest Pipe Line Company. El Paso, although not a California enterprise, supplied over half of the natural gas used in California; all the other natural gas was supplied by California sources. No gas was sold in California by Pacific Northwest, although it was a strong, experienced company within the Northwest area and had attempted several times to enter the California market. United States claimed that the acquisition of Pacific by El Paso constituted a violation of § 7 of the Clayton Act, as amended, because the effect would be to remove competition between the two companies within California. The defense was raised that (a) California was not a "section" of the country within the Clayton Act, (b) the sale of natural gas was not a line of commerce, and (c) the acquisition did not lessen competition when there had not been any prior sales by Pacific within the area. Decide. [*United States v El Paso Natural Gas Co.,* 376 US 651 (1964)]

12. The Aluminum Company of America, Alcoa, acquired the stock and assets of the Rome Cable Corporation. The United States brought suit claiming a violation of amended § 7 of the Clayton Act. In the year before the merger, Rome produced 1.3 percent of the aluminum conductors of the industry, consisting of .3 percent of bare aluminum conductors and 4.7 percent of insulated aluminum conductors. Rome also produced copper conductors.

Alcoa did not produce any copper conductors but produced 27.8 percent of aluminum conductors, consisting of 32.5 percent of the bare aluminum conductors and 11.6 percent of the insulated aluminum conductors.

The conductors are used principally for electric power transmission lines, with bare or lightly insulated aluminum being generally used for overhead lines, and heavily insulated copper being almost exclusively used for underground lines. The District Court held that the relative line of commerce was conductor wire, whether aluminum or copper, and whether insulated or not. It further held that the merger did not tend to lessen competition within this particular line of commerce. Was it correct? [*United States v Aluminum Company of America,* 377 US 271 (1964)]

12

Regulation of Contracts and Licenses

§ 12:1. TYING CONTRACTS

The Clayton Act prohibits the tying or tie-in sale or lease by which the person buying or renting goods agrees to use with such goods other materials sold or leased by the other party. The Act also prohibits exclusive dealer agreements by which a dealer agrees not to handle a competitor's articles. These tying and exclusive dealer arrangements are not absolutely prohibited, but only where their effect "may be to substantially lessen competition or tend to create a monopoly in any line of commerce." By virtue of this qualification, a provision that a person leasing machinery shall use only the materials furnished by the lessor is a lawful restriction if the nature of the materials and the machine is such that the machine will not operate with the materials produced or offered by any other person. Where, however, the materials furnished by any other competitor would be equally satisfactory, the agreement is illegal. Thus an agreement that the lessee of office machinery should only use the paper sold by the lessor for that type of office machine was illegal where it was shown that any other seller could supply paper of suitable quality.

The partial prohibition of tying and exclusive dealer agreements is expressly stated by the statute to be limited by the right of any seller to "select [the seller's] own customers in bona fide transactions and not in restraint of trade." There has also been a judicial trend to approve such agreements where the seller did not hold a dominant position in the market.

(a) Tying of unrelated enterprises

NORTHERN PACIFIC RAILWAY COMPANY v UNITED STATES

356 US 1 (1958)

The Northern Pacific Railway Company owns large tracts of land which it had received as federal grants to aid its original construction. It sold and leased several million acres of this land by deeds and leases that contained "preferential routing clauses" by which the grantees and lessees agreed to ship any of their produce or manufactured goods on the Northern Pacific, as long as it offered rates and services equal to any competing carrier. The United States government brought suit against the railroad to have the "preferential routing clauses" declared void as violations of the Sherman Antitrust Act.

OPINION BY BLACK, J.

. . . There are certain agreements or practices which because of their pernicious effect on competition and lack of any redeeming virtue are conclusively presumed to be unreasonable and therefore illegal without elaborate inquiry as to the precise harm they have caused or the business excuse for their use. This principle of per se unreasonableness not only makes the type of restraints which are proscribed by the Sherman Act more certain to the benefit of everyone concerned, but it also avoids the necessity for an incredibly complicated and prolonged economic investigation into the entire history of the industry involved, as well as related industries, in an effort to determine at large whether a particular restraint has been unreasonable—an inquiry so often wholly fruitless when undertaken. Among the practices which the courts have heretofore deemed to be unlawful in and of themselves are price fixing, . . . division of markets, . . . ; group boycotts, . . . ; and tying arrangements, *International Salt Co. v United States,* 332 US 392. . . .

For our purposes a tying arrangement may be defined as an agreement by a party to sell one product but only on the condition that the buyer also purchases a different (or tied) product, or at least agrees that he will not purchase that product from any other supplier. Where such conditions are successfully exacted competition on the merits with respect to the tied product is inevitably curbed. Indeed "tying agreements serve hardly any purpose beyond the suppression of competition. . . ." They deny competitors free access to the market for the tied product, not because the party imposing the tying requirements has a better product or a lower price but because of his power or leverage in another market. At the same time buyers are forced to forego their free choice between competing products. For these reasons "tying agreements fare harshly under the laws forbidding restraints of trade. . . ." They are unreasonable in and of themselves whenever a party has sufficient economic power with respect to the tying product to appreciably restrain free competition in the market for the tied product and a "not insubstantial" amount of interstate commerce is affected. . . . Of course where the seller has no control or dominance over the tying product so that it does not represent an effectual weapon to pressure buyers into taking the tied item any restraint of trade attributable to such tying arrangements would obviously be insignificant at most. As a simple example, if one of a dozen food stores in a community were to refuse to sell flour unless the buyer also took sugar it would hardly tend to restrain competition in sugar if its competitors were ready and able to sell flour by itself.

In this case we believe the district judge was clearly correct in entering summary judgment declaring the defendant's "preferential routing" clauses unlawful restraints of trade. We wholly agree that the undisputed facts established beyond any genuine question that the defendant possessed substantial economic power by virtue of its extensive landholdings which it used as leverage to induce large numbers of purchasers and lessees to give it preference, to the exclusion of its competitors, in carrying goods or produce from the land transferred to them. Nor can there be any real doubt that a "not insubstantial" amount of interstate commerce was and is affected by these restrictive provisions. . . .

. . . The "preferential routing" clauses conferred no benefit on the purchasers or lessees. While they got the land they wanted by yielding their freedom to deal with competing carriers, the defendant makes no claim that it came any cheaper than if the restrictive clauses had been omitted. In fact any such price reduction in return for rail shipments would have quite plainly constituted an unlawful rebate to the shipper. So far as the Railroad was concerned its purpose obviously was to fence out competitors, to stifle competition. While this may have been exceedingly beneficial to its business, it is the very type of thing the Sherman Act condemns. In short, we are convinced that the essential prerequisites for treating the defendant's tying arrangements as unreasonable *per se* were conclusively established below and that the defendant has offered to prove nothing there or here which would alter this conclusion. . . .

[Judgment for the United States as the preferential routing clause was illegal]

§ 12:2. STOCK AND DIRECTOR CONTROL

The Clayton Act, as amended, also prohibits the purchase by a corporation of the stock of another corporation engaged in commerce where the effect may be to lessen competition substantially or to tend to create a monopoly. The Act states that this does not prohibit purchase merely for the purpose of investment or purchase where there is no lessening of competition. This section does not prohibit the creation of a subsidiary corporation or the acquisition of stock in another company, which, though manufacturing or selling the same or a similar article, does not sell within the same price range or within the same geographic market.

The Clayton Act does not prohibit the holding of stock in competing corporations by the same person. It is possible for a group of individuals to control several corporations by virtue of the fact that they hold the controlling shares in each of them. As far as any formal action is concerned, these corporations would be separate and independent; but, as they would all be run following the pattern established by the individuals holding the controlling shares in each of them, it is obvious that the same control would be present as if the corporations had joined in a prohibited monopoly. While the Clayton Act prohibits the director of one corporation from being a director of another competing corporation engaged in commerce, this prohibition is not effective in checking the monopoly potential of interlocking private stockholding.

§ 12:3. PATENTS

Congress is authorized by the Constitution to "promote the Progress of Science and useful Arts, by securing for limited Times to Authors and Inventors the exclusive Right to their respective Writings and Discoveries" [Art. I, § 8, Cl. 8].

(a) Patent rights and the antitrust law

The holder of a patent is given the exclusive right to manufacture, use, or sell the article or material covered by the patent for a period of 17 years. This is a legally authorized monopoly. The holder of the monopoly may refrain from making any use of the patent. This is frequently done in industries where the utilization of new articles covered by patents held by particular manufacturers would cause a serious dislocation of the industry or require the scrapping of large amounts of equipment because the new inventions would make existing equipment obsolete. While the holder of a patent is given a legally protected monopoly, this right does not give any power to control the resale price of the product.

In the case of the licensing of another person to manufacture under the patent, the holder may specify the price at which the licensee's product will be sold. Licensing agreements are illegal where the patentee by means of such agreements endeavors to require the purchaser of the patented article to use a particular nonpatented article, when any other article would be just as satisfactory. Here the patentholder is, in effect, using the patent as a weapon to compel observance of a restraint in the trade of the unpatented article.

(b) Cross licensing

UNITED STATES v SINGER MANUFACTURING CO.

374 US 174 (1963)

The Singer Sewing Machine Company and Swiss (Gegauf) and Italian (Vigorelli) sewing machine manufacturers joined together to prevent the sale of Japanese zigzag sewing machines in their respective countries. They agreed that each would apply in its own country for a patent of the widest possible scope, that they would not challenge the validity of such patents, and that each would give licenses to the others to use their respective patents. The United States brought a suit against the manufacturers on the ground that their cross licensing of patents and other agreements constituted an illegal conspiracy to exclude Japanese competition.

OPINION BY CLARK, J.

. . . First it may be helpful to set out what is not involved in this case. There is no claim by the Government that it is illegal for one merely to acquire a patent in order to exclude his competitors; or that the owner of a lawfully acquired patent cannot use the patent laws to exclude all infringers of the patent; or that a licensee cannot lawfully acquire the covering patent in order better to enforce it on his own account, even when the patent dominates an industry in which the licensee is the dominant firm. Therefore, we put all these matters aside without discussion.

What is claimed here is that Singer engaged in a series of transactions with Gegauf and Vigorelli for an illegal purpose, i.e., to rid itself and Gegauf, together, perhaps, with Vigorelli, of infringements by their common competitors, the Japanese manufacturers. . . .

By entwining itself with Gegauf and Vigorelli in such a program, Singer went far beyond its claimed purpose of merely protecting its own 401 machine —it was protecting Gegauf and Vigorelli, the sole licensees under the patent at the time, under the same umbrella. This the Sherman Act will not permit. As the Court held in *Frey & Son, Inc. v Cudahy Packing Co.,* 256 US 208, 210, . . . (1921), the conspiracy arises implicitly from the course of dealing of the parties, here resulting in Singer's obligation to enforce the patent to the benefit of all three parties. While there was no contract so stipulating, the facts as found by the trial court indicate a common purpose to suppress the Japanese machine competition in the United States through the use of the patent, which was secured by Singer on the assurances to Gegauf and its colicensee, Vigorelli, that such would certainly be the result. . . . It is this concerted action to restrain trade, clearly established by the course of dealings, that condemns the transactions under the Sherman Act. As we said in *United States v Parke, Davis & Co.* . . . 362 US at 44, "whether an unlawful combination or conspiracy is proved is to be judged by what the parties actually did rather than by the words they used." . . .

It is strongly urged upon us that application of the antitrust laws in this case will have a significantly deleterious effect on Singer's position as the sole remaining domestic producer of zigzag sewing machines for household use, the market for which has been increasingly preempted by foreign manufacturers. Whether economic consequences of this character warrant relaxation of the scope of enforcement of the antitrust laws, however, is a policy matter committed to congressional or executive resolution. It is not within the province of the courts, whose function is to apply the existing law. It is well settled that "beyond the limited monopoly which is granted, the arrangements by which the patent is utilized are subject to the general law," . . . and it "is equally well settled that the possession of a valid patent or patents does not give the patentee any exemption from the provisions of the Sherman Act beyond the limits of the patent monopoly. By aggregating patents in one control, the holder of the patents cannot escape the prohibitions of the Sherman Act." . . .

[Judgment for United States]

---

§ 12:4. FRANCHISE RESTRICTIONS

Antitrust questions arise in connection with vertical agreements, as between franchisors and franchisees. Any agreement between a franchisor and a franchisee that the latter will maintain specified prices for goods and services or will not sell below a specified minimum is per se a violation of the antitrust law. Other restrictions placed upon franchisees will be sustained if reasonable.

CONTINENTAL T. V. INC. v GTE SYLVANIA INC.

435 US 36 (1977)

GTE Sylvania manufactures television sets which are sold to the public through franchised dealers. Each dealer is required to sell Sylvania sets exclusively and to sell them only from the location designated in the dealer's franchise. Continental T. V. held such a franchise from Sylvania. Sylvania granted a franchise to another dealer with a location approximately one mile from Continental's location. Some time later Sylvania terminated Continental's franchise. In an action brought by Sylvania to collect money due, Continental filed a cross claim seeking damages on the ground that the provision restricting selling to a designated location violated the Sherman Antitrust Act. The District Court held that the restriction was per se a violation of the Sherman Act. The Court of Appeals sustained the restriction and Continental appealed to the Supreme Court.

OPINION BY POWELL, J.

We turn first to Continental's contention that Sylvania's restriction on retail locations is a per se violation of § 1 of the Sherman Act as interpreted in *Schwinn* [*United States v Arnold, Schwinn & Co.,* 388 US 365 (1967)]. The restrictions at issue in *Schwinn* were part of a three-tier distribution system comprising, in addition to Arnold, Schwinn & Co. (Schwinn), 22 intermediate distributors and a network of franchised retailers. Each distributor had a defined geographic area in which it had the exclusive right to supply franchised retailers. Sales to the public were made only through franchised retailers, who were authorized to sell Schwinn bicycles only from specified locations. . . . [In the *Schwinn* case, the Court] proceeded to articulate the following "bright line" per se rule of illegality for vertical restrictions:

"Under the Sherman Act, it is unreasonable for a manufacturer to seek to restrict and confine areas or persons with whom an article may be traded after the manufacturer has parted with dominion over it." . . .

In the present case, it is undisputed that title to the televisions passed from Sylvania to Continental. Thus, the *Schwinn* per se rule applies unless Sylvania's restriction on locations falls outside Schwinn's prohibition against a manufacturer's attempting to restrict a "retailer's freedom as to where and to whom it will resell the products." . . .

Sylvania argues that if *Schwinn* cannot be distinguished, it should be reconsidered. . . . We are convinced that the need for clarification of the law in this area justifies reconsideration. *Schwinn* itself was an abrupt and largely unexplained departure from *White Motor Co. v United States*, 372 US 253 . . . (1963), where only four years earlier the Court had refused to endorse a per se rule for vertical restrictions. Since its announcement, *Schwinn* has been the subject of continuing controversy and confusion. . . . In our view, the experience of the past ten years should be brought to bear on this subject of considerable commercial importance.

The traditional framework of analysis under § 1 of the Sherman Act is familiar and does not require extended discussion. Section 1 prohibits "every contract, combination . . . , or conspiracy, in restraint of trade or commerce." Since the early years of this century a judicial gloss on this statutory language has established the "rule of reason" as the prevailing standard of analysis. *Standard Oil Co. v United States*, 221 US 1 . . . (1911). Under this rule, the factfinder weighs all of the circumstances of a case in deciding whether a restrictive practice should be prohibited as imposing an unreasonable restraint on competition. Per se rules of illegality are appropriate only when they relate to conduct that is manifestly anticompetitive. As the Court explained in *Northern Pac. R. Co. v United States*, 356 US 1, 5, . . . (1958), "there are certain agreements or practices which because of their pernicious effect on competition and lack of any redeeming virtue are conclusively presumed to be unreasonable and therefore illegal without elaborate inquiry as to the precise harm they have caused or the business excuse for their use."

In essence, the issue before us is whether Schwinn's per se rule can be justified under the demanding standards of *Northern Pac. R. Co.* The Court's refusal to endorse a per se rule in *White Motor Co.* was based on its uncertainty as to whether vertical restrictions satisfied those standards. Addressing this question for the first time, the Court stated:

> We need to know more than we do about the actual impact of these arrangements on competition to decide whether they have such a "pernicious effect on competition and lack . . . any redeeming virtue" . . . and therefore should be classified as per se violations. . . .

The question remains whether the per se rule stated in *Schwinn* should be expanded . . . or abandoned in favor of a return to the rule of reason. We have found no persuasive support for expanding the per se rule. . . .

We revert to the standard articulated in *Northern Pac. R. Co.,* and reiterated in *White Motor,* for determining whether vertical restrictions must be "conclusively presumed to be unreasonable and therefore illegal without elaborate inquiry as to the precise harm they have caused or the business excuse for their use." . . . Such restrictions, in varying forms, are widely used in our free market economy. . . . There is substantial scholarly and judicial authority supporting their economic utility. There is relatively little authority to the contrary. Certainly, there has been no showing in this case, either generally or with respect to Sylvania's agreements, that vertical restrictions have or are likely to have a "pernicious effect on competition" or that they "lack . . . any redeeming virtue." . . . Accordingly, we conclude that the per se rule stated in *Schwinn* must be overruled. In so holding we do not foreclose the possibility that particular applications of vertical restrictions might justify per se prohibition under *Northern Pac. R. Co.* But we do make clear that departure from the rule-of-reason standard must be based upon demonstrable economic effect. . . .

In sum, we conclude that the appropriate decision is to return to the rule of reason that governed vertical restrictions prior to *Schwinn.* When anticompetitive effects are shown to result from particular vertical restrictions they can be adequately policed under the rule of reason, the standard traditionally applied for the majority of anticompetitive practices challenged under § 1 of the Act. . . .

[Judgment affirmed]

---

§ 12:5. HORIZONTAL MARKET ALLOCATION

Horizontal agreements made by sellers who would otherwise compete, by which they divide selling territory, will generally be held to be a per se violation of the Sherman Antitrust Act. This means that the very fact that there is such an agreement is illegal without regard to the intentions of the persons involved or the actual effect of their agreement.

(a) Market allocation by cooperative

UNITED STATES v TOPCO ASSOCIATES, INC.

405 US 596 (1972)

Topco Associates is a cooperative association formed by 25 small- and medium-sized regional supermarket chains. The association acted as purchasing agent for the members to purchase products which were resold by the members under private labels owned by the association. The members were given particular geographic areas in which they could sell these products and were prohibited from selling outside of those areas. The United States claimed that this market allocation was a violation of the Sherman Antitrust Act. The District Court sustained the allocation as reasonable and the United States appealed to the United States Supreme Court.

OPINION BY MARSHALL, J.

Topco was founded in the 1940's by a group of small, local grocery chains, independently owned and operated, that desired to cooperate to obtain high quality merchandise under private labels in order to compete more effectively with larger national and regional chains. . . . By 1967, their sales totaled more than $2.3 billion, a figure exceeded by only three national grocery chains.

Members of the association vary in the degree of market share that they possess in their respective areas. The range is from 1.5% to 16%, with the average being approximately 6%. . . . There is much evidence in the record that Topco members are frequently in as strong a competitive position in their respective areas as any other chain. . . .

It is apparent that from meager beginnings approximately a quarter of a century ago, Topco has developed into a purchasing association wholly owned and operated by member chains, which possess much economic muscle, individually as well as cooperatively. . . .

The Government maintains that [Topco's] scheme of dividing markets violates the Sherman Act because it operates to prohibit competition in Topco-brand products among grocery chains engaged in retail operations . . .

Topco essentially maintains that it needs territorial divisions to compete with larger chains; that the association could not exist if the territorial divisions were anything but exclusive; and that by restricting competition in the sale of Topco-brand goods, the association actually increases competition by enabling its members to compete successfully with larger regional and national chains.

The District Court . . . concluded that "whatever anti-competitive effect these practices may have on competition in the sale of Topco private label brands is far outweighed by the increased ability of Topco members to compete both with the national chains and other supermarkets operating in their respective territories." . . . The court held that Topco's practices were procompetitive and, therefore, consistent with the purposes of the antitrust laws. But we conclude that the District Court used an improper analysis in reaching its result.
. . .

While the Court has utilized the "rule of reason" in evaluating the legality of most restraints alleged to be violative of the Sherman Act, it has also developed the doctrine that certain business relationships are per se violations of the Act without regard to a consideration of their reasonableness. . . .

"There are certain agreements or practices which because of their pernicious effect on competition and lack of any redeeming virtue are conclusively presumed to be unreasonable and therefore illegal without elaborate inquiry as to the precise harm they have caused or the business excuse for their use. This principle of per se unreasonableness not only makes the type of restraints which are proscribed by the Sherman Act more certain to the benefit of everyone concerned, but it also avoids the necessity for an incredibly complicated and prolonged economic investigation into the entire history of the industry involved, as well as related industries, in an effort to determine at large whether a particular restraint has been unreasonable—an inquiry so often wholly fruitless when undertaken."

It is only after considerable experience with certain business relationships that courts classify them as per se violations of the Sherman Act. . . . One of the classic examples of a per se violation of § 1 is an agreement between competitors at the same level of the market structure to allocate territories in order to minimize competition. Such concerted action is usually termed a "horizontal" restraint, in contradistinction to combinations of persons at different levels of the market structure, e.g., manufacturers and distributors, which are termed "vertical" restraints. This Court has reiterated time and time again that "horizontal territorial limitations . . . are naked restraints of trade with no purpose except stifling of competition." . . . Such limitations are per se violations of the Sherman Act. . . .

We think that it is clear that the restraint in this case is a horizontal one, and, therefore, a per se violation of § 1. The District Court failed to make any determination as to whether there were per se horizontal territorial restraints in this case simply and applied a rule of reason in reaching its conclusions that the restraints were not illegal. . . . In so doing, the District Court erred. . . .

Whether or not we would decide this case the same way under the rule of reason used by the District Court is irrelevant to the issue before us. The fact is that courts are of limited utility in examining difficult economic problems. Our inability to weigh, in any meaningful sense, destruction of competition in one sector of the economy against promotion of competition in another sector is one important reason we have formulated per se rules.

In applying these rigid rules, the Court has consistently rejected the notion that naked restraints of trade are to be tolerated because they are well intended or because they are allegedly developed to increase competition. . . .

Antitrust laws in general, and the Sherman Act in particular, are the Magna Carta of free enterprise. They are as important to the preservation of economic freedom as the Bill of Rights is to the protection of our fundamental personal freedoms. And the freedom guaranteed each and every business, no matter how small, is the freedom to compete—to assert with vigor, imagination, devotion, and ingenuity whatever economic muscle it can muster. Implicit in such freedom is the notion that it cannot be foreclosed with respect to one sector of the economy because certain private citizens or groups believe that such foreclosure might promote greater competition in a more important sector of the economy.
. . .

The District Court determined that by limiting the freedom of its individual members to compete with each other, Topco was doing a greater good by fostering competition between members and other large supermarket chains. But, the fallacy in this is that Topco has no authority under the Sherman Act to determine the respective values of competition in various sectors of the economy. On the contrary, the Sherman Act gives to each Topco member and to each prospective member the right to ascertain for itself whether or not competition with other supermarket chains is more desirable than competition in the sale of Topco-brand products. Without territorial restrictions, Topco members may indeed "[cut] each other's throats." . . . But, we have never found this possibility sufficient to warrant condoning horizontal restraints of trade.

The Court has previously noted with respect to price fixing, another per se violation of the Sherman Act, that:

> The reasonable price fixed today may through economic and business changes become the unreasonable price of tomorrow. Once established, it may be maintained unchanged because of the absence of competition secured by the agreement for a price reasonable when fixed.

A similar observation can be made with regard to territorial limitations. . . .

There have been tremendous departures from the notion of a free-enterprise system as it was originally conceived in this country. These departures have been the product of congressional action and the will of the people. If a decision is to be made to sacrifice competition in one portion of the economy for greater competition in another portion, this too is a decision that must be made by Congress and not by private forces or by the courts. Private forces are too keenly aware of their own interests in making such decisions and courts are ill-equipped and ill-situated for such decision making. To analyze, interpret, and evaluate the myriad of competing interests and the endless data that would surely be brought to bear on such decisions, and to make the delicate judgment on the relative values to society of competitive areas of the economy, the judgment of the elected representatives of the people is required.

[Judgment reversed]

Questions for Discussion

1. What facts must be shown in order to prove a "tying contract" violation of the Sherman Act?

2. What determines when conduct is per se unreasonable and a violation of the Sherman Act, and when the answer depends upon the circumstances of the case?

3. What is the administrative advantage of determining that a practice is a per se violation of the Sherman Act?

4. Company *A* manufactured an article on which it held the patent. Company *B* manufactured another article on which it held the patent. Companies *A* and *B* gave each other a license to manufacture the other's patented article. Both companies agreed on the price at which both patented articles would be sold by either of them. They were then sued for violating the Sherman Antitrust Act.   (a) Were they guilty of a violation?   (b) To what extent is your answer affected by the reasonableness or unreasonableness of the prices fixed by Companies *A* and *B?*

5. How would the *Singer Manufacturing* case be decided if it is admitted that the patents of each of the parties to the agreement were valid?

6. Why did not the Court in the *GTE Sylvania* case condemn the franchisor's geographic allocation of markets to franchisees as a per se violation of the antitrust law?

7. What is the significance of the statement of the Court in the *GTE Sylvania* case that "in the present case, it is undisputed that title passed from Sylvania to Continental"?

8. Compare the *GTE Sylvania* case and the *Topco* case.

9. Why is a horizontal geographic market allocation subject to the per se rule, while a vertical allocation is governed by the rule of reason?

10. *N* leases electrically driven drill equipment to *B*. By the terms of the lease, *B* is required to lubricate the drills with *"N"* brand oil sold by *N*. *N* is prosecuted for violation of the Clayton Act. Is *N* guilty? [See *International Salt Company v United States,* 332 US 392 (1947)]

11. Various motion picture companies block-booked films with television stations; that is, they sold them the right to use a group or package of films and refused to allow the stations to purchase the films individually. The picture companies were sued by the United States on the ground that blocked booking was illegal as a tying of undesired films to the desired films, and thus restrained trade. The picture companies defended on the ground that (a) each film was held under a copyright and therefore the copyright holder had the right to sell or not as the holder chose; (b) a television station is not limited to showing only films, but could use other programs; (c) the purchase of one of the blocks of films was financed by a loan from the Latex Corporation under an agreement by which its commercials were to be shown, and that by booking a block of films, Latex was assured that there would be a sufficient number of them shown to provide a sufficient number of opportunities for the company's commercials; and (d) no one film company dominated the market. Decide. [*United States v Loew Incorporated,* 371 US 38 (1962)]

12. The Tampa Electric Company made a contract with the Nashville Coal Co. to purchase from the coal company all of the coal that would be needed for one of its generating plants for a 20-year period. Some time thereafter, the electric company claimed that the contract was illegal as an exclusive dealing contract in violation of § 3 of the Clayton Act, which makes it unlawful for any person engaged in interstate commerce to make a sale on the understanding that the purchaser shall not use the goods of a competitor of the seller where the effect of such sale may be to lessen competition substantially or tend to create a monopoly in any line of commerce. At the trial it was shown that the type of coal supplied was procurable by the buyer in an area of some 8 states, that there were approximately 700 producers, and that the quantity sold by the Nashville Coal Company to the Tampa Electric Company represented .77 percent of the production of this area. Was the contract illegal? [*Tampa Electric Co. v Nashville Coal Co.,* 365 US 320 (1961)]

13

Regulation of Pricing Practices

§ 13:1. PRICE DISCRIMINATION

The Clayton Act prohibits price discrimination between different buyers of commodities "where the effect of such discrimination may be substantially to lessen competition or tend to create a monopoly in any line of commerce." This is not an absolute prohibition of discrimination but a prohibition only where discrimination has a monopolizing effect. Discrimination is expressly authorized where it can be justified on the basis of: (1) difference in grade, quality, or quantity involved; (2) the cost or the transportation involved in making the sale; or (3) when the sale is made in good faith in order to meet competition.

The vagueness of these standards is apparent, and Congress in 1936 passed the Robinson-Patman Act to clarify these provisions. The latter Act permits price differentials based on differences in the cost of manufacturing, selling, and delivering caused by differences in methods or quantities. It is significant that the Federal Trade Commission is authorized to limit the quantity discounts that can be given if it finds that there are so few large quantity purchasers that a quantity reduction, even though justified by cost differential, gives too great an advantage to the large purchaser or tends to create a monopoly. Price differentials are also permitted because of deterioration of goods or because the seller in good faith is making a close-out sale of a particular line of goods. The Robinson-Patman Act reaffirms the right of a seller to select customers and to refuse to deal with anyone as long as the seller is acting in good faith and not for the purpose of restraining trade. The problem of determining comparative costs, after making proper allowance for differences in methods of accounting and differences in subsidiary costs in different areas, and the problem of determining the intention of the parties actually brought greater difficulties to an already difficult problem.

The federal law prohibits the furnishing of advertising or other services that, when rendered to one purchaser but not to the other, will have the effect of granting the former a price discrimination or lower rate. It made it illegal for a seller to accept any fee or commission in connection with the sale except for services actually rendered and unless such services are equally available to all on the same terms. The Act makes either the giving or the receiving of any illegal price discrimination a criminal offense. It also makes it a crime to sell goods at "unreasonably low prices for the purpose of destroying competition or eliminating a competitor."

(a) Local discrimination

MOORE v MEAD'S FINE BREAD COMPANY
348 US 115 (1955)

Moore ran a bakery in Santa Rosa, New Mexico. His business was wholly intrastate. His competitor, Mead's Fine Bread Company, was one of several corporations held under interlocking ownership and management and engaged in an interstate business. Mead cut the price of bread in half in Santa Rosa but made no price cut in any other place in New Mexico or any other state. As the result of this price-cutting, Moore was driven out of business. He then sued Mead for damages for violation of the Clayton and Robinson-Patman Acts. Mead claimed that the price-cutting was purely intrastate and therefore did not constitute a violation of the federal statutes.

OPINION BY DOUGLAS, J.

. . . Respondent is engaged in commerce, selling bread both locally and interstate. In the course of such business, it made price discriminations, maintaining the price in the *interstate* transactions and cutting the price in the *intrastate* sales. The destruction of a competitor was plainly established, as required by . . . the Clayton Act; and the evidence to support a finding of purpose to eliminate a competitor, as required by § 3 of the Robinson-Patman Act, was ample.

We think that the practices in the present case are . . . included within the scope of the antitrust laws. We have here an interstate industry increasing its domain through outlawed competitive practices. The victim, to be sure, is only a local merchant; and no interstate transactions are used to destroy him. But the beneficiary is an interstate business; the treasury used to finance the warfare is drawn from interstate, as well as local, sources which include not only respondent but also a group of interlocked companies engaged in the same line of business; and the prices on the interstate sales, both by respondent and by the other Mead companies, are kept high while the local prices are lowered. If this method of competition were approved, the pattern for growth of monopoly would be simple. As long as the price warfare was strictly intrastate, interstate business could grow and expand with impunity at the expense of local merchants. The competitive advantage would then be with the interstate combines, not by reason of their skills or efficiency but because of their strength and ability to wage price wars. The profits made in interstate activities would underwrite the losses of local price-cutting campaigns. No instrumentality of interstate commerce would be used to destroy the local merchant and expand the domain of the combine. But the opportunities afforded by interstate commerce would be employed to injure local trade. Congress, as guardian of the Commerce Clause, certainly has power to say that those advantages shall not attach to the privilege of doing an interstate business. . . .

It is, we think, clear that Congress by the Clayton Act and Robinson-Patman Act barred the use of interstate business to destroy local business, outlawing the price cutting employed by respondent. . . .

[Judgment for Moore]

(b) Discrimination to meet competition

STANDARD OIL COMPANY v FEDERAL TRADE COMMISSION

340 US 231 (1951)

Standard Oil Company sold gasoline in Detroit to four large "jobber" customers at a lower price than it did to many smaller buyers in the same area. The Federal Trade Commission ordered it to stop such price discrimination. Standard Oil claimed that it had granted the large jobbers the lower price in order to retain them as customers by meeting the prices of Standard Oil's competitors. The Commission rejected this as a defense. Standard Oil Company appealed.

OPINION BY BURTON, J.

. . . Since the effective date of the Robinson-Patman Act, June 19, 1936, petitioner has sold its Red Crown gasoline to its "jobber" customers at its tank-car prices. Those prices have been 1½¢ per gallon less than its tank-wagon prices to service station customers for identical gasoline in the same area. In practice, the service stations have resold the gasoline at the prevailing retail service station prices. Each of petitioner's so-called "jobber" customers has been free to resell its gasoline at retail or wholesale. Each, at some time, has resold some of it at retail. One now resells it only at retail. The others now resell it largely at wholesale. As to resale prices, two of the "jobbers" have resold their gasoline only at the prevailing wholesale or retail rates. The other two, however, have reflected, in varying degrees, petitioner's reductions in the cost of the gasoline to them by reducing their resale prices of that gasoline below the prevailing rates. The effect of these reductions has thus reached competing retail service stations in part through retail stations operated by the "jobbers" and in part through retail stations which purchased gasoline from the "jobbers" at less than the prevailing tank-wagon prices. The Commission found that such reduced resale prices "have resulted in injuring, destroying, and preventing competition between said favored dealers and retail dealers in respondent's [petitioner's] gasoline and other major brands of gasoline. . . ."

The heart of our national economic policy long has been faith in the value of competition. . . . Congress did not seek by the Robinson-Patman Act either to abolish competition or so radically to curtail it that a seller would have no substantial right of self-defense against a price raid by a competitor. For example, if a large customer requests his seller to meet a temptingly lower price offered to him by one of his seller's competitors, the seller may well find it essential, as a matter of business survival, to meet that price rather than to lose the customer. It might be that this customer is the seller's only available market for the major portion of the seller's product, and that the loss of this customer would result in forcing a much higher unit cost and higher sales price upon the seller's other customers. There is nothing to show a congressional purpose, in such a situation, to compel the seller to choose only between ruinously cutting its prices to all its customers to match the price offered to one, or refusing to meet the competition and then ruinously raising its prices to its remaining customers to cover increased unit costs. There is, on the other hand, plain language and established practice which permits a seller . . . to retain a customer by realistically meeting in good faith the price offered to that customer, without necessarily changing the seller's price to its other customers.

In a case where a seller sustains the burden of proof placed upon it to establish its defense . . . we find no reason to destroy that defense indirectly, merely because it also appears that the beneficiaries of the seller's price reductions may derive a competitive advantage from them or may, in a natural course of events, reduce their own resale prices to their customers. It must have been obvious to Congress that any price reduction to any dealer may always affect competition at that dealer's level as well as at the dealer's resale level, whether or not the reduction to the dealer is discriminatory. Likewise, it must have been obvious to Congress that any price reductions initiated by a seller's competitor would, if not met by the seller, affect competition at the beneficiary's level or among the beneficiary's customers just as much as if those reductions had been met by the seller. . . . We . . . conclude that Congress meant to permit the natural consequences to follow the seller's action in meeting in good faith a lawful and equally low price of its competitor. . . .

[Case remanded to lower court to determine whether Standard Oil Company had in fact reduced the price to some customers in good faith in order to meet competition]

§ 13:2. HORIZONTAL PRICE FIXING

Horizontal price fixing, that is, the fixing of prices between competitors, is a per se violation of the Sherman Act without regard to the reasonable or unreasonable character of the price that is fixed. It is immaterial whether this fixing of the price is made pursuant to a formal plan adopted by all producers involved or is merely an informal agreement among them.

In *United States v Trenton Potteries Co.,* 273 US 392 (1927), the Court declared:

"the aim and result of every price-fixing agreement, if effective, is the elimination of one form of competition. The power to fix prices, whether reasonably exercised or not, involves power to control the market and to fix arbitrary and unreasonable prices. The reasonable price fixed today may, through economic and business changes, become the unreasonable price of tomorrow. Once established it may be maintained unchanged because of the absence of competition secured by the agreement for a price reasonable when fixed. Agreements which create such potential power may well be held in themselves to be unreasonable or unlawful restraint, without the necessity of minute inquiry, whether a particular price is reasonable or unreasonable as fixed, and without placing on the government in enforcing the Sherman law the burden of ascertaining from day to day whether it has become unreasonable through the mere variation of economic conditions. Moreover, in the absence of express legislation requiring it, we should hesitate to adopt a construction making the difference between legal and illegal conduct in the field of business relations depend upon so uncertain a test as whether prices are reasonable—a determination which can be satisfactorily made only after a complete survey of our economic organization and a choice between rival philosophies.

§ 13:3. BASING-POINT AND ZONE-DELIVERED PRICING SYSTEMS

The producer's problem of maintaining price stability is complicated further when a geographic distribution of markets is involved. In such a case, in addition to the other competitive factors, each seller will be faced by a transportation cost of taking goods to the market, and this cost may be different than that of competitors whose plants are located at different geographical points.

In such cases, manufacturers often have sought to establish a standard price for convenience in advertising or in bookkeeping, or for the purpose of enabling them to assert a better control over the market. Sometimes sales are made at a price free on board the manufacturer's plant. Some manufacturers have followed a plan of selling at a fixed price, regardless of where the buyer was located, and of absorbing part or all of the freight to such point. Sometimes the fixed delivery price system is divided into uniform zones, so that all buyers in a particular zone may buy at the same price, with the manufacturer possibly bearing some of the transportation cost in computing price.

Such a price control system, however, is merely the price control of the individual manufacturer for the disposal of that manufacturer's own goods. In contrast with this, there developed a basing-point system of establishing a fixed price for the goods of all manufacturers within a given line of production. Thus, from 1900 to 1926, the steel industry used the single basing-point plan, also called the "Pittsburgh Plus Plan," under which the price of steel of any producer to any purchaser anywhere in the United States was quoted as the price of steel at Pittsburgh plus freight from Pittsburgh to the point of delivery, regardless of the route actually followed by the shipment. Under this plan, a person purchasing steel in California from a plant ten miles away would be required to buy at a price equal to the cost if the steel had been bought at Pittsburgh and the transportation cost of the steel from Pittsburgh to the place of purchase had been added. This single basing-point system was later replaced by a multiple basing-point system in which, instead of all deliveries being priced at "Pittsburgh plus," the country was zoned so that each purchaser would pay the price of a certain city within the zone, plus the cost of transportation from that city to the purchaser.

This multiple basing-point fixed price delivery system became fairly common in many of the bulk commodity industries. Here, because of the standardized quality of the product, there is little room for competition except in price. The transportation factor looms high because these products have great bulk that gives rise to a high transportation cost, yet sell at a relatively low price per unit volume. Unless the selling price can be made uniform, the industry is subject to continual price warfare. The same factors that have led the large commodity industries to establish monopolies and cartels have induced them to adopt multiple basing-point systems.

Such systems have the economic disadvantage of retarding the development of producers at points other than the basing point. A new producer coming into a new area nearer the consumer would not secure any competitive advantage by locating at that point if required to sell at a basing-point figure. In addition, the basing-point price system prevents the purchaser from reaping an economic advantage from purchasing from an existing nearby producer.

Both single and multiple basing-point systems have been condemned by the Supreme Court as illegal when they are based upon collusion between producers. The exact extent to which they are to be regarded as collusive is not clear. The Supreme Court has also sustained the action of the Federal Trade Commission in prohibiting the concerted use of a zone-pricing system.

§ 13:4. VERTICAL PRICE FIXING

(a) Resale price maintenance agreements

When a manufacturer sells goods to a distributor, can the distributor be compelled to agree that the goods will not be resold for less than a specified price? Such resale price maintenance agreements are now violations of the Sherman Antitrust Act. For some three decades this was not the law; such agreements then generally were valid and were protected by state fair trade acts and by the federal Miller-Tydings Act. In 1975, the federal Act was repealed, thus removing the protection which the federal law had given. Such resale price maintenance agreements today are illegal under the federal law. They are valid only in a few states with respect to intrastate sales. As intrastate sales represent such a slight segment of the national economy, it may be stated that resale price maintenance agreements are now illegal.

This is a per se, or unqualified, illegality and it is immaterial whether the price is reasonable or is fixed in good faith. The fact that there is a fixing of the price in itself makes the agreement to fix the price illegal. The rule of reason is not applied.

(b) Price fixing by economic pressure

In many instances, the seller has a bargaining power so superior to that of the buyer that the seller is able to dictate to the buyer the prices at which the goods will be resold. Such coerced price fixing may violate the federal antitrust law.

SIMPSON v UNION OIL CO.

377 US 13 (1964)

The Union Oil Company leased a gas service station to Simpson. As in the case of its other gas stations, the lease was for a year and was renewable thereafter until terminated by either party upon notice. Gas was not sold outright by Union to Simpson, but instead was delivered on "consignment," by which the title of the gas was retained by Union. The consignment agreement specified the resale prices for the gas. Simpson sold below these prices and because of this, Union terminated the lease at the end of the year. Simpson sued for an injunction to prevent Union from terminating the lease because of its price-cutting. From adverse decisions of the District Court and the Court of Appeals, he appealed to the United States Supreme Court.

OPINION BY DOUGLAS, J.

. . . If the "consignment" agreement achieves resale price maintenance in violation of the Sherman Act, it and the lease are being used to injure interstate commerce by depriving independent dealers of the exercise of free judgment whether to become consignees at all, or remain consignees, and, in any event, to sell at competitive prices. The fact that a retailer can refuse to deal does not give the supplier immunity if the arrangement is one of those schemes condemned by the antitrust laws. . . .

The exclusive requirement contracts struck down in *Standard Oil Co. v United States,* 337 US 293, . . . were not saved because the dealers need not have agreed to them, but could have gone elsewhere. If that were a defense, a supplier could regiment thousands of otherwise competitive dealers in resale price maintenance programs merely by fear of nonrenewal of short-term leases.

. . . A supplier may not use coercion on its retail outlets to achieve resale price maintenance. We reiterate that view, adding that it matters not what the coercive device is. . . .

Consignments perform an important function in trade and commerce, and their integrity has been recognized by many courts, including this one. . . .

One who sends a rug or a painting or other work of art to a merchant or a gallery for sale at a minimum price can, of course, hold the consignee to the bargain. A retail merchant may, indeed, have inventory on consignment, the terms of which bind the parties inter se. . . .

The interests of the Government . . . frequently override agreements that private parties make. Here we have an antitrust policy expressed in Acts of Congress. Accordingly, a consignment, no matter how lawful it might be as a matter of private contract law, must give way before the federal antitrust policy. . . . [And] § 1 of the Sherman Act [does not] tolerate agreements for retail price maintenance. . . .

Resale price maintenance of gasoline through the "consignment" device is increasing. The "consignment" device in the gasoline field is used for resale price maintenance. . . .

Dealers, like Simpson, are independent businessmen; and they have all or most of the indicia of entrepreneurs, except for price fixing. The risk of loss of the gasoline is on them, apart from acts of God. Their return is affected by the rise and fall in the market price, their commissions declining as retail prices drop. Practically the only power they have to be wholly independent businessmen, whose service depends on their own initiative and enterprise, is taken from them by the proviso that they must sell their gasoline at prices fixed by Union Oil. By reason of the lease and "consignment" agreement dealers are coercively laced into an arrangement under which their supplier is able to impose noncompetitive prices on thousands of persons whose prices otherwise might be competitive. The evil of this resale price maintenance program, . . . is its inexorable potentiality for and even certainty in destroying competition in retail sales of gasoline by these nominal "consignees" who are in reality small struggling competitors seeking retail gas customers.

As we have said, an owner of an article may send it to a dealer who may in turn undertake to sell it only at a price determined by the owner. There is nothing illegal about that arrangement. When, however, a "consignment" device is used to cover a vast gasoline distribution system, fixing prices through many retail outlets, the antitrust laws prevent calling the "consignment" an agency. . . .

Reliance is placed on *United States v General Electric Co.*, 272 US 476, . . . where a consignment arrangement was utilized to market patented articles. Union Oil correctly argues that the consignment in that case somewhat parallels the one in the instant case. The Court in the *General Electric* case did not restrict its ruling to patented articles; it, indeed, said that the use of the consignment device was available to the owners of articles "patented or otherwise." . . . But whatever may be said of the *General Electric* case on its special facts, involving patents, it is not apposite to the special facts here. . . .

The patent laws which give a 17-year monopoly on "making, using, or selling the invention" are in pari materia with the antitrust laws and modify them pro tanto. That was the ratio decidendi of the *General Electric* case. . . . We decline the invitation to end it. . . .

[Judgment for Simpson]

DISSENTING OPINION BY STEWART, J.

In *United States v General Electric,* 272 US 476, . . . this Court held that a bona fide consignment agreement of this kind does not violate the Sherman Act. . . . Possession of patent rights on the article allegedly consigned has no legal significance to an inquiry directed to ascertaining whether the burdens, risks, and rights of ownership actually remain with the principal or have passed to his agent. Nor is the power of a consignor to fix the prices at which his consignee sells augmented in any respect by the possession of a patent on the goods so consigned. It is not by virtue of a patent monopoly that a bona fide consignor may control the price at which his consignee sells; his control over price flows from the simple fact that the owner of goods, so long as he remains the owner, has the unquestioned right to determine the price at which he will sell them. . . .

It is clear, therefore, that the Court today overrules *General Electric.* . . . Today's upsetting decision carries with it the most severe consequences to a large sector of the private economy. We cannot be blind to the fact that commercial arrangements throughout our economy are shaped in reliance upon this Court's decisions elaborating the reach of the antitrust laws. Everyone knows that consignment selling is a widely used method of distribution all over the country. By our decision today outlawing consignment selling if it includes a price limitation, we inject severe uncertainty into commercial relationships established in reliance upon a decision of this Court explicitly validating this method of distribution. We create, as well, the distinct possibility that an untold number of sellers of goods will be subjected to liability in treble damage suits because they thought they could rely on the validity of this Court's decisions. . . .

---

§ 13:5. FIXING OF PRICES FOR SERVICES

No distinction is made under the Sherman Antitrust Act between the regulation of the price of goods and the regulation of the price of services. It is necessary of course that the services or the agreements relating to the services be such as to constitute interstate commerce. Thus it has been held that an agreement between a state-wide medical society and various county medical societies not to compete with each other in furnishing prepaid medical care on a contract basis through nonprofit organizations related only to intrastate commerce and was therefore not a restraint of trade in violation of the Sherman Act.[1]

(a) Real estate brokers

UNITED STATES v NATIONAL ASSOCIATION OF
REAL ESTATE BOARDS

339 US 485 (1950)

The United States brought an action to enjoin the National Association of Real Estate Boards, the Washington Real Estate Board, and others, from violating the Sherman Antitrust Act by fixing by agreement the rates to be charged by member brokers for their services. The defendants contended that the commission-fixing agreements did not violate the Sherman Act because their business was not subject to the Act. From a judgment in favor of the defendants, the United States appealed.

OPINION BY DOUGLAS, J.

. . . The prescribed rates are used in the great majority of transactions, although in exceptional situations a lower charge is made. But departure from the prescribed rates has not caused the Washington Board to invoke any sanctions. Hence the District Court called the rate schedules "nonmandatory."

. . . Price fixing is *per se* an unreasonable restraint of trade. It is not for the courts to determine whether in particular settings price fixing serves an honorable or worthy end. An agreement, shown either by adherence to a price schedule or by proof of consensual action fixing the . . . price, is itself illegal under the Sherman Act, no matter what end it was designed to serve. . . . And the fact that no penalties are imposed for deviations from the price schedules is not material. . . . Subtle influences may be just as effective as the threat or use of formal sanctions to hold people in line.

. . . The critical question is whether the business of a real estate agent is included in the word "trade" within the meaning of § 3 of the Act. . . . The fact that the business involves the sale of personal services rather than commodities does not take it out of the category of "trade" within the meaning of § 3 of the Act. . . .

. . . Wherever any occupation, employment, or business is carried on for the purpose of profit, or gain, or a livelihood, not in the liberal arts or in the learned professions, it is constantly called a trade. . . .

It is in that broad sense that "trade" is used in the Sherman Act. That has been the consistent holding of the decisions. The fixing of prices and other

---

[1] *United States v Oregon State Medical Society*, 343 US 326 (1952).

unreasonable restraints have been consistently condemned in case of services as well as goods. Transportation services. . . . , cleaning, dyeing, and renovating wearing apparel . . . , the procurement of medical and hospital services . . . , the furnishing of news or advertising services . . .—these indicate the range of business activities that have been held to be covered by the Act.

[Judgment for United States]

---

§ 13:6. STATUTORY CONTROL OF PRICES

As a special aspect of governmental control of prices, certain statutes are designed to prevent price-cutting wars. It has been provided by statute in a number of states that it is a crime to sell "below cost" for the purpose of injuring a competitor. Section 3 of the Robinson-Patman Act is even less specific in making it a crime to sell goods at "unreasonably low prices for the purpose of destroying competition or eliminating a competitor." Such statutes are held constitutional against the contention that the quoted terms are too vague to furnish a clear boundary line as to what is lawful and what is unlawful, even though the method of accounting followed affects the conclusion reached concerning whether it was a sale below cost or at a low price.

Questions for Discussion

1. Borden Dairy sold milk to chain store systems at a price subject to a flat discount, regardless of the quantity purchased. It sold to independent stores at a discount graduated to the quantity of milk sold, but the largest obtainable independent store discount did not reach the chain store flat discount. When it was claimed that this was an illegal price discrimination, Borden claimed that it was justified in treating these two classes differently because there was a cost differential between the two, as most of the independent stores required greater servicing of accounts, had more delivery and collection problems, and so forth. Was this discrimination justified? [*United States v Borden Co.,* 370 US 460 (1962)]

2. (a) Why is horizontal price fixing declared illegal without regard to whether the price is reasonable? (b) How does this rejection of "reasonable price" compare with the rule applicable to determining the rates to be allowed public utilities and carriers?

3. Because the Robinson-Patman Act is based upon the interstate commerce power, it follows that the prohibited discriminations must be directed against interstate transactions. Appraise this statement.

4. *X* owned and operated a number of ice plants throughout the state. *X* sold ice at these plants at a standard price. *Z* opened an ice plant in one of the cities in which *X* operated a plant. *X* then reduced prices in that city below prices in other cities in order to undersell *Z. Z* sued to enjoin *X* under the Robinson-Patman Act from cutting the price in this manner. *X* defended on the ground that the great bulk of sales were for local consumption and only a very small percentage was sold to refrigerated railroad cars or interstate motor trucks. Was this defense valid? [*Atlantic Co. v Citizens Ice and Coal Storage Co.,* 178 F2d 453 (CCA 5 1949)]

5. A New Jersey statute provides that no rebates, allowances, concessions, or benefits shall be given, directly or indirectly, to permit any person to obtain motor fuel from a retail dealer below the posted price or at a net price lower than the posted price applicable at the time of the sale. An action was brought by Fried, a retail gasoline dealer, to prevent the enforcement of the statute. He claimed that it was invalid because it was discriminatory in that it related only to the sale of gasoline, and that it denied due process by regulating the price. Was the law constitutional? [*Fried v Kervick,* 34 NJ 68, 167, A2d 380 (1961)]

6. Sun Oil sells gasoline retail in its own gas stations, as well as sells gas to independently owned gas stations. In selling to one independent, it gave that independent a price cut to enable it to meet the competition of other independent gas stations. The Federal Trade Commission claimed this was an unlawful price discrimination. Sun Oil defended on the ground that the price cut was made as authorized by the statute "in good faith to meet an equally low price of a competitor." Was this defense valid? [*Federal Trade Commission v Sun Oil Co.,* 371 US 505 (1963)]

7. Is it a violation of the Robinson-Patman Act to give one customer a special price when the customer threatens to go elsewhere if such a reduction is not given?

8. National Dairy was prosecuted for violation of § 3 of the Robinson-Patman Act, which makes it a crime to sell goods at "unreasonably low prices for the purpose of destroying competition or eliminating a competitor." It claimed that the statute was so vague that it was unconstitutional because it did not reasonably inform the citizen of the price that would constitute a crime. It was shown that in certain geographic areas, National Dairy sold milk below its production cost in order to compete with other dairies. Was the statute valid? [*United States v National Dairy Products Corp.,* 372 US 29; rehearing denied, 372 US 961 (1963)]

9. If selling on consignment is lawful and the consignor, as in the case of any owner, can specify the price at which the goods are to be sold, how can the exercise of such rights be deemed a violation of the Antitrust laws?

10. If you are sued for negligently running over a plaintiff at Tenth and Main Streets on January 5, 1980, can it be shown at the trial that you were in the habit of going through red lights at other times and other places? Does the *Simpson* case and other cases follow the same pattern or a different pattern than the answer to this question?

11. What is embraced by "trade" in the phrase "restraint of trade"?

12. (a) What is the legal difference between price fixing by the agreement of the parties and price fixing by the legislature? (b) What is the economic or social difference? (c) Does it make any difference if the agreement fixing the price is a one-sided agreement in which one party is forced to deal on the terms stipulated by the other party?

14

Regulation of Agriculture

§ 14:1. POWER TO REGULATE AGRICULTURE

The states, under their police power, may regulate agriculture. Prior to 1937, the Congress had no power to regulate agriculture. During this period some indirect promotion of agriculture took place through various federal programs designed to encourage farm growth and expansion. Farmers were aided by grants of free land or lands at low cost. Extensive research and educational programs were conducted by the national and state governments in order to make information about better ways of farming available to the farmer. Financial aid was given directly in the form of subsidies or bounties, or in the form of credit upon easier terms. Programs of electrification, flood control, and fertilizer production undertaken by the government contributed to the advancement of the farmer. The farmer's competitive position was further aided by a protective tariff on agricultural products and by the exemption of farmer's cooperatives from the operation of antitrust laws.

Since 1937, the federal government has been able to embark upon programs directly aimed at protecting or furthering agriculture on the ground that this is an economic need of the nation, and therefore within the scope of the new commerce power.

§ 14:2. QUANTITY OF PRODUCTION

In the early 30's, the farmers suffered from falling prices caused, in part, by surplus production. The demand for their products shrank, although their capacity to produce had increased. As part of Roosevelt's New Deal, Congress sought to limit farm production in order to maintain farm prices.

Some effort was made to dissuade the farmer from producing surplus crops and to encourage the disposal of the surplus by the granting of export subsidies or adoption of a food distribution plan, such as free lunches to school children or food stamps to the needy. These methods proved inadequate and the direct regulation of acreage under cultivation was begun by the federal government in the Agricultural Adjustment Act of 1933. In substance, this act gave a bounty to farmers voluntarily reducing their acreage and obtained the money for the payment of this bounty by imposing a tax on the processors of the farm products. Thus a wheat farmer would be paid a bounty for reducing the acreage under cultivation, and this bounty would be obtained by placing a tax on the miller of the flour. This law was held unconstitutional, although today, in view of the new interpretation of the commerce clause, it would be valid.

Congress amended the Act in 1938. This amendment sought to avoid the constitutional barrier raised against the Act of 1933 by basing the regulation upon the commerce power, which by that time had been liberally construed in the *Jones & Laughlin Steel Corporation* case.[1] The declared purpose of the Act of 1938 as set forth in its statement of policy was

> "to regulate interstate and foreign commerce in cotton, wheat, corn, tobacco and rice to the extent necessary to provide an orderly, adequate, and balanced flow of such commodities in interstate and foreign commerce through storage of reserve supplies, loans, marketing, quotas, assisting farmers to obtain, insofar as practicable, parity prices for such commodities and parity of income, and assisting consumers to obtain an adequate and steady supply of such commodities at fair prices.

Under this Act, the Secretary of Agriculture is authorized to determine the proper volume of production for the following year; that is, the amount which can be disposed of by sale in domestic and foreign markets. This amount, or quota, is then recommended to producers of the particular commodity, who vote on whether that quota should be adopted. If those opposing the quota are less than one third of those voting, the quota is effective for the nation for that year. This national quota is then divided among the states according to their past production and is then subdivided within each state among the various producers. Production in excess of an assigned quota subjects the farmer to a penalty, even if the excess production is consumed at home and is not sold in commerce. Farmers conforming to the quotas are permitted to receive subsidies for the maintenance of their prices and, if they store any excess production with the government, they are permitted to obtain loans on such excess as security.

---

[1] § 8:3.

(a) Agricultural Adjustment Act of 1938

WICKARD v FILBURN

317 US 111 (1942)

OPINION BY JACKSON, J.

The appellee [Filburn] filed his complaint against the Secretary of Agriculture of the United States, three members of the County Agricultural Conservation Committee for Montgomery County, Ohio, and a member of the State Agricultural Conservation Committee for Ohio . . . to enjoin enforcement against himself of the marketing penalty imposed by the amendment of May 26, 1941, to the Agricultural Adjustment Act of 1938, upon that part of his 1941 wheat crop which was available for marketing in excess of the marketing quota established for his farm. He also sought a declaratory judgment that the wheat marketing quota provisions of the Act as amended and applicable to him were unconstitutional because not sustainable under the Commerce Clause or consistent with the Due Process Clause of the Fifth Amendment. . . .

In July of 1940, pursuant to the Agricultural Adjustment Act of 1938, as then amended, there were established for the appellee's 1941 crop a wheat acreage allotment of 11.1 acres and a normal yield of 20.1 bushels of wheat an acre. . . . He sowed, however, 23 acres, and harvested from his 11.9 acres of excess acreage 239 bushels, which under the terms of the Act as amended on May 26, 1941, constituted farm marketing excess, subject to a penalty of 49 cents a bushel, or $117.11 in all. The appellee has not paid the penalty and he has not postponed or avoided it by storing the excess under regulations of the Secretary of Agriculture, or by delivering it up to the Secretary. The Committee, therefore, refused him a marketing card, which was, under the terms of Regulations promulgated by the Secretary, necessary to protect a buyer from liability to the penalty and upon its protecting lien.

The general scheme of the Agricultural Adjustment Act of 1938 as related to wheat is to control the volume moving in interstate and foreign commerce in order to avoid surpluses and shortages and the consequent abnormally low or high wheat prices and obstructions to commerce. Within prescribed limits and by prescribed standards the Secretary of Agriculture is directed to ascertain and proclaim each year a national acreage allotment for the next crop of wheat, which is then apportioned to the states and their counties, and is eventually broken up into allotments for individual farms. Loans and payments to wheat farmers are authorized in stated circumstances.

The Act provides further that whenever it appears that the total supply of wheat as of the beginning of any marketing year, beginning July 1, will exceed a normal year's domestic consumption and export by more than 35 percent, the Secretary shall so proclaim not later than May 15 prior to the beginning of such marketing year; and that during the marketing year a compulsory national marketing quota shall be in effect with respect to the marketing of wheat. Between the issuance of the proclamation and June 10, the Secretary must, however, conduct a referendum of farmers who will be subject to the quota to determine whether they favor or oppose it; and if more than one third of the farmers voting in the referendum do oppose, the Secretary must prior to the effective date of the quota by proclamation suspend its operation. . . .

It is urged that under the Commerce Clause . . . Congress does not possess the power it has in this instance sought to exercise. . . . The sum of this is that the Federal Government fixes a quota including all that the farmer may harvest for sale or for his own farm needs, and declares that wheat produced on excess acreage may neither be disposed of nor used except upon payment of the penalty or except it is stored as required by the Act or delivered to the Secretary of Agriculture.

Appellee says that this is a regulation of production and consumption of wheat. . . . In answer the Government argues that the statute regulates neither production nor consumption, but only marketing; . . .

In the *Shreveport Rate* cases . . . the Court held that railroad rates of an admittedly intrastate character and fixed by authority of the state might, nevertheless, be revised by the Federal Government because of the economic effects which they had upon interstate commerce. The opinion of Mr. Justice Hughes found federal intervention constitutionally authorized because of "matters having such a close and substantial relation to interstate traffic that the control is essential or appropriate to the security of that traffic, to the efficiency of the interstate service, and to the maintenance of the conditions under which interstate commerce may be conducted upon fair terms and without molestation or hindrance." . . .

Questions of federal power cannot be decided simply by finding the activity in question to be "production" nor can consideration of its economic effects be foreclosed by calling them "indirect." . . . "The commerce power is not confined in its exercise to the regulation of commerce among the states. It extends to those activities intrastate which so affect interstate commerce, or the exertion of the power of Congress over it, as to make regulation of them appropriate means to the attainment of a legitimate end, the effective execution of the granted power to regulate interstate commerce. . . . The power of Congress over interstate commerce is plenary and complete in itself, may be exercised to its utmost extent, and acknowledges no limitations other than are prescribed in the Constitution. . . . It follows that no form of state activity can constitutionally thwart the regulatory power granted by the commerce clause to Congress. Hence the reach of that power extends to those intrastate activities which in a substantial way interfere with or obstruct the exercise of the granted power." . . .

Whether the subject of the regulation in question was "production," "consumption," or "marketing" is, therefore, not material for purposes of deciding the question of federal power before us. . . . Even if appellee's activity be local and though it may not be regarded as commerce, it may still, whatever its nature, be reached by Congress if it exerts a substantial economic effect on interstate commerce and this irrespective of whether such effect is what might at some earlier time have been defined as "direct" or "indirect."

[The Court summarized] the economics of the wheat industry.

In the absence of regulation the price of wheat in the United States would be much affected by world conditions. During 1941 producers who cooperated with the Agricultural Adjustment program received an average price on the farm of about $1.16 a bushel as compared with the world market price of 40 cents a bushel. . . .

The effect of consumption of homegrown wheat on interstate commerce is due to the fact that it constitutes the most variable factor in the disappearance of the wheat crop. Consumption on the farm where grown appears to vary in an amount greater than 20 percent of average production. The total amount of wheat consumed as food varies but relatively little, and use as seed is relatively constant.

. . . The effect of the statute before us is to restrict the amount which may be produced for market and the extent as well to which one may forestall resort to the market by producing to meet his own needs. That appellee's own contribution to the demand for wheat may be trivial by itself is not enough to remove him from the scope of federal regulation where, as here, his contribution, taken together with that of many others similarly situated, is far from trivial. . . .

It is well established by decisions of this Court that the power to regulate commerce includes the power to regulate the prices at which commodities in that commerce are dealt in and practices affecting such prices. One of the primary purposes of the Act in question was to increase the market price of wheat and to that end to limit the volume thereof that could affect the market. It can hardly be denied that a factor of such volume and variability as home-consumed wheat would have a substantial influence on price and market conditions. This may arise because being in marketable condition such wheat overhangs the market and if induced by rising prices tends to flow into the market and check price increases. But if we assume that it is never marketed, it supplies a need of the man who grew it which would otherwise be reflected by purchases in the open market. Homegrown wheat in this sense competes with wheat in commerce. The stimulation of commerce is a use of the regulatory function quite as definitely as prohibitions or restrictions thereon. This record leaves us in no doubt that Congress may properly have considered that wheat consumed on the farm where grown if wholly outside the scheme of regulation would have a substantial effect in defeating and obstructing its purpose to stimulate trade therein at increased prices.

It is said, however, that this Act, forcing some farmers into the market to buy what they could provide for themselves, is an unfair promotion of the markets and prices of specializing wheat growers. It is of the essence of regulation that it lays a restraining hand on the self-interest of the regulated and that advantages from the regulation commonly fall to others. The conflicts of economic interest between the regulated and those who advantage by it are wisely left under our system to resolution by the Congress under its more flexible and responsible legislative process. Such conflicts rarely lend themselves to judicial determination. And with the wisdom, workability, or fairness, of the plan of regulation we have nothing to do. . . .

[Judgment against Filburn]

§ 14:3. CONSERVATION AND RECLAMATION

A secondary type of regulation of agriculture is found in the conservation and reclamation of farm lands. To the extent that a conservation measure restricts output, it can be regarded as an antisurplus measure. At the same time, some conservation and most reclamation measures have as their result an increased productivity, so that in effect the likelihood of a surplus is increased. This is particularly true where the reclamation calls back into cultivation land that was lying idle, or where farmers are moved from marginal or submarginal lands and resettled on lands having greater productivity.

Here we have illustrated the curious conflict that may often arise between the individual and the group. In a given year there may be a national wheat surplus, yet at the same time there may be wheat farmers working poor lands who are barely able to make a living because of the low production of their lands. To move these farmers from the marginal or submarginal land to land producing a higher yield of wheat would to some extent solve their problem, but it would also increase the national surplus. This, at least in theory, should cause a further decrease in the national wheat price and thus harm the wheat farmers as a group.

The problem becomes one of great difficulty because of the problem of balancing competing interests: the interest of the individual farmer against farmers as a group, the interest of farmers against society seeking food at low prices, the interest of society in maintaining the purchasing power of the farmer, and the interest of the community or the nation in having a sound agricultural economy and a well-nourished people.

Under the new interpretation of the commerce power and the war power, there is little constitutional difficulty in sustaining any system of federal conservation. State conservation laws are also valid, as long as they are not in conflict with federal laws or are not so written as to discriminate against interstate commerce or the citizens of other states in an unreasonable manner.

To the extent that conservation and reclamation preserve a steady water supply, prevent floods, and prevent the clogging of river channels with soil erosion, such measures may also be sustained under the federal power over navigable waterways.

§ 14:4 STANDARDS, MARKETING, AND PRICE

Both state and national governments may impose regulations on agriculture for the purpose of maintaining standards. The object of these standards may be to protect the purchasing public from physical harm or financial loss through the purchase of agricultural products of inferior quality or grade, to maintain standard grade levels in order to facilitate merchandising, or to maintain trade reputation. Under the doctrine of the supremacy of the federal powers when exercised in an area in which a state has concurrent power, the federal standards become effective even as to locally produced and locally sold farm products, in order to avoid an unfair competition by them with the interstate products that are subjected to the federal regulation.

The marketing of farm products may be regulated by requiring their inspection prior to sale, by limiting their sale to designated regulated markets, or by requiring that the product be marketed through a central or governmental agency. Where farm products are sold at private markets or exchanges, the business practices and the charges of persons furnishing their services at such markets and exchanges may be regulated. Here again there is the concurrent power of national and state governments, with the supremacy of the former when it acts.

While, for the greater part, price regulation of farm products has taken the form of subsidies to maintain the prices at a desired level, national and state government may regulate the prices of farm products. To date, this power has not been extensively used and has been confined to the field of establishing minimum prices. Under the reported decisions, however, there is no reason why such control cannot be extended as far as the national Congress or the state legislatures desire, nor is there any reason why the regulation cannot be the establishment of a maximum or an exact price, rather than merely a minimum. Again, the powers of the nation and the state are concurrent, with the supremacy of the national power being recognized not only as to sales in interstate commerce but also as to local sales that compete with the interstate sales.

Questions for Discussion

1. What has been the pattern of governmental regulation of agriculture?

2. Describe the operation of the antisurplus provisions of the Agricultural Adjustment Act of 1938.

3. Did the Court consider the wisdom of the Act in determining the constitutionality of the statute in *Wickard v Filburn*?

4. (a) Under what power can a state adopt a conservation or land reclamation law?　(b) What is the basis for a federal law?

5. Is a law limiting the number of acres under cultivation the most effective way of preventing a crop surplus?

6. To what extent may the price of farm products be controlled by government?

7. Assuming the power to regulate wheat sold in interstate commerce, what is the justification for regulating wheat grown and used for home consumption by the farmers who raised it?

8. Compare the legality of: (a) An agreement between manufacturers to restrict output.   (b) An agreement between members of a labor union to restrict output.   (c) An agreement between farmers to restrict output. (d) A statute providing that the Secretary of Agriculture may direct farmers to restrict their output, so that it will not exceed a quota fixed by the Secretary.

9. (a) Was the statute before the Court in *Wickard v Filburn* a regulation of production?   (b) Was it so considered by the Court?

10. What test did the Court apply in the *Wickard* case to determine whether the activity came within the regulatory scope of the commerce power?

11. Assume that Congress passes a law regulating in detail the methods of farming, the crops to be grown, and the quantities of each crop to be produced. The first section of the statute recites that improper farming methods have impaired the agricultural potential of the country and are likely to make it vulnerable in time of war, and that to remedy this danger the Act in question is adopted. Discuss the constitutionality of this statute under (a) the commerce power, (b) the general welfare power, and (c) the war power.

12. Assume that Congress passes a law which recites that farm tenancy is rising and is a threat to American democratic institutions, and that to correct this situation the law in question is adopted. The law then provides that anyone owning a farm in excess of 1,000 acres or owning a number of farms, the total acreage of which exceeds 1,000, must sell the surplus to the government at a fair value to be determined by legal proceedings. The Act further provides that the surplus lands thus acquired by the government will be divided into parcels of 100 acres each and be given free to tenant farmers, provided they live on the land and properly farm it for five years. Discuss the constitutionality of this law.

15

Regulation of Price

§ 15:1. NATURE OF THE PROBLEM

In its broadest sense, a price is the amount that a seller receives and the amount that a buyer pays for services or property. The purpose of price regulation may be to prevent the seller from securing an exorbitant price or to guarantee the receipt of a reasonable price. The regulation of prices may be inspired by the premise that, under the existing circumstances, either generally or with respect to a particular product, the natural laws of supply and demand do not result in the establishment of a price that is socially desirable. It may also be inspired by the premise that, due to monopolistic or other restrictive practices, the natural laws of supply and demand are not able to operate, and therefore government regulation must intervene to establish a fair price.

In addition to direct regulation of prices, there may be intentional or unintentional indirect regulation. The requirement that factories install fire escapes or safety devices, while not intended as a price regulation, may indirectly have that effect as the factory owners seek to place the greater cost of their plant upon the purchasers of their goods. Laws restricting the hours of work or excluding women and children from certain types of labor will also have the effect of raising the labor cost of a manufacturer, and this added cost may ultimately result in the purchaser's paying a greater price. An illustration of an intentional indirect regulation of price is the case of the national government's devaluing of the dollar in 1933 and 1934 in order to cause a rise of the price level. A similar approach is found in the Agricultural Adjustment Act of 1938, which sought to raise the price of various basic farm commodities by restricting the quantity produced.

§ 15:2. STATE REGULATION

The right of the state by virtue of its police power to enact laws for the general welfare, safety, health, and morals was early recognized in the case of public utilities. In addition to regulation of public utilities proper, the Supreme Court also sustained the right to regulate those businesses that were affected with a public interest. In *Munn v Illinois,* the Court sustained a maximum rate fixed by a state legislature for the charges of grain elevator operators. The Court rejected the argument that the grain elevator was merely private property devoted to a private business and held that it was affected with a public interest. The difficulty of defining the scope of this phrase "affected with a public interest" is seen in the conflict between the majority and the dissenting opinions.

(a) Business affected with a public interest

MUNN v ILLINOIS
94 US 113 (1876)

OPINION BY WAITE, C. J.

The question . . . is whether Illinois can . . . fix . . . the maximum . . . charges for the storage of grain in warehouses at Chicago and other places in the State having not less than one hundred thousand inhabitants, "in which grain is stored in bulk, and in which the grain of different owners is mixed together. . . ."

When one becomes a member of society, he necessarily parts with some rights or privileges which, as an individual not affected by his relations to others, he might retain. . . . This is the very essence of government. . . . From this source come the police powers, which . . . "are nothing more or less than the powers of government inherent in every sovereignty, . . . that is to say, . . . the power to govern men and things." Under these powers the government regulates the conduct of its citizens one towards another, and the manner in which each shall use his own property, when such regulation becomes necessary for the public good. . . .

This brings us to inquire as to the principles upon which this power of regulation rests, in order that we may determine what is within and what without its operative effect. Looking, then, to the common law, from whence came the right which the Constitution protects, we find that when private property is "affected with a public interest, it ceases to be *juris privati* only." . . . Property does become clothed with a public interest when used in a manner to make it of public consequence, and affect the community at large. When, therefore, one devotes his property to a use in which the public has an interest, he, in effect, grants to the public an interest in that use, and must submit to be controlled by the public for the common good, to the extent of the interest he has thus created. He may withdraw his grant by discontinuing the use; but, so long as he maintains the use, he must submit to the control. . . .

. . . "The great producing region of the West and Northwest sends its grain by water and rail to Chicago, where the greater part of it is shipped by vessel for transportation to the seaboard by the Great Lakes, and some of it is forwarded by railway to the Eastern ports. . . . Vessels, to some extent, are loaded in the Chicago harbor, and sailed through the St. Lawrence directly to Europe. . . . This business has created a demand for means by which the immense quantity of grain can be handled or stored, and these have been found in grain warehouses, which are commonly called elevators. . . . The grain warehouses . . . are located with the river harbor on one side and the railway tracks on the other; and the grain is run through them from car to vessel, or boat to car, . . ."

. . . In 1874 there were in Chicago fourteen warehouses adapted to this particular business, . . . owned by about thirty persons, nine business firms controlled them, and . . . the prices charged and received for storage were such "as have been from year to year agreed upon and established by the different elevators or warehouses in the city of Chicago." . . . Thus it is apparent that all the elevating facilities through which these vast productions "of seven or eight great States of the West" must pass on the way "to four or five of the States on the seashore" may be a "virtual" monopoly.

Under such circumstances it is difficult to see why, if the common carrier, or the miller, or the ferryman, or the innkeeper, or the wharfinger, or the baker, or the cartman, or the hackney-coachman, pursues a public employment and exercises "a sort of public office," these [grain warehouses] do not. . . . Their business most certainly "tends to a common charge, and has become a thing of public interest and use." . . . Certainly, if any business can be clothed "with a public interest, and cease to be *juris privati* only," this has been. It may not be made so by the operation of the Constitution of Illinois or this statute, but it is by the facts. . . .

[Judgment for Illinois, sustaining price control statute]

DISSENTING OPINION BY FIELD, J.

The question presented, therefore, is one of the greatest importance,— whether it is within the competency of a State to fix the compensation which an individual may receive for the use of his own property in his private business, and for his services in connection with it. . . .

. . . But it would seem from its opinion that the court holds that property loses something of its private character when employed in such a way as to be generally useful. The doctrine declared is that property "becomes clothed with a public interest when used in a manner to make it of public consequence, and

affect the community at large;" and from such clothing the right of the legislature is deduced to control the use of the property, and to determine the compensation which the owner may receive for it. When Sir Matthew Hale, and the
sages of the law in his day, spoke of property as affected by a public interest,
and ceasing from that cause to be *juris privati* solely, that is, ceasing to be held
merely in private right, they referred to property dedicated by the owner to
public uses, or to property the use of which was granted by the government, or
in connection with which special privileges were conferred. Unless the property
was thus dedicated, or some right bestowed by the government was held with
the property, . . . the property was not affected by any public interest so as to
be taken out of the category of property held in private right. But it is not in
any such sense that the terms "clothing property with a public interest" are used
in this case. From the nature of the business under consideration—the storage
of grain—which, in any sense in which the words can be used, is a private
business . . . it is clear that the court intended to declare that, whenever one
devotes his property to a business which is useful to the public,—"affects the
community at large,"—the legislature can regulate the compensation which the
owner may receive for its use, and for his own services in connection with it.
. . .

If this be sound law, . . . all property and all business in the State are held
at the mercy of a majority of its legislature. . . .

The power of the State over the property of the citizen under the constitutional guaranty is well defined. The State may take his property for public uses,
upon just compensation being made therefor. It may take a portion of his
property by way of taxation for the support of the government. It may control
the use and possession of his property, so far as may be necessary for the
protection of the rights of others, and to secure to them the equal use and
enjoyment of their property. . . . Except in cases where property may be destroyed to arrest a conflagration or the ravages of pestilence, or be taken under
the pressure of an immediate and overwhelming necessity to prevent a public
calamity, the power of the State over the property of the citizen does not extend
beyond such limits. . . .

§ 15:3. EXPANSION OF STATE POWER

For some time, the Supreme Court refused to extend the concept of businesses affected with a public interest to other businesses in which the public
was, in fact, vitally interested. The Court invalidated state limitations upon the
profit of theater ticket brokers, the rates charged by private employment agencies, and the price of gasoline.

At this point, regulation was confined to public utilities proper, or to those
businesses that the Court considered so like public utilities that they could be
classified with them. Such price regulations as were permitted were designed to
set a ceiling on the charges that could be made by the businesses regulated in
order to protect the public from exorbitant rates. With the advent of the 1929

Depression, a new era in price regulation began. In the case of *Nebbia v New York,* the Supreme Court held that a business could be affected with a public interest, although it was neither a monopoly nor held a franchise and was not like a public utility, and that the regulation of prices was not limited to setting maximum prices but also permitted the establishment of minimum prices below which distributors could not resell the products of the business. Here the regulation is not to protect the consumer from exorbitant prices but to insure the producer a fair return. Again, the conflict between the majority and the dissenting opinions found in the *Munn* case is repeated.

(a) Nullification of public interest concept

NEBBIA v NEW YORK

291 US 502 (1934)

OPINION BY ROBERTS, J.

The Legislature of New York established . . . a Milk Control Board with power . . . to "fix minimum and maximum . . . retail prices to be charged by . . . stores to consumers for consumption off the premises where sold." The Board fixed 9 cents as the price to be charged by a store for a quart of milk. Nebbia, the proprietor of a grocery store . . . sold two quarts and a 5-cent loaf of bread for 18 cents; and was convicted for violating the Board's order. . . .

The question for decision is whether the Federal Constitution prohibits a state from so fixing the selling price of milk. . . .

Under our form of government the use of property and the making of contracts are normally matters of private and not of public concern. The general rule is that both shall be free of governmental interference. But neither property rights nor contract rights are absolute; for government cannot exist if the citizen may at will use his property to the detriment of his fellows, or exercise his freedom of contract to work them harm. Equally fundamental with the private right is that of the public to regulate it in the common interest. . . .

The Fifth Amendment, in the field of federal activity, and the Fourteenth, as respects state action, do not prohibit governmental regulation for the public welfare. They merely condition the exertion of the admitted power, by securing that the end shall be accomplished by methods consistent with due process. And the guaranty of due process, as has often been held, demands only that the law shall not be unreasonable, arbitrary, or capricious, and that the means selected shall have a real and substantial relation to the object sought to be attained. It results that a regulation valid for one sort of business, or in given circumstances, may be invalid for another sort, or for the same business under other circumstances, because the reasonableness of each regulation depends upon the relevant facts.

The milk industry in New York has been the subject of longstanding and drastic regulation in the public interest. The legislative investigation of 1932 was persuasive of the fact that for this and other reasons unrestricted competition aggravated existing evils, and the normal law of supply and demand was insufficient to correct maladjustments detrimental to the community. The inquiry disclosed destructive and demoralizing competitive conditions and unfair trade practices which resulted in retail price-cutting and reduced the income of the farmer below the cost of production. We do not understand the appellant to deny that in these circumstances the legislature might reasonably consider further regulation and control desirable for protection of the industry and the consuming public. That body believed conditions could be improved by preventing destructive pricecutting by stores which, due to the flood of surplus milk, were able to buy at much lower prices than the larger distributors and to sell without incurring the delivery costs of the latter. In the order of which complaint is made the Milk Control Board fixed a price of 10 cents per quart for sales by a distributor to a consumer, and 9 cents by a store to a consumer, thus recognizing the lower costs of the store, and endeavoring to establish a differential which would be just to both. In the light of the facts the order appears not to be unreasonable or arbitrary, or without relation to the purpose to prevent ruthless competition from destroying the wholesale price structure on which the farmer depends for his livelihood, and the community for an assured supply of milk.

But we are told that because the law essays to control prices it denies due process. Notwithstanding the admitted power to correct existing economic ills by appropriate regulation of business, even though an indirect result may be a restriction of the freedom of contract or a modification of charges for services or the price of commodities, the appellant urges that direct fixation of prices is a type of regulation absolutely forbidden. . . . The argument runs that the public control of rates or prices is *per se* unreasonable and unconstitutional, save as applied to businesses affected with a public interest; that a business so affected is one in which property is devoted to an enterprise of a sort which the public itself might appropriately undertake, or one whose owner relies on a public grant or franchise for the right to conduct the business, or in which he is bound to serve all who apply; in short, such as is commonly called a public utility; or a business in its nature a monopoly. The milk industry, it is said, possesses none of these characteristics, and, therefore, not being affected with a public interest, its charges may not be controlled by the state. Upon the soundness of this contention the appellant's case against the statute depends.

We may as well say at once that the dairy industry is not, in the accepted sense of the phrase, a public utility. We think the appellant is also right in asserting that there is in this case no suggestion of any monopoly or monopolistic practice. It goes without saying that those engaged in the business are in no way dependent upon public grants or franchise for the privilege of conducting their activities. But if, as must be conceded, the industry is subject to regulation in the public interest, what constitutional principle bars the state from correcting existing maladjustments by legislation touching prices? We think there is no such principle. The due process clause makes no mention of sales or of prices any more than it speaks of business or contracts or buildings or other incidents

of property. The thought seems nevertheless to have persisted that there is
something peculiarly sacrosanct about the price one may charge for what he
makes or sells, and that, however able to regulate other elements of manufacture
or trade, with incidental effect upon price, the state is incapable of directly
controlling the price itself. This view was negatived many years ago. *Munn v
Illinois,* 94 US 113. . . .

Many other decisions show that the private character of a business does not
necessarily remove it from the realm of regulation of charges or prices. The usury
laws fix the price which may be exacted for the use of money, although no
business more essentially private in character can be imagined than that of
loaning one's personal funds. . . . Insurance agents' compensation may be regulated, though their contracts are private, because the business of insurance is
considered one properly subject to public control. . . . Statutes prescribing in the
public interest the amounts to be charged by attorneys for prosecuting certain
claims, a matter ordinarily one of personal and private nature, are not a deprivation of due process. . . . A stockyards corporation, "while not a common carrier,
nor engaged in any distinctively public employment, is doing a work in which
the public has an interest," and its charges may be controlled. . . . Private contract
carriers, who do not operate under a franchise, and have no monopoly of the
carriage of goods or passengers, may, since they use the highways to compete
with railroads, be compelled to charge rates not lower than those of public
carriers for corresponding services, if the state, in pursuance of a public policy
to protect the latter, so determines. . . .

It is clear that there is no closed class or category of businesses affected with
a public interest, and the function of courts in the application of the Fifth and
Fourteenth Amendments is to determine in each case whether circumstances
vindicate the challenged regulation as a reasonable exertion of governmental
authority or condemn it as arbitrary or discriminatory. . . . The phrase "affected
with a public interest" can, in the nature of things, mean no more than that an
industry, for adequate reason, is subject to control for the public good. . . .

So far as the requirement of due process is concerned, and in the absence
of other constitutional restriction, a state is free to adopt whatever economic
policy may reasonably be deemed to promote the public welfare, and to enforce
that policy by legislation adapted to its purpose. The courts are without authority either to declare such policy, or, when it is declared by the legislature, to
override it. . . . With the wisdom of the policy adopted, with the adequacy or
practicability of the law enacted to forward it, the courts are both incompetent
and unauthorized to deal. . . .

The law-making bodies have in the past endeavored to promote free competition by laws aimed at trusts and monopolies. The consequent interference with
private property and freedom of contract has not availed with the courts to set
these enactments aside as denying due process. Where the public interest was
deemed to require the fixing of minimum prices, that expedient has been sustained. If the law-making body within its sphere of government concludes that
the conditions or practices in an industry make unrestricted competition an
inadequate safeguard of the consumer's interests, produce waste harmful to the

public, threaten ultimately to cut off the supply of a commodity needed by the public, or portend the destruction of the industry itself, appropriate statutes passed in an honest effort to correct the threatened consequences may not be set aside because the regulation adopted fixes prices reasonably deemed by the legislature to be fair to those engaged in the industry and to the consuming public. And this is especially so where, as here, the economic maladjustment is one of price, which threatens harm to the producer at one end of the series and the consumer at the other. The Constitution does not secure to anyone liberty to conduct his business in such fashion as to inflict injury upon the public at large, or upon any substantial group of the people. Price control, like any other form of regulation, is unconstitutional only if arbitrary, discriminatory, or demonstrably irrelevant to the policy the legislature is free to adopt, and hence an unnecessary and unwarranted interference with individual liberty.

Tested by these considerations we find no basis in the due process clause of the Fourteenth Amendment for condemning the provisions of the Agriculture and Markets Law here drawn into question.

[Judgment for New York]

DISSENTING OPINION BY McREYNOLDS, J.

Is the milk business so affected with public interest that the Legislature may prescribe prices for sales by stores? This Court has approved the contrary view; has emphatically declared that a State lacks power to fix prices in similar private businesses. . . .

Regulation to prevent recognized evils in business has long been upheld as permissible legislative action. But fixation of the price at which "A," engaged in an ordinary business, may sell, in order to enable "B," a producer, to improve his condition, has not been regarded as within legislative power. This is not regulation, but management, control, dictation—it amounts to the deprivation of the fundamental right which one has to conduct his own affairs honestly and along customary lines. The argument advanced here would support general prescription of prices for farm products, groceries, shoes, clothing, all the necessities of modern civilization, as well as labor, when some legislature finds and declares such action advisable and for the public good. This Court has declared that a State may not by legislative fiat convert a private business into a public utility. . . . And if it be now ruled that one dedicates his property to public use whenever he embarks on an enterprise which the Legislature may think is desirable to bring under control, this is but to declare that rights guaranteed by the Constitution exist only so long as supposed public interest does not require their extinction. To adopt such a view, of course, would put an end to liberty under the Constitution. . . .

Not only does the statute interfere arbitrarily with the rights of the little grocer to conduct his business according to standards long accepted—complete destruction may follow; but it takes away the liberty of 12 million consumers to buy a necessity of life in an open market. It imposes direct and arbitrary burdens upon those already seriously impoverished with the alleged immediate design of affording special benefits to others. To him with less than 9 cents it says—You cannot procure a quart of milk from the grocer although he is anxious to accept what you can pay and the demands of your household are urgent! A superabundance; but no child can purchase from a willing storekeeper below the figure appointed by three men at headquarters! And this is true although the storekeeper himself may have bought from a willing producer at half that rate and must sell quickly or lose his stock through deterioration. The fanciful scheme is to protect the farmer against undue exactions by prescribing the price at which milk disposed of by him at will may be resold! . . .

(b) Appraisal of the Nebbia doctrine

It should also be noted that the Supreme Court which decided the *Nebbia* case in 1934 was not the New Deal Court, nor even the old Court subjected to the influence of the New Deal controversy. It was the same strict constructionist Court that, in *Hammer v Dagenhart*, § 8:5(a), had limited the power of Congress over commerce and, in *Adkins v Children's Hospital*, § 4:6, had exalted freedom of contract by invalidating a minimum wage law for women. It was the Court that, in the two years after the *Nebbia* case, was to declare unconstitutional many of the federal New Deal laws and was not to show any leaning toward the new "federalism" until three years later in the *Jones & Laughlin Steel Corporation* case.

This is particularly significant because it indicates that the trend seen in the *Nebbia* case cannot be regarded as a swing of the pendulum to the "left," but as a new basic doctrine that is established in our constitutional law. The exact meaning of this doctrine cannot be determined because it is difficult to deny the argument of the dissent that the broad definition of "affected with a public interest" brings within the regulatory power virtually all modern business enterprise. It is difficult to see in what respect farming, steel production, mining, and the other great basic industries that supply our modern economic system are not to be deemed affected with a public interest. In truth, it would appear that the *Nebbia* case, in attempting to define "affected with a public interest" in a manner sufficiently broad to sustain price regulation, destroyed that concept. In *Olsen v Nebraska*, 313 US 236 (1941), the Court later refers to the concept of "affected with a public interest" as "discarded in *Nebbia v New York*." In *Cities Service Gas Co. v Peerless Oil & Gas Co.*, 340 US 179 (1950), the Court sustained the state fixing of minimum prices for natural gas at the wellhead without invoking expressly any concept of "affected with a public interest." The Court simply commented that "like any other regulation, a price fixing order is lawful if substantially related to a legitimate end sought to be attained," and cited the *Nebbia* case. The doctrine of the *Nebbia* case has been, in effect, carried forward by the decisions sustaining the federal regulation of the selling price of interstate milk and coal.

While the *Nebbia* case sustained state price regulation, the rising federal power of price regulation may be exercised so as to restrict the area of operation of state law. While a state may require a distributor to pay a local producer a minimum price, it cannot constitutionally regulate the price that the distributor pays to a producer in another state, even though the goods are resold locally. This confines state regulation of resale price to goods purchased by the seller within the state. If Congress desires, it can exclude the state from even this area of regulation in order to remove differentials between the price that the federal government has set on such commodities in interstate commerce and the price that the state has set in local sales. In addition to price regulation as discussed above, legislation is valid which regulates price in the negative sense of prohibiting sales below cost, or at a low price, for the purpose of harming competitors.[1]

§ 15:4. FEDERAL REGULATION UNDER THE COMMERCE POWER

Under the commerce power, the national Congress has created the Interstate Commerce Commission, which among other things regulates the rates that may be charged by interstate carriers. As such carriers have a natural monopoly because of the capital investment required and have a legal monopoly by virtue of their government franchise, the courts find little difficulty in sustaining the legality of regulating the rates charged by them. Here, the object of the rate or price regulation is to prevent the customers or the public from being charged exorbitant prices. Government interference is justified on the ground that, because of the natural and legal monopoly factors, the natural forces of supply and demand do not adjust the rates to a proper level.

On a somewhat similar basis, a federal regulation of the charges made by commission brokers at the great cattle exchanges was sustained. At these exchanges, cattle brought from one state would be held over long enough to be sold, after which they were shipped to other states for ultimate slaughter, packing, and final sale to the public. It was found that at such an exchange, which, in the words of the Court, was as a throat through which flowed interstate commerce, a number of evil practices had arisen, including exorbitant charges by brokers for their services in connection with the sale and temporary holdover of the cattle. In order to protect the flow of interstate commerce from this danger, Congress was held to have the authority under the commerce power to regulate such commissions. Similar federal control has been sustained over the grain exchanges.

The most significant extension of this power to regulate prices of services or labor under the commerce power is found in the establishment of minimum wages by the Federal Fair Labor Standards Act. This ability of Congress to reach beyond the facilities of interstate transportation into the local areas of production is sustained under the new interpretation of the commerce clause.

Under the commerce power, Congress can regulate the price of commodities that are sold in interstate transactions or that move through interstate commerce channels. This power has been sustained with respect to the regulation of the

---

[1] § 13:6.

price of milk and of coal. Congress also has authorized the Federal Power Commission to fix the rates for interstate transmission and transfer of electricity and natural gas.

The power to regulate the prices of interstate commodities is held to include the power to regulate the prices of local goods that compete with the goods which have moved through interstate commerce. Thus the power to regulate the price of interstate milk gives Congress the power to regulate the price of milk produced and sold in the state of its production, where that local milk competes in the local markets with the interstate milk. Stated differently, if an article commonly moves in interstate commerce, Congress may regulate the sale price of that commodity throughout the country, without regard to whether the particular unit of the commodity being sold has itself been in interstate commerce or not.

(a) Interstate commerce

UNITED STATES v ROCK ROYAL COOPERATIVE, INC.

307 US 533 (1939)

The Agricultural Marketing Agreement Act of 1937 authorizes the Secretary of Agriculture to designate milk marketing areas and to prescribe minimum prices to be paid to producers within that area.

OPINION BY REED, J.

These appeals involve the validity of Order No. 27 of the Secretary of Agriculture, issued under the Agricultural Marketing Agreement Act of 1937, . . . regulating the handling of milk in the New York metropolitan area. . . .

. . . The challenge is to the regulation "of the price to be paid upon the sale by a dairy farmer who delivers his milk to some country plant." It is urged that the sale, a local transaction, is fully completed before any interstate commerce begins and that the attempt to fix the price or other elements of that incident violates the Tenth Amendment. But where commodities are bought for use beyond state lines, the sale is a part of interstate commerce. We have likewise held that where sales for interstate transportation were commingled with intrastate transactions, the existence of the local activity did not interfere with the federal power to regulate inspection of the whole. Activities conducted within state lines do not by this fact alone escape the sweep of the Commerce Clause. Interstate commerce may be dependent upon them. Power to establish quotas for interstate marketing gives power to name quotas for that which is to be left within the state of production. Where local and foreign milk alike are drawn into a general plan for protecting the interstate commerce in the commodity from the interferences, burdens and obstructions, arising from excessive surplus and the social and sanitary evils of low values, the power of the Congress extends also to the local sales.

This power over commerce when it exists is complete and perfect. It has been exercised to fix a wage scale for a limited period, railroad tariffs and fees and charges for live-stock exchanges. . . .

[Judgment for United States, sustaining federal price regulation]

(b) Local goods

UNITED STATES v WRIGHTWOOD DAIRY CO.

315 US 110 (1942)

Acting under the Agricultural Marketing Agreement Act of 1937, the Secretary of Agriculture defined a Chicago milk sale area and established a minimum price to be paid producers. Application of the price-fixing regulations to milk produced, sold, and purchased within the state was challenged on the ground that only the sales price of commodities moving in interstate commerce could be regulated.

OPINION BY STONE, J.

. . . Competitive practices which are wholly intrastate may be reached by the Sherman Act . . . because of their injurious effect on the interstate commerce. . . . So too the marketing of a local product in competition with that of a like commodity moving interstate may so interfere with interstate commerce or its regulation as to afford a basis for Congressional regulation of the intrastate activity. It is the effect upon the interstate commerce or its regulation, regardless of the particular form which the competition may take, which is the test of the federal power. . . .

. . . The marketing of intrastate milk which competes with that shipped interstate will tend seriously to break down price regulation of the latter. . . .

It is no answer to suggest . . . that the federal power to regulate intrastate transactions is limited to those who are engaged also in interstate commerce. . . . It is the effect upon interstate commerce or upon the exercise of the power to regulate it, not the source of the injury, which is the criterion of Congressional power. . . .

We conclude that the national power to regulate the price of milk moving interstate into the Chicago, Illinois, marketing area, extends to such control of intrastate transactions there as is necessary and appropriate to make regulation of the interstate commerce effective; and that it includes authority to make like regulations for the marketing of intrastate milk whose sale and competition with the interstate milk affects its price structure so as in turn to affect adversely the Congressional regulation.

[Judgment for United States, sustaining federal price regulation as to local goods competing with interstate goods]

§ 15:5. FEDERAL REGULATION UNDER THE WAR POWER

The war power confers upon Congress the power to fix any and all prices, including wages and rents. This not only may be done during the actual period of hostilities but may be made effective during the prior preparatory period. The power to fix the prices does not end with the cessation of hostilities but continues thereafter for a reasonable period until the economic dislocation caused by the war has been corrected.

It must appear that either preparation for, prosecution of, or recovery from war underlies the regulation. In a truly normal time, this power could not be exercised. Here a difficult question arises in view of the fact that modern war is such a total war, enlisting not only all manpower but also all commodities. It therefore becomes difficult to say that a regulation, which if effective would place an industry on a sound basis and enable the government to be sure of a source of supply, is not in a sense a proper preparation for war. In sustaining the TVA, the Supreme Court has already recognized that a law may be valid as a preparation for war, even though at the time there is no reason to suspect that there will be a particular war. The right to prepare for war includes the right to be generally prepared in the event that a war does arise.

In regulating prices under the war power, greater latitude would probably be permitted the Congress than under the commerce power. While it would be necessary to establish some link between the regulation and war, it would not be necessary to show that the regulated article or service was in interstate commerce or competed with goods or services in interstate commerce. As under the commerce power, it would not be necessary to adopt a regulation applicable throughout the United States. As illustrating the latter point, the National Rent Control Act was held constitutional, even though it applied only to restricted areas and not to the entire nation.

Questions for Discussion

1. Would a statute of the type involved in *Munn v Illinois* violate the equal protection clause by exempting areas having less than 100,000 population?

2. Can the decision in *Munn v Illinois* be justified without invoking the social compact theory of government?

3. How does the *Nebbia* decision compare with *Munn v Illinois?*

4. Congress adopts a law fixing the price for the sale of potatoes throughout the United States. Is this law constitutional? Explain.

5. (a) Would it make any difference to your answer to Question 4 if Congress established a national potato administrator and gave the administrator authority to divide the country into potato-marketing zones and to fix the price in each zone?   (b) Would it make any difference if the administrator established a different price for each zone?

6. Does the *Nebbia* case redefine the phrase "affected with a public interest" or does it hold that, in determining the validity of price regulation, it is no longer necessary to determine whether the enterprise is "affected with a public interest"?

7. Was the *Nebbia* decision made before or after the broadened interpretation of the commerce and the due process clauses of the Constitution?

8. (a) When is property affected with a public interest under the principles of *Munn v Illinois?*   (b) Can you answer the objection of the dissenting opinion to the definition given by the majority to "business affected with a public interest"?

9. (a) A proposal is made in Congress to fix all food prices at the 1914 level to enable the community to purchase necessary foods. Would this law be constitutional?   (b) Assume that it is also proposed as part of this plan to give all food producers a government subsidy equal to the difference between the current price of food and the 1914 prices. Would this law be constitutional? If constitutional, what social or political effects might result?

10. Congress adopts a law fixing the price of bread at a higher price than would otherwise be obtained in the open market. The sellers of food claim that the law is unconstitutional because it selects a particular commodity and does not regulate prices generally. Is the law constitutional?

11. How does the Court define "due process" in the *Nebbia* case?

12. Assume that a law of Congress establishes a price for the sale of sugar. Is the law unconstitutional if it does not yield a fair return to the sugar producer or manufacturer? Is the law unconstitutional as to the purchasing public if the return to the producers or manufacturers is more than a fair return?

13. If the Sherman antitrust law had been in effect in 1876, could the problem faced in *Munn v Illinois* have been met by compelling the grain elevator operators to cease their practice of fixing prices by agreement?

14. (a) Compare the dissenting opinion in *Munn v Illinois* with the majority opinion in *Nebbia v New York.*   (b) Compare the majority opinion in *Munn v Illinois* with the dissenting opinion in *Nebbia v New York.*

15. (a) Did the regulation in the *Nebbia* case violate the equal protection clause because it established a different price for a sale by a distributor than by a store?   (b) How great was the difference between the prices allowed each of these two types of sellers?   (c) How would it affect your answer if the difference had been ten times as great as it was?

16. Congress passes a law fixing commodity prices at such a level that the producers will obtain a 20 percent profit. The statute recites in its preamble that Congress adopts such a law because it believes that the best insurance against future depression is to enable producers to set aside a surplus fund. A citizens' committee brings a suit to have the law declared unconstitutional. They point out that the return allowed the producers is several times greater than the legal rate of interest and more than could be obtained by making investments in the security market. Is the law constitutional?

17. A state legislature decides that excessive rates are being charged by insurance companies. It adopts a law prescribing a schedule of premiums that may be charged by insurance companies and making it a crime to charge greater amounts. The *X* Insurance Company charges higher premiums than allowed by the statute. The company is prosecuted under the statute and defends by claiming that the statute is unconstitutional. Is the company correct? [*German Alliance Insurance Co. v Lewis,* 233 US 389 (1914)]

18. The Pennsylvania legislature authorized the Utility Commission to issue temporary rate orders, pending the final decision of fair value and reasonable rates. The statute further provided that if the final rate allowed was in excess of that permitted by the temporary order, the utility would be allowed an additional increase to make up the difference. Is the Act constitutional? [*Driscoll v Edison Light and Power Co.,* 307 US 104 (1939)]

19. What conflicting interests are involved in the *Nebbia* type of statute? Is the same class benefited by the statute of the *Nebbia* case as in *Munn v Illinois?*

20. The Transportation Act of 1920 directed the Interstate Commerce Commission to fix such rates for carriers as would permit them to earn "an aggregate annual net railway operating income equal, as nearly as may be, to a fair return upon the aggregate value of the property of such carriers held for and used in the service of transportation" and that in arriving at a fair value the Commission should consider "all the elements of value recognized by the law of the land for rate-making purposes."

The Transportation Act of 1933 provided that "in the exercise of its power to prescribe just and reasonable rates the Commission shall give due consideration, among other factors, to the effect of rates on the movement of traffic; to the need, in the public interest, of adequate and efficient railway transportation service at the lowest cost consistent with the furnishing of such service; and to the need of revenues sufficient to enable the carriers, under earnest, economic, and efficient management, to provide such service."   (a) What is the difference between these two provisions?   (b) Why was the change made?   (c) Which standard do you prefer?

16

The Financial Powers

§ 16:1. THE TAXING POWER

The Federal Constitution provides that "Congress shall have Power To lay and collect Taxes, Duties, Imposts and Excises, to pay the Debts and provide for the common Defense and general Welfare of the United States:" . . . [Art. I, § 8, Cl. 1] Subject to the express and implied limitations arising from the Constitution, the states may impose such taxes as they desire and as their own individual constitutions permit. The extent to which political subdivisions may tax is determined by the constitution and the statutes of each state, subject to the limitations arising from the federal Constitution. In addition to express constitutional limitations, both national and local taxes are subject to the unwritten limitation that they be imposed for a public purpose.

The federal government is subject to certain limitations on the form of the taxes imposed by it. Capitation or poll taxes and all direct taxes must be apportioned among the states according to the census-determined population. [Art. I, § 9, Cl. 4] Today, direct taxes include taxes on real estate or personal property and taxes imposed on persons because of their ownership of property. Income taxes, to the extent that they tax the income from property, are direct, although by virtue of the Sixteenth Amendment their apportionment is no longer required.

All other taxes imposed by the federal government are regarded as indirect taxes. These include customs duties, taxes on consumption (such as gasoline and cigarette taxes), taxes on the exercise of a privilege (such as an amusement tax), taxes on the transmission of property upon death (such as estate or inheritance taxes), taxes upon the privilege of making a gift (such as gift taxes), or taxes upon the privilege of employing workers (such as the federal employer's social security tax). In the case of a federal tax upon the exercise of a privilege, it is immaterial whether the privilege arises by virtue of a state or a federal law.

The only restriction upon the form of indirect federal taxes is that they be uniform throughout the continental United States and the incorporated territories. This requirement of uniformity does not prohibit a progressively graduated tax, by which the greater the monetary value of the tax base, the greater the rate of tax. The requirement of uniformity also is not violated by a provision allowing credits against the federal tax for taxes paid to a state, even though the amount of the federal tax paid will vary from state to state, depending upon the existence of a state tax for which credit is allowable.

Congress is also prohibited from imposing taxes on goods exported from any state for shipment to a foreign country or on the bills of lading, insurance policies, or charter parties executed for such shipment. Further, Congress may not give preference by any tax law to the ports of one state over those of another and may not require vessels bound to or from one state to enter, clear, or pay taxes in another. [Art. I, § 9]

The taxing power of the states and the political subdivisions is generally subject to the limitations contained in state constitutions or statutes. In addition, each state is prohibited from levying

"without the Consent of the Congress, . . . any Imposts or Duties on Imports or Exports, except what may be absolutely necessary for executing its inspection Laws: and the net Produce of all Duties and Imposts, laid by any State on Imports or Exports, shall be for the Use of the Treasury of the United States; and all such Laws shall be subject to the Revision and the Control of the Congress. [Art. I, § 10, Cl. 2]

(a) Federal Social Security Act

STEWARD MACHINE CO. v DAVIS

301 US 548 (1937)

The Federal Social Security Act of 1935 provided for the payment of unemployment compensation from a fund created in part by the taxation of the employers. The tax was challenged as unconstitutional by the Steward Machine Company.

OPINION BY CARDOZO, J.

. . . The tax, which is described in the statute as an excise, is laid with uniformity throughout the United States as a duty, an impost or an excise upon the relation of employment.

1. We are told that the relation of employment is one so essential to the pursuit of happiness that it may not be burdened with a tax. Appeal is made to history. From the precedents of colonial days we are supplied with illustrations of excises common in the colonies. They are said to have been bound up with the enjoyment of particular commodities. Appeal is also made to principle or the analysis of concepts. An excise, we are told, imports a tax upon a privilege; employment, it is said, is a right, not a privilege, from which it follows that employment is not subject to an excise. Neither the one appeal nor the other leads to the desired goal.

As to the argument from history: Doubtless there were many excises in colonial days and later that were associated, more or less intimately, with the enjoyment or the use of property. . . . But in truth other excises were known, and known since early times. Thus in 1695 (6 & 7 Wm. III. c. 6), Parliament passed an act which granted "to His Majesty certain Rates and Duties upon Marriage, Births and Burials," all for the purpose of "carrying on the War against France with Vigour." . . . In 1777, before our Constitutional Convention, Parliament laid upon employers an annual "duty" of 21 shillings for "every male Servant" employed in stated forms of work. Revenue Act of 1777, 17 George III. c. 39. . . . A statute of Virginia passed in 1780 [imposed] . . . a tax of three pounds, six shillings and eight pence to be paid for every male tithable above the age of twenty-one years (with stated exceptions), and a like tax for "every white servant whatsoever, except apprentices under the age of twenty-one years." 10 Hening's Statutes of Virginia, p. 244. Our colonial forbears knew more about ways of taxing than some of their descendants seem to be willing to concede.

The historical prop failing, the prop or fancied prop of principle remains. We learn that employment for lawful gain is a "natural" or "inherent" or "inalienable" right, and not a "privilege" at all. But natural rights, so called, are as much subject to taxation as rights of less importance. An excise is not limited to vocations or activities that may be prohibited altogether. It is not limited to those that are the outcome of a franchise. It extends to vocations or activities pursued as of common right. What the individual does in the operation of a business is amenable to taxation just as much as what he owns, at all events if the classification is not tyrannical or arbitrary. . . . Indeed, ownership itself . . . is only a bundle of rights and privileges invested with a single name. . . . "A state is at liberty, if it pleases, to tax them all collectively, or to separate the faggots and lay the charge distributively." . . . Employment is a business relation, if not itself a business. It is a relation without which business could seldom be carried on effectively. The power to tax the activities and relations that constitute a calling considered as a unit is the power to tax any of them. The whole includes the parts. . . .

[Judgment against the Steward Machine Company, holding the statute constitutional]

(b) State enterprises

NEW YORK v UNITED STATES
326 US 572 (1946)

OPINION BY FRANKFURTER, J.

. . . The United States brought this suit to recover taxes assessed against the State of New York on the sale of mineral waters taken from Saratoga Springs, New York. The State claims immunity from this tax on the ground that "in the bottling and sale of the said waters the defendant State of New York was engaged in the exercise of a usual, traditional and essential governmental function." . . .

. . . The fear that one government may cripple or obstruct the operations of the other early led to the assumption that there was a reciprocal immunity of the instrumentalities of each from taxation by the other. It was assumed that there was an equivalence in the implications of taxation by a State of the governmental activities of the National Government and the taxation by the National Government of State instrumentalities. This assumed equivalence was nourished by the phrase of Chief Justice Marshall that "the power to tax involves the power to destroy." *McCulloch v Maryland,* . . . To be sure, it was uttered in connection with a tax of Maryland which plainly discriminated against the use by the United States of the Bank of the United States as one of its instruments. What he said may not have been irrelevant in its setting. But Chief Justice Marshall spoke at a time when social complexities did not so clearly reveal as now the practical limitations of a rhetorical absolute. . . . The phrase was seized upon as the basis of a broad doctrine of intergovernmental immunity, while at the same time an expansive scope was given to what were deemed to be "instrumentalities of the government" for purposes of tax immunity. As a result, immunity was until recently accorded to all officers of one government from taxation by the other, and it was further assumed that the economic burden of a tax on any interest derived from a government imposes a burden on that government so as to involve an interference by the taxing government with the functioning of the other government. . . .

In the meantime, cases came here, as we have already noted, in which States claimed immunity from a federal tax imposed generally on enterprises in which the State itself was also engaged. This problem did not arise before the present century, partly because State trading did not actively emerge until relatively recently, and partly because of the narrow scope of federal taxation. . . . Immunity from a federal tax on a dispensary system, whereby South Carolina monopolized the sale of intoxicating liquors, was denied by drawing a line between taxation of the historically recognized governmental functions of a State, and business engaged in by a State of a kind which theretofore had been pursued by private enterprise. . . . That there is a Constitutional line between the State as government and the State as trader, was still more recently made the basis of a decision sustaining a liquor tax against Ohio. "If a state chooses to go into the business of buying and selling commodities, its right to do so may be conceded so far as the Federal Constitution is concerned; but the exercise of the right is not the performance of a governmental function. . . . When a state enters the market place seeking customers it divests itself of its quasi sovereignty pro tanto, and takes on the character of a trader, so far, at least, as the taxing power of the federal government is concerned." . . .

When this Court came to sustain the federal taxing power upon a transportation system operated by a State, it . . . edged away from reliance on a sharp distinction between the "governmental" and the "trading" activities of a State, by denying immunity from federal taxation to a State when it "is undertaking a business enterprise of a sort that is normally within the reach of the federal taxing power and is distinct from the usual governmental functions that are immune from federal taxation in order to safeguard the necessary independence of the state." . . . But this likewise does not furnish a satisfactory guide for dealing with such a practical problem as the constitutional power of the United States over State activities. To rest the federal taxing power on what is "normally" conducted by private enterprise in contradiction to the "usual" governmental functions is too shifting a basis for determining constitutional power and too entangled in expediency to serve as a dependable legal criterion. The essential nature of the problem cannot be hidden by an attempt to separate manifestations of indivisible governmental powers. . . .

In the older cases, the emphasis was on immunity from taxation. The whole tendency of recent cases reveals a shift in emphasis to that of limitation upon immunity. They also indicate an awareness of the limited role of courts in assessing the relative weight of the factors upon which immunity is based. Any implied limitation upon the supremacy of the federal power to levy a tax like that now before us, in the absence of discrimination against State activities, brings fiscal and political factors into play. The problem cannot escape issues that do not lend themselves to judgment by criteria and methods of reasoning that are within the professional training and special competence of judges. Indeed the claim of implied immunity by States from federal taxation raises questions not wholly unlike provisions of the Constitution, such as that of Art. IV, § 4, guaranteeing States a republican form of government, . . . which this Court has deemed not within its duty to adjudicate.

We have already held that by engaging in the railroad business a State cannot withdraw the railroad from the power of the federal government to regulate commerce. . . . Surely the power of Congress to lay taxes has impliedly no less a reach than the power of Congress to regulate commerce. There are, of course, State activities and State-owned property that partake of uniqueness from the point of view of intergovernmental relations. These inherently constitute a class by themselves. Only a State can own a Statehouse; only a State can get income by taxing. These could not be included for purposes of federal taxation in any abstract category of taxpayers without taxing the State as a State. But so long as Congress generally taps a source of revenue by whomsoever earned and not uniquely capable of being earned only by a State, the Constitution of the United States does not forbid it merely because its incidence falls also on a State. If Congress desires, it may of course leave untaxed enterprises pursued by States for the public good while it taxes like enterprises organized for private ends. . . .

The process of Constitutional adjudication does not thrive on conjuring up horrible possibilities that never happen in the real world and devising doctrines sufficiently comprehensive in detail to cover the remotest contingency. . . . We reject limitations upon the taxing power of Congress derived from such untenable criteria as "proprietary," against "governmental" activities of the States, or historically sanctioned activities of government or activities conducted merely for profit, and find no restriction upon Congress to include the States in levying a tax exacted equally from private persons upon the same subject matter.

[Judgment for United States, rejecting state claim of immunity from federal taxation]

---

§ 16:2. REGULATORY TAXATION

Apart from constitutional provision, a tax may be adopted either for the purpose of raising revenue or as a method of regulating or prohibiting the sale of a particular article or the doing of certain acts, or a combination of both purposes. Will the court examine the tax law to determine whether it is a regulatory law? Will the constitutionality of the tax be affected if the court concludes that its purpose is regulation?

If the object of the tax is a regulation that could be imposed by the government directly as a regulation, it is immaterial whether the court would make such inquiry, for it will conclude that, since the power existed to regulate, a tax could be used as the means of enforcing the regulation. If the purpose of the tax statute is merely to enforce a regulation that cannot be made openly as such, the tax may be held unconstitutional. This limitation on the tax power is less significant today in view of the fact that, if a state law is concerned, the state through its police power has a wide ability to impose regulations, and that, if a national law is concerned, the broadened interpretation of the commerce clause will probably give the national government power to make the regulation in question if it chooses to do so.

In a number of instances the Supreme Court has refused to consider the ulterior regulatory purpose of tax laws, even though such purpose was readily apparent. Thus the Supreme Court sustained a 10 percent tax on state bank notes imposed for the purpose of driving them out of existence; a tax of 10 cents a pound on margarine colored to resemble butter;[1] and a $200 annual license fee on vendors of firearms, with an additional $200 tax on the sale of each machine

---

[1] *A. Magnano Co. v Hamilton,* 292 US 40 (1934).

gun, sawed-off shotgun, and silencer.[2] The federal tariff is held valid in spite of its prohibitive effect.

In contrast, however, the Supreme Court has held unconstitutional a federal law attempting to end child labor by imposing a tax on the profits of employers employing child labor,[3] a law imposing a $1,000 annual tax on persons selling liquor in violation of a state prohibition law, and a tax on the processors of farm products levied to raise a fund to pay farmers to reduce their production.[4]

With the subsequent expansion of the commerce power,[5] the problem considered here of whether a hidden motive of regulation will invalidate a tax law has become academic. Today the Congress can directly impose regulations on local activities affecting the economic welfare of the nation, and it has the choice of imposing such regulation in the form of a direct regulation, or in the indirect form of a tax or penalty upon those not conforming to the federal statute.

(a) Federal Narcotics Act

In *United States* v *Doremus,* the Supreme Court was confronted with a federal law imposing a license tax on persons selling narcotics. The obvious purpose of the law was to obtain federal control of the illicit drug traffic. Such trade could not be directly prohibited by Congress. The annual tax, or license fee, of each vendor was, for many years, $1, although later this was increased to $25. The validity of the statute was brought before the Supreme Court when the tax was only $1 and the gross proceeds of the tax were much less than the cost of its administration.

UNITED STATES v DOREMUS

249 US 86 (1919)

OPINION BY DAY, J.

. . . From an early day the court has held that the fact that other motives may impel the exercise of federal taxing power does not authorize the courts to inquire into that subject. If the legislation enacted has some reasonable relation to the exercise of the taxing authority conferred by the Constitution, it cannot be invalidated because of the supposed motives which induced it. . . .

Nor is it sufficient to invalidate the taxing authority given to the Congress by the Constitution that the same business may be regulated by the police power of the State. . . .

The act may not be declared unconstitutional because its effect may be to accomplish another purpose as well as the raising of revenue. If the legislation

---

[2]*Sonzinsky v United States,* 300 US 506 (1937).
[3]*Bailey v Drexel Furniture Co.,* 259 US 20 (1922).
[4]*United States v Butler,* 297 US 1 (1936).
[5]See § 8:1, 3.

is within the taxing authority of Congress—that is sufficient to sustain it.
. . .

. . . Considering the full power of Congress over excise taxation the decisive question here is: Have the provisions in question any relation to the
raising of revenue? That Congress might levy an excise tax upon such dealers . . . cannot be successfully disputed. The provisions of Sec. 2, to which
we have referred, aim to confine sales to registered dealers and to those dis-
pensing the drugs as physicians, and to those who come to dealers with legitimate prescriptions of physicians. Congress, with full power over the subject, short of arbitrary and unreasonable action which is not to be assumed,
inserted these provisions in an act specifically providing for the raising of
revenue. Considered of themselves, we think they tend to keep the traffic
aboveboard and subject to inspection by those authorized to collect the revenue. They tend to diminish the opportunity of unauthorized persons to obtain the drugs and sell them clandestinely without paying the tax imposed
by the federal law. . . .

We cannot agree with the contention that the provisions of Sec. 2, controlling the disposition of these drugs in the ways described, can have nothing to
do with facilitating the collection of revenue, as we should be obliged to do if
we were to declare this act beyond the power of Congress to impose excise taxes.
. . .

[Judgment for United States, holding federal tax law constitutional]

---

§ 16:3. THE BORROWING POWER

Congress is authorized "to borrow Money on the credit of the United
States." [Art. I, § 8, Cl. 2] No limitation is prescribed to the purposes for which
the United States can borrow.

Obligations of the United States issued to those lending money to the
United States are binding, and the Congress cannot attempt to repudiate
them or to make them repayable in a less valuable currency than called for
by the obligations without violating the legal rights of the holders. Accordingly, it is unconstitutional for Congress to provide that the holders of
United States bonds that specify repayment in gold should be paid in dollars
having a smaller gold content than the amount of gold specified in the
bonds.

The states have an inherent power to borrow money as an incident of the
police power. State constitutions and statutes may impose a limit on the amount
that can be borrowed. Frequently, these limitations are evaded by the creation
of independent authorities or districts which borrow money by issuing bonds.
The bonded indebtedness of such independent authorities and districts is not
regarded as a debt of the state and therefore is not subject to the limitations
applicable to state borrowing.

(a) Devaluation of federal gold bonds

PERRY v UNITED STATES

294 US 330 (1935)

The holder of four $10,000 United States liberty bonds brought suit against the United States in the Court of Claims. The bonds provided that "the principal and interest hereof are payable in United States gold coin of the present standard of value." When the bonds were issued and purchased by the plaintiff, a dollar was valued in gold at 25.8 grains .9 fine. When the bonds were presented for redemption, the gold content of the dollar had been reduced to 15⁵/₂₁ grains of gold .9 fine. The United States refused to redeem the bonds in gold coin and offered to pay $10,000 in legal tender, which was paper currency based on the reduced gold content. The bondholder brought suit to be paid an amount of the devaluated paper currency that would have the same total gold content as $10,000 of paper currency having the former gold content.

OPINION BY HUGHES, C. J.

. . . The Joint Resolution of June 5, 1933 . . . declared that provisions requiring "payment in gold or a particular kind of coin or currency" were "against public policy," and provided that "every obligation, heretofore or hereafter incurred . . . shall be discharged "upon payment, dollar for dollar, in any coin or currency which at the time of payment is legal tender for public and private debts." This enactment was expressly extended to obligations of the United States, and provisions for payment in gold, "contained in any law authorizing obligations to be issued by or under authority of the United States," were repealed.

There is no question as to the power of Congress to regulate the value of money, that is, to establish a monetary system and thus to determine the currency of the country. The question is whether the Congress can use that power so as to invalidate the terms of the obligations which the Government has theretofore issued in the exercise of the power to borrow money on the credit of the United States. In attempted justification of the Joint Resolution in relation to the outstanding bonds of the United States, the Government argues that "earlier Congresses could not validly restrict the 73rd Congress from exercising its constitutional powers to regulate the value of money, borrow money, regulate foreign and interstate commerce"; and, from this premise, the Government seems to deduce the proposition that when, with adequate authority, the Government borrows money and pledges the credit of the United States, it is free to ignore that pledge and alter the terms of its obligations in case a later Congress finds their fulfillment inconvenient. The Government's contention thus raises a question of far greater importance than the particular claim of the plaintiff. On that reasoning, if the terms of the Government's bond as to the standard of payment can be repudiated, it inevitably follows that the obligation as to the amount to be paid may also be repudiated. The contention necessarily imports that the Congress can disregard the obligations of the Government at its discretion and that, when the Government borrows money, the credit of the United States is an illusory pledge.

We do not so read the Constitution. . . . To say that the Congress may withdraw or ignore that pledge, is to assume that the Constitution contemplates a vain promise, a pledge having no other sanction than the pleasure and convenience of the pledgor. This Court has given no sanction to such a conception of the obligations of our Government. . . .

The argument in favor of the Joint Resolution, as applied to government bonds, is in substance that the Government cannot by contract restrict the exercise of a sovereign power. But the right to make binding obligations is a competence attaching to sovereignty. In the United States, sovereignty resides in the people, who act through the organs established by the Constitution. . . . The Congress as the instrumentality of sovereignty is endowed with certain powers to be exerted on behalf of the people in the manner and with the effect the Constitution ordains. The Congress cannot invoke the sovereign power of the people to override their will as thus declared. The powers conferred upon the Congress are harmonious. The Constitution gives to the Congress the power to borrow money on the credit of the United States, an unqualified power, a power vital to the Government,—upon which in an extremity its very life may depend. The binding quality of the promise of the United States is of the essence of the credit which is so pledged. . . . The fact that the United States may not be sued without its consent is a matter of procedure which does not affect the legal and binding character of its contracts. While the Congress is under no duty to provide remedies through the courts, the contractual obligation still exists and, despite infirmities of procedure, remains binding upon the conscience of the sovereign.

. . . The action is for breach of contract. As a remedy for breach, plaintiff can recover no more than the loss he has suffered and of which he may rightfully complain. He is not entitled to be enriched.

. . . Plaintiff has not shown or attempted to show, that in relation to buying power he has sustained any loss whatever. . . .

[Judgment for United States because plaintiff did not prove what loss had been sustained]

§ 16:4. SPENDING POWER

The federal government may use tax money and borrowed money "to pay the Debts and provide for the common Defense and general Welfare of the United States." . . . [Article 1, § 8, Cl. 1] From the earliest days of the Constitution, there was disagreement over whether there was any limitation on the power of the United States to spend the money which it raised by taxation or borrowing. Madison claimed that the money of the United States could only be spent on a subject which could be directly regulated or legislated upon by

Congress. Hamilton claimed that, as long as the money was spent for a public purpose rather than a private purpose, it was immaterial whether the Congress could legislate directly upon the object for which the money was spent.

This controversy came to the fore when the federal government embarked upon a program of granting subsidies to the states. This plan was attacked as a method of bribing the states to do for the national government that which the national government could not legally, under the Constitution, do itself or require the states to do. At first the subsidy plan was sustained by the Supreme Court on the technical ground that no one could show any legal injury and therefore had no standing to sue. The Court, in *United States v Butler,* [6] although then invalidating the law under consideration, approved the broader Hamiltonian view of the spending power that it finally adopted in the social security cases.

It must be remembered that the matter soon became academic, for the Supreme Court shortly interpreted the commerce power as authorizing the Congress to regulate anything required by the general welfare of the nation. When this conclusion had been reached, it was immaterial whether the Hamiltonian view had been adopted, for Congress under its commerce power could regulate anything and therefore, even under the Madisonian view, could have spent money for anything.

(a) Federal Social Security Act

HELVERING v DAVIS

301 US 619 (1937)

The Federal Social Security Act of 1935 imposed a tax on both employer and employee to create a fund for the payment of old-age benefits to employees. The constitutionality of these provisions was challenged.

OPINION BY CARDOZO, J.

The Social Security Act . . . is challenged once again . . .

Congress may spend money in aid of the "general welfare" . . . The conception of the spending power advocated by Hamilton and strongly reinforced by Story has prevailed over that of Madison. . . . Yet difficulties are left when the power is conceded. The line must still be drawn between one welfare and another, between particular and general. Where it shall be placed cannot be known through a formula in advance of the event. There is a middle ground or certainly a penumbra in which discretion is at large. The discretion, however, is not confided to the courts. The discretion belongs to Congress, unless the choice is clearly wrong, a display of arbitrary power, not an exercise of judgment. This is now familiar law. "When such a contention comes here we natu-

---

[6] 297 US 1 (1936).

rally require a showing that by no reasonable possibility can the challenged legislation fall within the wide range of discretion permitted to Congress." . . . Nor is the concept of the general welfare static. Needs that were narrow or parochial a century ago may be interwoven in our day with the well-being of the nation. What is critical or urgent changes with the time.

The purge of nation-wide calamity that began in 1929 has taught us many lessons. Not the least is the solidarity of interests that may once have seemed to be divided. Unemployment spreads from state to state. . . . Spreading from state to state, unemployment is an ill not particular but general, which may be checked, if Congress so determines, by the resources of the nation. . . . The ill is all one, or at least not greatly different, whether men are thrown out of work because there is no longer work to do or because the disabilities of age make them incapable of doing it. . . .

Congress did not improvise a judgment when it found that the award of old-age benefits would be conducive to the general welfare. . . . [The court then discussed the extensive committee hearings and reports that preceded the adoption of the Social Security Act and on which it was based. The court also emphasized the conclusion of both national and state investigations that the number of persons over 65 is increasing proportionately as well as absolutely and that in an increasingly industrialized economy such persons are increasingly less able to support themselves.]

The problem is plainly national in area and dimensions. Moreover, laws of the separate states cannot deal with it effectively. Congress, at least, had a basis for that belief. . . . Apart from the failure of resources, states and local governments are at times reluctant to increase so heavily the burden of taxation to be borne by their residents for fear of placing themselves in a position of economic disadvantage as compared with neighbors or competitors. . . . A system of old-age pensions has special dangers of its own, if put in force in one state and rejected in another. The existence of such a system is a bait to the needy and dependent elsewhere, encouraging them to migrate and seek a haven of repose. Only a power that is national can serve the interests of all.

Whether wisdom or unwisdom resides in the scheme of benefits set forth in [the old age provisions] it is not for us to say. The answer to such inquiries must come from Congress, not the courts . . . [The objection was made that the Social Security Act would adopt a paternalistic philosophy that might be contrary to the political philosophy of individual states.] . . . One might ask with equal reason whether the system of protective tariff is to be set aside whenever local policy prefers the rule of laissez faire. The issue is a closed one. It was fought out long ago. When money is spent to promote the general welfare, the concept of welfare or the opposite is shaped by Congress, not the states. So the concept be not arbitrary, the locality must yield. Constitution, Art. VI, Par. 2. . . .

[Statute held valid. Justices McReynolds and Butler dissented on the ground that the "Provisions of the Act . . . are repugnant to the Tenth Amendment."]

§ 16:5. THE CURRENCY POWER

The Constitution authorizes Congress "to coin Money, regulate the Value thereof" and "provide for the Punishment of counterfeiting the Securities and . . . Coin of the United States." [Art. 1, § 8, Cls. 5, 6] This federal power is made exclusive by prohibiting the states from coining money, emitting bills of credit, or making anything but gold and silver coins legal tender in payment of debts. [Art. 1, § 10]

The national government can determine what shall be legal tender and is not restricted to the use of metallic money. Congress can establish such base as it desires for the issue of paper currency and may change the base of existing currency, even though this interferes with, or makes impossible, the performance of private contracts calling for a different type of money.

(a) Paper currency

JUILLIARD v GREENMAN

110 US 421 (1884)

United States paper notes issued during the Civil War, the famous "greenbacks," were, under the authority of a federal statute, redeemed by the government and then reissued or put back into circulation and declared by the statute to be legal tender. A debtor offered to pay his creditor with this paper currency. The creditor refused to accept this payment and sued the debtor for the amount of the debt. The question before the Court was whether such paper currency could be made legal tender.

OPINION BY GRAY, J.

. . . That clause of the Constitution which declares that "the Congress shall have the power to lay and collect taxes, duties, imposts and excises, to pay the debts and provide for the common defence and general welfare of the United States," either embodies a grant of power to pay the debts of the United States, or presupposes and assumes that power as inherent in the United States as a sovereign government. . . . The government is to pay the debt of the Union, and must be authorized to use the means which appear to itself the most eligible to effect that object. . . .

The power "to borrow money on the credit of the United States" is the power to raise money for the public use on a pledge of the public credit, and may be exercised to meet either present or anticipated expenses and liabilities of the government. It includes the power to issue in return for the money borrowed, the obligations of the United States in any appropriate form, of stock, bonds, bills or notes; . . . Congress has authority to issue these obligations in a form adapted to circulation from hand to hand in the ordinary transactions of commerce and business. In order to promote and facilitate such circulation, to adapt them to use as currency, and to make them more current in the market, it may provide for their redemption in coin or bonds, and may make them receivable in payment of debts to the government.

. . . Congress has the power to issue the obligations of the United States in such form, and to impress upon them such qualities as currency for the purchase of merchandise and the payment of debts, as accord with the usage of sovereign governments. The power . . . was a power universally understood to belong to sovereignty, in Europe and America, at the time of the framing and adoption of the Constitution of the United States. . . . The exercise of this power not being prohibited to Congress by the Constitution, it is included in the power expressly granted to borrow money on the credit of the United States. . . .

The power of making the notes of the United States a legal tender in payment of private debts, being included in the power to borrow money and to provide a national currency, is not defeated or restricted by the fact that its exercise may affect the value of private contracts. . . .

So, under the power to coin money and to regulate its value, Congress may (as it did with regard to gold by the act of June 28th, 1834, ch. 95, and with regard to silver by the act of February 28th, 1878, ch. 20) issue coins of the same denomination as those already current by law, but of less intrinsic value than those, by reason of containing a less weight of the precious metals, and thereby enabled debtors to discharge their debts by the payment of coins of the less real value. A contract to pay a certain sum in money, without any stipulation as to the kind of money in which it shall be paid, may always be satisfied by payment of that sum in any currency which is lawful money at the place and time at which payment is to be made. . . .

Congress, as the legislature of a sovereign nation, being expressly empowered by the Constitution "to lay and collect taxes, to pay the debts and provide for the common defence and general welfare of the United States," and "to borrow money on the credit of the United States," and "to coin money and regulate the value thereof and of foreign coin;" and being clearly authorized, as incidental to the exercise of those great powers, to emit bills of credit, to charter national banks, and to provide a national currency for the whole people, in the form of coin, treasury notes, and national bank bills; and the power to make the notes of the government a legal tender in payment of private debts being one of the powers belonging to sovereignty in other civilized nations, and not expressly withheld from Congress by the Constitution; we are irresistibly impelled to the conclusion that the impressing upon the treasury notes of the United States the quality of being legal tender in payment of private debts is an appropriate means, conducive and plainly adapted to the execution of the undoubted powers of Congress, consistent with the letter and spirit of the Constitution, and therefore, within the meaning of that instrument, "necessary and proper for carrying into execution the powers vested by this Constitution in the government of the United States."

Such being our conclusion in matter of law, the question whether at any particular time, in war or in peace, the exigency is such, by reason of unusual and pressing demands on the resources of the government, or of the inadequacy of the supply of gold and silver coin to furnish the currency needed for the uses of the government and of the people, that it is, as matter of fact, wise and expedient to resort to this means, is a political question, to be determined by Congress when the question of exigency arises, and not a judicial question, to be afterwards passed upon by the courts. . . .

[Congress had power to make the paper currency legal tender]

(b) Devaluation of private gold bonds

NORMAN v B. & O. R. R. CO.

294 US 240 (1935)

OPINION BY HUGHES, C. J.

These cases present the question of the validity of the Joint Resolution of the Congress of June 5, 1933, with respect to the "gold clauses" of private contracts for the payment of money. . . .

This resolution . . . declares that "every provision contained in or made with respect to any obligation which purports to give the obligee a right to require payment in gold or a particular kind of coin or currency, or in an amount in money of the United States measured thereby" is "against public policy." Such provisions in obligations thereafter incurred are prohibited. The Resolution provides that "Every obligation, heretofore or hereafter incurred, whether or not any such provision is contained therein or made with respect thereto, shall be discharged upon payment, dollar for dollar, in any coin or currency which at the time of payment is legal tender for public and private debts."

. . . The suit was brought upon a coupon of a bond made by the Baltimore and Ohio Railroad Company. . . . The bond provided that the payment of principal and interest "will be made . . . in gold coin of the United States of America of or equal to the standard of weight and fineness existing on February 1, 1930." The coupon in suit, for $22.50, was payable on February 1, 1934. The complaint alleged that on February 1, 1930, the standard weight and fineness of a gold dollar of the United States as a unit of value "was fixed to consist of twenty-five and eight-tenths grains of gold, nine-tenths fine," . . . and by the order of the President . . . , the standard unit of value of a gold dollar of the United States "was fixed to consist of fifteen and five-twenty-firsts grains of gold, nine-tenths fine," from and after January 31, 1934. On presentation of the coupon, defendant refused to pay the amount in gold or the equivalent of gold in legal tender of the United States which was alleged to be, on February 1, 1934, according to the standard of weight and fineness existing on February 1, 1930, the sum of $38.10, and plaintiff demanded judgment for that amount. . . .

We are of the opinion that the gold clauses now before us were not contracts for payment in gold coins as a commodity, or in bullion, but were contracts for the payment of money. The bonds were severally for the payment of one thousand dollars. We also think that, fairly construed, these clauses were intended to afford a definite standard or measure of value, and thus to protect against a depreciation of the currency and against the discharge of the obligation by a payment of lesser value than that prescribed. When these contracts were made they were not repugnant to any action of the Congress. . . . Congress may make treasury notes legal tender in payment of debts previously contracted, as well as of those subsequently contracted, whether that authority be exercised in course of war or in time of peace.

. . . Contracts, however express, cannot fetter the constitutional authority of the Congress. Contracts may create rights of property, but when contracts deal with a subject matter which lies within the control of the Congress, they have a congenital infirmity. Parties cannot remove their transactions from the reach of dominant constitutional power by making contracts about them. . . .

This principle has familiar illustration in the exercise of the power to regulate commerce. If shippers and carriers stipulate for specified rates, although the rates may be lawful when the contracts are made, if Congress through the Interstate Commerce Commission exercises its authority and prescribes different rates, the latter control and override inconsistent stipulations in contracts previously made. . . .

The same reasoning applies to the constitutional authority of the Congress to regulate the currency and to establish the monetary system of the country. If the gold clauses now before us interfere with the policy of the Congress in the exercise of that authority they cannot stand.

. . . Whether they may be deemed to be such an interference depends upon an appraisement of economic conditions and upon determinations of questions of fact. With respect to those conditions and determinations, the Congress is entitled to its own judgment. We may inquire whether its action is arbitrary or capricious, that is, whether it has reasonable relation to a legitimate end. If it is an appropriate means to such an end, the decision of the Congress as to the degree of the necessity for the adoption of that means, is final. . . .

We are not concerned with consequences, in the sense that consequences, however serious, may excuse an invasion of constitutional right. We are concerned with the constitutional power of the Congress over the monetary system of the country and its attempted frustration. Exercising that power, the Congress has undertaken to establish a uniform currency, and parity between kinds of currency, and to make that currency, dollar for dollar, legal tender for the payment of debts. In the light of abundant experience, the Congress was entitled to choose such a uniform monetary system, and to reject a dual system, with respect to all obligations within the range of the exercise of its constitutional authority. The contention that these gold clauses are valid contracts and cannot be struck down proceeds upon the assumption that private parties, and states and municipalities, may make and enforce contracts which may limit that authority. Dismissing that untenable assumption, the facts must be faced. We think that it is clearly shown that these clauses interfere with the exertion of the power granted to the Congress and certainly it is not established that the Congress arbitrarily or capriciously decided that such an interference existed.

[Judgment against Norman]

Questions for Discussion

1. (a) Can taxes be imposed by the United States? by the states? by counties? by cities? by school districts? (b) If so, what is the source of the power of each of these units to tax? (c) What is the source of limitations on the power of each of these units to tax?

2. Does the Constitution authorize Congress to issue paper currency? What is the historical explanation for the form of the constitutional provision governing currency?

3. What effect did the existence of war have on the federal power with respect to the issuance of paper currency?

4. What is the nature of an income tax?

5. Does the due process clause protect a business from being destroyed by taxation?

6. A statute imposes a tax on margarine, but not on butter. Because of the tax, margarine can only be sold at a price higher than butter to avoid loss. Does the statute violate the equal protection clause?

7. A federal tax is imposed on the right to use an automobile. It is claimed that it is unconstitutional because the right to use an automobile on state highways is conferred by state law. Decide.

8. What is the basis for the decision in the *Perry* case that an obligation of the United States cannot be repudiated?

9. (a) Were the gold clauses valid when made? (b) Why does not the Court apply the prohibition against *ex post facto* laws? (c) What effect does the concept of freedom of contract have on this decision?

10. What are the limitations on the spending of tax money?

11. The federal government determines that in order to obtain stability in the gasoline industry, the retail sale price of gasoline should be regulated to eliminate a two-cent differential between the East Coast and the West Coast. Instead of adopting a law directly regulating the price, Congress adopts a gasoline tax law and provides that the tax should be three cents per gallon in the area where the price is lower and one cent per gallon in the area where the price is higher. Would this tax be constitutional?

12. State *Z* decides to eradicate evils connected with the business of selling liquor by creating a state monopoly of liquor stores. It refuses to pay federal taxes due from liquor stores throughout the country on the ground that it is running the enterprise as a government and is not subject to taxation. Decide. Does the fact that the state government maintains a monopoly of the business affect your answer? [*South Carolina v United States,* 199 US 437 (1905)]

13. The United States passed a tariff law which imposed rates so high that its purpose was obviously protection. The act was attacked as unconstitutional in attempting to regulate manufacturing. Is the act unconstitutional? [*Hampton v United States,* 276 US 394 (1928)]

14. Heald was the executor of a deceased person who had lived in Washington, D. C. Heald refused to pay federal tax owed by the estate on the ground that the tax had been imposed by an act of Congress, but that, since residents of the District of Columbia had no vote in Congress, the tax law was necessarily adopted without their representation. In addition to having no voice in the adoption of the tax laws, the proceeds from taxes collected in the District were paid into the general treasury of the United States and were not maintained as a separate District of Columbia fund. Heald objected that the tax law was void as contrary to the Constitution because it amounted to taxation without representation. Decide. [*Heald v District of Columbia,* 259 US 114 (1922)]

15. The University of Georgia built a stadium in which football games were held. It received a profit from the sale of admission tickets and used this profit to defray the expenses of its educational program. The federal tax collector sought to collect the amusement tax from the admissions to the football games. The university claimed that the admissions were not subject to tax, since the profits were not privately received but were used for education, which was a regular function of the state government. The university contended that to tax the admissions when so used interfered with the state's functions. Were the admissions taxable? [*Allen v Regents of the University of Georgia,* 304 US 439 (1938)]

16. The dollar was devalued by Congress in order to aid domestic debtors and to increase foreign trade. The plan was that, by lowering the value of the dollar, prices would be maintained at a higher level, thus enabling the debtors to pay off their debts in dollars of the same purchasing power as those that they had borrowed. Foreign trade was to be aided, since the foreign currencies would have a greater purchasing power relative to the cheaper American dollar and this would induce foreign countries to purchase more heavily within the United States. Does Congress have the power to undertake such economic planning? Can it do so under the guise of regulating currency?

17. Louisiana adopted a law under which the tax on chain stores increased with the number of stores operated by the chain, without regard to whether they were within Louisiana or within other states. The A & P Company refused to pay the tax on the ground that it was unconstitutional and also interfered with interstate commerce. Decide. [*Great A & P Tea Co. v Grosjean,* 301 US 412 (1937)]

18. (a) In the event that the national debt rose to such a level that it could never be repaid, would the *Perry* case permit the calling of a constitutional convention or the adoption of a constitutional amendment that would expressly authorize the repudiation of all preexisting debts of the United States?   (b) Would it make any difference if a "corporate reorganization" of the United States was authorized by the convention or constitutional amendment, under which reorganization all debts were not repudiated in full but were modified as to term, interest rate, or medium of currency in which payable?

19. (a) Is there any way in which the parties to a contract can assure themselves that payment will be made in currency of the same value as the currency that was legal tender at the time their debt was contracted?   (b) Is there any way that they can provide that the same gold content shall be paid irrespective of devaluation of the dollar?

20. When the Supreme Court handed down the decision in *Norman v Baltimore & Ohio RR Co.,* one of the dissenting judges orally announced from the bench that the decision amounted to "a repudiation of national obligations" and "a breaking of solemn pledges," and that "as for the Constitution, it does not seem too much to say that it is gone."   (a) Do you agree with these statements?   (b) Do they mean that this case goes farther than any other case?   (c) How does this case compare with decisions under the commerce clause? with the decision in *Nebbia v New York,* § 15:3?

17

The War Power and
the Foreign Affairs Power

§ 17:1. THE WAR POWER

The Constitution confers the national war power upon the Congress [Art. I, § 8, Cls. 10 to 16]. Except to the extent necessary to repel invasion, or in the event of imminent danger that will not admit of delay [Art. I, § 10, Cl. 3], the states are denied any war power. The federal war power includes the power to do everything reasonably necessary to the prosecution of the war, and the courts have shown very little desire to interfere with the congressional or presidential determination of what is reasonably necessary. The power to wage war is a "power to wage war successfully and thus it permits the harnessing of the entire energies of the people in a supreme cooperative effort to preserve the nation," as Chief Justice Hughes declared in *Home B. & L. Assn v Blaisdell,* 290 US 398 (1934). The absence of any real constitutional limitation upon the war power was recognized by Hamilton in the *Federalist:* "The circumstances that endanger the safety of nations are infinite, and for this reason no constitutional channels can safely be imposed on the power to which the care of it is committed."[1]

The Congress may not only draft soldiers, but it may subject private industry to any regulation it deems appropriate, or it may seize private plants and transportational facilities. If Congress chooses to obtain war materials through contracts made with private plants, it may provide for any type of contract and may authorize the renegotiation of the contracts in order to

---

[1]Quoted with approval in *Lichter v United States,* 334 US 742 (1948).

recapture excess profits realized by the contractor. If the government desires, it may construct and operate its own production plants and transportational facilities. Congress may establish price, rationing, and prohibition controls of everything that is related to the war effort or to the maintaining of the national economy or security.

The war power is not restricted to the time of actual war but may be used in advance to prepare for war, even though there is no immediate threat of danger. It may be exercised after hostilities have ceased in order to bind up the wounds of economic dislocation caused by the war, even though such effects may last for years. It must be recognized that, in an era of total war, it is difficult to claim that a bona fide element of war preparation is not present in any regulation of business. There is no significant industry or business whose strengthening cannot plausibly be claimed as legitimate preparation for war. Also, because of the increasing complexity of our economic system, the repercussions of war are felt many years after the conclusion of hostilities. The question of the duration of war power confronted the Supreme Court in the following case in determining the validity of a rent control law passed after the termination of hostilities.

(a) Federal Rent Control Act

WOODS v CLOYD W. MILLER CO.

333 US 138 (1948)

The United States Rent Control Act of 1947 was claimed unconstitutional because it was adopted after the president had proclaimed the termination of hostilities of World War II.

OPINION BY DOUGLAS, J.

. . . We conclude that the war power sustains this legislation. . . . The war power includes the power "to remedy the evils which have arisen from its rise and progress" and continues for the duration of that emergency. Whatever may be the consequences when war is officially terminated, the war power does not necessarily end with the cessation of hostilities. . . . Prohibition laws which were enacted after the Armistice in World War I were sustained as exercises of the war power because they conserved manpower and increased efficiency of production in the critical days during the period of demobilization, and helped to husband the supply of grains and cereals depleted by the war effort. . . .

The legislative history of the present Act makes abundantly clear that there has not yet been eliminated the deficit in housing which in considerable measure was caused by the heavy demobilization of veterans and by the cessation or reduction in residential construction during the period of hostilities due to the allocation of building materials to military projects. Since the war effort contributed heavily to that deficit, Congress has the power even after the cessation of hostilities to act to control the forces that a short supply of the needed articles created. If that were not true . . . the result would be paralyzing. It would render Congress powerless to remedy conditions the creation of which necessarily followed from the mobilization of men and materials for successful prosecution of the war. So to read the Constitution would be to make it self-defeating.

We recognize the force of the argument that the effects of war under modern conditions may be felt in the economy for years and years, and that if the war power can be used in days of peace to treat all the wounds which war inflicts on our society, it may not only swallow up all other powers of Congress but largely obliterate the Ninth and Tenth Amendments as well. There are no such implications in today's decision. We deal here with the consequences of a housing deficit greatly intensified during the period of hostilities by the war effort. Any power, of course, can be abused. But we cannot assume that Congress is not alert to its constitutional responsibilities. And the question whether the war power has been properly employed in cases such as this is open to judicial inquiry.

. . . Here it is plain from the legislative history that Congress was invoking its war power to cope with a current condition of which the war was a direct and immediate cause. . . .

[Judgment for Woods, sustaining the federal rent control statute]

§ 17:2. THE FOREIGN AFFAIRS POWER

Within the area of the 50 states, the national government shares the power of governing with the states. Domestically, it is a dual, or federal, governmental system. Internationally, the 50 states have no legal existence and it is the national government alone that exists. As such, the national government has the full power of a sovereign government to make treaties and to enter into foreign relations. [Art. II, § 2, Cl. 2; Art. I, § 10, Cls. 1, 3]

(a) Supremacy of federal power

UNITED STATES v BELMONT
301 US 324 (1937)

A Russian corporation deposited money with Belmont, a private banker, in New York. Following the Russian Revolution of 1917, the assets of the corporation were confiscated by the Soviet government. In 1933, the Soviet government made an agreement with the President of the United States with respect to the settlement of claims, and as part of the settlement the Soviet government assigned to the United States the money on deposit with Belmont. The United States sued Belmont for the money. The defense was raised that, according to the New York law, the decree of confiscation by the Soviet government was not recognized, and therefore the Soviet government could not assign the right to the deposit to the United States.

OPINION BY SUTHERLAND, J.

. . . We are of [the] opinion that no state policy can prevail against the international compact here involved.

. . . We take judicial notice of the fact that coincident with the assignment set forth in the complaint, the President recognized the Soviet Government, and normal diplomatic relations were established between that government and the Government of the United States, followed by an exchange of ambassadors. The effect of this was to validate, so far as this country was concerned, all acts of the Soviet Government here involved from the commencement of its existence. The recognition, establishment of diplomatic relations, the assignment, and agreements with respect thereto, were all parts of one transaction, resulting in an international compact between the two governments. That the negotiations, acceptance of the assignment and agreements and understandings in respect thereof were within the competence of the President may not be doubted. Governmental power over internal affairs is distributed between the national government and the several states. Governmental power over external affairs is not distributed, but is vested exclusively in the national government. And in respect of what was done here, the Executive had authority to speak as the sole organ of that government. The assignment and the agreements in connection therewith did not, as in the case of treaties, as that term is used in the treaty making clause of the Constitution (Art. II, § 2), require the advice and consent of the Senate.

A treaty signifies "a compact made between two or more independent nations with a view to the public welfare." . . . But an international compact, as this was, is not always a treaty which requires the participation of the Senate. There are many such compacts, of which a protocol, a modus vivendi, a postal convention, and agreements like that now under consideration are illustrations. . . .

Plainly, the external powers of the United States are to be exercised without regard to state laws or policies. The supremacy of a treaty in this respect has been recognized from the beginning. Mr. Madison, in the Virginia Convention, said that if a treaty does not supersede existing state laws, as far as they contravene its operation, the treaty would be ineffective. . . . And while this rule in respect of treaties is established by the express language of cl. 2, Art VI, of the Constitution, the same rule would result in the case of all international compacts and agreements from the very fact that complete power over international affairs is in the national government and is not and cannot be subject to any curtailment or interference on the part of the several states. . . . In respect of all international negotiations and compacts, and in respect of our foreign relations generally, state lines disappear. As to such purposes the State of New York does not exist. Within the field of its powers, whatever the United States rightfully undertakes, it necessarily has warrant to consummate. And when judicial authority is invoked in aid of such consummation, state constitutions, state laws, and state policies are irrelevant to the inquiry and decision. It is inconceivable that any of them can be interposed as an obstacle to the effective operation of a federal constitutional power. . . .

[Judgment for the United States]

§ 17:3. EFFECT OF TREATY POWER ON LEGISLATIVE POWER

Some treaties are self-executing and are fully effective from the time of agreement. Other treaties are executory and require adoption of laws by the participating nations to carry out and give effect to the terms of the treaty. No provision is found in the federal Constitution concerning the scope of the legislative power of Congress when it is adopting laws to carry out treaties. Hence, it is concluded that a statute called for by a treaty is valid even though the statute, if adopted by Congress without such an antecedent treaty, would be invalid as beyond the domestic legislative powers. Otherwise stated, Congress, when legislating "nationally," has only the powers given to it by the Constitution; when legislating "internationally" to carry out a treaty, Congress has the full law-making power of an independent sovereign nation not limited by any constitution.

§ 17:4. SOCIAL REFORM BY TREATY

The implications of the doctrine of treaty legislation are far-reaching. Extended to its logical conclusion, it would permit the execution of treaties with foreign nations designed to further international welfare and then sustain the validity of federal laws adopted to carry out such provisions, without regard to whether the laws would be constitutional without the treaties. Prior to the modern extension of the commerce power, this treaty and statute combination offered a possible means of outlawing child labor and of making the various other social reforms that Congress could not make directly. It was suggested that the president and the Senate should make a treaty prohibiting child labor, and then that Congress should adopt a federal law outlawing child labor within the United States under the authority of the treaty power. The extension of the commerce power, however, has made it unnecessary to resort to this device, as Congress is now able to regulate the most substantial part of the economic and the social area and to achieve by direct regulation reforms that were formerly prohibited. The problem of treaty legislation may be revived, however, in the field of human or personal rights if the United Nations should adopt a declaration or agreement binding on the United States and all its members, requiring the members to observe and maintain specified standards with respect to human and personal rights within their respective territories.

Questions for Discussion

1. (a) What is the extent of the national war power? (b) What is the extent of the state war power?

2. Are there any limitations on the regulations that may be imposed on business during wartime?

3. How does the executive compact in the *Belmont* case differ from a formal treaty (a) as to procedure and (b) as to effect?

4. Does the war power give Congress the authority to provide for the complete socialization or nationalization of all industries in time of war?

5. Is the question of what is used for war a judicial decision that the courts will pass upon or a political question that they will not decide?

6. Is the scope of the treaty-making power defined by the Constitution?

7. What limitations are there on the treaty power? On statutes adopted to carry out treaties?

8. A federal law may be sustained under the war power, even though it relates to postwar recovery. How long after a war has ended can this power be exercised?

9. (a) Are there any limitations on a wartime supply or price rationing system?   (b) Can such a system be adopted in peacetime?

10. (a) When Congress adopts a statute to carry out the terms of a treaty, does it make any difference if the subject regulated by the treaty and the statute is a business enterprise in which private citizens have money invested, such as factories, mines, or farms? Does it make any difference if the subject is one that does not represent investments and business, such as the preservation of migratory birds?   (b) Can a distinction be made between the two on the ground that the benefits to be attained would be great compared to the comparative insignificance of the restraint imposed?

11. Compare the national-state relation with respect to domestic matters within the United States and foreign matters with other countries.

12. In the *Woods* case, the Court stated: "Since the war effort contributed heavily to [the deficit of housing facilities], Congress has the power even after the cessation of hostilities to act to control the forces that a short supply of the needed articles created. If that were not true . . . the result would be paralyzing. . . . So to read the Constitution would make it self-defeating. . . ." (a) What do you think of this as a constitutional argument? (b) How does it compare with the approach of the Court in *Schechter v United States*, § 8:2(b), and *NLRB v Jones & Laughlin Steel Corp.*, § 8:2(c)?

18

The Power of Eminent Domain

§ 18:1. TAKING FOR A PUBLIC PURPOSE

Governments may take property without the consent of the owners by eminent domain. Lands and buildings, regardless of how the title to them is held, are all subject to the power of eminent domain. The right of government to take property for eminent domain is not affected by the existence of contracts between the owner of the property and third parties. The fact that the owner holds the property in trust for others, or for the general public, does not bar its taking by eminent domain.

Both the United States and the individual states possess the power to take private property as an implied power of government traditionally held by the sovereign. In the case of the federal government, the power must be exercised to accomplish or to aid the furthering of an object within the scope of the expressed federal powers. Such a purpose is necessarily for a public use. The federal eminent domain power may be exercised within a state without regard to whether the state consents to the federal government's exercising that power. It is not necessary that the federal government directly exercise the power of eminent domain. It may confer it upon a corporation that has been created to carry out the governmental purpose.

A state exercising the power of eminent domain must do so for a public purpose or a public use. If it fails to do so and takes property for a private or a nonpublic use, the taking will be held unconstitutional as depriving the former owner of property without due process of law.

The concept of what constitutes a public use is not clearly defined. Property is clearly taken for a public use when it is taken by the government and used for essential government buildings. The power may, however, be conferred upon a political subdivision or a private corporation. A railroad authorized to acquire its right of way by eminent domain is regarded as taking property for a public use, even though the corporation is a private railroad that intends to make profit through the operations of the road over the right of way, and even though the public will have no right to use that property unless it pays the railroad a fare or a freight charge. The courts have endeavored to define public use in terms of governmental function; that is, if the purpose is regarded as one which a government may properly undertake itself, then the taking of land for that purpose, whether by the government itself, a private corporation, or a semipublic corporation, is also regarded as a public use. This, however, is not a clear definition because the scope of governmental functions is itself a changing concept, as society moves from a negative police state to a positive paternalistic state. Irrigation and drainage works and gas, electric, and water supply works are regarded as being sufficiently within the public use area that government may use the power of eminent domain to acquire property for that purpose or may grant private enterprisers the right of taking property for such use.

As an illustration of the limitation upon the public use concept, it is generally held that excess land, that is, more land than is needed for an improvement, cannot be taken by eminent domain with the object of thereafter reselling the unnecessary surplus. However, this does not preclude the condemnation of an entire blighted area for redevelopment purposes, with the intention of selling any surplus areas that should not be required for the completed project.

The requirement that a taking be for a public purpose is, to a large extent, nullified in practice by the principle that the determination of Congress as to whether a purpose is public is virtually final. While the courts have the power to review the Congressional determination, the rule is followed that "when Congress has spoken . . . 'its decision is entitled to deference until it is shown to involve an impossibility.' "[1]

(a) Redevelopment project

BERMAN v PARKER

348 US 26 (1954)

The District of Columbia Redevelopment Act authorizes the taking of land by eminent domain in order to clear blighted or slum areas and authorizes the use of such land for redevelopment projects. The agency under the Act declared a certain area to be blighted and proceeded to acquire the land. Berman and others owned a department store within the area. They claimed that the Act was unconstitutional as to them because the building was not used as a dwelling and

---

[1] *United States v Welch,* 327 US 546 (1946).

did not contribute to the blighted character of the surrounding neighborhood. They brought an action to prevent the condemnation of their store.

OPINION BY DOUGLAS, J.

. . . Appellants . . . claim that their property may not be taken constitutionally for this project. It is commercial, not residential property; it is not slum housing. . . . To take for the purpose of ridding the area of slums is one thing; it is quite another, the argument goes, to take a man's property merely to develop a better balanced, more attractive community. . . .

We do not sit to determine whether a particular housing project is or is not desirable. . . . In the present case, the Congress and its authorized agencies have made determinations that take into account a wide variety of values. It is not for us to reappraise them. If those who govern the District of Columbia decide that the Nation's Capital should be beautiful as well as sanitary, there is nothing in the Fifth Amendment that stands in the way. . . .

In the present case, Congress and its authorized agencies attack the problem of the blighted parts of the community on an area rather than on a structure-by-structure basis. That, too, is opposed by appellants. They maintain that since their building does not imperil health or safety nor contribute to the making of a slum or a blighted area, it cannot be swept into a redevelopment plan by the mere dictum of the Planning Commission or the Commissioners. The particular uses to be made of the land in the project were determined with regard to the needs of the particular community. The experts concluded that if the community were to be healthy, if it were not to revert again to a blighted or slum area, as though possessed of a congenital disease, the area must be planned as a whole. It was not enough, they believed, to remove existing buildings that were insanitary or unsightly. It was important to redesign the whole area so as to eliminate the conditions that cause slums—the overcrowding of dwellings, the lack of parks, the lack of adequate streets and alleys, the absence of recreational areas, the lack of light and air, the presence of outmoded street patterns. It was believed that the piecemeal approach, the removal of individual structures that were offensive, would be only a palliative. The entire area needed redesigning so that a balanced, integrated plan could be developed for the region, including not only new homes but also schools, churches, parks, streets, and shopping centers. In this way it was hoped that the cycle of decay of the area could be controlled and the birth of future slums prevented.

. . . It is the need of the area as a whole which Congress and its agencies are evaluating.

. . . It is not for the courts to oversee the choice of the boundary line nor to sit in review on the size of a particular project area. Once the question of the public purpose has been decided, the amount and character of land to be taken for the project and the need for a particular tract to complete the integrated plan rests in the discretion of the legislative branch. . . .

The District Court indicated grave doubts concerning the Agency's right to take full title to the land as distinguished from the objectionable buildings located on it. . . . We do not share those doubts. If the Agency considers it necessary in carrying out the redevelopment project to take full title to the real property involved, it may do so. It is not for the courts to determine whether it is necessary for successful consummation of the project that unsafe, unsightly, or unsanitary buildings alone be taken or whether title to the land be included, any more than it is the function of the courts to sort and choose among the various parcels selected for condemnation.

The rights of these property owners are satisfied when they receive that just compensation which the Fifth Amendment exacts as the price of the taking.

[Judgment against Berman]

---

§ 18:2. WHAT AMOUNTS TO A TAKING

By the express provision of the Fifth Amendment and the interpretation of the due process clause of the Fourteenth Amendment, just compensation must be made whenever property is taken by eminent domain; that is, for a public use.

Where the government takes exclusive physical possession of property, no question arises but that it has been "taken." The government, without actually taking possession of the property, may carry on activities of such a nature in its vicinity as to interfere with the use of the property by its owner and to reduce its value. Under such circumstance, a question arises as to whether there has been a "taking" for which compensation must be made. It is held that there is a "taking" if the activity of the government or the body having power of eminent domain so damages or so materially impairs the use of the property of the private owner that it in effect has taken away or destroyed a substantial part or all of its value. The fact that the owner technically holds the title to the now worthless or greatly depreciated land does not deprive the owner of the right to compensation.

(a) Loss of value

UNITED STATES v CAUSBY

328 US 256 (1946)

OPINION BY DOUGLAS, J.

. . . The problem presented is whether respondents' property was taken within the meaning of the Fifth Amendment, by frequent and regular flights of army and navy aircraft over respondents' land at low altitudes. . . .

Respondents own 2.8 acres near an airport outside of Greensboro, North Carolina. . . . The 30 to 1 safe glide angle approved by the Civil Aeronautics Authority passes over this property at 83 feet, which is 67 feet above the house, 63 feet above the barn and 18 feet above the highest tree.

. . . Since the United States began operations in May, 1942, its four-motored heavy bombers, other planes of the heavier type, and its fighter planes have frequently passed over respondents' land and buildings in considerable number and rather close together. They come close enough at times to appear barely to miss the tops of the trees and at times so close to the tops of the trees as to blow the old leaves off. The noise is startling. And at night the glare from the planes brightly lights up the place. As a result of the noise, respondents had to give up their chicken business. . . . The result was the destruction of the use of the property as a commercial chicken farm. Respondents are frequently deprived of their sleep and the family has become nervous and frightened. Although there have been no airplane accidents on respondents' property, there have been several accidents near the airport and close to respondents' place. These are the essential facts found by the Court of Claims. On the basis of these facts, it found that respondents' property had depreciated in value. It held that the United States had taken an easement over the property on June 1, 1942, . . .

It is ancient doctrine that a common-law ownership of the land extended to the periphery of the universe—*Cujus est solum ejus est usque ad coelum.* [The owner of the soil owns to the sky.] But that doctrine has no place in the modern world. The air is a public highway, as Congress has declared. Were that not true, every transcontinental flight would subject the operator to countless trespass suits. Common sense revolts at the idea. To recognize such private claims to the airspace would clog these highways, seriously interfere with their control and development in the public interest, and transfer into private ownership that to which only the public has a just claim.

. . . If, by reason of the frequency and altitude of the flights, respondents could not use this land for any purpose, their loss would be complete. It would be as complete as if the United States had entered upon the surface of the land and taken exclusive possession of it.

We agree that in those circumstances there would be a taking. Though it would be only an easement of flight which was taken, that easement, if permanent and not merely temporary, normally would be the equivalent of a fee interest. It would be a definite exercise of complete dominion and control over the surface of the land. . . . The owner's right to possess and exploit the land —that is to say, his beneficial ownership of it—would be destroyed.

. . . The path of glide for airplanes might reduce a valuable factory site to grazing land, an orchard to a vegetable patch, a residential section to a wheat field. Some value would remain. But the use of airspace immediately above the land would limit the utility of the land and cause a diminution in its value.

. . .

We have said that the airspace is a public highway. Yet it is obvious that if the landowner is to have full enjoyment of the land, he must have exclusive control of the immediate reaches of the enveloping atmosphere. Otherwise buildings could not be erected, trees could not be planted, and even fences could not be run. The principle is recognized when the law gives a remedy in case overhanging structures are erected on adjoining land. The landowner owns at least as much of the space above the ground as he can occupy or use in connection with the land. . . . The fact that he does not occupy it in a physical sense—by the erection of buildings and the like—is not material. As we have said, the flight of airplanes, which skim the surface but do not touch it, is as much an appropriation of the use of the land as a more conventional entry upon it. We would not doubt that if the United States erected an elevated railway over respondents' land at the precise altitude where its planes now fly, there would be a partial taking, even though none of the supports of the structure rested on the land. The reason is that there would be an intrusion so immediate and direct as to subtract from the owner's full enjoyment of the property and to limit his exploitation of it. While the owner does not in any physical manner occupy the stratum of airspace or make use of it in the conventional sense, he does use it in somewhat the same sense that space left between buildings for the purpose of light and air is used. The superadjacent airspace at this low altitude is so close to the land that continuous invasions of it affect the use of the surface of the land itself. We think that the landowner, as an incident to his ownership, has a claim to it and that invasions of it are in the same category as invasions of the surface.

[Judgment for Causby]

(b) Seizure in labor dispute

UNITED STATES v PEWEE COAL COMPANY

341 US 114 (1951)

During World War II, the president ordered the seizure of coal mines to avert a national strike. The government held and operated the mine of the Pewee Coal Co. from May 1 to October 12, 1943. After the mine was restored to the Pewee Company, it brought suit in the Court of Claims to recover compensation on the theory that its property had been taken and that the measure of damages was its total operating loss for the period of the government seizure. The Court of Claims held that there was a taking but allowed damages for only $2,241.26 on the basis that that amount was the portion of the operating loss which was attributable to government operation of the mine through compliance with a wage increase order of the War Labor Board. The United States appealed.

OPINION BY BLACK, J.

. . . To convince the operators, miners and public that the United States was taking possession for the bona fide purpose of operating the mines, the Government formally and ceremoniously proclaimed that such was its intention. It required mine officials to agree to conduct operations as agents for the Government; required the American flag to be flown at every mine; required placards reading "United States Property!" to be posted on the premises; and appealed to the miners to dig coal for the United States as a public duty. Under these circumstances and in view of the other facts which were found, it should not and will not be assumed that the seizure of the mines was a mere sham or pretense to accomplish some unexpressed governmental purpose instead of being the proclaimed actual taking of possession and control. In *United States v United Mine Workers,* 330 US 258, there had been a government seizure of the mines under presidential and secretarial orders, which, insofar as here material, were substantially the same as those issued in the present case. We rejected the contention of the mine workers that "the Government's role in administering the bituminous coal mines [was] for the most part fictional and for the remainder nominal only." We treated that seizure as making the mines government facilities "in as complete a sense as if the Government held full title and ownership." . . . It follows almost as a matter of course from our holding in *United Mine Workers* that the Government here "took" Pewee's property and became engaged in the mining business.

. . . Having taken Pewee's property, the United States became liable under the Constitution to pay just compensation. Ordinarily, fair compensation for a temporary possession of a business enterprise is the reasonable value of the property's use. . . . But in the present case, there is no need to consider the difficult problems inherent in fixing the value of the use of a going concern because Pewee neither claimed such compensation nor proved the amount. It proceeded on the ground that the Fifth Amendment requires the United States to bear operating losses incurred during the period the Government operates private property in the name of the public without the owner's consent. . . .

Like any private person or corporation, the United States normally is entitled to the profits from, and must bear the losses of, business operations which it conducts. When a private business is possessed and operated for public use, no reason appears to justify imposition of losses sustained on the person from whom the property was seized. This is conceptually distinct from the Government's obligation to pay fair compensation for property taken, although in cases raising the issue, the Government's profit and loss experience may well be one factor involved in computing reasonable compensation for a temporary taking. Of course, there might be an express or implied agreement between the parties that the Government should not receive operating profits nor bear the losses, in which event the general principle would be inapplicable. . . .

Where losses resulting from operation of property taken must be borne by the Government, it makes no difference that the losses are caused in whole or in part by compliance with administrative regulations requiring additional wages to be paid. With or without a War Labor Board order, when the Government increased the wages of the miners whom it employed, it thereby incurred the expense. Moreover, it is immaterial that governmental operation resulted in a smaller loss than Pewee would have sustained if there had been no seizure of the mines. Whatever might have been Pewee's losses had it been left free to exercise its own business judgment, the crucial fact is that the Government chose to intervene by taking possession and operating control. By doing so, it became the proprietor and, in the absence of contrary arrangements, was entitled to the benefits and subject to the liabilities which that status involves. . . .

[Judgment affirmed]

CONCURRING OPINION BY REED, J.

I agree that in this case there was a "taking" by eminent domain that requires the Government to pay just compensation to the owner of the property for its use. However, it is impossible for me to accept the view that the "taking" in this case requires the United States to bear all operating losses during the period it controls the property without the owner's consent or agreement. Such a view would lead to disastrous consequences where properties necessarily taken for the benefit of the Nation have a long record of operating losses, *e. g.,* certain railroads, coal mines, or television broadcasting stations. The question of who bears such losses is not, I think, "conceptually distinct" from the question of just compensation. Losses or profits on the temporary operation after the declaration or judgment of taking are factors to be taken into consideration in determining what is just compensation to the owner.

This is a temporary taking. The relatively new technique of temporary taking by eminent domain is a most useful administrative device: many properties, such as laundries, or coal mines, or railroads, may be subjected to public operation only for a short time to meet war or emergency needs, and can then be returned to their owners. However, the use of the temporary taking has spawned a host of difficult problems, . . . especially in the fixing of the just compensation. Market value, despite its difficulties, provides a fairly acceptable test for just compensation when the property is taken absolutely.

. . . But in the temporary taking of operating properties, . . . market value is too uncertain a measure to have any practical significance. The rental value for a fully functioning railroad for an uncertain period is an unknowable quantity. . . . The most reasonable solution is to award compensation to the owner as determined by a court under all the circumstances of the particular case.

Temporary takings can assume various forms. There may be a taking in which the owners are ousted from operation, their business suspended, and the property devoted to new uses. . . . A second kind of taking is where, as here, the Government, for public safety or the protection of the public welfare, "takes" the property in the sense of assuming the responsibility of its direction and employment for national purposes, leaving the actual operations in the hands of its owners as government officials appointed to conduct its affairs with the assets and equipment of the controlled company. Examples are the operation of railroads, motor carriers, or coal mines. . . .

When in a temporary taking, no agreement is reached with the owners, the courts must determine what payments the Government must make. Whatever the nature of the "taking," the test should be the constitutional requirement of "just compensation." However, there is no inflexible requirement that the same incidents must be used in each application of the test.

So far as the second kind of temporary "taking" is concerned, the Government's supervision of a losing business for a temporary emergency ought not to place upon the Government the burden of the losses incurred during that supervision unless the losses were incurred by governmental acts, *e. g.,* if the business would not have been conducted at all but for the Government, or if extra losses over what would have been otherwise sustained were occasioned by Government operations. Where the owner's losses are what they would have been without the "taking," the owner has suffered no loss or damage for which compensation is due. . . . The measure of just compensation has always been the loss to the owner, not the loss or gain to the Government. . . .

(c) Restriction on use

UNITED STATES v CENTRAL EUREKA MINING COMPANY
357 US 155 (1958)

In order to divert miners and mining equipment from gold mining to other, more essential, forms of mining, the War Production Board issued Order L-208 in 1942, classifying gold mining as nonessential and ordering all gold mines to shut down. After World War II, Central Eureka Mining Company, which was one of the gold mines closed down by the government order, brought suit in the Court of Claims against the United States to recover compensation for the loss sustained by the closing of the mine.

OPINION BY BURTON, J.

. . . It is clear from the record that the Government did not occupy, use, or in any manner, take physical possession of the gold mines or of the equipment connected with them. Cf. *United States v Pewee Coal Co.,* 341 US 114, ... All that the Government sought was the cessation of the consumption of mining equipment and manpower in the gold mines and the conservation of such equipment and manpower for more essential war uses. The Government had no need for the gold or the gold mines.

. . . Traditionally, we have treated the issue as to whether a particular governmental restriction amounted to a constitutional taking as being a question properly turning upon the particular circumstances of each case. . . . The mere fact that the regulation deprives the property owner of the most profitable use of his property is not necessarily enough to establish the owner's right to compensation. . . . In the context of war, we have been reluctant to find that degree of regulation which, without saying so, requires compensation to be paid for resulting losses of income. . . . The reasons are plain. War, particularly in modern times, demands the strict regulation of nearly all resources. It makes demands which otherwise would be insufferable. But wartime economic restrictions, temporary in character, are insignificant when compared to the widespread uncompensated loss of life and freedom of action which war traditionally demands.

We do not find in the temporary restrictions here placed on the operation of gold mines a taking of private property that would justify a departure from the trend of the above decisions. The WPB here sought, by reasonable regulation, to conserve the limited supply of equipment used by the mines and it hoped that its order would divert available miners to more essential work. Both purposes were proper objectives; both matters were subject to regulation to the extent of the order. L-208 did not order any disposal of property or transfer of men. . . . The damage to the mine owners was incidental to the Government's lawful regulation of matters reasonably deemed essential to the war effort. . . .

[Judgment for United States]

DISSENTING OPINION BY HARLAN, J.

I dissent because I believe that the Fifth Amendment to the Constitution requires the Government to pay just compensation to the respondents for the temporary "taking" of their property accomplished by WPB Order L-208. . . .

L-208 was the only order promulgated during World War II which by its terms required a lawful and productive industry to shut down at a severe economic cost. . . . As a result of the Order the respondents were totally deprived of the beneficial use of their property. Any suggestion that the mines could have been used in such a way (that is, other than to mine gold) so as to remove them from the scope of the Order would be chimerical. Not only were the respondents completely prevented from making profitable use of their property, but the Government acquired all that it wanted from the mines—their complete immobilization and the resulting discharge of the hardrock miners. It is plain that as a practical matter the Order led to consequences no different from those that would have followed the temporary acquisition of physical possession of these mines by the United States.

In these circumstances making the respondents' right to compensation turn on whether the Government took the ceremonial step of planting the American Flag on the mining premises, cf. *United States v Pewee Coal Co.*, 341 US 114, 116, . . . is surely to permit technicalities of form to dictate consequences of substance. In my judgment the present case should be viewed precisely as if the United States, in order to accomplish its purpose of freeing gold miners for essential work, had taken possession of the gold mines and allowed them to lie fallow for the duration of the war. Had the Government adopted the latter course it is hardly debatable that respondents would have been entitled to compensation. See *United States v Pewee Coal Co.*, . . .

(d) Wartime destruction

UNITED STATES v CALTEX
344 US 149 (1952)

Caltex and other oil companies had terminal facilities in Manila harbor in the Philippine Islands at the outbreak of World War II. In order to prevent these facilities from falling into the control of the advancing enemy, the United States Army notified Caltex and the other oil companies that the facilities were requisitioned by the army and then demolished them. After the war, Caltex and the other companies sued the United States in the Court of Claims for compensation. From a decision in their favor, the United States appealed.

OPINION BY VINSON, C.J.

. . . *United States v Pacific R. Co.,* 120 US 227 (1887), . . . involved bridges which had been destroyed during the War Between the States by a retreating Northern Army to impede the advance of the Confederate Army. Though the point was not directly involved, the Court raised the question of whether this act constituted a compensable taking by the United States and answered it in the negative:

> The destruction or injury of private property in battle, or in the bombardment of cities and towns, and in many other ways in the war, had to be borne by the sufferers alone as one of its consequences. Whatever would embarrass or impede the advance of the enemy, as the breaking up of roads, or the burning of bridges, or would cripple and defeat him, as destroying his means of subsistence, were lawfully ordered by the commanding general. Indeed, it was his imperative duty to direct their destruction. The necessities of the war called for and justified this. The safety of the state in such cases overrides all considerations of private loss.

. . . The common law had long recognized that in times of imminent peril —such as when fire threatened a whole community—the sovereign could, with immunity, destroy the property of a few that the property of many and the lives of many more could be saved. And what was said in the *Pacific Railroad* case was later made the basis for the holding in *Juraqua Iron Co. v United States,* 212 US 297 (1909), where recovery was denied to the owners of a factory which had been destroyed by American soldiers in the field in Cuba because it was thought that the structure housed the germs of a contagious disease.

Had the army hesitated, had the facilities only been destroyed after retreat, respondents would certainly have no claims to compensation. The Army did not hesitate. It is doubtful that any concern over the legal niceties of the situation entered into the decision to destroy the plants promptly while there was yet time to destroy them thoroughly. Nor do we think it legally significant that the destruction was effected prior to withdrawal. The short of the matter is that this property, due to the fortunes of war, had become a potential weapon of great significance to the invader. It was destroyed, not appropriated for subsequent use. It was destroyed that the United States might better and sooner destroy the enemy.

The terse language of the Fifth Amendment is no comprehensive promise that the United States will make whole all who suffer from every ravage and burden of war. This Court has long recognized that in wartime many losses must be attributed solely to the fortunes of war, and not to the sovereign. No rigid rules can be laid down to distinguish compensable losses from noncompensable losses. Each case must be judged on its own facts. But the general principles laid down in the *Pacific Railroad* case seem especially applicable here. Viewed realistically, then, the destruction of respondents' terminals by a trained team of engineers in the face of their impending seizure by the enemy was no different than the destruction of the bridges in the *Pacific Railroad* case. Adhering to the principles of that case, we conclude that the court below erred in holding that respondents have a constitutional right to compensation on the claims presented to this Court.

[Judgment for United States]

DISSENTING OPINION BY DOUGLAS, J., in which BLACK, J., concurs.

I have no doubt that the military had authority to select this particular property for destruction. But whatever the weight of authority may be, I believe that the Fifth Amendment requires compensation for the taking. The property was destroyed, not because it was in the nature of a public nuisance, but because its destruction was deemed necessary to help win the war. It was as clearly appropriated to that end as animals, food, and supplies requisitioned for the defense effort. As the Court says, the destruction of this property deprived the enemy of a valuable logistic weapon.

It seems to me that the guiding principle should be this: Whenever the Government determines that one person's property—whatever it may be—is essential to the war effort and appropriates it for the common good, the public purse, rather than the individual, should bear the loss. . . .

---

§ 18:3. MEASUREMENT OF DAMAGES

The property owner is not entitled to compensation for every depreciation caused to the owner's property. No compensation need be made for what are termed indirect or consequential damages from the exercise of otherwise proper governmental powers. When compensation is made, the body taking the property must pay the fair value of the property taken or the amount of the depreciation determined as of the date that the taking occurred.

(a) Market value

UNITED STATES v MILLER

317 US 369 (1943)

The United States took land of Miller by eminent domain. The compensation due by the United States was determined by a district court. Its decision was reversed by the circuit court of appeals. An appeal was then taken to the Supreme Court.

OPINION BY ROBERTS, J.

. . . The Fifth Amendment of the Constitution provides that private property shall not be taken for public use without just compensation. Such compensation means the full and perfect equivalent in money of the property taken. The owner is to be put in as good position pecuniarily as he would have occupied if his property had not been taken.

It is conceivable that an owner's indemnity should be measured in various ways depending upon the circumstances of each case and that no general formula should be used for the purpose. In an effort, however, to find some practical standard, the courts early adopted, and have retained, the concept of market value. The owner has been said to be entitled to the "value", the "market value", and the "fair market value" of what is taken. The term "fair" hardly adds anything to the phrase "market value," which denotes what "it fairly may be believed that a purchaser in fair market conditions would have given," or, more concisely, "market value fairly determined."

. . . Where, for any reason, property has no market, resort must be had to other data to ascertain its value; and, even in the ordinary case, assessment of market value involves the use of assumptions, which make it unlikely that the appraisal will reflect true value with nicety. It is usually said that market value is what a willing buyer would pay in cash to a willing seller. Where the property taken, and that in its vicinity, has not in fact been sold within recent times, or in significant amounts, the application of this concept involves, at best, a guess by informed persons.

Again, strict adherence to the criterion of market value may involve inclusion of elements which, though they affect such value, must in fairness be eliminated in a condemnation case, as where the formula is attempted to be applied as between an owner who may not want to part with his land because of its special adaptability to his own use, and a taker who needs the land because of its peculiar fitness for the taker's purposes. These elements must be disregarded by the fact finding body in arriving at "fair" market value.

Since the owner is to receive no more than indemnity for his loss, his award cannot be enhanced by any gain to the taker. Thus although the market value of the property is to be fixed with due consideration of all its available uses, its special value to the condemnor as distinguished from others who may or may not possess the power to condemn, must be excluded as an element of market value. . . .

There is, however, another possible element of market value, which is the bone of contention here. Should the owner have the benefit of any increment of value added to the property taken by the action of the public authority in previously condemning adjacent lands? If so, were the lands in question so situated as to entitle respondents to the benefit of this increment?

Courts have had to adopt working rules in order to do substantial justice in eminent domain proceedings. One of these is that a parcel of land which has been used and treated as an entity shall be so considered in assessing compensation for the taking of part or all of it.

This has begotten subsidiary rules. If only a portion of a single tract is taken the owner's compensation for that taking includes any element of value arising out of the relation of the part taken to the entire tract. Such damage is often, though somewhat loosely, spoken of as severance damage. On the other hand, if the taking has in fact benefited the remainder, the benefit may be set off against the value of the land taken.

As respects other property of the owner consisting of separate tracts adjoining that affected by the taking, the Constitution has never been construed as requiring payment of consequential damages; and unless the legislature so provides, as it may, benefits are not assessed against such neighboring tracts for increase in their value.

If a distinct tract is condemned, in whole or in part, other lands in the neighborhood may increase in market value due to the proximity of the public improvement erected on the land taken. Should the Government, at a later date, determine to take these other lands, it must pay their market value as enhanced by this factor of proximity. If, however, the public project from the beginning included the taking of certain tracts but only one of them is taken in the first instance, the owner of the other tracts should not be allowed an increased value for his lands which are ultimately to be taken any more than the owner of the tract first condemned is entitled to be allowed an increased market value because adjacent lands not immediately taken increased in value due to the projected improvement.

The question then is whether the respondents' lands were probably within the scope of the project from the time the Government was committed to it. If they were not, but were merely adjacent lands, the subsequent enlargement of the project to include them ought not to deprive the respondents of the value added in the meantime by the proximity of the improvement. If, on the other hand, they were, the Government ought not to pay any increase in value arising from the known fact that the lands probably would be condemned. . . .

[Judgment of the circuit court of appeals reversed because it had not observed the distinctions stated in the Supreme Court's opinion, and judgment of the district court affirmed]

Questions for Discussion

1. What is the importance of "public purpose" or "public use" in connection with eminent domain?

2. When a law is adopted prohibiting the manufacture of intoxicating liquor, is the owner of a brewery entitled to compensation on the grounds that the government has taken the brewery because, as a practical matter, the building cannot be used for any other purpose?

3. The state of N erects a public electric power plant. The dam of the plant causes water to back up and flood neighboring farmland. The owners demand compensation for their land. The state refuses to pay the owners on the ground that they still own their land, and that the state has not taken it from them and does not receive any benefit from it. Decide.

4. The Congress of the United States grants a charter to a new transcontinental railroad corporation and gives it authority to take private property by eminent domain for the purpose of building its roadbed and operating facilities. The corporation proceeds to take property of B by eminent domain. B seeks an injunction on the ground that the statute is unconstitutional because: (a) Congress cannot authorize a private corporation to exercise the power of eminent domain.   (b) The condemning of land for a privately owned railroad is not the taking of land for a public purpose. Decide and discuss the merits of each of these contentions.

5. What are the arguments for and against compensation in the *Caltex* case?

6. The United States wanted to purchase an interest in land owned by the Bodcaw Company. The company and the United States could not agree on the price, and the United States then took the land by eminent domain. Bodcaw claimed that, in addition to compensation for the value of the land taken, it should be awarded approximately $20,000 to cover the cost of an appraisal, which it had made of the interest that the United States had taken, and the fees paid to witnesses. Was Bodcaw entitled to this additional $20,000? [*United States v Bodcaw Company,*   US   , 59 L Ed 2d 257 (1979)]

7. With respect to condemnation for redevelopment, (a) can an entire area be taken on the basis that it is a blighted area? (b) can a property owner within an area which is predominantly blighted object to the condemnation on the ground that the owner's particular property is in excellent condition?

8. Is there a taking within the eminent domain concept when the government takes a steel mill in wartime (a) to keep it permanently and use it as a steel mill?   (b) to keep it for the duration of a war and use it as a steel mill? (c) to keep it temporarily until a labor dispute is settled and to continue it in operation as a steel mill during that period?

9. Appraise the dissenting opinion of Chief Justice Harlan in the *Pewee* case.

10. Compare the concept of "public purpose" in eminent domain, "public purpose" in government spending, and "business affected with a public interest" in the regulation of business. Do these three concepts have the same meaning? Have they changed in meaning during the past century?

11. *X* owns land in Utah. There is no water supply on the land. The nearest water supply is a river one-half mile away. To reach the river, it is necessary to cross the land belonging to *Z*. A statute of Utah provides that a land-locked property owner may construct an irrigation ditch across neighboring land and that this may be done by exercising the power of eminent domain. When *X* proceeds to construct a ditch on *Z*'s land, *Z* objects, refuses to accept compensation for such taking, and claims that the statute is unconstitutional, since the ditch would benefit *X* alone and is therefore not a public purpose for which eminent domain may be exercised. Decide. [*Himonas v Denver & RGWR*, (CCA 10) 179 F2d 171 (1949)]

12. What kind of property is subject to eminent domain? Can the owner of property block the exercise of eminent domain by placing the property in trust or by making a contract to sell it to another person?

13. In the *Pewee* case, the Court stressed that the government actually took possession of the mine and was operating it. Does this mean that the people in management, in the office, and in the mines were government employees or soldiers who displaced the former private workers?

14. The United States developed a hydroelectric plant on the non-navigable Grand River, a tributary of the navigable Arkansas River, as part of a comprehensive plan for the regulation of navigation, the control of floods, and the production of power on the Arkansas River. The Grand River Dam Authority, established by the Oklahoma legislature to develop hydroelectric power on the Grand River, protested on the ground that the federal project took away from it the ability to do what it was authorized to do by the state law. It claimed that the action of the federal government took away the hydroelectric power that it was to use and destroyed its franchise. The Authority claimed that this constituted a taking of its property by eminent domain and that it was entitled to compensation for such loss. Was it correct? [*United States v Grand River Dam Authority*, 363 US 229 (1960)]

15. The Long Island Water-Supply Co. was a privately owned water works that was under contract to supply water to various local political subdivisions. Eminent domain proceedings were brought to take certain land, including the land of the water works. It claimed that its property could not be taken by eminent domain because that would make it unable to perform its contracts with the local governments. Was this a valid defense? [*Long Island Water-Supply Co. v Brooklyn*, 166 US 685 (1897)]

16. A state highway commission exercised its power to take land by eminent domain. It took land owned by *M*. There were buildings on the land that could be removed and placed on other land owned by *M* that was not affected by the taking by eminent domain. The commission made an award of eminent domain compensation to *M* in an amount equal to the value of the land without buildings, plus the cost to *M* of moving the existing buildings to the other land. *M* objected to this standard of damages. Decide. [*Proctor v State Highway & Public Works Commission,* 230 NC 687, 55 SE 2d 479 (1949)]

19

Government Ownership of Business

§ 19:1. THE BACKGROUND

In a sense, government ownership of what would ordinarily be deemed a private business represents the ultimate in the regulation of private business. Government ownership may affect private business in one of three different ways. The operation of business by the government may remove a potential customer from other private enterprises. For example, the United States government maintains its own printing office, which deprives private printing houses of a very large customer. Government ownership may go a step further and sell goods or services to the public in competition with private enterprises that furnish the same goods or services to the public. This can be illustrated by the Tennessee Valley Authority, through which the United States government sells electrical power to public and private consumers in competition with private electrical power plants. The final stage of government ownership exists when the government maintains a monopoly of a particular type of enterprise, so that the private enterpriser cannot enter that field even if the enterpriser is willing to face the competition of the government-operated business. This total absorption by the government of a field of enterprise is more characteristic of nationalization or socialization programs than it has been of government ownership of business in the United States to date.

It is significant to note that, in the instances in which government in the United States has embarked upon government ownership, the move has rarely been influenced by a doctrine of state socialization. Three other factors have been more important in bringing government into the operation of business.

The first factor which has always been significant is that government is able to operate a business which private industry could not operate at a profit. This does not mean that governmental operation is more efficient than private enterprise, but only that private enterprise, in the last analysis, cannot exist unless it makes a profit, whereas government activity does not have to meet this standard. If the people of the nation or a state wish their government to offer a particular service, that service can be rendered at a loss and the deficit can be made up from public funds. The United States Postal System illustrates this situation, for the mail traffic in certain areas is so small that a private enterprise would not wish to furnish service to those areas.

The second significant factor in government ownership is that reform movements, convinced rightly or wrongly that certain evils in private management cannot be eliminated, have taken the business away from private hands and placed it under the government. This has been typical of many of the state moves to acquire and run industry.

The third factor in government operation of business has been the inability of government to transfer to private ownership enterprises entered into during times of war or emergency. This is true of the TVA, which began in 1917 as a plant for the generation of electricity. The electricity was to be used to make nitrates for explosives, for use in World War I. The actual working facilities were not completed until 1926. Partly because there was no feasible way of disposing of this large investment, the federal government began active development and operation of the TVA as a hydroelectric plant. In this connection it should be noted, however, that the advent of the New Deal was responsible to a large degree for expanding the TVA as a desirable asset, rather than regarding it as a liability to be scrapped as soon as possible.

Every proposal for government ownership naturally brings forth the protests of those who will be adversely affected by the activity or the competition of the government, in addition to those who object as a sincere matter of principle. A government caring for the welfare of all its peoples cannot lightly make a change that will have the effect of depriving a substantial segment of society of its existing means of obtaining a livelihood, or that will substantially depreciate the value of its investment. The economic misfortune of any segment of society soon is shared by other segments as the result of the reduced purchasing power of the group first adversely affected. A government therefore must proceed carefully, so that the sum of government ownership is a benefit to the public.

On behalf of public ownership of industry, it is claimed that it eliminates the need for regulation of private industry by government agencies. The difficulties found in regulation of business, particularly in the field of rate-making for utilities, are certainly such that it is desirable to avoid them if possible. It is answered, however, that the happy solution of avoiding them by government ownership of the business is not as happy as it first seems; for the net result, it is claimed, is lowered efficiency and lowered productivity because of a lower caliber of leadership, divided responsibility, and "red tape."

It is claimed that government ownership would make it safe to permit extensive integration of industry, with resultant large-scale economies that would benefit the public. Waste in advertising and in duplication of plant facilities and railroads are pointed out as cost items of a system of free enterprise that would be eliminated by government ownership. This is answered by the contention that service to the public would in fact deteriorate if there were no longer the incentive between competing, although duplicating, enterprisers.

It is claimed that government-owned plants could be financed at a lower interest rate because of the lower risk resulting from the backing of the government. This, however, might have the dangerous effect of encouraging unhealthy overexpansion of government-owned enterprises.

It is urged that government ownership of industry would eliminate much of the present labor-management conflict. It is doubtful whether labor is desirous of this possible solution for the conflict. The right of government employees to strike has been generally denied and, in recent years, has been expressly prohibited. The Taft-Hartley Amendment of 1947 to the Wagner Labor Relations Act provides that a striking federal employee shall be discharged, shall lose civil service status, if any, and may not be rehired by the government for a period of three years. It is likely that organized labor would prefer to retain its right to wage economic war.

It is urged that government ownership would make the goal of industry the greatest service for the greatest number, rather than profit. This would be offset by the danger that operation of business at a loss, in order to give greater services, merely would mean the imposing of a greater tax burden on the rest of the community and on the remaining private businesses. In addition, there is the great danger that the government industries would have their policies affected by the whims and accidents of political fortune.

§ 19:2. THE TENNESSEE VALLEY AUTHORITY

Government ownership has been carried further by the states than by the national government, although the activities of the latter have served to draw more attention and comment. Different states or political subdivisions have at various times maintained publicly owned fuel yards, utilities, coal mines, grain elevators, banks, and housing projects. Examples of United States government ownership of business are the United States Government Printing Office, the United States Post Office, the Inland Waterways Corporation, the Panama Canal Railroad, and the Tennessee Valley Authority.

The TVA is of particular interest in connection with these problems because of the extent and the breadth of its operation. As previously stated, it began its career as a nitrate production plant to aid in World War I; it was not until the New Deal came into power that the project was broadened into a plan for the development of the Tennessee Valley watershed. To carry out this plan, a corporation was created of which the United States government is the sole stockholder. This corporation, the Tennessee Valley Authority, is managed by three directors who are appointed by the President of the United States. The project has as its purposes the control of floods along the Tennessee Valley, with the accompanying conservation and elimination of soil erosion; the improvement of water transportation by increasing the area of navigability of the Tennessee river; the manufacture and sale of fixed nitrogen for fertilizer use; and the production of electrical power in surplus quantities for sale to political subdivisions, corporations, and individuals.

The express plan, as set forth in the statute creating the TVA, was to further the domestic and agricultural use of electricity by furnishing power to such consumers at the lowest possible rates. In order to insure that TVA-produced electricity would find its way to the consumers at a low rate, TVA was given authority to require that any business or enterprise purchasing electrical power from it should not charge more than stated maximum prices upon making a resale of that power to ultimate consumers. It was also an objective of President Roosevelt, although not expressly stated in the statute, that the operations at TVA would show reasonable costs for producing electricity, and that TVA operations could therefore serve as a yardstick in determining what rates should be allowed by utilities commissions for private electrical energy producers.

As a result of TVA operation, material advance has been made in the control of floods in the Tennessee Valley and a real service has been done to the farms and thus, indirectly, to the nation. The bulk of goods transported by water and the length of navigable waterways in the valley have also increased.

It is difficult to assess the net benefit of the TVA to the area and to the nation. Water transportation has been increased, but this may mean that to that extent, transportation by other means has been injured. This would be true unless it could be shown that the area has produced such an additional bulk of goods that the increase in transportation was not at the expense of other existing means. It is claimed that private electrical power companies have been injured by the government competition. This would certainly appear to be a reasonable claim, as the government electrical output has been sold at a substantially lower figure than that of private enterprise. The difficulty with the contention of private industry in this respect is that it assumes that, had it not been for the government's offering the electricity at a lower price, the government's customers would have bought the electricity from the private enterprise at the higher price. The fact that the new government users had not been purchasing electricity from the private enterprisers before TVA began its operation, or if they had, had been purchasing at much lower consumption levels, suggests that the government consumers would not have patronized private enterprise to any greater extent. If this is true, government industry does not necessarily compete with private industry because, though the same service or commodity is being sold, it is being sold at different economic levels that would not mix if left to themselves. Of course, this is merely a generalization, and it is undoubtedly true that many of the persons now using TVA electricity would have come to use the electricity furnished by private enterprise in time, although it seems clear that the rate at which they would have turned to privately produced electricity would have been much slower because of its greater cost.

The value of TVA as a yardstick in determining reasonable production costs merely has led to another debate. This has been due to the fact that TVA is not limited merely to the production of electrical energy but, as indicated above, has a number of different activities. In order to determine its cost of producing electrical energy, it is necessary to place a valuation on the property that it has devoted to that purpose. At this point two unknown factors enter the equation, because it is difficult, if not impossible, to determine just how much of the TVA plant should be allocated to electrical energy production and how much should be regarded as devoted to flood control, conservation, improvement of navigation, and other activities engaged in by TVA. Any figure would be more or less an arbitrary decision or reasonable guess; yet a difference of five or ten percent in the guess or the allocation could make a very substantial difference in determining what the reasonable rate or cost would be. In addition to this question of allocation, there is also the question of placing a value on what has been allocated, and here again we are faced with the difficulty of valuing property for rate-making purposes.

Because of these uncertainties in the calculation, there is ample ground for the claim of TVA's critics that it is not producing electrical energy at a lower-than-private cost and still making a profit. They can claim, as they have done, that, if a different allocation and a different valuation were placed upon the property used for the purpose of making electrical energy, it would really be shown that the production of electricity was costing the government a greater amount, and that unless the rates were raised so that they were comparable to those charged by private enterprise, TVA would operate at a loss. If this contention is correct, it means that the rates charged by private enterprises are reasonable and also means that the government, in furnishing electricity at a lower rate, is not obtaining an economic benefit but is merely furnishing services at a loss that is made up by the general body of taxpayers. In view of the fact that so many uncertainties and so many points of expert opinion are involved, it is impossible for the private citizen to determine where the truth lies.

§ 19:3. CONSTITUTIONALITY OF GOVERNMENT OWNERSHIP

Speaking generally, there is no constitutional barrier against government ownership and operation of business. If the government is building a new plant or buying an existing plant, the question of constitutionality is merely one of the spending power. As long as the purpose of the expenditure is for a public purpose or for the general welfare, the expenditure will be held valid. While it has always been readily assumed that there were certain purposes that were not public or not for the general welfare, which were clearly distinguished from those that were public or for the general welfare, it would seem that it is increasingly difficult to prohibit a government from entering into any particular business on the ground that to do so is not in furtherance of a public purpose or does not advance the general welfare. Manifestly, this represents a change in our philosophy of government and economics but, as Justice Holmes repeatedly complained, the Constitution does not incorporate and preserve any particular theory of economics.

As stated by the Supreme Court in *Puget Sound Power & Light Company v Seattle,* 291 US 619 (1934), "the decisions of this Court leave no doubt that a state may, in the public interest, constitutionally engage in a business commonly carried on by private enterprise, levy a tax to support it . . . and compete with private interests engaged in a like activity." The private enterprise that is faced with government competition cannot claim exemption from such taxation. As stated by the Court, it cannot be claimed that the public body "upon entering the business forfeited its power to tax any competitor."

In a world periodically the subject of wars and war scares, it could be urged that the government should own and operate the essential industries which produce for war in order to insure that the government will have a large supply of needed war materials at a low cost. The extension made to the war power repels any argument that such a program could not be followed in what would be considered normal peacetime. While technically the war power is possessed only by the national government, it is likely that the police power of the states to advance the general welfare would be regarded as authorizing action designed to further defense by the states.

If the question is not one of government beginning a new factory or plant but of acquiring the ownership of an existing plant or industry, the power of eminent domain will come into play if the property is not voluntarily sold to the government. If the enterprise is deemed a purpose sufficiently public to warrant the expenditure of tax money for its operation, then it will also be held to be sufficiently public to justify its being taken from the private ownership by use of the power of eminent domain. When this is done, however, the government, whether state or national, must make reasonable compensation to the owners for the value of the property taken. Because of this constitutional restriction, it is impossible in the United States for government to expropriate private enterprise. The government cannot take private industry away from its owners without making compensation for such taking.

In the case of the United States, it must also be remembered that, as a sovereign nation, it may acquire land or any other property by any means. It may do so by war, purchase, treaty, discovery and occupation, or eminent domain. Congress is authorized to "dispose of and make all needful rules and regulations respecting the territory or other property belonging to the United States."

This "property" power embraces the product of industrial activity. The power to dispose of it permits Congress to compete with private enterprise and to dispose of its product at any price it chooses, without regard to whether the price is below cost or not. No constitutional privilege of the private enterpriser is violated by being underbid by the government.

(a) Tennessee Valley Authority

ASHWANDER v TVA
297 US 288 (1936)

OPINION BY HUGHES, C. J.

. . . The Tennessee Valley Authority, . . . entered into a contract with the Alabama Power Company, providing (1) for the purchase by the Authority from the Power Company of certain transmission lines, substations, and auxiliary properties for $1,000,000; (2) for the purchase by the Authority from the Power Company of certain real property for $150,000; (3) for an interchange of hydro-electric energy, and, in addition, for the sale by the Authority to the Power Company of its "surplus power," on stated terms; and (4) for mutual restrictions as to the areas to be served in the sale of power. . . .

The Alabama Power Company is a corporation organized under the laws of Alabama, and is engaged in the generation of electric energy and its distribution generally throughout that state, its lines reaching 66 counties. The transmission lines to be purchased by the Authority extend from Wilson Dam, at the Muscle Shoals plant owned by the United States on the Tennessee river in northern Alabama, into seven counties in that state, within a radius of about 50 miles. These lines serve a population of approximately 190,000, including about 10,000 individual customers, or about one-tenth of the total number served directly by the Power Company. The real property to be acquired by the Authority (apart from the transmission lines above mentioned and related properties) is adjacent to the area known as the "Joe Wheeler dam site," upon which the Authority is constructing the Wheeler Dam.

The contract . . . also provided for cooperation between the Alabama Power Company and the Electric Home & Farm Authority, Inc., a subsidiary of the Tennessee Valley Authority, to promote the sale of electrical appliances. . . . The Congress may not, "under the pretext of executing its powers, pass laws for the accomplishment of objects not intrusted to the government." . . . The government's argument recognizes this essential limitation. The government's contention is that the Wilson Dam was constructed, and the power plant connected with it was installed, in the exercise by the Congress of its war and commerce powers; that is, for the purposes of national defense and the improvement of navigation.

Wilson Dam . . . was begun in 1917 and completed in 1926. Authority for its construction is found in § 124 of the National Defense Act of June 3, 1916. . . . It authorized the President . . . "to construct, maintain, and operate" on any such site "dams, locks, improvements to navigation, power houses, and other plants and equipment or other means than water power as in his judgment is the best and cheapest, necessary or convenient for the generation of electrical or other power and for the production of nitrates or other products needed for munitions of war and useful in the manufacture of fertilizers and other useful products." The President was authorized to lease or acquire by condemnation or otherwise such lands as might be necessary and there was further provision that "the products of such plants shall be used by the President for military and naval purposes to the extent that he may deem necessary, and any surplus which he shall determine is not required shall be sold and disposed of by him under such regulations as he may prescribe." . . .

We may take judicial notice of the international situation at the time the act of 1916 was passed, and it cannot be successfully disputed that the Wilson Dam and its auxiliary plants, including the hydroelectric power plant, are, and were intended to be, adapted to the purposes of national defense. While the District Court found that there is no intention to use the nitrate plants or the hydroelectric units installed at Wilson Dam for the production of war materials in time of peace, "the maintenance of said properties in operating condition and the assurance of an abundant supply of electric energy in the event of war, constitute national defense assets." This finding has ample support.

The act of 1916 also had in view "improvements to navigation." Commerce includes navigation. "All America understands, and has uniformly understood," said Chief Justice Marshall in *Gibbons v Ogden*, . . . "the word 'commerce,' to comprehend navigation." The power to regulate interstate commerce embraces the power to keep the navigable rivers of the United States free from obstructions to navigation and to remove such obstructions when they exist. "For these purposes," said the Court in *Gilman v Philadelphia*, . . . "Congress possesses all the powers which existed in the States before the adoption of the national Constitution, and which have always existed in the Parliament in England." . . .

The Tennessee river is a navigable stream, although there are obstructions at various points because of shoals, reefs, and rapids. The improvement of navigation on this river has been a matter of national concern for over a century. Recommendation that provision be made for navigation around Muscle Shoals was made by the Secretary of War, John C. Calhoun, in his report transmitted to the Congress by President Monroe in 1824, and, from 1852, the Congress has repeatedly authorized projects to develop navigation on that and other portions of the river, both by open channel improvements and by canalization. The Wilson Dam project, adopted in 1918, gave a 9-foot slack water development, for 15 miles above Florence, over the Muscle Shoals rapids, and, as the District Court found, "flooded out the then existing canal and locks which were inadequate." The District Court also found that a "high dam of this type was the only feasible means of eliminating this most serious type obstruction to navigation." By the act of 1930, after a protracted study by the Corps of Engineers of the United States Army, the Congress adopted a project for a permanent improvement of the main stream "for a navigable depth of 9 feet."

While, in its present condition, the Tennessee river is not adequately improved for commercial navigation, and traffic is small, we are not at liberty to conclude either that the river is not susceptible of development as an important waterway, or that Congress has not undertaken that development, or that the construction of the Wilson Dam was not an appropriate means to accomplish a legitimate end.

The Wilson Dam and its power plant must be taken to have been constructed in the exercise of the constitutional functions of the federal government.

. . . The government acquired full title to the dam site, with all riparian rights. The power of falling water was an inevitable incident of the construction of the dam. That water power came into the exclusive control of the federal government. The mechanical energy was convertible into electric energy, and the water power, the right to convert it into electric energy, and the electric energy thus produced constitute property belonging to the United States. . . .

Authority to dispose of property constitutionally acquired by the United States is expressly granted to the Congress by § 3 of article IV of the Constitution. This section provides:

"The Congress shall have Power to dispose of and make all needful Rules and Regulations respecting the Territory or other Property belonging to the United States; and nothing in this Constitution shall be so construed as to Prejudice any Claims of the United States, or of any particular State."

To the extent that the power of disposition is thus expressly conferred, it is manifest that the Tenth Amendment is not applicable. And the Ninth Amendment . . . in insuring the maintenance of the rights retained by the people does not withdraw the rights which are expressly granted to the Federal Government. The question is as to the scope of the grant and whether there are inherent limitations which render invalid the disposition of property with which we are now concerned.

. . . The argument is stressed that, assuming that electrical energy generated at the dam belongs to the United States, the Congress has authority to dispose of this energy only to the extent that it is a surplus necessarily created in the course of making munitions of war or operating the works for navigation purposes; that is, that the remainder of the available energy must be lost or go to waste. We find nothing in the Constitution which imposes such a limitation. It is not to be deduced from the mere fact that the electrical energy is only potentially available until the generators are operated. The government has no less right to the energy thus available by letting the water course over its turbines than it has to use the appropriate process to reduce to possession other property within its control, as, for example, oil which it may recover from a pool beneath its land, and which is reduced to possession by boring oil wells and otherwise might escape its grasp. . . . And it would hardly be contended that, when the government reserves coal on its lands, it can mine and dispose of it only for the purpose of heating public buildings or for other governmental operations. . . . Or that when the government extracts the oil it has reserved, it has no constitutional power to sell it. Our decisions recognize no such restriction . . . the United States owns the coal, or the silver, or the lead, or the oil, it obtains from its lands, and it lies in the discretion of Congress, acting in the public interest, to determine of how much of the property it shall dispose.

We think the same principle is applicable to electrical energy. . . . Suppose for example, that in the erection of a dam for the improvement of navigation, it became necessary to destroy a dam and power plant which had previously been erected by a private corporation engaged in the generation and distribution of energy. . . . Would anyone say that, because the United States had built its own dam and plant in the exercise of its constitutional functions . . . no power could be supplied to communities and enterprises dependent on it . . . because . . . the supply to the communities and enterprises . . . must be limited to the slender amount of surplus unavoidably involved in the operation of the navigation works? . . .

. . . The constitutional provision is silent as to the method of disposing of property belonging to the United States. That method, of course, must be an appropriate means of disposition according to the nature of the property, it must be one adopted in the public interest as distinguished from private or personal ends, and we may assume that it must be consistent with the foundation principles of our dual system of government and must not be contrived to govern the concerns reserved to the states. . . .

The transmission lines which the Authority undertakes to purchase from the Power company lead from the Wilson dam to a large area within about 50 miles of the dam. . . . They furnish a method of reaching a market. The alternative method is to sell the surplus energy at the dam, and the market there appears to be limited to one purchaser. . . . We know of no constitutional ground upon which the federal government can be denied the right to seek a wider market.

. . . The argument is earnestly presented that the government by virtue of its ownership of the dam and power plant could not establish a steel mill and make and sell steel products, or a factory to manufacture clothing or shoes for the public, and thus attempt to make its ownership of energy, generated at its dam, a means of carrying on competitive commercial enterprises, and thus drawing to the federal government the conduct and management of business having no relation to the purposes for which the federal government was established. . . . The government is not using . . . the energy generated at the dam to manufacture commodities of any sort for the public. The government is disposing of the energy itself which simply is the mechanical energy, incidental to falling water at the dam, converted into the electrical energy which is susceptible of transmission. The question here is simply as to the acquisition of the transmission lines as a facility for the disposal of that energy. . . .

[Judgment sustaining constitutionality of the TVA and the validity of its contract with the Alabama Power Company]

§ 19:4. SCOPE OF THE TVA DOCTRINE

There would seem to be no effective limitation on the power of the government to dispose of its property on any terms it sees fit. It may sell at any price it desires without regard to the production cost or to the cost or sale price of like property by private enterprise. It may lease its property or give it away.

While two limitations were recognized in the *TVA* case, these limitations appear ineffective. The case stated that the disposition must be made to further public interest rather than private interest. This limitation is not any clearer in connection with the disposition of government property than it is in the case of the disposition of money by means of the spending power. It appears so broad as to be no limitation at all.

The Court also stated that the disposition must be "consistent" with the basic principles of "our dual system of government." This was one of the last times that this doctrine of "dual federalism" made its appearance. By this is meant the peculiar interpretation found in several of the Supreme Court decisions that, not only must a particular power be delegated to Congress, but, in addition, the exercise of that power must not be in derogation of rights reserved to the states by the Tenth Amendment. This double barrel concept of the Tenth Amendment has been abandoned, and it is now recognized that the Tenth Amendment merely affirms what necessarily follows from the fact that Congress can only exercise those powers which have been delegated to it—of necessity, all others remain with the states from which the national government derived its powers. That the Tenth Amendment has been violated follows automatically from the conclusion that a power has not been given Congress. The latter question is not affected by the consideration that the power is reserved to the states if not granted to Congress. This second limitation is accordingly meaningless today.

A third limitation may be implied from the *TVA* opinion; namely, that the government cannot acquire the property solely for the purpose of disposing of it. It is unlikely that the government would at any time set itself up as a distributor to purchase goods from private sources with the object of resale to the public, although even this could no doubt be sustained under the commerce power if evils in marketing and distribution existed that could be eliminated by government acting as the distributor. Sales of property will in all likelihood result, with the exception of such incidental matters as the sale of war surplus, either from the government's purchasing surplus goods, such as farm goods, as a means of maintaining prices, or from the government's establishing publicly owned essential industries and then selling the surplus products, as in the TVA. Neither of these most likely forms of competition with private enterprise would be condemned by the third limitation stated above.

In view of the later interpretations of the commerce power, there would be seem to be little significance today in the statement by the Court in the *TVA* case that "the government is not using the water power at the Wilson Dam to establish any industry or business. It is not using the energy generated at the dam to manufacture commodities of any sort for the public. . . ." Economically, there is little merit to a distinction between the sale of electricity or the sale of loaves of bread at a cheaper rate than supplied by private enterprise. From the standpoint of private enterprise, the nature and effect of the competition is the same. If it should be held that the production of bread was a matter vital to the national health and security or a desirable way of disposing of a surplus wheat crop, the suggested limitation is not likely to be controlling.

While there is a distinction between the *TVA* case and those just posed, the limitation is one that may be readily avoided. There would be few enterprises in which the government could not take some part of the output and then have on its hands a surplus that it could sell under the authority of the *TVA* decision. This has added significance when it is realized that many modern industrial plants must be run at a certain production level in order to achieve efficiency of operation. It may very well be that, in slack periods, the government consumption would not consume the entire output when production is maintained at the level of greatest efficiency. It would not necessarily follow that the government would be required to curtail, and thus decrease the efficiency of, production. There is apparently no limitation that would prevent it from making the most efficient use of the taxpayer's money by maintaining the higher level of production and then selling the surplus under the authority of the *TVA* case.

The *TVA* decision attains added significance when considered in the light of the Atomic Energy Control Act of 1946. Under this law, the federal government nationalized all fissionable materials and has the monopoly of their use for peacetime productive purposes as well as military purposes. If the full economic potential of atomic energy can be realized, it would be possible for all the industries and all the homes in the United States to pipe in all their heat, power, and light from one gigantic government atomic energy plant. Private enterprise in the traditional types of heat, power, and light could not compete with such an enterprise.

§ 19:5. ACQUISITION OF EXISTING ENTERPRISE

Government ownership may arise from the government's building a new enterprise, which it then owns. In contrast, the government may wish to acquire ownership of an already existing business. This can be done either by taking the enterprise by eminent domain,[1] in which case just compensation must be made for the value of the property taken, or by purchasing the enterprise from its owner.

(a) Purchase of private enterprise

GREEN v FRAZIER

253 US 233 (1920)

OPINION BY DAY, J.

This is an action by taxpayers of the state of North Dakota . . . to enjoin the enforcement of certain state legislation. . . .

The legislation involved consists of . . . (1) An act creating an Industrial Commission of North Dakota, . . . which is authorized to conduct and manage on behalf of that state certain utilities, industries, enterprises, and business projects, to be established by law. . . . (2) The Bank of North Dakota Act

---

[1]See Ch. 18.

..., which establishes a bank under the name of "The Bank of North Dakota," operated by the state. . . . (3) An act providing for the issuing of bonds of the state in the sum of $2,000,000, the proceeds of which are to constitute the capital of the Bank of North Dakota. . . . (4) An act providing for the issuing of bonds in the sum of not exceeding $10,000,000, to be known as "Bonds of North Dakota, Real Estate Series" . . . for the purpose of raising money to procure funds for the Bank of North Dakota. . . . (5) An act declaring the purpose of the state of North Dakota to engage in the business of manufacturing and marketing farm products, and to establish a warehouse, elevator, and flour mill system under the name of "North Dakota Mill & Elevator Association," to be operated by the state. . . . The purpose is declared that the state shall engage in the business of manufacturing farm products and for that purpose shall establish a system of warehouses, elevators, flour mills, factories, plants, machinery and equipment, owned, controlled, and operated by it under the name of the "North Dakota Mill & Elevator Association." The Industrial Commission is placed in control of the association, with full power, and it is authorized to acquire by purchase, lease, or right of eminent domain, all necessary property or properties, etc.; to buy, manufacture, store, mortgage, pledge, sell, and exchange all kinds of raw and manufactured farm food products, and by-products, and to operate exchanges, bureaus, markets and agencies within and without the state, and in foreign countries. . . . An appropriation is made out of state funds, together with the funds procured from the sale of state bonds, to be designated as the capital of the association. (6) An act providing for the issuing of bonds of the state of North Dakota in a sum not exceeding $5,000,000, to be known as "Bonds of North Dakota, Mill & Elevator Series," . . . to be issued and sold for the purpose of carrying on the business of the Mill & Elevator Association. . . . (7) The Home Building Act declares the purpose of the state to engage in the enterprise of providing homes for its residents and to that end to establish a business system operated by it under the name of "The Home Building Association of North Dakota."

. . . This legislation was adopted under the broad power of the state to enact laws raising by taxation such sums as are deemed necessary to promote purposes essential to the general welfare of its people. Before the adoption of the Fourteenth Amendment this power of the state was unrestrained by any federal authority. That amendment introduced a new limitation upon state power into the federal Constitution. The states were forbidden to deprive persons of life, liberty or property without due process of law. . . .

The due process of law clause contains no specific limitation upon the right of taxation in the states, but it has come to be settled that the authority of the states to tax does not include the right to impose taxes for merely private purposes.

. . . What is a public purpose has given rise to no little judicial consideration. Courts, as a rule, have attempted no judicial definition of a "public" as distinguished from a "private" purpose, but have left each case to be determined by its own peculiar circumstances. . . .

With the wisdom of such legislation, and the soundness of the economic policy involved we are not concerned. Whether it will result in ultimate good or harm it is not within our province to inquire.

We come now to examine the grounds upon which the Supreme Court of North Dakota held this legislation not to amount to a taking of property without due process of law. The questions involved were given elaborate consideration in that court, and it held, concerning what may in general terms be denominated the "banking legislation," that it was justified for the purpose of providing banking facilities, and to enable the state to carry out the purposes of the other acts, of which the Mill & Elevator Association Act is the principal one. It justified the Mill & Elevator Association Act by the peculiar situation in the state of North Dakota, and particularly by the great agricultural industry of the state. It estimated from facts of which it was authorized to take judicial notice, that 90 percent of the wealth produced by the state was from agriculture, and stated that upon the prosperity and welfare of that industry other business and pursuits carried on in the state were largely dependent; that the state produced 125 million bushels of wheat each year. The manner in which the present system of transporting and marketing this great crop prevents the realization of what are deemed just prices was elaborately stated. It was affirmed that the annual loss from these sources (including the loss of fertility to the soil and the failure to feed the by-products of grain to stock within the state), amounted to $55 million to the wheat raisers of North Dakota. It answered the contention that the industries involved were private in their nature, by stating that all of them belonged to the state of North Dakota, and therefore the activities authorized by the legislation were to be distinguished from business of a private nature having private gain for its objective.

As to the Home Building Act, that was sustained because of the promotion of the general welfare in providing homes for the people, a large proportion of whom were tenants moving from place to place. It was believed and affirmed by the Supreme Court of North Dakota that the opportunity to secure and maintain homes would promote the general welfare, and that the provisions of the statutes to enable this feature of the system to become effective would redound to the general benefit.

As we have said, the question for us to consider and determine is whether this system of legislation is violative of the federal Constitution because it amounts to a taking of property without due process of law. The precise question herein involved so far as we have been able to discover has never been presented to this court. The nearest approach to it is found in *Jones v City of Portland,* 245 US 217, . . . in which we held that an act of the state of Maine authorizing cities or towns to establish and maintain wood, coal and fuel yards for the purpose of selling these necessaries to the inhabitants of cities and towns, did not deprive taxpayers of due process of law within the meaning of the Fourteenth Amendment. In that case we reiterated the attitude of this court towards state legislation, and repeated what had been said before, that what was or was not a public use was a question concerning which local authority, legislative and judicial, had especial means of securing information to enable them to form a judgment; and particularly, that the judgment of the highest court of the state, declaring a given use to be public in its nature, would be accepted by this court unless clearly unfounded. In that case the previous decisions of this court, sustaining this proposition, were cited with approval, and a quotation was made from the opinion of the Supreme Court of Maine justifying the legislation under the conditions prevailing in that state. We think the principle of that decision is applicable here.

. . . In many instances states and municipalities have in late years seen fit to enter upon projects to promote the public welfare which in the past have been considered entirely within the domain of private enterprise.

Under the peculiar conditions existing in North Dakota, which are emphasized in the opinion of its highest court, if the state sees fit to enter upon such enterprises as are here involved, with the sanction of its constitution, its legislature and its people, we are not prepared to say that it is within the authority of this court, in enforcing the observance of the Fourteenth Amendment, to set aside such action by judicial decision.

[Judgment against the taxpayers, sustaining state ownership of the industries involved]

---

§ 19:6. INTERGOVERNMENTAL RELATIONS

To what extent is a government-owned enterprise to be treated by other governments as a government activity or a private enterprise? Where the enterprise is one that is ordinarily conducted by private enterprise and, as such, is subject to a federal tax, it is clear that the enterprise will remain subject to that tax without regard to the fact of its public ownership. The converse should also be true, that a federal enterprise is subject to a local tax that would be imposed if the federal activity were privately operated.

Regarding governmental regulations, an enterprise owned by a state or a political subdivision must conform to the same federal regulations as it would if it were privately owned, where it is a type of enterprise that is ordinarily privately owned. It would seem that the converse is also true for a federally owned enterprise, although if the local regulation interferes with the federal program, the doctrine of federal supremacy will prevail over the local regulation.

The experience with the TVA has not given a definitive answer to the questions of tax liability and governmental regulation. The question of tax liability has been avoided by the practice of the TVA of voluntarily paying such local taxes as it would be required to pay if it were privately owned. In addition to avoiding the question of constitutionality of a state tax on a federally owned enterprise, this policy also avoids the objection that TVA operations cannot be used as a yardstick because of a favored tax status.

Local utility commissions have already asserted jurisdiction over contracts made by the TVA. Just how far this jurisdiction will extend, and to what extent state regulation will be permitted by the Court to conflict with the federal objectives of the TVA project remain for future determination.

(a) Applicability of federal statute

PARDEN v TERMINAL RAILWAY OF THE ALABAMA STATE DOCKS DEPARTMENT

377 US 184 (1964)

Parden and others were injured while working on the terminal railroad owned by the State of Alabama. They brought suit against the railroad by filing a petition setting forth their claims. The State of Alabama, which voluntarily appeared in the action as a defendant, raised the objection that there was no liability because the railroad was owned by the state and the state could not be sued without its consent. From decisions sustaining the immunity of the state, the petitioners appealed.

OPINION BY BRENNAN, J.

. . . The question in this case is whether a State that owns and operates a railroad in interstate commerce may successfully plead sovereign immunity.
. . .

The Terminal Railway is wholly owned and operated by the State of Alabama through its State Docks Department, and has been since 1927. Consisting of about 50 miles of railroad tracks in the area adjacent to the State Docks at Mobile, it serves those docks and several industries situated in the vicinity, and also operates an interchange railroad with several privately owned railroad companies. It performs services for profit under statutory authority authorizing it to operate "as though it were an ordinary common carrier." . . . It conducts substantial operations in interstate commerce. It has contracts and working agreements with the various railroad brotherhoods in accordance with the Railway Labor Act, 45 USC § 151 et seq.; maintains its equipment in conformity with the Federal Safety Appliance Act, 45 USC § 1 et seq.; and complies with the reporting and bookkeeping requirements of the Interstate Commerce Commission. It is thus indisputably a common carrier by railroad engaging in interstate commerce.

Petitioners contend that it is consequently subject to this suit under the Federal Employers' Liability Act. That statute provides that "every common carrier by railroad while engaging in commerce between any of the several States . . . shall be liable in damages to any person suffering injury while he is employed by such carrier in such commerce," and that "under this chapter an action may be brought in a district court of the United States. . . ." 45 USC §§ 51, 56. Respondents rely, as did the lower courts in dismissing the action, on sovereign immunity—the principle that a State may not be sued by an individual without its consent. . . .

We think that Congress, in making the FELA applicable to "every" common carrier by railroad in interstate commerce, meant what it said. That congressional statutes regulating railroads in interstate commerce apply to such railroads whether they are state owned or privately owned is hardly a novel proposition; it has twice been clearly affirmed by this Court. . . .

. . . If Congress made the judgment that, in view of the dangers of railroad work and the difficulty of recovering for personal injuries under existing rules, railroad workers in interstate commerce should be provided with the right of action created by the FELA, we should not presume to say, in the absence of express provision to the contrary, that it intended to exclude a particular group of such workers from the benefits conferred by the Act. To read a "sovereign immunity exception" into the Act would result, moreover, in a right without a remedy; it would mean that Congress made "every" interstate railroad liable in damages to injured employees but left one class of such employees—those whose employers happen to be state owned—without any effective means of enforcing that liability. We are unwilling to conclude that Congress intended so pointless and frustrating a result. We therefore read the FELA as authorizing suit in a Federal District Court against state-owned as well as privately owned common carriers by railroad in interstate commerce.

Respondents contend that Congress is without power, in view of the immunity doctrine, thus to subject a State to suit. We disagree. Congress enacted the FELA in the exercise of its constitutional power to regulate interstate commerce. . . . While a State's immunity from suit by a citizen without its consent has been said to be rooted in "the inherent nature of sovereignty," . . . the States surrendered a portion of their sovereignty when they granted Congress the power to regulate commerce. . . .

. . . A State's operation of a railroad in interstate commerce "must be in subordination to the power to regulate interstate commerce, which has been granted specifically to the national government. The sovereign power of the states is necessarily diminished to the extent of the grants of power to the federal government in the Constitution. . . . There is no such limitation upon the plenary power to regulate commerce [as there is upon the federal power to tax state instrumentalities]. The state can no more deny the power if its exercise has been authorized by Congress than can an individual." . . .

. . . Our conclusion is simply that Alabama, when it began operation of an interstate railroad approximately 20 years after enactment of the FELA, necessarily consented to such suit as was authorized by that Act. By adopting and ratifying the Commerce Clause, the States empowered Congress to create such a right of action against interstate railroads; by enacting the FELA in the exercise of this power, Congress conditioned the right to operate a railroad in interstate commerce upon amenability to suit in federal court as provided by the Act; by thereafter operating a railroad in interstate commerce, Alabama must be taken to have accepted that condition and thus to have consented to suit. "By engaging in interstate commerce by rail [the State] has subjected itself to the commerce power, and is liable for a violation of the . . . Act, as are other carriers. . . ."

. . .

Our conclusion that this suit may be maintained is in accord with the common sense of this Nation's federalism. A State's immunity from suit by an individual without its consent has been fully recognized by the Eleventh Amendment and by subsequent decisions of this Court. But when a State leaves the sphere that is exclusively its own and enters into activities subject to congressional regulation, it subjects itself to that regulation as fully as if it were a private person or corporation. . . . It would surprise our citizens, we think, to learn that petitioners, who in terms of the language and purposes of the FELA are on precisely the same footing as other railroad workers, must be denied the benefit of the Act simply because the railroad for which they work happens to be owned and operated by a State rather than a private corporation. It would be even more surprising to learn that the FELA does make the Terminal Railway "liable" to petitioners, but, unfortunately, provides no means by which that liability may be enforced. Moreover, such a result would bear the seeds of a substantial impediment to the efficient working of our federalism. States have entered and are entering numerous forms of activity which, if carried on by a private person or corporation, would be subject to federal regulation. . . . In a significant and increasing number of instances, such regulation takes the form of authorization of lawsuits by private parties. To preclude this form of regulation in all cases of state activity would remove an important weapon from the congressional arsenal with respect to a substantial volume of regulable conduct. Where, as here, Congress by the terms and purposes of its enactment has given no indication that it desires to be thus hindered in the exercise of its constitutional power, we see nothing in the Constitution to obstruct its will.

[Judgment for Parden and co-workers, holding the federal statute applicable to a state-owned railroad]

Questions for Discussion

1. What rule did the Court establish in the *Frazier* case for determining whether the purpose of a law is public or private?

2. How would the Court have decided the *Frazier* case if a federal instead of a state law had been involved?

3. (a) What is the constitutional basis for ownership of a private industry by the United States? by a state?   (b) Does it make any difference to your answer if it is wartime? depression? peacetime?

4. What is the basis for the decision in the *TVA* case?

5. Would the *TVA* be constitutional if it had been constructed in peacetime and operated in peacetime?

6. (a) What are the objectives of the *TVA?*   (b) What is the constitutional basis for seeking to achieve each of these objectives?

7. Discuss the value of the *TVA* as a yardstick for measuring electrical energy production costs.

8. What is the organization of the *TVA?* By whom is it owned? By whom is it controlled?

9. In *Ashwander v TVA,* the Court stated: "While, in its present condition, the Tennessee River is not adequately improved for commercial navigation, and traffic is small, we are not at liberty to conclude either that the river is not susceptible of development as an important waterway, or that Congress has not undertaken that development, or that the construction of the Wilson Dam was not an appropriate means to accomplish a legitimate end." Compare this with the approach in *McCulloch v Maryland,* § 3:3(a).

10. How does government ownership of a business affect private enterprise?

11. (a) Is it desirable to maintain private ownership even though government ownership may be more efficient? (b) Does this problem bear any relation to the question of whether small enterprise should be maintained even though big enterprise may be more efficient?

12. Does *Ashwander v TVA* authorize the United States to enter the farming business? the coal business? the mining business generally?

13. City *A* operates a chain of auto service stations that compete with private auto service stations. The city stations sell gasoline, oil, and services at a lower price than the private stations. The private stations seek an injunction to stop the operation of the public stations on the ground that the law authorizing their operation is unconstitutional because: (a) The city has no authority to enter such a business, as it is not affected with a public interest. (b) The city cannot spend public money for the purpose of running such a business. (c) The private stations are deprived of their property without due process of law, as the city is able to undersell them. (d) The city is guilty of unfair methods of competition by underselling the private concerns, as it can make up any deficit from the tax money. (e) The city cannot operate public service stations if it taxes the private stations. Decide and discuss each of the objections.

14. Is the doctrine of *Ashwander v TVA* limited to extractive industries that involve the removal of a substance contained in land owned by the United States?

15. Is there any limitation on the power recognized in *Ashwander v TVA?* Discuss.

16. A coalyard is owned and operated by City *X.* Can the United States tax this property and make it subject to regulations imposed on all privately owned coalyards?

17. A chain of coalyards is owned and operated throughout the United States by the United States government.   (a) Can a state tax the property of such coalyards located within its boundaries?   (b) Can a state make its trade regulations apply to the national coalyards?

18. How does the *Parden* case avoid the immunity of a state from suit?

19. (a) Can Congress constitutionally adopt a law providing that whenever any war surplus materials are sold by the United States to private citizens, the purchasers cannot make a resale of the materials at a price greater than the price of purchase from the government plus 10 percent? (b) Would the statute be constitutional if it prohibited resale by the purchaser under any condition?

20. California owns the Belt Railroad that serves San Francisco Harbor and, through connections with other lines, handles interstate traffic. It is a common carrier and files tariffs with the Interstate Commerce Commission. A collective bargaining agreement was entered into between the state and the employees of the Belt Railroad. A number of employees later presented claims arising under the agreement to the National Railroad Adjustment Board. The board refused to exercise jurisdiction over the matter, on the theory that the Railway Labor Act did not apply to a state-owned railroad. The employees then brought an action against the board to compel it to exercise jurisdiction. Decide. [*California v Taylor,* 353 US 553 (1957)]

In this part, consideration will be given to the modern use of administrators in exercising the powers of government which have been discussed in the earlier chapters. Successive chapters will deal with the power of administrators to adopt rules, to make investigations, and to determine disputed issues, and the extent to which a court will reverse the conclusion of an administrator.

20

Administrative Rule Making

§ 20:1. PERSPECTIVE

Large areas of the American economy are governed by federal administrative agencies, created to carry out the general policies specified by Congress. A contract must be in harmony with public policy, not only as declared by Congress and the courts, but also as applied by the appropriate administrative agency. For example, a contract to market particular goods might not be prohibited by any statute or court decision but it may still be condemned by the Federal Trade Commission as an unfair method of competition. When the proper commission has made its determination, a contract not in harmony therewith, such as a contract of a carrier charging a higher or a lower rate than that approved by the Interstate Commerce Commission, is illegal. Other federal administrative agencies include the Civil Aeronautics Board, the Federal Communications Commission, the Federal Maritime Commission, the Federal Power Commission, the National Labor Relations Board, and the Securities and Exchange Commission. The law governing these agencies is known as *administrative law.* State administrative agencies may also affect business and the citizen, because state agencies may have jurisdiction over fair employment practices, workers' compensation claims, and the renting of homes and apartments.

The structure of government common in the states and the national government is a division into three branches—executive, legislative, and judicial—with the lawmaker selected by popular vote, and with the judicial branch acting as the superguardian to prevent either the executive or the legislative branch from exceeding the proper spheres of their respective powers. In contrast, members of administrative agencies are ordinarily appointed (in the case of federal agencies, by the President of the United States with the consent of two thirds of Congress), and the major agencies combine legislative, executive, and judicial powers, in that they may make the rules, police the community to see that the rules are obeyed, and sit in judgment to determine whether there have been violations of their rules.

Although an appeal to the courts may be taken from the action of an administrative agency, to a large degree the agency is not subject to control by the courts. The subject matter involved is ordinarily so technical, and the agency is clothed with such discretion, that courts will not reverse agency action unless it can be proved arbitrary and capricious. Very few agency decisions are reversed on this ground.

(a) "Administrator" defined

The administrator may be an agency or commission of a few or many persons or the head of an executive department of the United States government. The name or size is not important. It is the function of "administering" which is here considered; and, for the sake of brevity, the term *administrator* will be used to refer to all these administrators as a general class, without indicating the number of persons or the structure of the agency involved.

(b) Decentralization of administrative functions

In order to meet the objection that the exercise of executive, legislative, and judicial powers by the same administrator is a potential threat to impartiality, some steps have been taken toward decentralizing the administrative functions. Thus the prosecutorial power of the National Labor Relations Board was severed from the board and entrusted to an independent General Counsel by the Labor-Management Relations Act of 1947. In a number of agencies, such as the Federal Trade Commission, the judicial function is assigned to Administrative Law Judges.

§ 20:2. LEGISLATIVE POWER OF ADMINISTRATORS

The modern administrator has power to make the laws that regulate a particular segment of life or industry. Congress, or the state legislature, can make laws. It therefore seemed an improper transfer or delegation of power for the lawmaker to set up a separate body or agency and give to it the power to make the laws. The same forces that led society initially to create the administrator caused society to clothe the administrator with the power to make the laws. Practical expediency gradually prevailed in favor of the conclusion that if we want the administrator to do a job, we must grant the administrator sufficient power to do so.

In the early days of administrative regulation, the legislative character of the administrative rules was not clearly perceived, largely because the administrator's sphere of power was so narrow that the administrator was, in effect, merely a thermostat. That is, the lawmaker told the administrator when to do what, and all that the administrator did was to act in the manner specified by such a program. For example, the cattle inspector was told to take certain steps when it was determined that cattle had hoof-and-mouth disease. Here it was clear that the lawmaker had set the standard, and the administrator merely "swung into action" when the specified factual situation existed.

The next step in the growth of the administrative power was to authorize the cattle inspector to act upon finding that cattle had a contagious disease, leaving it to the inspector to formulate a rule or guide as to what diseases were contagious. Here again, the discretionary and the legislative aspects of the administrator's conduct were obscured by the belief that the field of science would define "contagious," leaving no area of discretionary decision to the administrator.

Today's health commission, an administrator, is authorized to make such rules and regulations for the protection or improvement of the common health as it deems desirable. Its rules thus make the "health law." In regulating various economic aspects of national life, the administrator is truly the lawmaker.

(a) Statement of goal or policy

It is now sufficient for a legislature to authorize an administrator to grant licenses "as public interest, convenience, or necessity requires"; "to prohibit unfair methods of competition"; to regulate prices so that they "in [the administrator's] judgment will be generally fair and equitable"; to prevent "profiteering"; "to prevent the existence of intercorporate holdings which unduly or unnecessarily complicate the structure [or] unfairly or inequitably distribute voting power among security holders"; and to renegotiate government contracts to prevent "excessive profits."

(b) Changing technology and the administrator's authority

The authority of an administrator is not limited to the technology existing when the administrator was created. To the contrary, the sphere in which the administrator may act expands with new scientific developments. For this reason it has been held that although community cable television (CATV) was developed after the Federal Communication Commission was created by the Federal Communications Act of 1934, the commission can regulate CATV. This power to regulate includes both the mechanical aspects of broadcasting and reception and also the content of the broadcast. Thus the commission may require such systems to originate local programs (cablecasting) in order to serve the local communities, in addition to their activity of transmitting programs from a distance.[1]

---

[1]*United States v Midwest Video Corp.*, 406 US 649 (sustaining a commission regulation which provided that "no CATV system having 3,500 or more subscribers shall carry the signal of any

§ 20:3. NECESSITY FOR DELEGATION OF RULE-MAKING AUTHORITY

In a relatively simple or primitive community, society can content itself with the adoption of rules or law decrees prohibiting certain lines of conduct and specifying the penalty to be imposed for the violation of those standards. In such a state, the conduct that is permitted and the conduct that is prohibited are relatively clearly divided. It is not necessary to correlate the economic conditions or other circumstances to determine whether a practice is condemned. The classification or division between that which is lawful and that which is unlawful is both universal and static.

To illustrate, larceny has for centuries been set apart as being unlawful conduct. While technicalities arise as to the precise definition of larceny, for practical purposes it is a course of conduct that may be readily separated or isolated from other forms of conduct. A prohibition against larceny is likewise a universal concept within the particular community or state; that is, the conduct is condemned to the same extent regardless of the geographic place of its commission. Larceny is also larceny independently of the conduct of any other party or of the community in which it is committed. Moreover, there is virtually no need to change the standard of larceny at any particular moment. It is true that the course of law has been to widen the definition of larceny beyond that of the common law, so as to include takings that were not condemned at the common law. This has been done by expanding the nature of property that may be the subject of larceny, and the persons who may commit it. This growth has been the work of several centuries and, from the standpoint of any one year, presents a static rather than a dynamic picture.

(a) Details of administration

As we move into the more modern era of regulation, particularly the regulation of business, the picture changes. The horizon of the lawmaker widens. Now the lawmaker attempts not merely to prohibit specific types of conduct but to regulate enterprises or activities generally, in the interest of achieving a social betterment. It is no longer possible or desirable for the lawmaker to prescribe every detail. When a statute based on the policy that prices should be "reasonable" or that licenses should be granted where required by the "public interest" is adopted, it becomes impossible for the lawmaker to give a precise definition of "reasonable" or "public interest." The practice has therefore developed of appointing or selecting an administrator, who is charged with the duty of making regulations to carry out the legislative purpose of maintaining reasonable prices or of granting licenses in the public interest.

---

television broadcast station unless the system also operates to a significant extent as a local outlet by cablecasting and has available facilities for local production and presentation of programs other than automated services").

Had the lawmaker not been willing to entrust this authority to the administrator, it would have been necessary for the statute to specify in detail every factual situation in which the price would be reasonable or the issuance of a license would be in the public interest. The inability of the lawmaker, however farsighted, to foresee every possible contingency is obvious. Even assuming such an ability, the statute would be so long and detailed that few persons would be able to know its full meaning. By delegating authority to the administrator, the legislative body is free to confine its attention to the basic or underlying principles of policy, leaving to the administrator the task of filling out the details.

(b) Expert administration

In addition to the necessity of the situation, which requires the delegation of regulation or rule-making authority to the administrator, there is also the advantage to be gained of administration by an expert. An administrator properly qualified for the position will have a far greater knowledge of the subject than could be expected of the lawmaker. The regulation by the administrator should therefore be better than the amateur regulation by the lawmaker. This is not intended to belittle the lawmaker, but is merely a recognition of the fact that each member of a lawmaking body cannot have the experience and the knowledge of a specialist in every field of business that the government may wish to regulate. It is also a recognition of the fact that, if a business is to be regulated, the person making the regulation cannot know too much about that business.

Of course, if the administrator is not competent, these benefits will not be obtained. If the administrator is not expert in the field, not alert to change, not quick to realize the good or the bad effects of a particular regulation, confusion, hardship, and partisanship as great as though the matter was not in the hands of an administrator may result. This obviously is not an argument against delegating legislative authority, but is merely an argument to exert all the power of a democracy to make certain that those authorized to administer are competent to do so.

(c) Flexibility of administration

This delegation of authority to the administrator is further necessitated by the fact that what is "reasonable" or in the "public interest" depends upon an accurate prediction of future situations. A sudden shortage or an unexpected surplus may throw out of line any prior rigid fixing of a "reasonable price." The regulation must therefore be dynamic rather than static, and it would be unsatisfactory and would produce great injustice for the lawmaker to fix a rigid price. The necessity for correlation of the regulation to changing factors demands a flexibility of regulation that cannot be possessed by a lawmaking body meeting only at intervals.

The flexibility of administration made possible by regulation by an administrator is also desirable from the standpoint of the mechanics of regulation. The period of the regulation of modern business has been comparatively short. While we have obtained considerable experience in certain lines of regulation, there are many fields recently embarked on in which regulation necessarily has been made on the basis of trial and error. In the absence of prior experience, no other course is available than to adopt the regulation that appears the best, and then to modify it from time to time as experience dictates. To do this requires both a day-to-day surveillance of the workings of the regulation and the ability to change the regulation quickly, as wisdom dictates. A statute cannot provide this flexibility. All lawmaking bodies in the United States meet at intervals. In many of the states, the legislature meets only every other year. Under such a system, regulation by the lawmaker necessarily assumes a spasmodic, intermittent character and currently cannot be adjusted to change with the times.

(d) Localized administration

The administrative regulation may also lack the universality of a traditional statute. It may be necessary to divide the country into areas or zones to regulate price within the separate units. A "reasonable" price for one area of supply or competition may be unreasonable for another. It would be extremely difficult, if not impossible, for a lawmaking body to devise a law with such variations.

§ 20:4. LEGISLATIVE NATURE OF RULE MAKING

Before considering the validity of a statute authorizing an administrator to adopt rules, it is necessary to determine the nature of the function of rule making. Since the regulation of the administrator will govern the community in the same manner as an Act of Congress or other appropriate legislature, authorizing an administrator to adopt rules, in effect, gives the administrator power to make laws. In adopting a regulation, the administrator exercises a legislative, rather than an executive or judicial, function. It is true that the administrator is not given the power to make laws generally and must keep within the area prescribed by the lawmaker; nevertheless, within the area of permitted action, the administrator is making law. This at first does violence to constitutional provisions and traditional concepts of governmental powers divided into three branches—executive, legislative, and judicial—and of the exclusive domain of the publicly elected lawmaker. In contrast, in the field of regulation we find an administrator, generally not elected, generally unknown to the public, making the laws. Because of this conflict between the necessity of administration and constitutional and traditional policies, the courts for a long time have been reluctant to admit the legislative nature of the administrative function when the administrator prescribes general rules for future conduct that will apply to all persons coming within their field of operation.

The rule may be either a rule of conduct, as that term is generally used, or it may be a rule of conduct as to a specific thing, such as a rule fixing rents, prices, or production quotas. Conduct is regulated by specifying the price at which an article is to be sold just as much as when the sale itself is prohibited.

The legislative nature of the rule-making function was recognized in *Prentis v Atlantic Coastline Co.,* 211 US 210 (1908), where, in speaking of the Interstate Commerce Commission, Justice Holmes stated:

> . . . we think it equally plain that the proceedings drawn in question here are legislative in their nature, and none the less so that they have taken place with a body which at another moment, or in its principal or dominant aspect, is a court. . . . A judicial inquiry investigates, declares, and enforces liabilities as they stand on present or past facts and under laws supposed already to exist. That is its purpose and end. Legislation, on the other hand, looks to the future and changes existing conditions by making a new rule to be applied thereafter to all or some part of those subject to its power. The establishment of a rate is the making of a rule for the future, and therefore is an act legislative, not judicial, in kind.
> . . .

(a) Rule making and the federal Administrative Procedure Act

The legislative nature of the rule-making function is also recognized by the federal Administrative Procedure Act,[2] which, in a general way, provides that the administrator, in adopting regulations, shall follow a procedure of notice, hearing, and inquiry similar to that followed by a legislative body. The Act provides in this connection that:

> Sec. 4. Except to the extent that there is involved (1) any military, naval, or foreign affairs function of the United States or (2) any matter relating to agency management or personnel or to public property, loans, grants, benefits, or contracts—
> (a) NOTICE.—General notice of proposed rule making shall be published in the Federal Register (unless all persons subject thereto are named and either personally served or otherwise have actual notice thereof in accordance with law) and shall include (1) a statement of the time, place, and nature of public rule making proceedings; (2) reference to the authority under which the rule is proposed; and (3) either the terms or substance of the proposed rule or a description of the subjects and issues involved. Except where notice or hearing is required by statute, this subsection shall not apply to interpretative rules, general statements of policy, rules of agency organization, procedure, or practice, or in any situation in which the agency for good cause finds (and incorporates the finding and a brief statement of the reasons therefor in the rules issued) that notice and public procedure thereon are impracticable, unnecessary, or contrary to the public interest.

---

[2]This Act establishes uniform procedure for all federal administrators not otherwise regulated.

(b) PROCEDURES.—After notice required by this section, the agency shall afford interested persons an opportunity to participate in the rule making through submission of written data, views, or arguments with or without opportunity to present the same orally in any manner; and, after consideration of all relevant matter presented, the agency shall incorporate in any rules adopted a concise general statement of their basis and purpose. Where rules are required by statute to be made on the record after opportunity for an agency hearing, the requirements of sections 7 and 8 shall apply in place of the provisions of this subsection.

(c) EFFECTIVE DATES.—The required publication or service of any substantive rule (other than one granting or recognizing exemption or relieving restriction or interpretative rules and statements of policy) shall be made not less than thirty days prior to the effective date thereof except as otherwise provided by the agency upon good cause found and published with the rule.

(d) PETITIONS.—Every agency shall accord any interested person the right to petition for the issuance, amendment, or repeal of a rule.

(b) Rules as "law of the state"

UNITED STATES v HOWARD

352 US 212 (1957)

The Congress made it a federal crime to transport fish in interstate commerce from a state if such transportation was "contrary to the law of the state." Howard transported fish from Florida. No Florida statute made it unlawful, but such transportation violated a rule of the Florida Game and Fresh Water Fish Commission. Howard was prosecuted for violating the federal statute. She claimed that she had not violated the statute because no Florida "law" prohibited such transportation.

OPINION BY REED, J.

. . . The sole question presented is whether Rule 14.01 of the Commission's regulations, . . . is a "law" of the State of Florida as that term is used in the Federal Act.

This Court has repeatedly ruled, in other circumstances, that orders of state administrative agencies are the law of the State. . . . In *Grand Trunk R. Co. v Indiana R. Comm'n,* 221 US 400, 403, the Court stated, citing *Prentis v Atlantic Coast Line Co.,* 211 US 210, 226: "the order [of the Indiana Railroad Commission] . . . is a law of the State within the meaning of the contract clause of the Constitution. . . ." And, in *Lake Erie & W. R. Co. v Public Utilities Comm'n,* 249 US 422, 424, it was said that an order of the state public utilities commission "being legislative in its nature . . . is a state law within the meaning of the Constitution of the United

States and the laws of Congress regulating our jurisdiction." A similar statement may be found in *Arkadelphia Co. v St. Louis S. W. R. Co.,* 249 US 134, 141. . . .

Appellee argues that the rules of the Florida Commission are so subject to change that they lack sufficient substance and permanence to be the "law" of Florida. We need not decide now whether a state agency could make a rule of such a temporary nature and so unaccompanied by the procedural niceties of rule making that the declaration should not be considered the law of the State for purposes of a statute such as the Black Bass Act. . . .

Accordingly we hold that the phrase "law of the State," as used in this Act, is sufficiently broad to encompass the type of regulation used in Florida. . . .

[Judgment for United States]

§ 20:5. CONSTITUTIONALITY OF DELEGATION OF RULE-MAKING POWER

Apart from the question of the desirability of delegating authority to the administrator in a particular case, the question arises, under both national and state constitutions, whether a particular delegation by the lawmaker to the administrator is constitutional. In the case of the Federal Constitution, there is the express limitation of Article I that "all legislative powers herein granted shall be vested in a Congress of the United States."

The delegation of legislative powers also runs counter to the traditional American principle of a tripartite government consisting of executive, legislative, and judicial branches. This division of powers was inspired by the desire to prevent rule by a tyrant. If governmental powers are all concentrated in one person or one group, it then depends merely upon the goodness of their natures whether government is or is not tyrannical. If, on the other hand, no one person or group has more than a segment of the governing powers, it is clear that each segment will serve as a check to block potential tyranny on the part of the other. This theory of tripartite division of governmental powers is defeated in part by a statute that delegates the power of one segment to another.

On this basis, laws by which the Congress authorized the president to do certain acts after making certain determinations have been attacked as unconstitutional on the ground that they destroyed the division of powers between the Congress and the president by entrusting to the latter those which belong to the former. Where the delegation is made to a separate or independent administrator, this problem of destroying the fundamental division of power is not presented in such an acute form. If the Congress chooses to give part of its power to a separate agency, this does not increase the power of either the executive or the judicial branch. In such case, the argument against delegation is fundamentally that the body entrusted with the original duty cannot shirk that duty or permit it to be performed by anyone else.

In the earlier years, when the administrators performed relatively simple tasks, the lawmaker generally instructed the administrator in exactly what should be done when certain facts existed. In this period, therefore, it was necessary to find in the statute a standard to govern the administrator. Today the field of administrative regulation is too complex for the establishment of a statutory standard, and the lawmaker must be content with stating an objective or policy to the administrator and then allowing the administrator to do whatever the latter deems proper in order to achieve that objective or carry out the policy. Today the courts generally hold that there is no improper delegation if the lawmaker has established the policy for the administrator to follow, although many cases will find that the statutes in question declare both a standard and a policy. That is, such cases give recognition to both the earlier test of a statutory standard and the modern test of a statutory policy. There is even authority that the law is moving into a third stage, in which neither a standard nor a policy need be declared, and it is sufficient to create an administrator to regulate a given area of the economy and then to allow the administrator to decide what rules should be adopted and what policies should be followed.

Although the constitutionality of delegation has been much litigated, there have only been three instances in which the United States Supreme Court has invalidated an Act of Congress for that reason.[3] The significance of these cases may be readily discounted, for the reason that the condemnation of the statutes in question on the ground of improper delegation was merely part of a general condemnation of those statutes because they exceeded the bounds of the federal commerce power, as that power was then interpreted. With the changing concept of that power,[4] it appears unlikely that the statutes in question would be invalidated on the sole ground of delegation.

With respect to state legislation, the doctrine of nondelegation has greater vitality, and a number of state laws have been declared void on that ground. Many state courts continue to require a standard to be specified, although a few have recognized the impracticality of so doing as the complexity of regulation and of the economy increases.[5]

(a) Prescribing the policy for price control

YAKUS v UNITED STATES

321 US 414 (1944)

Acting under the Emergency Price Control Act of 1942, as amended by the Inflation Control Act of 1942, the Price Control Administrator fixed maximum prices for specified commodities. Certain dealers were convicted for selling these commodities at prices above the set levels. The dealers claimed that the law was unconstitutional in delegating the legislative power of Congress to the Price Administrator.

---

[3]*A.L.A. Schechter Poultry Corp v United States,* § 8:2(b). *Carter v Carter Coal Co.,* § 8:2(c). *Panama Refining Co. v Ryan,* 293 US 388 (1935).

[4]See Chapter 8.

[5]*Pressman v Barnes,* 209 Md 544, 121 A 2d 816 (1956).

OPINION BY STONE, C. J.

... The Emergency Price Control Act provides for the establishment of the Office of Price Administration under the direction of a Price Administrator appointed by the President, and sets up a comprehensive scheme for the promulgation by the Administrator of regulations or orders fixing such maximum prices of commodities and rents as will effectuate the purpose of the Act and conform to the standards which it prescribes. The Act was adopted as a temporary wartime measure, and provides in § 1(b) for its termination on June 30, 1943, unless sooner terminated by Presidential proclamation or concurrent resolution of Congress. By the amendatory act of October 2, 1942, it was extended to June 30, 1944.

Section 1(a) declares that the Act is "in the interest of the national defense and security and necessary to the effective prosecution of the present war," and that its purposes are:

> to stabilize prices and to prevent speculative, unwarranted, and abnormal increases in prices and rents; to eliminate and prevent profiteering, hoarding, manipulation, speculation, and other disruptive practices resulting from abnormal market conditions or scarcities caused by or contributing to the national emergency; to assure that defense appropriations are not dissipated by excessive prices; to protect persons with relatively fixed and limited incomes, consumers, wage earners, investors, and persons dependent on life insurance, annuities, and pensions, from undue impairment of their standard of living; to prevent hardships to persons engaged in business, . . . and to the Federal, State, and local governments, which would result from abnormal increases in prices; to assist in securing adequate production of commodities and facilities; to prevent a post emergency collapse of values; . . .

The standards which are to guide the Administrator's exercise of his authority to fix prices, so far as now relevant, are prescribed by § 2(a) and by § 1 of the amendatory Act of October 2, 1942, and Executive Order 9250. . . . By § 2(a) the Administrator is authorized, after consultation with representative members of the industry so far as practicable, to promulgate regulations fixing prices of commodities which "in his judgment will be generally fair and equitable and will effectuate the purposes of this Act" when, in his judgment, their prices "have risen or threaten to rise to an extent or in a manner inconsistent with the purposes of this Act."

The section also directs that

> So far as practicable, in establishing any maximum price, the Administrator shall ascertain and give due consideration to the prices prevailing between October 1 and October 15, 1941 (or if, in the case of any commodity, there are no prevailing prices between such dates, or

the prevailing prices between such dates are not generally representative because of abnormal or seasonal market conditions or other cause, then to the prices prevailing during the nearest two-week period in which, in the judgment of the Administrator, the prices for such commodity are generally representative) . . . and shall make adjustments for such relevant factors as he may determine and deem to be of general applicability, including. . . . Speculative fluctuations, general increases or decreases in costs of production, distribution, and transportation, and general increases or decreases in profits earned by sellers of the commodity or commodities, during and subsequent to the year ended October 1, 1941.

By the Act of October 2, 1942, the President is directed to stabilize prices, wages and salaries "so far as practicable" on the basis of the levels which existed on September 15, 1942, except as otherwise provided in the Act. By Title I, § 4 of Executive Order No. 9250, he has directed "all departments and agencies of the Government" "to stabilize the cost of living in accordance with the Act of October 2, 1942." . . .

Congress enacted the Emergency Price Control Act in pursuance of a defined policy and required that the prices fixed by the Administrator should further that policy and conform to standards prescribed by the Act. The boundaries of the field of the Administrator's permissible action are marked by the statute. It directs that the prices fixed shall effectuate the declared policy of the Act to stabilize commodity prices so as to prevent war-time inflation and its enumerated disruptive causes and effects. In addition the prices established must be fair and equitable, and in fixing them the Administrator is directed to give due consideration, so far as practicable, to prevailing prices during the designated base period, with prescribed administrative adjustments to compensate for enumerated disturbing factors affecting prices. In short the purposes of the Act specified in § 1 denote the objective to be sought by the Administrator in fixing prices—the prevention of inflation and its enumerated consequences. The standards set out in § 2 define the boundaries within which prices having that purpose must be fixed. It is enough to satisfy the statutory requirements that the Administrator finds that the prices fixed will tend to achieve that objective and will conform to those standards, and that the courts in an appropriate proceeding can see that substantial basis for those findings is not wanting.

The Act is thus an exercise by Congress of its legislative power. In it Congress has stated the legislative objective, has prescribed the method of achieving that objective—maximum price fixing—and has laid down standards to guide the administrative determination of both the occasions for the exercise of the price-fixing power, and the particular prices to be established. . . .

The Constitution as a continuously operative charter of government does not demand the impossible or the impracticable. It does not require that Congress find for itself every fact upon which it desires to base legislative action or that it make for itself detailed determinations which it has declared to be prerequisite to the application of the legislative policy to particular facts and circumstances impossible for Congress itself properly to investigate. The essentials of the legislative function are the determination of the legislative policy and its formulation and promulgation as a defined and binding rule of conduct—here the rule, with penal sanctions, that prices shall not be greater than those fixed by maximum price regulations which conform to standards and will tend to further the policy which Congress has established. These essentials are preserved when Congress has specified the basic conditions of fact upon whose existence or occurrence, ascertained from relevant data by a designated administrative agency, it directs that its statutory command shall be effective. It is no objection that the determination of facts and the inferences to be drawn from them in the light of the statutory standards and declaration of policy call for the exercise of judgment, and for the formulation of subsidiary administrative policy within the prescribed statutory framework. . . .

Nor does the doctrine of separation of powers deny to Congress power to direct that an administrative officer properly designated for that purpose have ample latitude within which he is to ascertain the conditions which Congress has made prerequisite to the operation of its legislative command. Acting within its constitutional power to fix prices it is for Congress to say whether the data on the basis of which prices are to be fixed are to be confined within a narrow or a broad range. In either case the only concern of courts is to ascertain whether the will of Congress has been obeyed. This depends not upon the breadth of the definition of the facts or conditions which the administrative officer is to find but upon the determination whether the definition sufficiently marks the field within which the Administrator is to act so that it may be known whether he has kept within it in compliance with the legislative will.

. . . Congress is not confined to that method of executing its policy which involves the least possible delegation of discretion to administrative officers. . . . It is free to avoid the rigidity of such a system, which might well result in serious hardship, and to choose instead the flexibility attainable by the use of less restrictive standards. . . . Only if we could say that there is an absence of standards for the guidance of the Administrator's action, so that it would be impossible in a proper proceeding to ascertain whether the will of Congress has been obeyed, would we be justified in overriding its choice of means for effecting its declared purpose of preventing inflation.

The standards prescribed by the present Act, with the aid of the "statement of the considerations" required to be made by the Administrator, are sufficiently definite and precise to enable Congress, the courts and the public to ascertain whether the Administrator, in fixing the designated prices, has conformed to those standards. . . . Hence we are unable to find in them an unauthorized delegation of legislative power. The authority to fix prices only when prices have risen or threaten to rise to an extent or in a manner inconsistent with the purpose of the Act to prevent inflation is no broader than the authority to fix maximum prices when deemed necessary to protect consumers against unreasonably high prices . . . or the authority to take possession of and operate telegraph lines whenever deemed necessary for the national security or defense . . . or the authority to suspend tariff provisions upon findings that the duties imposed by a foreign state are "reciprocally unequal and unreasonable" . . . [These had been sustained by the Court.]

The directions that the prices fixed shall be fair and equitable, that in addition they shall tend to promote the purposes of the Act, and that in promulgating them consideration shall be given to prices prevailing in a stated base period, confer no greater reach for administrative determination than the power to fix just and reasonable rates . . . or the power to approve consolidations in the "public interest" . . . or the power to regulate radio stations engaged in chain broadcasting "as public interest, convenience or necessity requires" . . . or the power to prohibit "unfair methods of competition" . . . or the direction that in allotting marketing quotas among states and producers due consideration be given to a variety of economic factors . . . or the similar direction that in adjusting tariffs to meet differences in costs of production the President "take into consideration" "in so far as he finds practicable" a variety of economic matters . . . or the similar authority, in making classifications within an industry, to consider various named and unnamed "relevant factors" and determine the respective weights attributable to each. . . . [These had been sustained by the Court in earlier decisions.]

[Judgment for United States]

Justice Roberts dissented on the ground that the "purpose, or 'standard,' [of the Act] seems to permit adoption by the Administrator of any conceivable policy."

(b) Prescribing the policy for dissolution of holding companies

AMERICAN POWER & LIGHT CO. v SECURITIES AND EXCHANGE COMMISSION

329 US 90 (1946)

The Securities and Exchange Commission Act authorized the Securities and Exchange Commission to order the dissolution of holding companies in certain industries when they served no useful economic purpose. The validity of the Act was challenged on the ground that it did not establish an adequate standard for the guidance of the Commission in exercising this power.

OPINION BY MURPHY, J.

. . . We . . . reject the claim that [the Securities and Exchange Commission Act] . . . constitutes an unconstitutional delegation of legislative power to the

Securities and Exchange Commission because of an alleged absence of any standards for guidance in carrying out its functions.

[The Act] . . . itself provides that the Commission shall act so as to insure that the corporate structure or continued existence of any company in a particular holding company system does not "unduly or necessarily complicate the structure" or "unfairly or inequitably distribute voting power among security holders." It is argued that these phrases are undefined by the act, are legally meaningless in themselves and carry with them no historically defined concepts. As a result, it is said, the Commission is forced to use its unlimited whim to determine compliance or noncompliance with [the Act] . . .; and in framing its orders, the Commission has unfettered discretion to decide whose property shall be taken or destroyed and to what extent. Objection is also made on the score that no standards have been developed or announced by the Commission which justify its action in this case.

These contentions are without merit. Even standing alone, standards in terms of unduly complicated corporate structures and inequitable distributions of voting power cannot be said to be utterly without meaning, especially to those familiar with corporate realities. But these standards need not be tested in isolation. They derive much meaningful content from the purpose of the act, its factual background and the statutory context in which they appear. . . . These standards are certainly no less definite in nature than those speaking in other contexts in terms of "public interest," "just and reasonable rates," "unfair methods of competition" or "relevant factors." . . .

The judicial approval accorded these "broad" standards for administrative action is a reflection of the necessities of modern legislation dealing with complex economic and social problems. . . . The legislative process would frequently bog down if Congress were constitutionally required to appraise beforehand the myriad situations to which it wishes a particular policy to be applied and to formulate specific rules for each situation. Necessity therefore fixes a point beyond which it is unreasonable and impracticable to compel Congress to prescribe detailed rules; it then becomes constitutionally sufficient if Congress clearly delineates the general policy, the public agency which is to apply it, and the boundaries of this delegated authority. . . .

Nor is there any constitutional requirement that the legislative standards be translated by the Commission into formal and detailed rules of thumb prior to their application to a particular case. If that agency wishes to proceed by the more flexible case-by-case method, the Constitution offers no obstacle. All that can be required is that the Commission's actions conform to the statutory language and policy.

[Judgment for SEC, sustaining constitutionality of federal statute and affirming order of dissolution]

(c) Creating an administrator without prescribing policy

AMERICAN TRUCKING ASSOCIATIONS v UNITED STATES

344 US 298 (1953)

The practice developed for owners of trucks who drive their loaded trucks from one point to another to hire themselves and their trucks out to a common carrier, so that the return trip would not be made with empty trucks. The Interstate Commerce Commission concluded that these one-trip rentals made it possible for the carriers to operate in part without satisfying the requirements otherwise applicable to them. In order to stop this, the commission adopted a set of rules which provided that trucks could not be rented by a carrier for less than 30 days. A number of suits were brought to prevent the enforcement of these rules on the ground that they were not authorized by the Interstate Commerce Act and that this enforcement would cause financial loss and hardship.

OPINION BY REED, J.

. . . All agree that the rules . . . abolish trip-leasing. Unfortunate consequences are predicted for the public interest because the exempt owner-operator will no longer be able to hire himself out at will—in sum, that the industry's ability to serve a fluctuating demand will suffer and transportation costs accordingly go up. It is the Commission's position that the industry and the public will benefit directly because of the stabilization of conditions of competition and rate schedules, and that in fact the continued effectiveness of the Commission's functions under the Motor Carrier Act is dependent on regulation of leasing and interchange. Needless to say, we are ill equipped to weigh such predictions of the economic future. Nor is it our function to act as a super-commission. So we turn to the legal considerations. . . .

Here, appellants have framed their position as a broadside attack on the Commission's asserted power. All urge upon us the fact that nowhere in the Act is there an express delegation of power to control, regulate or affect leasing practices, and it is further insisted that in each separate provision of the Act granting regulatory authority there is no direct implication of such power. Our function, however, does not stop with a section-by-section search for the phrase "regulation of leasing practices" among the literal words of the statutory provisions. As a matter of principle, we might agree with appellants' contentions if we thought it a reasonable canon of interpretation that the draftsmen of acts delegating agency powers, as a practical and realistic matter, can or do include specific consideration of every evil sought to be corrected. But no great acquaintance with practical affairs is required to know that such prescience, either in fact or in the minds of Congress, does not exist. . . . Its very absence, moreover, is precisely one of the reasons why regulatory agencies such as the Commission are created, for it is the fond hope of their authors that they bring to their work the expert's familiarity with industry conditions which members of the delegating legislatures cannot be expected to possess. . . .

Moreover, we must reject at the outset any conclusion that the rules as a whole represent an attempt by the Commission to expand its power arbitrarily; there is clear and adequate evidence of evils attendant on trip-leasing. The purpose of the rules is to protect the industry from practices detrimental to the maintenance of sound transportation services consistent with the regulatory system. Sections 216(b) and 218(a) of the Act, for instance, require the filing of a just and reasonable rate schedule by each common carrier, and the violation of these rates and the demoralization of rate structures generally are a probable concomitant of current leasing practices. Section 204(a)(2) requires the Commission to impose rules relating to safety of operation for vehicles and drivers. These are likewise threatened by the unrestricted use of nonowned equipment by the common carriers. And the requirements of continuous service . . . of observance of authorized routes and termini . . . and the prohibitions of rebates [all matters expressly governed by the Interstate Commerce Act] also may be ignored through the very practices here proscribed.

So the rules in question are aimed at conditions which may directly frustrate the success of the regulation undertaken by Congress. Included in the Act as a duty of the Commission is that "to administer, execute, and enforce all provisions of this part, to make all necessary orders in connection therewith, and to prescribe rules, regulations, and procedure for such administration." § 204(a)(6). And this necessary rule-making power, coterminous with the scope of agency regulation itself, must extend to the "transportation of passengers or property by motor carriers engaged in interstate or foreign commerce and to the procurement of and the provision of facilities for such transportation," regulation of which is vested in the Commission. . . .

We hold then that the promulgation of these rules for authorized carriers falls within the Commission's power, despite the absence of specific reference to leasing practices in the Act. . . . This result . . . is foreshadowed . . . by *United States v Pennsylvania R. Co.,* 323 US 612. That case validated an order requiring railroads to lease cars to a competing carrier by sea, in spite of the inability of the Commission to ground its action on some specific provision of the Act. . . . This Court pointed to the fact that the "unquestioned power of the Commission to require establishment of [through] routes would be wholly fruitless, without the correlative power to abrogate the Association's rule which prohibits the interchange." . . . There is evidence here that convinces us that that regulation of leasing practices is likewise a necessary power; in fact, we think its exercise more crucial than in *United States v Pennsylvania R. Co.* The enforcement of only one phase of the Act was there endangered; here, practically the entire regulatory scheme is affected by trip-leasing.

[Judgment for United States, sustaining the ICC regulation]

§ 20:6. DELEGATION TO NONGOVERNMENTAL BODIES OR PERSONS

In some instances, the lawmaker will not merely establish an administrator with power to make regulations but will also provide that an administrative regulation cannot go into effect until a certain percentage of persons affected by the regulation agree thereto. Thus a production quota regulation of the administrator may require the approval of two thirds of the producers before it becomes effective. Such a requirement is imposed for a variety of reasons. It may be done to make the administrative program more acceptable to, or popular with, the persons regulated by giving them a part in the promulgation of the program. It may be designed as a check upon the administrator. Again, it may be intended as an indirect way of pooling the experience or judgment of a wide number of persons in the formulation of the program.

Against such delegation, it may be argued that rules which have the effect of laws are being made by persons who are neither the duly elected lawmakers nor even administrators created by statutes adopted by such lawmakers. Moreover, objection may be made that the procedure has an element of class discrimination when the nongovernmental group whose consent is required does not represent a cross section of all society, as when merely the wheat producers, but not the millers, distributors, bakers, or consumers, are permitted to vote on the quantity of wheat to be produced. Under the present federal theory, such objections are without merit, and it is constitutional to provide for the adoption of an administrative rule with the consent of a specified percentage of a specified class of persons. There is a conflict over the validity of state laws making such provision.

(a) Cooperation between administrators and producers

UNITED STATES v ROCK ROYAL COOPERATIVE, INC.

307 US 533 (1939)

The Agricultural Marketing Agreement Act of 1937, described in the portion of this opinion set forth under § 15:4(a), was further challenged as making an unconstitutional delegation of legislative power by requiring two thirds of the producers to approve a quota proposed by the Secretary of Agriculture.

OPINION BY REED, J.

. . . Under Section 8c(9)(B) of the Act it is provided that any order shall become effective notwithstanding the failure of 50 percent of the handlers to approve a similar agreement, if the Secretary of Agriculture with the approval of the President determines, among other things, that the issuance of the order is approved by two thirds of the producers interested or by interested producers of two thirds of the volume produced for the market of the specified production area. By subsection (19) it is provided that for the purpose of ascertaining whether the issuance of such order is approved "the Secretary may conduct a referendum among producers." The objection is made that this is an unlawful delegation to producers of the legislative power to put an order into effect in a market. In considering this question, we must assume that the Congress had the power to put this Order into effect without the approval of anyone. Whether producer approval . . . is necessary or not, . . . a requirement of such approval would not be an invalid delegation.

[Judgment for United States]

§ 20:7. PUBLICITY AND ADMINISTRATIVE ACTIVITY

(a) Open meetings

The Government in the Sunshine Act of 1976 requires most of the meetings of the major administrative agencies to be open to the public.[6] The object of this statute is to enable the public to know what is being done and to prevent administrative misconduct by making the administrator aware that the public is watching.

(b) Public participation in adoption of regulations

In some instances, nongovernmental bodies or persons play a part in furnishing information or opinions that may ultimately affect the adoption or nature of the rule adopted by the administrator. This pattern of cooperation with the administrator may be illustrated by the Federal Trade Commission practice, begun in 1919, of calling together members of each significant industry so that the members can discuss which practices are fair trade practices and which are not. The conclusions of these conferences are not automatically binding on the Federal Trade Commission, but they serve as a valuable means of bringing to the commission detailed information respecting the conduct of the particular industry or business in question. Under the Federal Trade Commission practice, the rules of fair practice agreed to at a trade conference may be approved or disapproved by the commission. When the rules are approved, a further distinction is made between those rules that are "affirmatively approved" by the commission and those that are merely "accepted as expressions of the trade." In the case of the former, the commission will enforce compliance by the members of the industry. In the case of the latter, the commission will accept the practices as fair trade practices but will not enforce compliance by persons not willing to comply.

---

[6]PL 94-409, 90 Stat 1241, 5 USC § 552.

(c) Public knowledge of regulations

When the administrator adopts a regulation, a practical problem arises as to how to inform the public of its existence. Some regulations will have already attracted such public attention that the news media will give the desired publicity. The great mass of regulations, however, do not attract this attention. In order to provide publicity for all regulations, the Federal Register Act provides that an administrative regulation is not binding until it is printed in the *Federal Register*. This is a government publication, published five days a week, in which are printed all administrative regulations, all presidential proclamations and executive orders, and such other documents and classes of documents as the president or Congress may from time to time direct.

The Federal Register Act provides that the printing of an administrative regulation in the *Federal Register* is sufficient to give notice of the contents of the regulation to any person subject thereto or affected thereby. This means that no one can claim ignorance of the published regulation as an excuse.

Every five years, each agency of the national government is required to file "a complete codification of all documents which, in the opinion of the agency, have general applicability and legal effect" and which are then in force. This is a reasonably satisfactory solution to the problem in the case of a big business that has an attorney or a legal staff to examine the *Register*. In the case of a smaller business that cannot afford an attorney or does not have a legal staff, the *Federal Register* is not a satisfactory solution, although it is difficult to determine what further step, if any, could be taken by the government. A number of states have statutes similar to the Federal Register Act.

FEDERAL CROP INSURANCE CORP. v MERRILL

332 US 380 (1947)

Administrative regulations adopted under the Federal Wheat Crop Insurance Act were published in the *Federal Register* but were in fact unknown to the applicant for insurance. He claimed that he was not bound by them.

OPINION BY FRANKFURTER, J.

. . . Just as everyone is charged with knowledge of the United States Statutes at Large, Congress has provided that the appearance of rules and regulations in the *Federal Register* gives legal notice of their contents. . . . Accordingly, the Wheat Crop Insurance Regulations were binding on all who sought to come within the Federal Crop Insurance Act, regardless of actual knowledge of what is in the Regulations or of the hardship resulting from innocent ignorance.

[Judgment against Merrill]

Questions for Discussion

1. To what extent may ordinary citizens be present at meetings of the important federal administrative agencies?

2. Why is it constitutional to provide that a statute shall not go into effect until approved by a certain percentage of those affected?

3. To what extent may legislative power be delegated? Are there any limitations on the power?

4. Why is it desirable to delegate rule-making authority to the administrator?

5. What are the legal and practical objections to delegation?

6. Appraise the merits of the argument that an administrator's decision should not be regarded as the law of the state because it may be so readily changed.

7. State and compare the opposing arguments that can be made about whether a state administrative rule is a law of the state.

8. (a) How does the administrator inform the public of regulations that have been adopted?   (b) Is the problem the same in the case of a health officer as in the case of a public utility commission?

9. (a) What does the Federal Register Act provide with regard to the publication of regulations?   (b) What are the disadvantages of this method?   (c) Can you suggest a better method?

10. (a) Why does the Administrative Procedure Act provide for a hearing when the administrator proposes to make rules?   (b) Is the hearing a legislative or a judicial function?

11. How does the Court define the legislative process or function in the *Yakus* case?

12. The owner of a business violates a federal regulation applicable to the business. The owner raises the defense that the owner had no knowledge of the regulation. Is this a valid defense?

13. On the basis of the *American Trucking Association* case, would the Interstate Commerce Commission have authority to stop riots in a given city on the ground that the rioting was interfering with the movement of interstate trains?

14. (a) Is a statute constitutional that sets forth the policy to be followed by the administrator?   (b) Has the requirement that the administrator conform to a "standard" been replaced by the broader view that it is sufficient for Congress to define the general policy? See *American Power & Light Co. v Securities Exchange Commission.*

15. Can the administrator apply rules adopted after a particular case has been begun? Is the administrator restricted to the rules that existed before the action was taken?

16. Is the Court correct in stating in *United States v Rock Royal Cooperative* that the standards there considered give ample assurance that the various factors will be considered by the Secretary?

17. A federal statute applicable to the District of Columbia created a board for the condemnation of unsanitary buildings and conferred upon the board "jurisdiction and authority to examine into the sanitary conditions of all buildings in said District, to condemn those buildings which are in such insanitary condition as to endanger the health or lives of the occupants thereof or of persons living in the vicinity, and to cause all buildings to be put into sanitary conditions or to be vacated, demolished, and removed. . . ." Acting under this authority, the board condemned a building. The owner claimed that the law was unconstitutional in failing to establish standards for the guidance of the board. Decide. [*Keys v Madesen,* (CA DistCol) 179 F2d 40 (1949)]

18. (a) In the *Yakus* case, does the Court indicate whether it is necessary that the Court agree with the price administrator about the amount of the price to be established?   (b) If the administrator sets a price of seven cents per unit, would the Court reverse if it believed that the fair price should be eight cents or six cents instead?

19. What type of administrator is the Federal Trade Commission? Is it legislative, executive, or judicial? Discuss.

20. In *United States v Morton Salt Co.,* 338 US 632 (1950), the Court stated: "The Administrative Procedure Act was framed against a background of rapid expansion of the administrative process as a check upon administrators whose zeal might otherwise have carried them to excesses not contemplated in legislation creating their offices. It created safeguards even narrower than the constitutional ones, against arbitrary official encroachment upon private rights. . . ." To what extent is this policy seen in the Administrative Procedure Act quoted in § 20:4(a)?

21

Administrative Investigation

§ 21:1. POWER TO INVESTIGATE

The modern administrator has executive power to investigate and to require persons to appear as witnesses and to produce relevant papers. Thus the administrator may investigate in order to see if there is any violation of the law or of its rules generally, to determine whether there is need for the adoption of additional rules, to ascertain the facts with respect to a particular suspected or alleged violation, and to determine whether its decisions are being obeyed.

To aid the administrator in making investigations, the power to issue subpoenas is typically given. Under some statutes, the administrator must apply to a court for a subpoena.

In general, the subpoena is the same as in an ordinary lawsuit. It is employed to compel witnesses to testify and to produce relevant papers. However, the subpoena is in many cases issued more freely than in a lawsuit. The administrative subpoena power has broadened greatly, so that such orders may be issued as incidental to an administrative investigation whether or not the determination of the right of particular parties is involved and without regard to whether it is probable that the person subpoenaed has been violating an administrative regulation.

In order to protect the individual from the improper use of information secured by administrative investigations, it is often made a criminal offense for an administrator to disclose or make improper publication of any information obtained from an investigation.

(a) Subpoena power

ENDICOTT JOHNSON CORP. v PERKINS

317 US 501 (1943)

The Walsh-Healey Act requires that contracts to supply the United States materials at a cost greater than $10,000 specify that the contractor shall pay employees in the manufacture of the materials not less than the minimum wages set by the Secretary of Labor nor employ them for more than 40 hours a week except with the permission of the Secretary, in which case wages of not less than 1½ times the basic hourly rate must be paid. Endicott Johnson Corporation had several contracts in excess of $10,000 to supply shoes to the United States. The contracts conformed to the Act and specified the plants in which the shoes were to be made. The Secretary of Labor made an investigation which showed minor wage violations in the plants named in the contract. The Secretary of Labor then ordered the corporation to produce records of wages and hours in other plants that were physically separate from the plants in which the contracts were being performed, because the Secretary "had reason to believe" that the employees in those plants were also covered by the contracts. The corporation refused to produce the records on the ground that the subpoena power extended only to the plants specified in the contracts.

OPINION BY JACKSON, J.

. . . The Secretary is directed "to administer the provisions of this Act" and empowered to "make investigations and findings as herein provided, and prosecute any inquiry necessary to his functions." . . . And that he may the better and the more fairly discharge his functions, he is authorized to hold hearings "on complaint of a breach or violation of any representation or stipulation" and "to issue orders requiring the attendance and testimony of witnesses and the production of evidence under oath. . . . In such case of contumacy, failure, or refusal of any person to obey such an order," the District Court of the United States "shall have jurisdiction to issue to such person an order requiring such person to appear before him or representative designated by him, to produce evidence if, as, and when so ordered, and to give testimony relating to the matter under investigation or in question; and any failure to obey such order of the court may be punished by said court as a contempt thereof." . . .

The Act directs the Secretary to administer its provisions. It is not an Act of general applicability to industry. It applies only to contractors who voluntarily enter into competition to obtain government business on terms of which they are fairly forewarned by inclusion in the contract. . . .

The matter which the Secretary was investigating and was authorized to investigate was an alleged violation of this Act and these contracts. Her scope would include determining what employees these contracts and the Act covered. . . . But because she sought evidence of underpayment before she made a decision on the question of coverage and alleged that she "had reason to believe" the employees in question were covered, the District Court refused to order its production, tried the issue of coverage itself, and decided it against the Secretary. This ruling would require the Secretary, in order to get evidence of violation, either to allege she had decided the issue of coverage before the hearing or to sever the issues for separate hearing and decision. The former would be of dubious propriety, and the latter of doubtful practicality. The Secretary is given no power to investigate mere coverage, as such, or to make findings thereon except as incident to trial of the issue of violation. No doubt she would have discretion to take up the issues of coverage for separate and earlier trial if she saw fit. Or, in a case such as the one revealed by the pleadings in this one, she might find it advisable to begin by examining the payroll, for if there were no underpayments found, the issue of coverage would be academic. On the admitted facts of the case, the District Court had no authority to control her procedure or to condition enforcement of her subpoenas upon her first reaching and announcing a decision on some of the issues in her administrative proceeding.

[Judgment against Endicott Johnson Corp.]

DISSENTING OPINION BY MURPHY, J., IN WHICH ROBERTS, J., CONCURS

Because of the varied and important responsibilities of a quasijudicial nature that have been entrusted to administrative agencies in the regulation of our political and economic life, their activities should not be subjected to unwarranted and ill-advised intrusions by the judicial branch of the government. Yet, if they are freed of all restraint upon inquisitorial activities and are allowed uncontrolled discretion in the exercise of the sovereign power of government to invade private affairs through the use of the subpoena, to the extent required or sought in situations like the one before us and other inquiries of much broader scope, under the direction of well-meaning but over-zealous officials they may at times become instruments of intolerable oppression and injustice. This is not to say that the power to enforce their subpoenas should never be entrusted to administrative agencies, but thus far Congress, for unstated reasons, has not seen fit to confer such authority upon any agency which it has created. So here, while the Secretary of Labor is empowered to administer the Walsh-Healey Act, to "prosecute any inquiry necessary to his functions," and "to issue orders requiring the attendance and the testimony of witnesses and the production of evidence under oath," he alone cannot compel obedience of those orders. "Jurisdiction" so to do is conferred upon the district courts of the United States and it is our immediate task to delineate the proper function of those courts in the exercise of this jurisdiction. Specifically the question is: What is the duty of the courts when the witness or party claims the proceeding is without authority of law?

This Court, in recognition of the drastic nature of the subpoena power and the possibilities of severe mischief inherent in its use, has insisted that it be kept within well-defined channels. . . . In conditioning enforcement of the Secretary's administrative subpoenas upon application therefor to a district court, Congress evidently intended to keep the instant subpoena power within limits, and clearly must have meant for the courts to perform more than a routine ministerial function in passing upon such applications. If this were not the case, it would have been much simpler to lodge the power of enforcement directly with the Secretary, or else to make disregard of his subpoenas a misdemeanor. . . .

The Government concedes that the district courts are more than mere rubber stamps of the agencies in enforcing administrative subpoenas and lists as examples of appropriate defenses, claims that a privilege of the witness, like that against self-incrimination, would be violated; or that the subpoena is unduly vague or unreasonably oppressive; or that the hearing is not of the kind authorized; or that the subpoena was not issued by the person vested with the power; or that it is plain on the pleadings that the evidence sought is not germane to any lawful subject of inquiry. But the Government insists that the issue of "coverage," i. e., whether the Act extends to plants of petitioner's establishment which manufactured materials used in making complete shoes but not named in the contracts, is not a proper ground for attack in this case. I think it is.

If petitioner [Endicott Johnson Corp.] is not subject to the Act as to the plants in question, the Secretary has no right to start proceedings or to require the production of records with regard to those plants. In other words, there would be no lawful subject of inquiry, and under present statutes giving the courts jurisdiction to enforce administrative subpoenas, petitioner is entitled to a judicial determination of this issue before its privacy is invaded. . . .

It is within the competence and authority of the court to inquire and satisfy itself whether there is probable legal justification for the proceeding, before it exercises its judicial authority to require a witness or a party to reveal his private affairs or be held in contempt.

Just how much of a showing of statutory coverage should be required to satisfy the district court, and just how far it should explore the question, are difficult problems, to be solved best by a careful balancing of interests and the exercise of a sound and informed discretion. If the proposed examination under the subpoena or the proceeding itself would be relatively brief and of a limited scope, any doubt should ordinarily be resolved in favor of the agency's power. If it promises to be protracted and burdensome to the party, a more searching inquiry is indicated. A formal finding of coverage by the agency, which the Secretary did not make here, should be accorded some weight in the court's deliberation, unless wholly wanting in either legal or factual support, but it should not be conclusive. In short, the responsibility resting upon the court in this situation is not unlike that of a committing magistrate on preliminary examination to determine whether an accused should be held for trial.

With these considerations in mind, let us turn to the facts of this case. Petitioner has willingly complied with all demands of the Secretary relating to the plants of its establishment, named in the contracts, in which the shoes were manufactured. It resists the application for enforcement of the subpoenas directing the production of records of other plants, not named in the contracts, in which some component parts for the shoes were manufactured, on the ground that the Walsh-Healey Act does not extend to those plants. It is true that petitioner voluntarily entered into the contracts with the Government, but those referred only to the specific plants where the finished product was made. And, it was not until 1939, after all the contracts were completed, that the Secretary issued rulings specifically dealing with "integrated establishments." The mere fact that petitioner voluntarily contracted with reference to some plants does not necessarily mean that the Secretary is free to investigate petitioner's entire business without let or hindrance. That depends upon whether or not the Act extends to those other plants. Petitioner was entitled to have this question determined by the district court before the subpoena was enforced over its objection. . . . Under the facts of this case the district court should not be compelled mechanically to enforce the Secretary's subpoena, in the exercise of its statutory jurisdiction. It should first satisfy itself that probable cause exists for the Secretary's contention that the Act covers the plants in question.

(b) Production of papers

Many federal agencies are empowered to procure documents as an incident to making an investigation. This power is possessed by the Federal Trade Commission, the Federal Maritime Commission, the National Science Foundation, the Treasury Department, the Department of Agriculture, the Department of the Army, the Department of Labor, and the Veterans' Administration.

ST. REGIS PAPER COMPANY v UNITED STATES

368 US 208 (1961)

The Federal Trade Commission is empowered under § 6(b) of the Federal Trade Commission Act to require certain corporations to furnish reports or written answers to specific questions. A corporation that fails to do so is subject to a penalty of $100 for each day of delay. The Federal Trade Commission directed the St. Regis Paper Company to furnish a copy of its census reports and to answer certain questions. It did not furnish all the information requested, and the Commission sought an order against it in the district court. The district court, which found that some of the requests had been satisfied and that some were too vague to be enforced, refused to assess the statutory penalty for delay, but required the submission of copies of the census reports. The Court of Appeals affirmed the district court except that, in addition, it directed the entry of the statutory penalty. St. Regis filed a petition for the Supreme Court to review the case.

OPINION BY CLARK, J.

. . . Among the items ordered enforced and with which the petitioner still refuses to comply are requests for file copies of certain reports previously made to the Census Bureau. The petitioner claims each of these to be confidential. There is a conflict between the Courts of Appeal on the point. . . .

. . . The government agencies are at loggerheads on the problem, the Department of Commerce, Census Bureau, and the Bureau of the Budget believe that the copies are not subject to legal process, while the Federal Trade Commission and the Antitrust Division of the Department of Justice, which filed this suit, contend to the contrary. The Solicitor General, "fully recognizing the delicate balance of opposing considerations," has concluded "on balance" that the copies are not subject to compulsive production. . . . We do not agree. . . .

[The Court then set forth the reason for concluding that production of the reports could be compelled.]

The District Court held that since the Commission orders were "partially defective," petitioner had a valid reason for challenging them, and therefore no forfeitures accrued. Petitioner supports this holding by asserting that many of the items included in the Commission's orders were held unenforceable by the District Court, and that . . . forfeiture should not be imposed for noncompliance with substantially defective orders. The Court of Appeals disagreed, holding that forfeiture had occurred and that the daily penalty began to run 30 days after the notice of default on the first set of the Commission's orders [on June 20, 1959]. We agree with the Court of Appeals and conclude that the single daily penalty runs until the date of our stay, February 7, 1961.

. . . Here petitioner might have delayed accrual of the forfeitures pending determination of the merits or obtained a separate judicial determination of the validity of the orders before the penalties began to accrue, as we point out infra. Rather than attempting such procedures it defied large parts of the orders. It cannot now be heard to complain because such defiance was in error. . . .

Upon the commencement of the action by the Government, petitioner might have then sought a stay, as it did when the decision went against it in the Court of Appeals. Moreover, after the entry of the notices of default by the Commission, petitioner might have itself sought relief before the § 10 forfeitures began to accrue instead of waiting for the Attorney General to sue for their collection. . . . "We are not prepared to say that courts would be powerless" to act where such orders appear suspect and ruinous penalties would be sustained pending a good faith test of their validity. There the record did not present and the Court did not determine "whether the Declaratory Judgment Act, the Administrative Procedure Act, or general equitable powers of the courts would afford a remedy if there were shown to be a wrong, or what the consequences would be if no chance is given for a test of reasonable objections to such an order." . . .

The petitioner has pursued none of these remedies, and we could not therefore say that it had "no chance" to prevent the running of the forfeiture pending a test of the validity of the orders. . . .

This Court cannot forgive statutory penalties once they legally attach and, finding no grounds upon which we can strike them down, the judgment of the Court of Appeals is [affirmed].

[Judgment affirmed]

DISSENTING OPINION BY BLACK, J., IN WHICH WHITTAKER AND STEWART, JJ., CONCUR

I dissent from the Court's holdings (1) that petitioner's copies of census reports submitted to the Census Bureau are not privileged from production by § 9 of the Census Act, and (2) that for its refusal to produce these copies and to answer certain of many questions asked it by the Federal Trade Commission, petitioner must pay a penalty of $100 for each day since that refusal up to the time, many months later, when this Court granted a stay as to future penalties.

. . .

The petitioner is being penalized $100 per day for its failure to produce copies of its census reports along with answers to certain of the voluminous questions propounded to it by the Federal Trade Commission. Many questions had already been answered prior to the time penalties began to run. The District Court has held that a very substantial number of the other questions asked need not be answered, and I do not understand that this Court now holds otherwise. So far as the Commission's demand for production of the census reports is concerned, petitioner could quite reasonably have felt that it was under no obligation to comply because of the Government's numerous promises that these reports would be treated as confidential. Indeed, the very position taken by petitioner as to the privileged nature of its census reports was held to be correct in the *Dilger* case, decided just three weeks before the District Court decision in this case. All of this plainly shows, I think, that, with regard to some of the information sought, indeed a very substantial part of it, there was a serious, good-faith controversy concerning the Commission's power to compel disclosure. Under these circumstances I agree with the District Court's conclusion that these heavy statutory penalties should not have been imposed. It is practically the universal rule that laws imposing penalties of this kind should be strictly, not expansively, construed. Applying that standard, I am by no means sure that the penalty provisions of the statute upon which this judgment rests can be construed so as to justify the penalties here at all.

I would reverse this judgment.

(c) Antitrust Civil Process Act

The federal Antitrust Civil Process Act is an example of the extent to which administrative investigation is authorized. The Act authorizes the Attorney General or the Assistant Attorney General in charge of the Antitrust Division of the Department of Justice to make a civil investigative demand (CID) on any person believed to have knowledge relevant to any civil antitrust investigation, such as an investigation before bringing a suit to enjoin a monopolistic practice, or an investigation made upon receiving a premerger notification. The person so notified can be compelled to produce relevant documents, furnish written answers to written questions, or appear in person and give oral testimony.[1]

---

[1]Antitrust Civil Process Act of 1962, as amended by the Antitrust Improvement Act of 1976, §§ 101, 102, PL 94–435, 90 Stat 1383, 15 USC § 1311 et seq.

§ 21:2. INVESTIGATION FOR RULE MAKING

When the administrator is seeking information as a guide in the formulation of a rule, the problem is the same as that of a legislative body conducting an examination or holding a hearing to determine the facts in drafting a statute. In the case of a legislative body, it is recognized that the power to legislate carries with it by necessary implication the right to obtain information appropriate to a determination of matters within the scope of the authority to legislate. Under some statutes, a duty is placed upon the administrator to make certain types of investigations or to hold certain types of hearings before adopting specified classes of rules.

(a) Grant of authority

SMITH v INTERSTATE COMMERCE COMMISSION

245 US 33 (1917)

Section 13 of the Interstate Commerce Act, as amended, gave the Interstate Commerce Commission

> full authority and power at any time to institute an inquiry, on its own motion, in any case and as to any matter or thing concerning which a complaint is authorized to be made, to or before said Commission by any provision of this Act, or concerning which any question may arise under any of the provisions of this Act, or relating to the enforcement of any provisions of this Act.

The Interstate Commerce Commission sought to compel the appellant, the president of the Louisville & Nashville Railroad, to answer questions about efforts to maintain a monopoly, the expenditure of money of the railroad for political purposes, and the method followed in charging such expenditures in the company's books.

OPINION BY MCKENNA, J.

The fundamental contention of appellant is that the Interstate Commerce Commission has no power to ask the questions in controversy and in emphasis of this he asserts "the inquiry was confined exclusively to supposed political activities and efforts to suppress competition." And these, it is further asserted, "are not matters which the Commission 'is legally entitled to investigate.'"

. . .

The Interstate Commerce Act confers upon the Commission powers of investigation in very broad language and this court has refused by construction to limit it so far as the business of the carriers is concerned and their relation to the public. And it would seem to be a necessary deduction from the cases that the investigating and supervising powers of the Commission extend to all of the activities of carriers and to all sums expended by them which could affect in any way their benefit or burden as agents of the public. If it be grasped thoroughly and kept in attention that they are public agents, we have at least the principle which should determine judgment in particular instances of regulation or investigation; and it is not far from true—it may be it is entirely true, as said by the Commission—that "there can be nothing private or confidential in the activities and expenditures of a carrier engaged in interstate commerce."

Turning to the specialties of the Interstate Commerce Act we find there that all charges and treatment of all passengers and property shall be just and reasonable, and there is a specific prohibition of preferences and discriminations in all the ways that they can be executed, with corresponding regulatory power in the Commission. And authority and means are given to enable it to perform its duty. By Section 12 it is authorized to inquire into the management of the business of carriers and keep itself informed as to the manner and method in which the same is conducted, and has the right to obtain from the carriers full and complete information. It may . . . institute an inquiry of its own motion, and may . . . require detailed accounts of all the expenditures and revenues of carriers and a complete exhibit of their financial operations and prescribe the forms of accounts, records and memoranda to be kept. And it is required to report to Congress all data collected by it.

It would seem to be an idle work to point out the complete comprehensiveness of the language of these sections and we are not disposed to spend any time to argue that it necessarily includes the power to inquire into expenditures and their proper assignment in the accounts, and the questions under review, we have seen, go no further. They are incidental to an investigation as to the "manner and method" . . . in which the business of the carriers is conducted; they are in requisition of a detailed account of their expenditures and revenues and an exhibit of their financial operations . . . and the answers to them may be valuable as information to Congress. . . .

A limitation, however, is deduced from Section 13. It is said to be confined to cases where an inquiry is instituted "as to any matter or thing concerning which a complaint is authorized to be made, . . . or concerning which any question may arise under any of the provisions" of the act "or relating to the enforcement of any of the provisions" of the act. . . . The objection overlooks the practical and vigilant function of the Commission. . . .

The expenditures of the carriers essentially concern their business. Section 20 declares it and gives the Commission power to require a detail of them, and necessarily not only of their amount but purpose and how charged. And the Commission must have power to prevent evasion of its orders and detect in any formal compliance or in the assignment of expenses a "possible concealment of forbidden practices."

It may be said that our comments are not applicable to questions . . . which relate to the expenditure of money in Alabama "in a campaign against rate reduction." That is, those questions are not directed to "political activities" strictly so called, nor to the suppression of competition. They are directed, however, to the use of funds in a campaign against state legislative action. But this, appellant asserts, is at the farthest an attempt to "influence legislation or to mold public opinion" and that there is nothing in the Interstate Commerce Act "which forbids it or gives to the Commission any power to investigate the subject." . . .

Abstractly speaking, we are not disposed to say that a carrier may not attempt to mold or enlighten public opinion, but we are quite clear that its conduct and the expenditures of its funds are open to inquiry. If it may not rest inactive and suffer injustice, it may not on the other hand use its funds and its power in opposition to the policies of government. Beyond this generality it is not necessary to go. The questions in the case are not of broad extent. They are quite special, and we regard them, as the learned judge of the court below regarded them, as but incident to the amount of expenditures and to the manner of their charge upon the books of the companies. This, we repeat, is within the power of the Commission. The purpose of an investigation is the penetration of disguises or to form a definite estimate of any conduct of the carriers that may in any way affect their relation to the public. We cannot assume that an investigation will be instituted or conducted for any other purpose. . . .

[Judgment for ICC]

---

§ 21:3. INVESTIGATION FOR ENFORCEMENT

In the case of the more complex forms of business regulation, the action of the administrator is a continuing action, and investigation becomes a continuing process to determine the effectiveness of the administrator's regulation and whether the parties have complied with the administrative decision. Investigation for the purpose of determining compliance will, as a practical matter, assume a narrower scope than investigation for rulemaking, but the extent to which the investigation may go within the proper area can be regarded as the same in each case.

(a) Compliance with court order

UNITED STATES v MORTON SALT CO.

338 US 632 (1950)

As the result of proceedings originating before the Federal Trade Commission, the Morton Salt Company and others were ordered by the Supreme Court to cease certain practices, with respect to the pricing, producing, and marketing of salt, and to file with the Commission a report showing compliance with this order. The Federal Trade Commission thereafter ordered the Morton Salt Company to furnish additional reports on its method of operation in order to determine whether the company was continuing to comply with the order. The company challenged the authority of the Federal Trade Commission to require the additional reports.

OPINION BY JACKSON, J.

. . . [Subsequent to the filing of an initial report directed by the original decree] the Commission ordered additional and highly particularized reports to show continuing compliance with the decree. This was done without application to the court, was not authorized by any provision of its decree, and is not provided for in § 5 of the statute under which the Commission's original cease and desist order had issued. . . .

The Trade Commission Act is one of several in which Congress, to make its policy effective, has relied upon the initiative of administrative officials and the flexibility of the administrative process. Its agencies are provided with staffs to institute proceedings and to follow up decrees and police their obedience. While that process at times is adversary, it also at times is inquisitorial. These agencies are expected to ascertain when and against whom proceedings should be set in motion and to take the lead in following through to effective results. It is expected that this combination of duty and power always will result in earnest and eager action but it is feared that it may sometimes result in harsh and overzealous action.

To protect against mistaken or arbitrary orders, judicial review is provided. Its function is dispassionate and disinterested adjudication, unmixed with any concern as to the success of either prosecution or defense. Courts are not expected to start wheels moving or to follow up judgments. Courts neither have, nor need, sleuths to dig up evidence, staffs to analyze reports, or personnel to prepare prosecutions for contempts. . . .

This case illustrates the difference between the judicial function and the function the Commission is attempting to perform. The respondents argue that since the Commission made no charge of violation either of the decree or the statute, it is engaged in a mere "fishing expedition" to see if it can turn up evidence of guilt. We will assume for the argument that this is so. Courts have often disapproved the employment of the judicial process in such an enterprise. Federal judicial power itself extends only to adjudication of cases and controversies and it is natural that its investigative powers should be jealously confined to these ends. The judicial subpoena power not only is subject to specific constitutional limitations, which also apply to administrive orders, such as those against self-incrimination, unreasonable search and seizure, and due process of law, but also is subject to those limitations inherent in the body that issues them because of the provisions of the Judiciary Article of the Constitution.

We must not disguise the fact that sometimes, especially early in the history of the federal administrative tribunal, the courts were persuaded to engraft judicial limitations upon the administrative process. The courts could not go fishing, and so it followed neither could anyone else. . . . It must not be forgotten that the administrative process and its agencies are relative newcomers in the field of law and that it has taken and will continue to take experience and trial and error to fit this process into our system of judicature. More recent views

have been more tolerant of it than those which underlay many older decisions.
. . .

The only power that is involved here is the power to get information from those who best can give it and who are most interested in not doing so. Because judicial power is reluctant if not unable to summon evidence until it is shown to be relevant to issues in litigation, it does not follow that an administrative agency charged with seeing that the laws are enforced may not have and exercise powers of original inquiry. It has a power of inquisition, if one chooses to call it that, which is not derived from the judicial function. It is more analogous to the Grand Jury, which does not depend on a case or controversy for power to get evidence but can investigate merely on suspicion that the law is being violated, or even just because it wants assurance that it is not. When investigative and accusatory duties are delegated by statute to an administrative body, it, too, may take steps to inform itself as to whether there is probable violation of the law.

. . . Even if one were to regard the request for information in this case as caused by nothing more than official curiosity, nevertheless law-enforcing agencies have a legitimate right to satisfy themselves that corporate behavior is consistent with the law and the public interest.

Of course a governmental investigation into corporate matters may be of such a sweeping nature and so unrelated to the matter properly under inquiry as to exceed the investigatory power. . . . But it is sufficient if the inquiry is within the authority of the agency, the demand is not too indefinite and the information sought is reasonably relevant. "The gist of the protection is in the requirement, expressed in terms, that the disclosure sought shall not be unreasonable." . . . Nothing on the face of the Commission's order transgressed these bounds. . . . In upholding this order upon this record, we are not to be understood as holding such orders exempt from judicial examination or as extending a license to exact as reports what would not reasonably be comprehended within that term as used by Congress in the context of this Act. . . .

[Judgment for United States]

---

§ 21:4. CONSTITUTIONAL LIMITATIONS ON INVESTIGATION

With the exception of the searching of premises, such as a factory building, the Constitution does not impose any significant limitation on the power of an administrator to conduct an investigation.

(a) Inspection of premises

In general, a person has the same protection against unreasonable search and seizure by an administrative officer as that person has against unreasonable search and seizure by a police officer. Thus the administrator must have a search warrant in order to inspect a building over the objection of the occupant when the administrator is seeking to see if there have been any violations of the building or fire code, or of factory safety regulations.

In contrast, when the danger of concealment is great, a warrantless search is validly made of the premises of a business which is highly regulated, as that of selling liquor or firearms. Similarly, the recipient of welfare who claims an additional allowance because of a dependent child can be required to allow a welfare investigator to enter a dwelling without a warrant to determine that there was in fact such a dependent child.

(b) Production of papers

For the most part, the constitutional guarantee against unreasonable search and seizure does not afford much protection for papers and records against investigation by an administrator, since that guarantee does not apply in the absence of an actual seizure. That is, a subpoena to testify or to produce records cannot be opposed on the ground that it is a search and seizure, as the constitutional protection is limited to cases of actual search and seizure rather than the obtaining of information by compulsion.

The protection afforded by the guarantee against self-incrimination is likewise narrow. It cannot be invoked (1) when the person compelled to present self-incriminating evidence is given immunity from future prosecution; nor can it be claimed as to (2) corporate records, even though the officer or employee of the corporation who produces them would be incriminated thereby; nor for (3) records which by law must be kept by the person subject to the administrative investigation.

(c) Production of records required by law

SHAPIRO v UNITED STATES

335 US 1 (1948)

Shapiro was a wholesaler of fruit and produce. The Price Administrator, acting under the federal Emergency Price Control Act, subpoenaed him to produce his business records. Under protest of constitutional privilege, he furnished the records. He was later prosecuted for making illegal tying sales, contrary to the Emergency Price Control Regulations. The evidence on which the prosecution was based was obtained from information found in the records that he had been required to produce before the administrator. He claimed that he was entitled to immunity from prosecution for any matter arising out of those records. His claim of privilege was overruled, and he was convicted. He appealed from the conviction.

OPINION BY VINSON, C. J.

... The Circuit Court of Appeals ruled that the records which petitioner was compelled to produce were records required to be kept by a valid regulation under the Price Control Act; that thereby they became public documents, as to which no constitutional privilege against self-incrimination attaches.

... The language of the statute and its legislative history, viewed against the background of settled judicial construction of the immunity provision, indicate that Congress required records to be kept as a means of enforcing the statute and did not intend to frustrate the use of those records for enforcement action by granting an immunity bonus to individuals compelled to disclose their required records to the Administrator.

... A corporate officer has no such constitutional privilege as to corporate records in his possession, even though they contain entries made by himself which disclose his crime. . . .

> The physical custody of incriminating documents does not of itself protect the custodian against their compulsory production. The question still remains with respect to the nature of the documents and the capacity in which they are held. It may yet appear that they are of a character which subjects them to the scrutiny demanded and that the custodian has voluntarily assumed a duty which overrides his claim of privilege. . . . The principle applies not only to public documents in public offices, but also to *records required by law to be kept in order that there may be suitable information of transactions which are the appropriate subjects of governmental regulation and the enforcement of restrictions validly established. There the privilege, which exists as to private papers, cannot be maintained.*

As illustrations of documents meeting this "required records" test, the Court cited with approval state supreme court decisions that business records kept under requirements of law by private individuals in *unincorporated* enterprises were " 'public documents, which the defendant was required to keep, not for his private uses, but for the benefit of the public, and for public inspection.' "

. . .

It may be assumed at the outset that there are limits which the Government cannot constitutionally exceed in requiring the keeping of records which may be inspected by an administrative agency and may be used in prosecuting statutory violations committed by the record-keeper himself. But no serious misgiving that those bounds have been overstepped would appear to be evoked when there is a sufficient relation between the activity sought to be regulated and the public concern so that the Government can constitutionally regulate or forbid the basic activity concerned, and can constitutionally require the keeping of particular records, subject to inspection by the Administrator. . . . [Shapiro was therefore not deprived of any right by the use of his records.]

[Conviction affirmed]

Questions for Discussion

1. Can an administrator require the production of papers by the person being investigated?

2. Does investigation for rule making differ from an investigation to determine the rights of parties?

3. An administrator is subject to the same limitations on the production of papers as a court. Appraise this statement.

4. An administrative agency can put the regulated enterprise on probation. Appraise this statement.

5. What limitation on the investigatory power is recognized in the *Smith* case?

6. Do you think it desirable that an administrator have the power of investigation approved in the *Smith* case?

7. What is the function or scope of inquiry of a court when an administrator applies to it for a subpoena?

8. Discuss the *Endicott* case with reference to the advantages and disadvantages of the Court's decision.

9. Is the Court, in the *St. Regis* case, affected in any way by a concept similar to contributory negligence?

10. Were the records in the *Shapiro* case public documents?

11. By federal statute, the Internal Revenue Service can issue a summons to a bank to produce documents relating to a taxpayer. This summons may only be used for the purpose of determining whether the taxpayer is liable for additional taxes and may not be issued once the Internal Revenue Service has recommended to the Department of Justice that the taxpayer should be criminally prosecuted. An IRS agent issued a summons to the LaSalle National Bank. It refused to supply the papers requested by the summons on the ground that the agent was actually trying to find evidence on which to base a criminal prosecution of a taxpayer. If that was so, was the bank required to honor the summons and produce the requested documents? [*United States v LaSalle National Bank,* 437 US 298 (1978)]

12. The Occupational Safety and Health Act of 1970 (OSHA) is designed to protect workers from occupational hazards. An OSHA inspector entered the premises of Barlow's, Inc., to see if there were any improper hazards. He did not have a search warrant. Barlow's brought an action to enjoin a search or examination of the premises without a search warrant. It claimed that the Fourth Amendment required that the inspector show "probable cause" to a court and obtain a search warrant before examining the premises. Was Barlow's correct? [*Marshall v Barlow's, Inc.,* 436 US 307 (1978)]

22

Administrative Determination of Issues and Enforcement

§ 22:1. PATTERN OF ADMINISTRATIVE PROCEDURE

At the beginning of the era of modern regulation of business, the administrator was, to a large extent, a minor executive or police officer charged with the responsibility of enforcing the laws applicable to limited factual situations. The health officer empowered to condemn and destroy diseased cattle was typical. In view of the need for prompt action, and because of the relative simplicity of the fact determination to be made, it was customary for the administrator to exercise summary powers; that is, upon finding cattle that the administrator believed diseased, the cattle could be killed immediately without delaying to find their true owner or without holding a formal hearing to determine whether they were in fact diseased.

As we come down to the present day, the exercise of summary powers becomes the exceptional case. Today it is permitted mainly in connection with the fraudulent use of the mails or the sending of improper matter such as lottery tickets or obscene matter through the mails, the enforcement of navigation regulations and tax laws, and the exercise of the police power in order to protect the public health and safety. As the regulation of business assumes the aspect of economic rather than health or safety regulation, the need for immediate action by the administrator diminishes, if not disappears, when the administrator acts to determine whether particular conduct comes within the scope of a regulation or whether there has been a violation thereof. Accordingly, concepts of due process generally require that some notice be given those who will be adversely affected and that some form of hearing be held at which they may present their case. As a practical matter, also, the more complicated the nature of the determinations to be made, the longer the period of investigation and deliberation required.

In the more modern type of regulation, the proceedings before the administrator tend to follow the general pattern of an action in the law court. It is commonly provided that either a private individual aggrieved by the conduct of another or the administrator may present a complaint. This complaint is served on the alleged wrongdoer, who is allowed to file an answer. There may be other phases of pleading between the parties and the administrator, but eventually the matter comes before the administrator to be heard. After a hearing, the administrator makes a decision and enters an order either dismissing the complaint or directing the adverse party to do or not to do certain acts. This order is generally not self-executing and, in order to enforce it, provision is generally made for an application by the administrator to a court. Sometimes the converse is provided, so that the order of the administrator becomes binding upon the adverse party unless an appeal is taken to a court within a stated period for a review of the order.

The complaint filing and prehearing stage of the procedure may be more detailed than just stated. In many of the modern administrative statutes, provision is made for an examination of the informal complaint by some branch of the administrator to determine whether it presents a case coming within the scope of the administrator's authority. It is also commonly provided that an investigation be made by the administrator to determine whether the facts are such as warrant a hearing of the complaint. If it is decided that the complaint is within the jurisdiction of the administrator and that the facts appear to justify it, a formal complaint is issued and served on the adverse party, and an answer is filed as above stated.

With the rising complexity of the subjects regulated by administrative procedure, the trend is increasingly toward greater preliminary examination upon the basis of an informal complaint. Cutting across these procedures are the practical devices of informal settlement and consent decrees. In many instances, the alleged wrongdoer will be willing to change the offending practices or conduct upon being informally notified that a complaint has been made. It is therefore sound public relations, as well as expeditious handling of the matter, for the administrator to inform the alleged wrongdoer of the charge made prior to the filing of any formal complaint in order to provide the opportunity to settle the matter voluntarily. A matter that has already gone into the formal hearing stage may also be terminated by agreement, and a stipulation or consent decree may be entered or filed setting forth the terms of the agreement.

A further modification of this general pattern is made in the case of the Interstate Commerce Commission. Complaints received by the commission are referred to the Bureau of Informal Cases, which endeavors to secure an amicable adjustment with the carrier. If this cannot be done, the complainant is notified that it will be necessary to file a formal complaint. At this stage of the proceedings, the parties can expedite the matter by agreeing that the case may be heard on the pleadings alone. If this is done, the complainant files a pleading or memorandum, to which the defendant files an answering memorandum, the plaintiff then filing a reply or rebuttal memorandum. If the parties do not agree to this procedure, a hearing is held after the pleadings have been filed.

§ 22:2. DELEGATION OF JUDICIAL POWER

Paralleling the unsuccessful argument that the power to make rules cannot be delegated to the administrator[1] is the assertion that the administrator cannot be given the power to make judicial determinations, on the theory that only a body with judicial power can make determinations affecting matters of private right. In the federal area, this argument has never been sustained.[2] In the state courts, it has sometimes been held that there was an improper delegation of judicial power when the power is given to an administrator to determine matters involving common-law rights and liabilities, but not when questions relating to new administrative rights are determined. One court has held that even in the latter case the power to make a judicial determination cannot be conferred.[3] Generally, however, the state decisions follow the federal rule.

§ 22:3. NECESSITY OF NOTICE AND HEARING

In order to satisfy the requirements of due process, it may be necessary for the administrator to give notice and to hold a hearing. This raises two questions, whether notice and hearing are necessary and, if they are, whether satisfactory notice and hearing has been given and allowed. The courts have attempted to define the necessity for notice and hearing in terms of whether the administrator exercises a legislative or a judicial function. In the case of the legislative function, the administrator makes a determination or adopts a rule to govern future cases. In the case of a judicial function, the administrator applies the existing law to the facts of a particular case to determine the liability of the parties. If the function exercised by the administrator is judicial or quasijudicial, notice and hearing are required. Although rate making is classified as a legislative function, notice and hearing are also required, as in the case of a judicial function.

If due process requires a notice and hearing, this does not necessarily take place at the administrative level. In some instances, it is held that a notice given the party affected after the administrator makes a decision and a hearing held before a court on appeal from the decision of the administrator are sufficient notice and hearing. The same is true where the administrative determination cannot be enforced by the administrator but only by an action at law against the party affected. Here it is held that the notice to the person that a suit has been brought and the opportunity for a hearing in that suit satisfy the requirements of due process.

---

[1]See § 20:1.
[2]*Sunshine Anthracite Coal Co. v Adkins,* 310 US 381 (1940).
[3]*State ex rel Hovey Concrete Products Co. v Mechem,* 63 NM 250, 316 P2d 1069 (1957).

(a) Abolition of railroad grade crossings

SOUTHERN RAILWAY v VIRGINIA

290 US 190 (1933)

A state statute authorized an administrator to order railroads to eliminate grade crossings whenever, in the administrator's opinion, this was necessary for the public safety and convenience. No express provision was made for a notice or a hearing on the question of the necessity of eliminating grade crossings, and no provision was made for a review of the officer's decision other than that which was afforded by resorting to the injunction power of a court.

OPINION BY MCREYNOLDS, J.

... The Highway Commissioner, without prior notice, advised [the railroad] that in his opinion public safety and convenience required elimination of the grade crossing. . . .

As authoritatively interpreted the challenged Act permits the Highway Commissioner—an executive officer—without notice or hearing to command a railroad company to abolish any designated grade crossing and construct an overhead when, in his opinion, necessary for public safety and convenience. His opinion is final upon the fundamental question whether public convenience and necessity require the elimination, unless what the Supreme Court denominates "arbitrary" exercise of the granted power can be shown. Upon petition, filed within sixty days, the Corporation Commission may consider the proposed plans and approve or modify them, but nothing more. The statute makes no provision for review by any court. But the Supreme Court [of the state] has declared that a court of equity may give relief under an original bill where "arbitrary" action can be established.

As construed and applied, we think the statute conflicts with the Fourteenth Amendment.

Certainly, to require abolition of an established grade crossing and the outlay of money necessary to construct an overhead would take the railway's property in a very real sense. This seems plain enough. . . .

If we assume that by proper legislation a State may impose upon the railways the duty of eliminating grade crossings, when deemed necessary for public safety and convenience, the question here is whether the challenged statute meets the requirements of due process of law. Undoubtedly, it attempts to give an administrative officer power to make final determination in respect of facts —the character of a crossing and what is necessary for the public safety and convenience—without notice, without hearing, without evidence; and upon this ex parte finding, not subject to general review, to ordain that expenditures shall be made for erecting a new structure. The thing so authorized is no mere police regulation. . . .

Counsel submit that the legislature, without giving notice or opportunity to be heard, by direct order might have required elimination of the crossing. Consequently, they conclude the same may be accomplished in any manner which it deems advisable without violating the Federal Constitution. But if we assume that a state legislature may determine what public welfare demands and by direct command require a railway to act accordingly, it by no means follows that an administrative officer may be empowered, without notice or hearing, to act upon his own opinion and ordain the taking of private property. There is an obvious difference between legislative determination and the finding of an administrative official not supported by evidence. In theory at least, the legislature acts upon adequate knowledge after full consideration and through members who represent the entire public. . . .

This court has often recognized the power of a state, acting through an executive officer or body, to order the removal of grade crossings; but in all these cases there was the right to a hearing and review by some court. . . .

The court below said: "The railroad is not without remedy. Should the power vested in the Highway Commissioner be arbitrarily exercised, equity's long arm will stay his hand." But, by sanctioning the order directing the Railway to proceed, it, in effect, approved action without hearing, without evidence, without opportunity to know the basis therefor. This was to rule that such action was not necessarily "arbitrary." There is nothing to indicate what that court would deem arbitrary action or how this could be established in the absence of evidence or hearing. In circumstances like those here disclosed no contestant could have full opportunity for relief in a court of equity. There would be nothing to show the grounds upon which the Commissioner based his conclusion. He alone would be cognizant of the mental processes which begot his urgent opinion.

The infirmities of the enactment are not relieved by an indefinite right of review in respect of some action spoken of as arbitrary. Before its property can be taken under the edict of an administrative officer the appellant is entitled to a fair hearing upon the fundamental facts. This has not been accorded. . . .

[Judgment for Southern Railway]

(b) Rate determination

CHICAGO, MILWAUKEE & ST. PAUL RAILWAY CO. v MINNESOTA
134 US 418 (1890)

A state commission was authorized to fix the rates to be charged by common carriers whenever it found that unreasonable rates were charged. If a carrier failed to comply with the order of the commission, the latter was authorized to obtain a writ of mandamus or court order to compel compliance. If the carrier then failed to comply with the court order, it could be punished for contempt. No provision was made for a hearing before the commission at which a carrier could offer evidence as to the reasonable character of the rate it charged.

OPINION BY BLATCHFORD, J.

. . . The supreme court of Minnesota . . . declares . . . that the rates recommended and published by the commission, if it proceeds in the manner pointed out by the act, are not simply advisory, nor merely *prima facie* equal and reasonable, but final and conclusive as to what are equal and reasonable charges; that the law neither contemplates nor allows any issue to be made or inquiry to be had as to their equality or reasonableness in fact; that, under the statute, the rates published by the commission are the only ones that are lawful, and therefore, in contemplation of law, the only ones that are equal and reasonable; and that, in [an enforcement] proceeding . . . under the statute, there is no fact to [deny] except the violation of law in not complying with the recommendations of the commission. In other words, although the railroad company is forbidden to establish rates that are not equal and reasonable, there is no power in the courts to stay the hands of the commission, if it chooses to establish rates that are unequal and unreasonable. This being the construction of the statute . . . it conflicts with the constitution of the United States. . . . It deprives the company of its right to a judicial investigation, by due process of law, under the forms and with the machinery provided by the wisdom of successive ages for the investigation judicially of the truth of a matter in controversy, and substitutes therefor, as an absolute finality, the action of a railroad commission which, in view of the powers conceded to it by the state court, cannot be regarded as clothed with judicial functions, or possessing the machinery of a court of justice. Under section 8 of the statute, which the supreme court of Minnesota says is the only one which relates to the matter of the fixing by the commission of general schedules of rates, and which section, it says, fully and exclusively provides for that subject, and is complete in itself, all that the commission is required to do is on the filing with it by a railroad company of copies of schedules of charges, to "find" that any part thereof is in any respect unequal or unreasonable, and then it is authorized and directed to compel the company to change the same, and adopt such charge as the commission "shall declare to be equal and reasonable;" and to that end it is required to inform the company in writing in what respect its charges are unequal and unreasonable. No hearing is provided for; no summons or notice to the company before the commission has found what it is to find, and declared what it is to declare; no opportunity provided for the company to introduce witnesses before the commission,—in fact, nothing which has the semblance of due process of law; and although, in the present case, it appears that, prior to the decision of the commission, the company appeared before it by its agent, and the commission investigated the rates charged by the company for transporting milk, yet it does not appear what the character of the investigation was, or how the result was arrived at. By the second section of the statute in question, it is provided that all charges made by a common carrier for the transportation of passengers or property shall be equal and reasonable. Under this provision, the carrier has a right to make equal and reasonable charges for such transportation. In the present case, the return alleged that the rate of charge fixed by the commission was not equal or reasonable, and the supreme court held that the statute deprived the company of the right to show that judicially. The question of the reasonableness of a rate of charge for transportation by a railroad company, involving, as it does, the element of reasonableness both as regards the company and as regards the public, is eminently a question for judicial investigation, requiring due process of law for its determination. If the company is deprived of the power of charging reasonable rates for the use of its property, and such deprivation takes place in the absence of an investigation by judicial machinery, it is deprived of the lawful use of its property, and thus, in substance and effect, of the property itself, without due process of law, and in violation of the constitution of the United States; . . .

[Judgment for Chicago, Milwaukee & St. Paul Railway Co.]

DISSENTING OPINION BY BRADLEY, J.

. . . The legislature might have fixed the rates in question. If it had done so, it would have done it through the aid of committees appointed to investigate the subject, to acquire information, to cite parties, to get all the facts before them, and finally to decide and report. No one could have said that this was not due process of law. And if the legislature itself could do this, acting by its committees, and proceeding according to the usual forms adopted by such bodies, I can see no good reason why it might not delegate the duty to a board of commissioners, charged, as the board in this case was, to regulate and fix the charges so as to be equal and reasonable. Such a board would have at its command all the means of getting at the truth, and ascertaining the reasonableness of fares and freights, which a legislative committee has. It might or it might not swear witnesses and examine parties. Its duties being of an administrative character, it would have the widest scope for examination and inquiry. All means of knowledge and information would be at its command; just as they would be at the command of the legislature which created it. Such a body, though not a court, is a proper tribunal for the duties imposed upon it. . . .

It is complained that the decisions of the board are final and without appeal. So are the decisions of the courts in matters within their jurisdiction. There must be a final tribunal somewhere for deciding every question in the world. Injustice may take place in all tribunals. All human institutions are imperfect,—courts as well as commissions and legislatures. Whatever tribunal has jurisdiction, its decisions are final and conclusive, unless an appeal is given therefrom. The important question always is, what is the lawful tribunal for the particular case? In my judgment, in the present case, the proper tribunal was the legislature, or the board of commissioners which it created for the purpose. . . .

§ 22:4. TIME FOR HEARING

While a hearing must be granted the carrier, it is not necessary that this hearing be held before the commission makes a determination of the rates. It is sufficient if an opportunity is given for a full hearing before the order fixing the rates becomes operative. It is thus constitutional to authorize a commission to fix the rate first and then grant a hearing on this proposed rate if the carrier applies for a hearing. If the carrier does not apply for the hearing, the procedure is not objectionable because in the particular case there was, in fact, no hearing. It is likewise constitutional to provide that at such a hearing the burden of proof shall be on the carrier to show that the rates proposed by the commission are unreasonable, rather than placing the burden on the commission to justify its rates as reasonable.

(a) Rent control

BOWLES v WILLINGHAM

321 US 503 (1944)

The Emergency Price Control Act of 1942 authorized the Price Control Administrator to fix maximum rentals for areas in which such control was, in the administrator's opinion, needed. A property owner sought to enjoin the enforcement of a rent order issued under the Act. It was claimed that the Act was unconstitutional because there was no hearing provided prior to the entry of a rent order.

OPINION BY DOUGLAS, J.

In June 1943, the Rent Director [Bowles] gave written notice to Mrs. Willingham that he proposed to decrease the maximum rents for three apartments owned by her, and which had not been rented on April 1, 1941, but were first rented in the summer of 1941, on the ground that the first rents for these apartments received after April 1, 1941 were in excess of those generally prevailing in the area for comparable accommodations on April 1, 1941. Mrs. Willingham filed objections to that proposed action together with supporting affidavits. The Rent Director thereupon advised her that he would proceed to issue an order reducing the rents. . . .

It is finally [argued] that the Act violates the Fifth Amendment because it makes no provision for a hearing to landlords before the order or regulation fixing rents becomes effective. Obviously, Congress would have been under no necessity to give notice and provide a hearing before it acted, had it decided to fix rents on a national basis the same as it did for the District of Columbia. See 55 Stat. 788. We agree with the Emergency Court of Appeals . . . that Congress need not make that requirement when it delegates the task to an administrative agency. In *Bi-Metallic Investment Co. v State Board,* 239 US 441, a suit was brought by a taxpayer and landowner to enjoin a Colorado Board from putting in effect an order which increased the valuation of all taxable property in Denver 40 percent. Such action, it was alleged, violated the Fourteenth Amendment as the plaintiff was given no opportunity to be heard. Mr. Justice Holmes, speaking for the court, stated:

> Where a rule of conduct applies to more than a few people it is impracticable that every one should have a direct voice in its adoption. The Constitution does not require all public acts to be done in town meeting or an assembly of the whole. General statutes within the state power are passed that affect the person or property of individuals, sometimes to the point of ruin, without giving them a chance to be heard. Their rights are protected in the only way that they can be in a complex society, by their power, immediate or remote, over those who make the rule.

We need not go so far in the present case. Here Congress has provided for judicial review of the Administrator's action. To be sure, that review comes after the order has been promulgated; and no provision for a stay is made. . . . "Where only property rights are involved, mere postponement of the judicial enquiry is not a denial of due process, if the opportunity given for the ultimate judicial determination of the liability is adequate. . . . Delay in the judicial determination of property rights is not uncommon where it is essential that government needs be immediately satisfied."

. . . Congress was dealing here with the exigencies of war time conditions and the insistent demands of inflation control. . . . Congress chose not to fix rents in specified areas or on a national scale by legislative fiat. It chose a method designed to meet the needs for rent control as they might arise and to accord some leeway for adjustment within the formula which it prescribed. At the same time, the procedure which Congress adopted was selected with the view of eliminating the necessity for "lengthy and costly trials with concomitant dissipation of the time and energies of all concerned in litigation rather than in common war effort." . . . To require hearings for thousands of landlords before any rent control order could be made effective might have defeated the program of price control. Or Congress might well have thought so. National security might not be able to afford the luxuries of litigation and the long delays which preliminary hearings traditionally have entailed.

We fully recognize . . . that "even the war power does not remove constitutional limitations safeguarding essential liberties." . . . But where Congress has provided for judicial review after the regulations or orders have been made effective it has done all that due process under the war emergency requires. . . .

[Judgment for Bowles]

§ 22:5. NATURE OF HEARING

When a hearing is required, to what extent must it conform to the standards observed in a court trial? Certain requirements of a court trial should be observed at the administrative hearing if the testimony of witnesses is presented. Experience and common sense have shown that certain devices or procedures of a court trial are aids in the determination of the truth. At the hearing before the administrator, witnesses should be sworn, or affirmed, in the same manner as in a jury trial. Persons against whom testimony is given should have the privilege of confronting or facing those who have testified against them. The right to cross-examine the opposing witnesses and to offer evidence in rebuttal of their testimony should be preserved. Similarly, the right to make objections to the proceedings and to the introduction of evidence, and to obtain rulings either in the course of the hearing or in the opinion or report filed by the administrator, should also be observed.

The various privileges against testifying must also be honored before the administrator. Communications between husband and wife, physician and patient, attorney and client, which are deemed "privileged" in an action in a law court, must also be regarded as privileged before an administrator. In consequence, a witness may refuse to testify on what was said because that statement was a privileged communication because of the relationship of the speaker to the witness. Similarly, the guarantee against self-incrimination applies to a witness testifying before the administrator.

When it is provided that the administrator is not bound by the rules of evidence or by procedure applicable to a proceeding before a law court, the question arises whether any procedure is valid or whether some limitation is imposed in place of those that would bind a court. That there must be some limitations was recognized in *Interstate Commerce Commission v Louisville & Nashville Railroad,* 227 US 88 (1913), in which the court stated:

> . . . the more liberal the practice in admitting testimony, the more imperative the obligation to preserve the essential rules of evidence by which rights are asserted or defended. In such cases the Commissioners cannot act upon their own information, as could jurors in primitive days. All parties must be fully apprised of the evidence submitted or to be considered, and must be given opportunity to cross-examine witnesses, to inspect documents, and to offer evidence in explanation or rebuttal. In no other way can a party maintain its rights or make its defense. In no other way can it test the sufficiency of the facts to support the findings; for otherwise, even though it appeared that the order was without evidence, the manifest deficiency could always be explained on the theory that the Commission had before it extraneous, unknown but presumptively sufficient information to support the finding.

(a) The administrator as judge

The fact that the administrator hearing the case had already investigated the matter does not disqualify the administrator from hearing and determining the case. In order to meet the objection that the exercise of executive, legislative, and judicial powers by the same administrator is a potential threat to impartiality, some steps have been taken toward decentralizing the administrative functions. Thus the prosecutorial power of the National Labor Relations Board was severed from the Board by the Labor-Management Relations Act of 1947 and entrusted to an independent General Counsel. In a number of agencies, such as the Federal Trade Commission, the judicial function is assigned to Administrative Law Judges.

WITHROW v LARKIN

421 US 35 (1975)

Larkin was a doctor licensed under the laws of Wisconsin. The state medical licensing board conducted an investigation, after which it concluded that a hearing should be held by it to determine whether Larkin's license to practice should be suspended. Larkin claimed that his constitutional rights would be violated if the same body which had investigated the case against him would also act as judge to determine whether his license should be suspended. He brought a lawsuit against Withrow and the other members of the licensing board to enjoin them from holding the hearing. An injunction was granted, and Withrow and the other members of the board appealed to the United States Supreme Court.

OPINION BY WHITE, J.

. . . Concededly, a "fair trial in a fair tribunal is a basic requirement of due process." . . .

The contention that the combination of investigative and adjudicative functions necessarily creates an unconstitutional risk of bias in administrative adjudication has a . . . difficult burden of persuasion to carry. It must overcome a presumption of honesty and integrity in those serving as adjudicators; and it must convince that, under a realistic appraisal of psychological tendencies and human weakness, conferring investigative and adjudicative powers on the same individuals poses such a risk of actual bias or prejudgment that the practice must be forbidden if the guarantee of due process is to be adequately implemented.

Very similar claims have been squarely rejected in prior decisions of this Court. . . .

More recently we have sustained against due process objection a system in which a Social Security examiner has responsibility for developing the facts and making a decision as to disability claims, and observed that the challenge to this combination of functions "assumes too much and would bring down too many procedures designed, and working well, for a government structure of great and growing complexity." . . .*

That is not to say that there is nothing to the argument that those who have investigated should not then adjudicate. The issue is substantial, it is not new, and legislators and others concerned with the operations of administrative agencies have given much attention to whether and to what extent distinctive administrative functions should be performed by the same persons. No single answer has been reached. Indeed, the growth, variety, and complexity of the administrative processes have made any one solution highly unlikely. Within the Federal Government itself, Congress has addressed the issue in several different ways, providing for varying degrees of separation from complete separation of functions to virtually none at all. For the generality of agencies, Congress has been content with § 5 of the Administrative Procedure Act, 5 USC § 554(d) [5 USCS § 554(d)], which provides that no employee engaged in investigating or prosecuting may also participate or advise in the adjudicating function, but which also expressly exempts from this prohibition "the agency or a member or members of the body comprising the agency."

. . . The case law, both federal and state, generally rejects the idea that the combination [of] judging [and] investigating functions is a denial of due process. . . ." Similarly, our cases . . . offer no support for the bald proposition applied in this case by the District Court that agency members who participate in an investigation are disqualified from adjudicating. . . .

When the Board instituted its investigative procedures, it stated only that it would investigate whether proscribed conduct had occurred. Later in noticing the adversary hearing, it asserted only that it would determine if violations had been committed which would warrant suspension of appellee's license. Without doubt, the Board then anticipated that the proceeding would eventuate in an adjudication of the issue; but there was no more evidence of bias or the risk of bias or prejudgment than inhered in the very fact that the Board had investigated and would now adjudicate. Of course, we should be alert to the possibilities of bias that may lurk in the way particular procedures actually work in practice. The processes utilized by the Board, however, do not in themselves contain an unacceptable risk of bias. The investigative proceeding

---

*The decisions of the courts of appeals touching upon this question of bias arising from a combination of functions are also instructive. In *Pangburn v Civil Aeronautics Board,* 311 F2d 349 (CA1 1962), the Board had the responsibility of making an accident report and also reviewing the decision of a trial examiner that the pilot involved in the accident should have his airline transport pilot rating suspended. The pilot claimed that his right to procedural due process had been violated by the fact that the board was not an impartial tribunal in deciding his appeal from the trial examiner's decision since it had previously issued its accident report finding pilot error to be the probable cause of the crash. The Court of Appeals found the Board's procedures to be constitutionally permissible: "We cannot say that the mere fact that a tribunal has had contact with a particular factual complex in a prior hearing, or indeed has taken a public position on the facts, is enough to place that tribunal under a constitutional inhibition to pass upon the facts in a subsequent hearing. We believe that more is required. Particularly is this so in the instant case where the Board's prior contact with the case resulted from its following the Congressional mandate to investigate and report the probable cause of all civil air accidents." Id., at 358. . . .

had been closed to the public, but appellee and his counsel were permitted to be present throughout; counsel actually attended the hearings and knew the facts presented to the Board. No specific foundation has been presented for suspecting that the Board had been prejudiced by its investigation or would be disabled from hearing and deciding on the basis of the evidence to be presented at the contested hearing. The mere exposure to evidence presented in nonadversary investigative procedures is insufficient in itself to impugn the fairness of the board members at a later adversary hearing. Without a showing to the contrary, state administrators, "are assumed to be men of conscience and intellectual discipline, capable of judging a particular controversy fairly on the basis of its own circumstances." . . .

We are of the view, therefore, that the District Court was in error when it entered the restraining order against the Board's contested hearing and when it granted the preliminary injunction based on the untenable view that it would be unconstitutional for the Board to suspend appellee's license "at its own contested hearing on charges evolving from its own investigation. . . ."

[Judgment reversed]

(b) Absence of jury trial

There is no constitutional right to a trial by jury before an administrator. The fact that the administrator's decision may involve large sums of money or impose fines does not alter this conclusion. The absence of a trial by jury does not constitute a denial of due process nor violate the constitutional guarantees of jury trials. The theory is that the statute creating the administrator creates a new right unknown to the common law, and that the right to a jury trial exists only when the right involved was recognized at common law.

ATLAS ROOFING CO., INC. v OCCUPATIONAL SAFETY AND HEALTH REVIEW COMMISSION
430 US 442 (1977)

Under the Occupational Safety and Health Act of 1970 (OSHA), an employer may be ordered to eliminate or abate an unsafe working condition. On failing to do so, a civil penalty may be assessed against the employer. Atlas Roofing was ordered to abate a specified working condition and a penalty was assessed against it for failing to do so. It claimed that the procedure which had been followed violated the guarantee of a jury trial declared by the Seventh Amendment of the federal Constitution:

> In suits at common law, where the value in controversy shall exceed twenty dollars, the right of trial by jury shall be preserved, and no fact tried by a jury shall be otherwise reexamined in any court of the United States, than according to the rules of the common law.

From a decision against Atlas, it appealed to the United States Supreme Court.

OPINION BY WHITE, J.

The issue . . . is whether, consistent with the Seventh Amendment, Congress may create a new cause of action in the Government for civil penalties enforceable in an administrative agency where there is no jury trial. . . .

After extensive investigation, Congress concluded, in 1970, that work-related deaths and injuries had become a "drastic" national problem. Finding the existing state statutory remedies as well as state common-law actions for negligence and wrongful death to be inadequate to protect the employee population from death and injury due to unsafe working conditions, Congress enacted the Occupational Safety and Health Act of 1970. . . . The Act created a new statutory duty to avoid maintaining unsafe or unhealthy working conditions, and empowers the Secretary of Labor to promulgate health and safety standards. Two new remedies were provided—permitting the Federal Government, proceeding before an administrative agency, (1) to obtain abatement orders requiring employers to correct unsafe working conditions and (2) to impose civil penalties on any employer maintaining any unsafe working condition. Each remedy exists whether or not an employee is actually injured or killed as a result of the condition, and existing state statutory and common-law remedies for actual injury and death remain unaffected.

Under the Act, inspectors, representing the Secretary of Labor, are authorized to conduct reasonable safety and health inspections. . . . If a violation is discovered, the inspector, on behalf of the Secretary, issues a citation to the employer fixing a reasonable time for its abatement and, in his discretion, proposing a civil penalty. . . . Such proposed penalties may range from nothing for de minimis and nonserious violations, to not more than $1,000 for serious violations, to a maximum of $10,000 for willful or repeated violations, . . .

If the employer wishes to contest the penalty or the abatement order, he may do so by notifying the Secretary of Labor within 15 days, in which event the abatement order is automatically stayed. . . . An evidentiary hearing is then held before an administrative law judge of the Occupational Safety and Health Review Commission. The Commission consists of three members, appointed for six-year terms, each of whom is qualified "by reason of training, education or experience" to adjudicate contested citations and assess penalties. . . . At this hearing the burden is on the Secretary to establish the elements of the alleged violation and the propriety of his proposed abatement order and proposed penalty; and the judge is empowered to affirm, modify, or vacate any or all of these items, giving due consideration in his penalty assessment to "the size of the business of the employer . . . , the gravity of the violation, the good faith of the employer, and the history of previous violations." . . . The judge's decision becomes the Commission's final and appealable order unless within 30 days a Commissioner directs that it be reviewed by the full Commission. . . .

If review is granted, the Commission's subsequent order directing abatement and the payment of any assessed penalty becomes final unless the employer timely petitions for judicial review in the appropriate court of appeals. . . . The Secretary similarly may seek review of Commission orders . . ., but, in either case, "the findings of the Commission with respect to questions of fact, if supported by substantial evidence on the record considered as a whole, shall be conclusive." . . . If the employer fails to pay the assessed penalty, the Secretary may commence a collection action in a federal district court in which neither the fact of the violation nor the propriety of the penalty assessed may be retried. . . . Thus, the penalty may be collected without the employer's ever being entitled to a jury determination of the facts constituting the violation. . . .

Congress has often created new statutory obligations, provided for civil penalties for their violation, and committed exclusively to an administrative agency the function of deciding whether a violation has in fact occurred. These statutory schemes have been sustained by this Court. . . .

In *NLRB v Jones & Laughlin Steel Corp.*, 301 US 1, . . . (1937), the Court squarely addressed the Seventh Amendment issue involved when Congress commits the factfinding function under a new statute to an administrative tribunal. Under the National Labor Relations Act, Congress had committed to the National Labor Relations Board in a proceeding brought by its litigating arm, the task of deciding whether an unfair labor practice had been committed and of ordering backpay where appropriate. The Court stated:

> The instant case is not a suit at common law or in the nature of such a suit. The proceeding is one unknown to common law. *It is a statutory proceeding.* Reinstatement of the employee and payment for time lost *are requirements* [*administratively*] *imposed for violation of the statute and are remedies appropriate to its enforcement.* The contention under the Seventh Amendment is without merit. . . .

This passage from *Jones & Laughlin* has recently been explained in *Curtis v Loether,* 415 US 189, . . . (1974), in which the Court held the Seventh Amendment applicable to private damages suits in federal courts brought under the housing discrimination provisions of the Civil Rights Act of 1968. The Court rejected the argument that *Jones & Laughlin* held the Seventh Amendment inapplicable to any action based on a statutorily created right even if the action was brought before a tribunal which customarily utilizes a jury as its factfinding arm. Instead, we concluded that *Jones & Laughlin* upheld

> congressional power to entrust enforcement of statutory rights to *an administrative process or specialized court of equity* free from the strictures of the Seventh Amendment. . . .

In sum, the cases . . . stand clearly for the proposition that when Congress creates new statutory "public rights," it may assign their adjudication to an administrative agency with which a jury trial would be incompatible, without violating the Seventh Amendment's injunction that jury trial is to be "preserved" in "suits at the common law." Congress is not required by the Seventh Amendment to choke the already crowded federal courts with new types of litigation or prevented from committing some new types of litigation to administrative agencies with special competence in the relevant field. This is the case even if the Seventh Amendment would have required a jury where the adjudication of those rights is assigned to a federal court of law instead of an administrative agency . . .

It is apparent from the history of jury trial in civil matters that factfinding, which is the essential function of the jury in civil cases, . . . was never the exclusive province of the jury under either the English or American legal systems at the time of the adoption of the Seventh Amendment; and the question whether a fact would be found by a jury turned to a considerable degree on the nature of the forum in which a litigant found himself. Critical factfinding was performed without juries in suits in equity, and there were no juries in admiralty, . . . neither was there in the military justice system. The jury was the factfinding mode in most suits in the common-law courts, but it was not exclusively so: condemnation was a suit at common law but constitutionally could be tried without a jury, . . .

The Seventh Amendment was declaratory of the existing law, for it required only that jury trial in suits at common law was to be "preserved." It thus did not purport to require a jury trial where none was required before. . . .

The point is that the Seventh Amendment was never intended to establish the jury as the exclusive mechanism for factfinding in civil cases. It took the existing legal order as it found it, and there is little or no basis for concluding that the Amendment should now be interpreted to provide an impenetrable barrier to administrative factfinding under otherwise valid federal regulatory statutes. We cannot conclude that the Amendment rendered Congress powerless —when it concluded that remedies available in courts of law were inadequate to cope with a problem within Congress' power to regulate—to create new public rights and remedies by statute and commit their enforcement, if it chose, to a tribunal other than a court of law—such as an administrative agency—in which facts are not found by juries. . . .

Congress found the common-law and other existing remedies for work injuries resulting from unsafe working conditions to be inadequate to protect the Nation's working men and women. It created a new cause of action, and remedies therefor, unknown to the common law, and placed their enforcement in a tribunal supplying speedy and expert resolutions of the issues involved. The Seventh Amendment is no bar to the creation of new rights or to their enforcement outside the regular courts of law. . . .

[Judgment affirmed]

(c) Basis for decision

UNITED STATES AND INTERSTATE COMMERCE COMMISSION v ABILENE & SOUTHERN RAILWAY CO.

265 US 274 (1924)

The examiner of the Interstate Commerce Commission informed the carrier that it might be necessary to refer to the annual reports of the carriers at a hearing that was to be held before the commission. The reports were not offered in evidence at the hearing, but the order of the commission on the division of rates was based in part upon the information contained in them. The order of the commission was attacked on this ground.

OPINION BY BRANDEIS, J.

. . . The plaintiffs contend that the order is void because it rests upon evidence not legally before the Commission. It is conceded that the finding rests, in part, upon data taken from the annual reports filed with the Commission by the plaintiff carriers pursuant to law; that these reports were not formally put in evidence; that the parts containing the data relied upon were not put in evidence through excerpts; that attention was not otherwise specifically called to them; and that objection to the use of the reports, under these circumstances was seasonably made by the carriers and was insisted upon. The parts of the annual reports in question were used as evidence of facts which it was deemed necessary to prove, not as a means of verifying facts of which the Commission, like a court, takes judicial notice. The contention of the Commission is that, because its able examiner gave notice that "no doubt it will be necessary to refer to the annual reports of all these carriers," its Rules of Practice permitted matter in the reports to be used as freely as if the data had been formally introduced in evidence.

The mere admission by an administrative tribunal of matter which under the rules of evidence applicable to judicial proceedings would be deemed incompetent does not invalidate its order. . . . But a finding without evidence is beyond the power of the Commission. Papers in the Commission's files are not always evidence in a case. . . . Nothing can be treated as evidence which is not introduced as such. . . . If the proceeding had been, in form, an adversary one commenced by the Orient system, that carrier could not . . . have introduced the annual reports as a whole. For they contain much that is not relevant to the matter in issue. . . . It would have been obliged to submit copies of such portions as it deemed material; or to make specific reference to the exact portion to be used. The fact that the proceeding was technically an investigation instituted by the Commission would not relieve the Orient, if a party to it, from this requirement. Every proceeding is adversary, in substance, if it may result in an order in favor of one carrier as against another. Nor was the proceeding under review any the less an adversary one, because the primary purpose of the Commission was to protect the public interest through making

provides that "any oral or documentary evidence may be received, but every agency shall as a matter of policy provide for the exclusion of irrelevant, immaterial, or unduly repetitious evidence. . . ."[5] This section omits the qualification of "competent" or any other term indicating that the administrative evidence is to be governed by the ordinary law court rules of evidence.

The outstanding exception to the rule of admissibility of administrative evidence is the provision of the National Labor-Management Relations Act that hearings before the Board "shall, so far as practicable, be conducted in accordance with the rules of evidence applicable in the district courts of the United States under the rules of civil procedure for such courts, adopted by the Supreme Court. . . ."[6] In actual application this provision may not be as restrictive as it first appears because of the qualification, "so far as practicable."

§ 22:7. WEIGHT OF ADMINISTRATIVE EVIDENCE

If the administrator is not bound by the rules of evidence, questions arise as to the effect to be given evidence that would otherwise be inadmissible. Is it to be given the same weight as evidence that would be admissible at a jury trial? May a determination before the administrator be made solely upon the basis of such evidence that would otherwise be inadmissible? To date no clear answer has been given by the courts.

(a) Weight of hearsay statements

CARROLL v KNICKERBOCKER ICE CO.

218 NY 435, 113 NE 507 (1916)

The decedent was employed delivering ice. The Workmen's Compensation Commission found that he had been fatally injured in the course of his employment and awarded workmen's compensation to his widow. The commission found that he had been fatally injured when an ice tong slipped and a large cake of ice struck him in the stomach, causing internal hemorrhage. The decedent was admitted to a hospital where, after developing delirium tremens, he died six days later. The award of compensation by the commission was challenged on the ground that there was not adequate evidence to establish that the decedent had been fatally injured in the course of his employment.

OPINION BY CUDDEBACK, J.

Section 21 of the Workmen's Compensation Law . . . provides that in any proceeding upon a claim for compensation . . . "it shall be presumed in the absence of substantial evidence to the contrary (1) that the claim comes within the provisions [of the law]. . . ." There was in this case substantial evidence to

---

[5]APA § 7(c).
[6]NLMRA § 10(b).

overcome the statutory presumption. A helper on the ice wagon and two cooks employed in the saloon where the ice was delivered testified before the commission that they were present at the time and place when it was alleged the plaintiff was injured, and that they did not see any accident whatsoever happen to him, and that they did not see any cake of ice fall. The physicians who subsequently examined the decedent testified that there were no bruises, discolorations, or abrasions on the surface of his body.

The finding of the commission is based solely on the testimony of witnesses who related what [the decedent] told them as to how he was injured. [His] wife testified that when he came home from his work he told her that he was putting a 300 pound cake of ice in Daly's cellar and the tong slipped and the ice came back on him. The physician who was called to treat the injured man at his home, a neighbor who dropped in, and the physicians at the hospital, where he was taken later in the day, testified that he made like statements to them.

The question is presented whether this hearsay testimony is sufficient under the circumstances of the case to sustain the finding of the commission. . . .

We have only to consider whether the law of this state excluding such testimony has been changed in cases coming within the Workmen's Compensation Law by Section 68 of that law. That section is as follows:

> Section 68. Technical rules of evidence or procedure not required. The commission or a commissioner or deputy commissioner in making an investigation or inquiry or conducting a hearing shall not be bound by common law or statutory rules of evidence or by technical or formal rules of procedure, except as provided in this chapter; but may make such investigation or inquiry or conduct such hearing in such manner as to ascertain the substantial rights of the parties.

This section has plainly changed the rules of evidence in all cases affected by the act. It gives the workmen's compensation commission free rein in making its investigations and in conducting its hearings and authorizes it to receive not only hearsay testimony, but any kind of evidence that may throw light on a claim pending before it. The award of the commission cannot be overturned on account of an alleged error in receiving evidence.

This is all true, but . . . Section 68 . . . does not make the hearsay testimony offered by the claimant sufficient ground to uphold the award which the commission made. That section does not declare the probative force of any evidence, but it does declare that the aim and end of the investigation by the commission shall be "to ascertain the substantial rights of the parties." No matter what latitude the commission may give to its inquiry, it must result in a determination of the substantial rights of the parties. Otherwise the statute becomes grossly unjust and a means of oppression.

The act may be taken to mean that while the commission's inquiry is not limited by the common law or statutory rules of evidence or by technical or formal rules of procedure, and it may in its discretion accept any evidence that is offered; still in the end there must be a residuum of legal evidence to support the claim before an award can be made. . . .

"There must be in the record some evidence of a sound, competent, and recognizedly probative character to sustain the findings and award made, else the findings and award must in fairness be set aside by [the] court."

It is not necessary to consider in this case the constitutional limitations upon the power of the legislature to change the rules of evidence. It is sufficient to say that the intention of the legislature as revealed in the Workmen's Compensation Law was not so revolutionary in character as to declare that an award can be sustained which is dependent altogether on hearsay testimony where the presumption created by Section 21 of the statute is overcome by substantial evidence.

The only substantial evidence before the Workmen's Compensation Commission was to the effect that no cake of ice slipped and struck the decedent, and there were no bruises or marks upon his body which indicated that he had been so injured. The findings to the contrary rest solely on the decedent's statement made at a time when he was confessedly in a high nervous state, which ended in his death from delirium tremens. Such hearsay testimony is no evidence. . . .

[Judgment for the Knickerbocker Ice Company]

DISSENTING OPINION BY SEABURY, J.

. . . I think the decision which is now the subject of review is correct. To sustain this award does not mean that the commission are obliged to act upon all hearsay evidence that is presented, but only that it may act upon it where the circumstances are such that the evidence offered is deemed by the commission to be trustworthy. . . .

The Workmen's Compensation Law is a new step in the field of social legislation. We should interpret it in accordance with the spirit which called it into existence. Our reverence for the traditional rules of our common-law system should not lead us to restrict it by subjecting it to the operation of these rules. This court is under no obligation to see to it that laws enacted to remedy abuses arising from new industrial and social conditions shall be made to square with ancient conceptions of the principles of the common law. . . . The difficulty in proving the cause of death in cases where the person injured dies as a result of the injury has long been recognized, and even in ordinary actions based on negligence the rules requiring proof of freedom from contributory negligence on the part of the deceased are relaxed to some extent. In the case now under consideration the injured man was taken from the place where he was working to his home, and into the presence of his wife and physician. The wife and physician naturally inquired as to how the accident happened, and the injured man told them. The evidence of these persons is now the only evidence available which can explain the cause of death. The commission examined and cross-examined these witnesses, and was satisfied that they correctly reported what the injured man had related shortly before his death and believed that the narrative which the injured man gave was correct. I think that the commission were justified in basing an award upon this testimony, and that the language of Section 68 . . . expressly authorized them so to do. . . .

We should frankly recognize that the commission are not limited by the common-law methods of proof, and that if they were satisfied that the so-called hearsay evidence that was offered was creditable they were justified in basing their award upon that evidence.

It is said in the prevailing opinion that: "this section does plainly permit the introduction of hearsay testimony . . . but still it does not . . . make hearsay testimony, unsupported by other evidence, sufficient ground to sustain such a finding of fact as the commission made in this case." The distinction sought to be made between admitting such evidence and basing an award upon it seems to me to be unreasonable and not to find support in anything contained in Section 68. In conceding that Section 68 sanctions the introduction of hearsay evidence the argument of the appellant is left without any foundation upon which to rest. If the legislature sanctioned the admission of this evidence it follows by necessary implication that it intended to authorize the commission to act upon it. In resting the judgment about to be rendered upon this ground the court concedes that evidence upon which the commission acted was legal evidence, but holds that it was insufficient to sustain an award. . . .

DISSENTING OPINION BY POUND, J.

I think that this case should not be disposed of by deciding that all evidence held to be objectionable as hearsay in the courts of this state is without probative force. . . .

Hearsay is said by old writers to be "of no value in the court of justice" . . . and "no evidence" . . . yet the rule against hearsay, even at common law, is subject to many exceptions, and is not inelastic either in statement or application. . . .

The rule and its exceptions are not always and everywhere the same. The decisions are not in harmony. What is admissible in one jurisdiction is sometimes excluded in another. In the same jurisdiction the exception at first formulated is sometimes limited or extended by later cases. In *Insurance Co. v. Mosley* (8 Wall 397) the question was whether the assured died from the effects of an accidental fall downstairs in the night or from natural causes. Assured had left his bed between 12 and 1 o'clock at night and it was held that his declaration to his wife when he came back that he had fallen down the back stairs and hurt himself badly were competent and sufficient proof of the fall because they were made so soon thereafter as to be in the nature of *res gestae*—declarations contemporaneous with the main fact and part thereof. The evidence was, nevertheless, the narrative by a person since deceased of a past, although a recent, event. This court . . . very properly characterized the *Mosley* case as "an extreme case" and . . . said "the distinction to be made [in such cases] is in the character of the declaration whether it is so spontaneous, or natural, an utterance as to exclude the idea of fabrication; or whether it be in the nature of narrative of what had occurred." . . . Can we say that evidence which the Supreme Court of the United States held competent and sufficient, i.e., the declarations of a deceased person made soon after the alleged accidental injury and under circumstances entitling them to credit, is not competent and sufficient proof before the industrial commission under the rule of Section 68 . . . which says that the commission shall not be bound by the common law rules of evidence? May not the commission, under this statute, adopt the rule of the Supreme Court of the United States and in its discretion give it an extremely liberal application and reject the stricter rule laid down by this court without being open to the charge of making an award on no evidence whatever? Could not "the substantial rights of the parties" be thereby ascertained? If it may go so far, we need only hold that where the common law rule against hearsay is not uniformly stated or applied, the commission may base an award upon evidence received under the exceptions to a rule most favorable to the claimant, without being bound by the decisions of this court thereon. I think that the evidence of Carroll's declarations to his wife when he came home from work and to the physician called to treat him might, without too violent a wrench to our established ideas, be held competent under the exception to the rule against hearsay applied to the *Mosley* case. In any event as pointed out by my brother Seabury in his opinion the evidence was legal and admissible. If it had any probative force, its weight was for the commission as triers of fact, and their decision thereon was final. . . . I think that we cannot say as a matter of law that it had no probative force under Section 68 of the act, but I do not thereby conclude that all hearsay has probative force, or that awards in contested cases may be allowed or disallowed on rumor or report to which the circumstances give no weight. It is not to be anticipated that the commission will become confused, waste time, lose sight of the main issue, and base awards or refuse them on haphazard hearsay, as our convention is that a jury might if it were permitted to hear everything relevant. . . .

§ 22:8. ENFORCEMENT OF ADMINISTRATIVE DETERMINATION

After the administrator has determined the matter, the industry or person affected thereby will often voluntarily comply with the decision of the administrator. In that event, the matter ends without further resort to the machinery of the law. If there is not such voluntary compliance, the question then arises as to who can do what to obtain the enforcement of the order or decision of the administrator.

Originally administrators were powerless to impose any punishment or to enforce their decisions. If the person regulated did not voluntarily comply with the administrator's decision, the administrator could only petition a court to order that person to obey. Within the last few decades, administrators have been increasingly given the power to impose a penalty and to issue orders which are binding on the regulated person, unless an appeal is taken to a court and the administrative decision reversed. As an illustration of the first, the Occupational Safety and Health Act of 1970 provides for the assessment of civil penalties against employers failing to put an end to dangerous working conditions when ordered to do so by the administrative agency created by that statute.[7] Likewise, environmental protection statutes adopted by states commonly give the state agency the power to assess a penalty for a violation of the environmental protection regulations.[8] As an illustration of the second type of administrative action, the Federal Trade Commission can issue a cease and desist order to stop a practice which it decides is improper. This order to stop is binding unless reversed on an appeal.

A question arises whether a private person or a competitor who would be benefited by the enforcement of the administrator's order may bring an action to compel enforcement. This is a question which is not readily answered, for it is held that the mere fact that someone would benefit by the enforcement of the administrative order does not give that person a right or standing to bring an action against the violator, either to recover damages for the violation of the administrative order or to compel compliance with it.

(a) National Labor Relations Act

AMALGAMATED UTILITY WORKERS v CONSOLIDATED EDISON CO.

309 US 261 (1940)

The National Labor Relations Board ordered the Consolidated Edison Company and its affiliates to desist from certain unfair labor practices. The board obtained an order from the court directing that the company observe the board's order. The company and its affiliates refused to do so. The Amalgamated Utilities Workers then began an action to punish the company and its affiliates for contempt in failing to comply with the order.

OPINION BY HUGHES, C. J.

Petitioner contends that the National Labor Relations Act "creates private rights"; that the Act recognizes the rights of labor organizations; and that it gives the parties upon whom these rights are conferred status in the courts for their vindication. . . .

Congress declared that certain labor practices should be unfair, but it prescribed a particular method by which such practices should be ascertained and prevented. By the express terms of the Act, the Board was made the exclusive agency for that purpose. Section 10(a) provides:

---

[7]*Lake Butler Apparel Co. v Secretary of Labor* (CA5 OSHA) 519 F2d 84.
[8]*Lloyd A. Fry Roofing Co. v Pollution Control Board,* 46 IllApp3d 412, 361 NE2d 23.

"The Board is empowered, as hereinafter provided, to prevent any person from engaging in any unfair labor practice (listed in Section 8) affecting commerce. This power shall be exclusive, and shall not be affected by any other means of adjustment or prevention that has been or may be established by agreement, code, law, or otherwise."

The Act then sets forth a definite and restricted course of procedure. . . . It is apparent that Congress has entrusted to the Board exclusively the prosecution of the proceeding by its own complaint, the conduct of the hearing, the adjudication and the granting of appropriate relief. The Board as a public agency acting in the public interest, not any private person or group, not any employee or group of employees, is chosen as the instrument to assure protection from the described unfair conduct in order to remove obstructions to interstate commerce.

When the Board has made its order, the Board alone is authorized to take proceedings to enforce it. For that purpose the Board is empowered to petition the Circuit Court of Appeals for a decree of enforcement. The court is to proceed upon notice to those against whom the order runs and with appropriate hearing. If the court, upon application by either party, is satisfied that additional evidence should be taken, it may order the Board, its member or agent, to take it. The Board may then modify its findings of fact and make new findings. The jurisdiction conferred upon the court is exclusive and its decree is final save as it may be reviewed in the customary manner. § 10(e). Again, the Act gives no authority for any proceeding by a private person or group, or by any employee or group of employees, to secure enforcement of the Board's order. The vindication of the desired freedom of employees is thus confided by the Act, by reason of the recognized public interest, to the public agency the Act creates. Petitioner emphasizes the opportunity afforded to private persons by § 10(f). But that opportunity is given to a person aggrieved by a final order of the Board which has granted or denied in whole or in part the relief sought. That is, it is an opportunity afforded to *contest* a final order of the Board, not to *enforce* it. The procedure on such a contest before the Circuit Court of Appeals is assimilated to that provided in § 10(e) when the Board seeks an enforcement of its order. But the assimilation does not change the nature of the proceeding under § 10(f), which seeks not to require compliance with the Board's order but to overturn it.

What Congress said at the outset, that the power of the Board to prevent any unfair practice as defined in the Act is exclusive, is thus fully carried out at every stage of the proceeding. . . .

In both Houses of Congress, the Committees were careful to say that the procedure provided by the bill was analogous to that set up by the Federal Trade Commission Act, § 5, which was deemed to be "familiar to all students of administrative law." That procedure, which was found to be prescribed in the public interest as distinguished from provisions intended to afford remedies to private persons, was fully discussed by this Court in *Federal Trade Commission v Klesner,* 280 US 19, 25, where it was said:

Section 5 of the Federal Trade Commission Act does not provide private persons with an administrative remedy for private wrongs. The formal complaint is brought in the Commission's name; the prosecution is wholly that of the government; and it bears the entire expense of the prosecution. A person who deems himself aggrieved by the use of an unfair method of competition is not given the right to institute before the Commission a complaint against the alleged wrongdoer. Nor may the Commission authorize him to do so. He may of course bring the matter to the Commission's attention and request it to file a complaint. But a denial of his request is final. And if the request is granted and a proceeding is instituted, he does not become a party to it or have any control over it.

That sort of procedure concerning unfair competition was contrasted with that provided by the Interstate Commerce Act in relation to unjust discrimination. We said that "in their bearing upon private rights" they are "wholly dissimilar." The Interstate Commerce Act, imposes upon the carrier many duties and creates in the individual corresponding rights. For the violation of the private right it affords "a private administrative remedy." The interested person can file as of right a complaint before the Interstate Commerce Commission and the carrier is required to make answer. . . . The present Act, drawn in analogy to the Federal Trade Commission Act, contains no such features.

. . . Congress has . . . created a public agency entrusted . . . with the exclusive authority for the enforcement of the provisions of the Act. . . .

We think that the provision of the National Labor Relations Act conferring exclusive power upon the Board to prevent any unfair labor practice, as defined,—a power not affected by any other means of "prevention that has been or may be established by agreement, code, law, or otherwise," necessarily embraces exclusive authority to institute proceedings for the violation of the court's decree directing enforcement. The decree in no way alters, but confirms, the position of the Board as the enforcing authority. It is the Board's order on behalf of the public that the court enforces. It is the Board's right to make that order that the court sustains. The Board seeks enforcement as a public agent, not to give effect to a "private administrative remedy." Both the order and the decree are aimed at the prevention of the unfair labor practice. If the decree of enforcement is disobeyed, the unfair labor practice is still not prevented. The Board still remains as the sole authority to secure that prevention. The appropriate procedure to that end is to ask the court to punish the violation of its decree as a contempt. As the court has no jurisdiction to enforce the order at the suit of any private person or group of persons, we think it is clear that the court cannot entertain a petition for violation of its decree of enforcement save as the Board presents it. As the Conference Report upon the bill stated, in case the unfair labor practice is resumed, "there will be immediately available to the Board an existing court decree to serve as a basis for contempt proceedings."

[Judgment for Consolidated Edison Company]

Questions for Discussion

1. (a) Describe the typical pattern of procedure before an administrator having authority to regulate business. (b) What trends have there been in such procedure during recent years?

2. Does the federal Constitution guarantee that the disputed facts on important matters be decided by a jury?

3. Why did the Court in the *Abilene* case hold that it was not enough to inform the parties that the commission would make use of the information contained in the annual reports?

4. The National Labor-Management Relations Act provides that unfair labor practice proceedings before the National Labor Relations Board "shall, so far as practicable, be conducted in accordance with the rules of evidence applicable in the district courts of the United States...." (a) Is this characteristic of modern administrative statutes? (b) Why was this provision adopted?

5. Does the majority opinion in the *Chicago, Milwaukee & St. Paul Railway Company* case require the holding of a hearing before there can be any price regulation?

6. What are the fundamentals of procedures that should be followed in an administrative hearing?

7. Is a public utility denied due process by the fact that the administrator who makes the regulation is also the one to hear and decide the case?

8. An administrator cannot decide a claim already investigated by the administrator because the United States Constitution guarantees that there be a separation of executive and judicial branches of government. Appraise this statement.

9. In the *Withrow* case, did the notice of the hearing before the board accuse Larkin of improper conduct?

10. What is the practical effect of placing the burden of disproving the reasonableness of the rates set by the administrator on the person affected by the order?

11. (a) In the *Carroll* case, to what extent was the majority of the Court affected by the fact that the "legally admissible" testimony was in conflict with the hearsay statements? (b) What decision would have been made if there was no testimony by other witnesses as to whether the cake of ice had slipped, or as to the condition of the decedent's body after the alleged injury?

12. What decision would have been made in the *Willingham* case in peacetime?

13. (a) Why did the Court in the *Abilene* case consider it important that the records be offered in evidence?   (b) Why cannot an administrator examine any records that the administrator chooses, as a book in the library?

14. When must an administrator give notice to the parties to be affected and hold a hearing before acting?

15. A state law provides that a tax commission shall assess taxes and that any taxpayer aggrieved by the assessment must appeal to the commission instead of to a court. Is this constitutional? [*Opinion of the Justices,* 96 NH 513, 68 A2d 859 (1949)]

16. A landowner applied to the zoning board for permission to erect a type of building not permitted by the zoning restrictions. The owner was not permitted to cross-examine the witness who testified against allowing such variation from the zoning regulations. The zoning board based its refusal on the ground that it had been its experience that, when cross-examination was permitted, it frequently resulted in personal and irrelevant quarrels between the examiner and the witness. The commission stated, however, that any questions that the owner might wish to ask the witness could be presented to the commission, which would in turn question the witness. The owner attacked the proceedings on the ground that he was improperly denied the right of cross-examination. Decide. [*Wadell v Board of Zoning Appeals,* 136 Conn 1, 68 A2d 152 (1949)]

17. Fagan was employed as a firefighter by the City of Newark. As part of his job, he delivered a fire extinguisher. When he returned, he complained that he had injured his arm and shoulder lifting the extinguisher and that he felt pain. There was no evidence by any other person as to what had happened. Fagan's report was noted on the fire company ledger, or log, by the firefighter in charge of keeping such records. Later Fagan died from a heart condition growing out of the arm and shoulder condition. When his widow sought workmen's compensation from the City of Newark, it raised the defense that there was no proof that Fagan had ever been injured while at work because his statement as to his injury, when repeated in court, was merely hearsay, and the notation of that hearsay statement on the fire company log did not give it any greater strength. Decide. [*Fagan v City of Newark,* 78 NJS 294, 188 A2d 427 (1963)]

18. Appraise the *Atlas Roofing* decision in terms of efficiency and expediency.

19. A commission holds a hearing to determine whether an employee is physically fit to perform the duties of the employee's job. The employee is present and takes part in the hearing. Thereafter, a later hearing, unknown to the employee, is held by the commission, which considers additional evidence on the basis of which it finds that the employee is not physically fit. The employee seeks a review of the decision on the ground that the commission acted improperly. Decide. [*English v City of Long Beach,* 35 Cal2d 155, 217 P2d 22 (1950)]

20. Teachers of the Hortonville School District were negotiating with the school district board to renew their employment contract. They could not agree on the terms of renewal. The teachers of the district went out on strike. This was a violation of the state law. When the striking teachers refused to return to work, the school board decided to consider disciplining the striking teachers. It did so, and fired them. The fired teachers claimed that they had been denied due process of law because the administrative board which disciplined them was not impartial, because of its association with the negotiation process. Were the teachers correct? [*Hortonville School District v Hortonville Education Association,* 426 US 482 (1976)]

23

Review of Administrative Action

§ 23:1. PROCEDURE

The modern concept of the administrator dates from the 30's. The statutes creating administrators which had been adopted in earlier years were typically fragmentary or primitive with respect to procedural matters. This frequently meant that the statute which authorized the administrator to make a determination did not state how the persons opposing that determination could obtain a review or reversal of that determination.

In contrast, statutes adopted during and since the early 30's have been much more detailed. Having the benefit of the experience of the earlier years, these later statutes provided definite patterns for obtaining a review. As in the case of the enforcement of the administrator's determination, a question arises under some statutes as to who may take the appeal which is authorized by the statute.

§ 23:2. WHO MAY OBTAIN REVIEW

As a general rule, only a party having a legally recognized interest in the proceedings has standing to obtain a review of the administrator's action. The mere fact that a person is interested or curious about the action of the administrator does not give standing to obtain a review. Even the fact that a person is affected or harmed by the administrative action does not give standing to obtain a review unless that interest in the matter is recognized as a legal interest. A number of statutes and the Federal Administrative Procedure Act avoid the distinction between being harmed in fact and being harmed in the eyes of the law by conferring the right of review upon "any person suffering legal wrong because of any agency action, or adversely affected or aggrieved by such action within the meaning of any relevant statute. . . ."[1]

§ 23:3. LIMITATIONS ON REVIEW

Although the modern statute gives the right to take an appeal from the action of the administrator, this does not mean that the administrator's action will be overruled. Certain limitations on review have developed which actually make it highly improbable that the reviewing court will reverse the administrator's decision. Typically, the court will merely verify that the administrator followed the procedure prescribed by the statute and acted in good faith in seeking to reach a decision. The fact that the court might disagree with the decision reached by the administrator, or that the court would have reached a different decision had it been the administrator, does not mean that the court will reverse the administrator.

§ 23:4. EXHAUSTION OF ADMINISTRATIVE REMEDY

As a procedural limitation upon review, a person objecting to any administrative action must first have exhausted any remedy available before the administrator.

As a general rule the courts refuse to review an administrative determination unless it is final. If, under the statute creating the office of the administrator, there is provision for a further appeal or review before the administrator or before another administrative body, this administrative remedy must first be exhausted before the court will review the matter. This rule has developed, in part, as a matter of common sense and orderly procedure. If the matter has not been finally concluded before the administrator, it is obviously too early to complain to the courts. The courts also have based their view upon a principle of comity: respect by the courts for another branch of the government, in this case the administrator, should compel the court to refrain from taking any action while the matter is still uncompleted before the administrator. For the court to step into the picture before the administrative phase had been completed would be regarded as impolite intermeddling.

Another reason for the courts' refusal to take action prior to the conclusion of the administrative phase is that, to a large extent, judicial review of administrative action has been, by injunction, issued by the court of equity. Traditionally, an injunction issues only when there is no other adequate remedy. By definition, there is another adequate remedy if the complainant has a right to appeal or to obtain a review within the administrative area. A complainant who has not exhausted this other remedy is not in a position to ask the court of equity to grant relief.

---

[1]APA § 10(a).

In certain instances, the doctrine of exhaustion of administrative remedy has not been observed. If it can be shown to the court that the administrative action would produce irreparable injury before the complainant could complete the appeal or other procedure before the administrative body, or that resort to administrative remedy would produce a multiplicity of suits, an injunction may be issued. The same conclusion is reached when the complainant is able to show that resort to the administrative remedy would be futile because it is manifestly inadequate, or because the administrator or administrative body refuses to act.

The exact limits of the exhaustion of the administrative remedies rule are not clearly defined. The result of an evolutionary process, it has at different times been stated in slightly different ways and has been limited at different points, so that its exact boundaries are not now precise.

(a) Tax assessment

FIRST NATIONAL BANK v WELD COUNTY

264 US 450 (1924)

OPINION BY SUTHERLAND, J.

. . . Under the Colorado statute . . . a bank is required to make a list of its shares, stating their market value, and of its shareholders for the information of the county assessor, who is thereupon directed to assess such shares for taxation in all respect the same as similar property belonging to other corporations and individuals. . . . If any taxpayer is of the opinion that his property has been assessed too high, or otherwise illegally assessed, he may appear before the assessor and have the same corrected. . . . The county commissioners of each county are constituted a Board of Equalization, with power to adjust and equalize the assessment among the several taxpayers.

. . . Plaintiff made and delivered to the County Assessor of Weld County the statement required by law. The Assessor thereupon fixed the value of its shares, as well as that of the shares of other banks within the county, at their full cash and market value; but fixed the assessed value of the property of the remaining taxpayers in the county at 61 percent for 1913 and 80 percent for 1914, of such cash and market value. . . . The Tax Commission determined that the property of the county as a whole had been underassessed and recommended a horizontal increase of 63 percent in 1913 and 25 percent in 1914, as necessary to bring it to the full cash value. This determination was approved by the State Board of Equalization, and the County Assessor was directed to make the increase with the result, as alleged, that plaintiff's assets, and those of all other banks in the county, were in fact assessed at an amount 63 percent in excess of their value for the year 1913 and 25 percent in excess thereof for the year 1914. In other counties of the State, either no increase of valuation was made, or the increase was comparatively small. The result was that the banks of Weld County were assessed and compelled to pay upon a valuation grossly in excess of that put upon other property in the same county, and likewise in excess of that put upon other banks in other counties of the state. It does not appear from the complaint that the plaintiff applied to any of the taxing authorities to reduce the assessment of its property or correct the alleged inequalities, prior to the final levy of the tax, but some time after such levy had been completed, it made application for abatement and rebate, which application was approved by the County Board but disallowed by the State Tax Commission.

We are met at the threshold of our consideration of the case with the contention that the plaintiff did not exhaust its remedies before the administrative boards and consequently cannot be heard by a judicial tribunal to assert the validity of the tax. We are of the opinion that this contention must be upheld.

. . .

It is further urged that it would have been futile to seek a hearing before the State Tax Commission because, first, no appeal to a judicial tribunal was provided in the event of a rejection of a taxpayer's complaint; and, second, because the time at the disposal of the Commission for hearing individual complaints was inadequate. But, aside from the fact that such an appeal is not a matter of right but wholly dependent upon the statute . . . we cannot assume that if application had been made to the Commission proper relief would not have been accorded by that body, in view of the statutory authority to receive complaints and examine into all cases where it is alleged that property has been fraudulently, improperly, or unfairly assessed. . . . Nor will plaintiff be heard to say that there was not adequate time for a hearing, in the absence of any effort on its part to obtain one. In any event the decision of the State Supreme Court . . . that such remedies were, in fact, available, is controlling here. . . .

Plaintiff not having availed itself of the administrative remedies afforded by the statutes as construed by the state court, it results that the question whether the tax is vulnerable to the challenge in respect of its validity upon any or all of the grounds set forth, is one which we are not called upon to consider.

. . .

[Judgment for Weld County]

---

§ 23:5. DISCRETION OF ADMINISTRATOR

When the statute gives the administrator discretion to act and the administrator has acted within the boundaries of that discretion, a court will never reverse the administrator because it personally would have exercised that discretion in a different manner. The great bulk of modern administrative determinations relate to matters which, by their economic or business-oriented nature, require the exercise of discretion rather than the application of a rigid predetermined rule to precisely determinable facts. This means that most administrative determinations relating to business are immune from reversal on appeal because the court will not re-exercise the discretion which the lawmaker gave to the administrator.

Thus the Supreme Court has said

. . . The very breadth of the statutory language precludes a reversal of the Commission's judgment save where it has plainly abused its discretion in these matters . . . Such an abuse is not present in this case. . . .

The Commission's conclusion here rests squarely in that area where administrative judgments are entitled to the greatest amount of weight by appellate courts. It is the product of administrative experience, appreciation of the complexities of the problem, realization of the statutory policy, and responsible treatment of the uncontested facts. It is the type of judgment which administrative agencies are best equipped to make and which justifies the use of the administrative process. . . . Whether we agree or disagree with the result reached, it is an allowable judgment which we cannot disturb.[2]

The Federal Administrative Procedure Act expressly excepts from the definition of reviewable acts "agency action [that] is by law committed to agency discretion."

(a) Unfair competition

MOOG INDUSTRIES v FEDERAL TRADE COMMISSION
355 US 411 (1958)

Moog Industries was ordered to stop certain pricing practices by the Federal Trade Commission. It raised the objection that its competitors were also guilty of the same practices and that Moog would be ruined if it were required to stop the practices without also requiring its competitors to stop such practices. The commission rejected this argument. Moog appealed.

OPINION BY THE COURT

The general question presented . . . is whether it is within the scope of the reviewing authority of a Court of Appeals to postpone the operation of a valid cease and desist order of the Federal Trade Commission against a single firm until similar orders have been entered against that firm's competitors. . . .

In view of the scope of administrative discretion that Congress has given the Federal Trade Commission, it is ordinarily not for courts to modify ancillary features of a valid Commission order. This is but recognition of the fact that in

---

[2]*Securities and Exchange Commission v Chenery Corporation,* 332 US 194 (1947).

". . . But it is the Commission, not the courts, which must be satisfied that the public interest will be served by renewing the license. And the fact that we might not have made the same determination on the same facts does not warrant a substitution of judicial for administrative discretion since Congress has confided the problem to the latter. . . ." *Federal Communications Commission v WOKO,* 329 US 223 (1946).

the shaping of its remedies within the framework of regulatory legislation, an agency is called upon to exercise its specialized, experienced judgment. Thus, the decision as to whether or not an order against one firm to cease and desist from engaging in illegal price discrimination should go into effect before others are similarly prohibited depends on a variety of factors peculiarly within the expert understanding of the Commission. Only the Commission, for example, is competent to make an initial determination as to whether and to what extent there is a relevant "industry" within which the particular respondent competes and whether or not the nature of that competition is such as to indicate identical treatment of the entire industry by an enforcement agency. Moreover, although an allegedly illegal practice may appear to be operative throughout an industry, whether such appearances reflect fact and whether all firms in the industry should be dealt with in a single proceeding or should receive individualized treatment are questions that call for discretionary determination by the administrative agency. It is clearly within the special competence of the Commission to appraise the adverse effect on competition that might result from postponing a particular order prohibiting continued violations of the law. Furthermore, the Commission alone is empowered to develop that enforcement policy best calculated to achieve the ends contemplated by Congress and to allocate its available funds and personnel in such a way as to execute its policy efficiently and economically.

The question, then, of whether orders such as those before us should be held in abeyance until the respondents' competitors are proceeded against is for the Commission to decide. . . . If the Commission has decided the question, its discretionary determination should not be overturned in the absence of a patent abuse of discretion. . . .

[Judgment for Federal Trade Commission]

(b) Production quota

SECRETARY OF AGRICULTURE v CENTRAL ROIG REFINING CO.

338 US 604 (1950)

Acting under the Sugar Act of 1948, the Secretary of Agriculture made quota allowances to sugar refiners in the Puerto Rico area. Appeals were taken from that action on the ground that the Act was unconstitutional and that, if constitutional, the Secretary had acted improperly in establishing the quota.

OPINION BY FRANKFURTER, J.

. . . In the course of this opinion all expressions of an economic character are to be attributed to those who have authority to make such economic judgments—the Congress and the Secretary of Agriculture—and are not to be deemed the independent judgments of the Court. It is not our right to pronounce economic views; we are confined to passing on the right of the Congress and the Secretary to act on the basis of entertainable economic judgments. . . .

By a series of enactments Congress addressed itself to what it found to be serious evils resulting from an uncontrolled sugar market. The central aim of this legislation was to rationalize the mischievous fluctuations of a free sugar market by the familiar device of a quota system. . . .

The volume of sugar moving to the continental United States market was controlled to secure a harmonious relation between supply and demand. To adapt means to the purpose of the sugar legislation, the Act of 1918 defines five domestic sugar-producing areas: two in the continental United States, Hawaii, Puerto Rico and the Virgin Islands. To each area is allotted an annual quota of sugar, specifying the maximum number of tons which may be marketed on the mainland from that area. § 202(a). A quota is likewise assigned to the Philippines. § 202(b). The balance of the needs of consumers in the continental United States, to be determined each year by the Secretary, § 201, is met by importation from foreign countries, predominantly from Cuba, of the requisite amount of sugar. § 202(c).

The quotas thus established apply to sugar in any form, raw or refined. In addition, § 207 of the Act establishes fixed limits on the tonnage of "direct consumption" or refined sugar which may be marketed annually on the mainland from the offshore areas as part of their total sugar quotas. But mainland refiners are not subject to quota limitations upon the marketing of refined sugar.

The Puerto Rican quota for "direct consumption" sugar is 126,033 tons. This figure had its genesis in the Jones-Costigan Act of 1934, which provided that the quota for each offshore area was to be the largest amount shipped to the mainland in any one of the three preceding years. . . . In the case of Puerto Rico this was computed by the Secretary at 126,033 tons. . . . By the Sugar Acts of 1937 and 1948, Congress embedded this amount in legislation. All the details for the control of a commodity like sugar could not, of course, be legislatively predetermined. Administrative powers are an essential part of such a regulatory scheme. The powers conferred by § 205(a) upon the Secretary of Agriculture raise some of the serious issues in this litigation. By that section Congress authorized the Secretary to allot the refined sugar quota as well as the inclusive allowance of a particular area among those marketing the sugar on the mainland from that area. The section provides that "Allotments shall be made in such manner and in such amounts as to provide a fair, efficient, and equitable distribution of such quota or proration thereof, by taking into consideration" three factors: (1) "processings of sugar . . . to which proportionate shares . . . pertained"; (2) past marketings; and (3) ability to market the amount allotted.

To help effectuate the marketing controls § 301 of the Act provides that certain payments will be made to farmers only if they limit the marketing of sugar cane or beets grown on their farms to a "proportionate share" of the quantity necessary to fill the area's quota, plus a normal carry-over. The relevance of this provision here is that processings of sugar grown within the "proportionate share" restriction are one of the three factors to be considered by the Secretary in the making of allotments under § 205(a).

On January 21, 1948, the Secretary issued Puerto Rico Sugar Order No. 18, 13 Fed.Reg. 310, allotting the 1948 Puerto Rican refined sugar quota among the various refineries of the island. Having satisfied himself of the need for an allotment the Secretary, in conformity with the procedural requirements of § 205(a), apportioned the quota among the individual refiners, setting forth in appropriate findings the manner in which he applied the three statutory standards for allotment.

As to "past marketings" he found that the proper measure was the average of the highest five years of marketings during the seven-year period of 1935–1941. While recognizing that ordinarily the most recent period of marketings furnished the appropriate data, he concluded that the period 1942–1947 was unrepresentative in that the war needs made those years abnormal and not a fair basis for purposes of the economic stabilization which was the aim of the 1948 Act. Shortages as to transportation, storage and materials, caused by the war, led to special government control. These circumstances resulted in hardships or advantages in varying degrees to different refiners, quite unrelated to a fair system of quotas for the post-war period.

Likewise as to "the ability . . . to market," the Secretary recognized that marketings during a recent period ordinarily furnished the best measure. But again he found that the derangements of the war years served to make that measure abnormal. He therefore concluded that a fairer guide to his judgment came from the highest marketings of any year during the 1935–1947 period, using, however, present plant capacity as a corrective.

The Secretary duly considered "the processings of sugar" to which proportionate shares pertained, but concluded that this factor could not fairly be applied. This was so because it referred to processings of raw sugar from sugar cane, whereas the three largest Puerto Rican refining concerns restricted themselves to refining raw sugar after it had already been processed. He felt bound, therefore, to give no weight to this factor in the sum he finally struck, and gave equal weight to past marketings and ability to market.

Availing themselves of § 205 (b), respondents, Central Roig Refining Company and Western Sugar Refining Company . . . appealed from the Secretary's order. . . .

In making quota allotments the Secretary of Agriculture must of course keep scrupulously within the limits set by the Sugar Act of 1948. In devising the framework of control Congress fixed the flat quotas for the sugar-producing areas. Congress could not itself, as a practical matter, allot the area quotas among individual marketers. The details on which fair judgment must be based are too shifting and judgment upon them calls for too specialized understanding to make direct congressional determination feasible. Almost inescapably the function of allotting the area quotas among individual marketers becomes an administrative function entrusted to the member of the Cabinet charged with oversight of the agricultural economy of the nation. He could not be left at large and yet he could not be rigidly bounded. Either extreme would defeat the control system. They could be avoided only by laying down standards of such breadth as inevitably to give the Secretary leeway for his expert judgment. Its exercise presumes a judgment at once comprehensive and conscientious. Accordingly, Congress instructed the Secretary to make allotments "in such manner and in such amounts as to provide a fair, efficient, and equitable distribution" of the quota.

In short, Congress gave the Secretary discretion commensurate with the legislative goal. Allocation of quotas to individual marketers was deemed an essential part of the regulatory scheme. The complexity of problems affecting raw and refined sugar in widely separated and economically disparate areas, accentuated by the instability of the differentiating factors, must have persuaded Congress of the need for continuous detailed administrative supervision. In any event, such is the plain purport of the legislation.

With respect to the Secretary's comparable function of fixing proportionate shares for farms under § 302 of the Act, the House Committee on Agriculture stated:

> In view of the differences in conditions of production obtaining in the various sugar-producing areas, the committee has not attempted to specify the exact manner in which the Secretary shall use production history. It is the judgment of the committee that considerable discretion should be left to the Secretary to deal with the varied and changing conditions in the various producing areas, in order to establish fair and equitable proportionate shares for farms in such areas. . . .

By way of guiding the Secretary in formulating a fair distribution of individual allotments, Congress directed him to exercise his discretion "by taking into consideration" three factors: past marketings, ability to market, and processings to which proportionate shares pertained. Plainly these are not mechanical or self-defining standards. They in turn imply wide areas of judgment and therefore of discretion. The fact that the Secretary's judgment is finally expressed arithmetically gives an illusory definiteness to the process of reaching it. Moreover, he is under a duty merely to take "into consideration" the particularized factors. The Secretary cannot be heedless of these factors in the sense, for instance, of refusing to hear relevant evidence bearing on them. But Congress did not think it was feasible to bind the Secretary as to the part his "consideration" of these three factors should play in his final judgment—what weight each should be given, or whether in a particular situation all three factors must play a quantitative share in his computation.

It was evidently deemed fair that in a controlled market each producer should be permitted to retain more or less the share of the market which he had acquired in the past. Accordingly, past marketings were to be taken into consideration in the Secretary's allotments. But the past is relevant only if it furnishes a representative index of the relative positions of different marketers. And there is no calculus available for determining whether a base period for measurement is fairly representative. Whether conditions have been so unusual as to make a period unrepresentative is not a matter of counting figures but of weighing imponderables. If he is to exercise the function of allotting a limited supply among avid contenders for it, the Secretary cannot escape the necessity of passing judgment on their relative competitive positions. For Congress announced that one of the main purposes justifying the making of allotments is "to afford all interested persons an equitable opportunity to market sugar." § 205 (a).

In directing the Secretary to take into consideration ability to market, Congress in effect charged the Secretary with making a forecast of the marketers' capacity to perform in the immediate future. Such a forecast no doubt draws heavily on experience, but history never quite repeats itself even in the vicissitudes of industry. Whether ability to market is most rationally measured by plant capacity or by past performance, whether, if the latter, the base period should be a year and what year or a group of years and what group—these are not questions to be dealt with as statistical problems. They require a disinterested, informed judgment based on circumstances themselves difficult of prophetic interpretation.

The proper mode of ascertaining "processings of sugar . . . to which proportionate shares . . . pertained" is not here in controversy. Perhaps this factor too implies choice. But the question common to all three standards is whether the Secretary may conclude, after due consideration, that in the particular situation before him it is not essential that each of the three factors be quantitatively reflected in the final allotment formula. Concededly, § 205 (a) empowers the Secretary to attribute influences to the three factors. Obviously one factor may be more influential than another in the sense of furnishing a better means of achieving a "fair, efficient, and equitable distribution." But it is not consonant with reason to authorize the Secretary to find in the context of the situation before him that a criterion has little value and is entitled to no more than nominal weight, but to find it unreasonable for him to conclude that this factor has no significance and therefore should not be at all reflected quantitatively.

Congress did not predetermine the periods of time to which the standards should be related or the respective weights to be accorded them. . . . Nor do the bare words of § 205 (a) confine the Secretary in the responsible exercise of discretion beyond the limitation inherent upon such delegated authority. He is not free to be capricious, to act without reason, that is, in relation to the attainment of the objects declared by § 205 (a). The very standards for his conduct, the attainment of "fair, efficient, and equitable distribution" preclude abstract or doctrinaire categories. A variety of plans of allotment may well conform to the statutory standards. But the choice among permissible plans is necessarily the Secretary's; he is the agency entrusted by Congress to make the choice.

These considerations dispose of this phase of the case. We would have to replace the Secretary's judgment with our own to hold that on the record before us he acted arbitrarily in reaching the conviction that the years 1935–1941 furnished a fairer measure of past marketings than the war years 1942–1947. Nor can we hold that it was baseless for him to decide that increased marketings during the war years may be taken to mean improved ability to market but decreased marketings do not justify the opposite conclusion. And it was within his province to exclude from his determination the processings of sugar to which proportionate shares pertained. It is not for us to reject the balance he struck on consideration of all the factors unless we can say that his judgment is not one that a fair-minded tribunal with specialized knowledge could have reached. This we cannot say. We conclude, therefore, that in issuing Order No. 18 the Secretary did not exceed the authority given him by Congress. . . .

It is a commonplace that reforms may bring in their train new difficulties. In any scheme of reform, their prevention or mitigation becomes a proper legislative concern. While ameliorating the effect of disorderly competition, market controls generate problems of their own, not encountered under a competitive system. Such new problems are not outside the comprehensive scope of the great Commerce Clause. Nor does the Commerce Clause impose requirements of geographic uniformity. . . . Congress may devise, as it has done in the Sugar Act of 1948, a national policy with due regard for the varying and fluctuating interests of different regions. . . .

. . . The Sugar Act of 1948 is claimed to offend the Due Process Clause of the Fifth Amendment because of the alleged discriminatory character and the oppressive effects of the refined sugar quota established by the Act. . . .

The use of quotas on refined sugar, legislatively apportioned to different geographic areas and administratively allocated to individual beneficiaries, is a device based on the Agricultural Adjustment Act of 1938, . . . The problem which confronted Congress was not the setting of quotas abstractly considered but so to fix their amount as to achieve approximate justice in the shares allotted to each area and the persons within it. To recognize the problem is to acknowledge its perplexities.

Congress was thus confronted with the formulation of policy peculiarly within its wide swath of discretion. It would be a singular intrusion of the judiciary into the legislative process to extrapolate restrictions upon the formulation of such an economic policy from those deeply rooted notions of justice which the Due Process Clause expresses. To fix quotas on a strict historical basis is hard on latecomers into the industry or on those in it who desire to expand. On the other hand, to the extent that newcomers are allowed to enter or old-timers to expand there must either be an increase in supply or a reduction in the quotas of others. Many other factors must plague those charged with the formulation of policy—the extent to which projected expansion is a function of efficiency or becomes a depressant of wage standards; the wise direction of capital into investments and the economic waste incident to what may be on the short or the long pull overexpansion of industrial facilities; the availability of a more suitable basis for the fixing of quotas, etc., etc. The final judgment is too apt to be a hodge-podge of considerations, including considerations that may well weigh with legislators but which this Court can hardly disentangle.

Suffice it to say that since Congress fixed the quotas on a historical basis it is not for this Court to reweigh the relevant factors and, perchance, substitute its notion of expediency and fairness for that of Congress. This is so even though the quotas thus fixed may demonstrably be disadvantageous to certain areas or persons. This Court is not a tribunal for relief from the crudities and inequities of complicated experimental economic legislation. . . .

Congress, it is insisted, has not established refined sugar quotas for the mainland refiners as it has for the offshore areas. Whatever inequalities may thereby be created this is not the forum for their correction for the all-sufficient reason that the extent and nature of inequalities are themselves controversial matters hardly meet for judicial solution. Thus, while the mainland refiners are legally free to purchase and refine all sugar within the raw sugar quota and Puerto Rico refiners are limited to their shares of the refined sugar quota, Congress apparently thought that Puerto Rico refiners operated at costs sufficiently low to insulate them from mainland competition. In addition, it is claimed that since the total supply of raw sugar permitted to enter the mainland market is limited the mainland refiners are in effect also subject to the refined sugar quota, although in contrast to the unchanging quotas of the territories the mainland quota will vary with changes in the total consumer demand. Because this demand tends to be stable, however, the mainland refiners' share of the refined sugar has not, it is urged, greatly expanded during the years when quotas were in effect. Congress might well have thought that relatively minor contractions and expansions in supply from year to year should thus be absorbed.

Plainly it is not the business of judges to sit in judgment on the validity or the significance of such views. The Act may impose hardships here and there; the incidence of hardship may shift in location and intensity. It is not for us to have views on the merits of this legislation. It suffices that we cannot say, as we cannot, that there is "discrimination of such an injurious character as to bring into operation the due process clause.". . . Expressions of dissatisfaction by the Executive and in some quarters of Congress that the refined sugar quotas were "arbitrary," "discriminatory," and "unfair" may reflect greater wisdom or greater fairness than the collective wisdom of Congress which put this Act on the statute books. But the issue was thrashed out in Congress; Congress is the place for its reconsideration. . . .

[Judgment for Secretary of Agriculture]

---

§ 23:6. QUESTIONS OF FACT

When the decision of the administrator is based on a finding of fact, the appellate court will not reverse the administrator if there is substantial evidence in the record before the administrator which, if believed, would support the conclusion of the administrator. For example, if the issue before the administrator is whether an employee was fired because of incompetence or because of membership in a labor union and there is evidence pointing both ways, a decision by the administrator either way will not be reversed by a court, even though the court would not have reached the same conclusion.

This is not a radical new rule, but merely the application to the administrative appeal of a principle which had been applied for centuries when an appeal was taken which attacked the findings of fact made by a jury. For example, there may be a right-angle collision between two automobiles at a street intersection.

The lawsuit between the two drivers may turn on whether a particular traffic light was red or green. Assume that some witnesses say it was red and some say it was green. If the jury chooses to believe the "red" witnesses, the jury will decide that the light was red and dispose of the lawsuit on that basis. No court will set this verdict aside on the ground that the court would have believed the "green" witnesses and would have decided the case on that basis. That is, the jury has a free hand to believe either the "red" witnesses or the "green" witnesses, and the jury's choice is accepted as final.

This is part of the concept that had evolved over the centuries by which the jury is the determiner of the facts. After following this rule for centuries in the case of jury trials, it was inevitable that the administrator would be given the same freedom of action in deciding facts, and that the administrator's determination of facts would be binding on the court as long as there was a reasonable basis, technically called "substantial evidence," in the record to support the administrative determination.

(a) Review de novo or record review

When an appeal is taken from the administrator to the court, should it be a review de novo or a record review? Under the *review de novo,* the court proceeds as though nothing had ever happened before the administrator. It hears the matter as though it were a new case and as though the court were the first governmental agency to have anything to do with the matter. This means that the court hears all the witnesses, decides the facts, and then applies the appropriate rule of law to the facts. In so doing, it completely ignores what the administrator had done or decided.

In contrast, when there is a *record review,* the appellate court, instead of going back to the beginning, will merely look over the record in the matter to see if there is any glaring error and to verify that there is evidence which supports the findings of fact and conclusions of the administrator. In general terms, the record in the matter is a log of the proceedings before the administrator and a copy of what was said at any administrative hearing. With the higher level administrators, this will be an exact word for word statement of every witness. The record will also include any papers submitted in evidence to the administrator.

The appeal from an administrator is typically a record review and not a review de novo. The practical reason for this is that the review de novo takes up so much time and increases the costs to the parties. Most significantly, the administrator was created to act in an area in which law-trained judges have no competence. It therefore does not make much sense to have the court go through a matter as to which, by definition, it is not competent to act. The most that a court can do is to double-check to see that there was no obvious error. This is the result obtained by the record review.

Because the typical review of the administrator is confined to examining the record, the reviewing court never hears or sees the witnesses; this explains why the reviewing court will not substitute its own opinion as to the credibility of witnesses or redecide the facts of the matter. The practical effect of confining appellate review to an examination of the record is that the proceeding before the administrator is the only "day in court" that is really important. It should not be treated as a mere dress rehearsal, which it would be if the review were de novo. If the matter before the administrator turns on questions of fact, such as why an employee was fired or whether a plant is unreasonably dangerous or pollutes the environment, the proceeding is ended with the administrator for all practical purposes, and the appeal is useless because the court on a record review will ordinarily not reverse the administrator. Ordinarily, the administrator will have followed the correct procedure and, ordinarily, there will be evidence in the record which supports the findings and conclusions of the administrator. If this is so, the administrator has the last word.

Some people feel that it is un-American to allow any branch of government other than a court to have the last word. The cherished concept of "the supremacy of the law" urges that result. In appraising the system, we must not overlook the fact that these principles, the application of which clothe the administrative decision with virtual finality, are not new. Again, we have principles that for centuries have been applied to jury trials. Consider again the case of the collision of two automobiles, with witnesses testifying differently as to the color of a traffic light. If an appeal is taken from the judgment entered upon the verdict of the jury, the higher court that decides the appeal does not hear the case all over again from the beginning and then make up its mind as though there never had been a trial in the lower court. Instead, the reviewing court limits itself to examining the record of the trial to see if the proper procedure was followed and if there is evidence in the record which, if believed, would support the verdict of the jury. The reviewing court does not substitute what it would have decided had it been the jury. Again, it was natural and inevitable to carry over these concepts of the "proper" scope of appellate review to the appeals that were taken from administrative action.

Contrary to the typical appellate record review pattern described above, the appeal from some administrators is taken to a trial court and the matter is heard de novo. The case of *Crowell v Benson* which follows below represents one of the exceptional instances in which a review de novo has been allowed. Particular attention should be paid to the dissenting opinion because of its thorough statement of the normal, or typical, scope of appellate review of administrative action.

CROWELL v BENSON

285 US 22 (1932)

Knudsen, a longshoreman, was injured at work. He filed a claim against Benson, as employer, under the Federal Longshoremen's and Harbor Workers' Compensation Act. Benson objected to the claim on the ground that Knudsen when injured was not acting as an employee of Benson and was not employed upon navigable waters of the United States. The Act did not apply if either objection was valid. Crowell, the administrator under the Act, rejected the objections and made an award to Knudsen. Benson brought an action against

Crowell to enjoin enforcement of the award. The lower court heard the issue of employment de novo, with the employee presenting additional evidence not presented before the administrator. Benson claimed that a review de novo on any issue was improper.

OPINION BY HUGHES, C. J.

. . . The act has two limitations that are fundamental. It deals exclusively with compensation in respect of disability or death resulting "from an injury occurring upon the navigable waters of the United States" if recovery "through workmen's compensation proceedings may not validly be provided by State law," and it applies only when the relation of master and servant exists. . . . The statute contains no express limitation attempting to preclude the court, in proceedings to set aside an order as not in accordance with law, from making its own examination and determination of facts whenever that is deemed to be necessary to enforce a constitutional right properly asserted. . . .

Apart from cases involving constitutional rights to be appropriately enforced by proceedings in court, there can be no doubt that the Act contemplates that, as to questions of fact arising with respect to injuries to employees within the purview of the Act, the findings of the deputy commissioner, supported by evidence and within the scope of his authority, shall be final. To hold otherwise would be to defeat the obvious purpose of the legislation to furnish a prompt, continuous, expert, and inexpensive method for dealing with a class of questions of fact which are peculiarly suited to examination and determination by an administrative agency specially assigned to that task. . . .

What has been said thus far relates to the determination of claims of employees within the purview of the Act. A different question is presented where the determinations of fact are fundamental or "jurisdictional," in the sense that their existence is a condition precedent to the operation of the statutory scheme. These fundamental requirements are that the injury occurs upon the navigable waters of the United States, and that the relation of master and servant exists. These conditions are indispensable to the application of the statute, not only because the Congress has so provided explicitly . . . but also because the power of the Congress to enact the legislation turns upon the existence of these conditions.

In amending and revising the maritime law, the Congress cannot reach beyond the constitutional limits which are inherent in the admiralty and maritime jurisdiction. Unless the injuries to which the Act relates occur upon the navigable waters of the United States, they fall outside that jurisdiction. . . . If the person injured was not an employee of the person sought to be held, or if the injury did not occur upon the navigable waters of the United States, there is no ground for an assertion that the person against whom the proceeding was directed could constitutionally be subjected, in the absence of fault upon his part, to the liability which the statute creates.

In relation to these basic facts, the question is not the ordinary one as to the propriety of provision for administrative determinations. Nor have we simply the question of due process in relation to notice and hearing. It is rather a question of the appropriate maintenance of the federal judicial power in requiring the observance of constitutional restrictions. It is the question whether the Congress may substitute for constitutional courts, in which the judicial power of the United States is vested, an administrative agency—in this instance a single deputy commissioner—for the final determination of the existence of the facts upon which the enforcement of the constitutional rights of the citizen depend. The recognition of the utility and convenience of administrative agencies for the investigation and finding of facts within their proper province, and the support of their authorized action, does not require the conclusion that there is no limitation of their use, and that the Congress could completely oust the courts of all determinations of fact by vesting the authority to make them with finality in its own instrumentalities or in the Executive department. That would be . . . to establish a government of a bureaucratic character alien to our system, wherever fundamental rights depend, as not infrequently they do depend, upon the facts, and finality as to facts becomes in effect finality in law. . . .

Assuming that the federal court may determine for itself the existence of these fundamental or jurisdictional facts, we come to the question,—Upon what record is the determination to be made? There is no provision of the statute which seeks to confine the court in such a case to the record before the deputy commissioner or to the evidence which he has taken. The remedy which the statute makes available is not . . . a review of his determination upon the record before him. The remedy is "through injunction proceedings mandatory or otherwise." . . . The question in the instant case is not whether the deputy commissioner has acted improperly or arbitrarily as shown by the record of his proceedings in the course of administration in cases contemplated by the statute, but whether he has acted in a case to which the statute is inapplicable. By providing for injunction proceedings, the Congress evidently contemplated a suit as in equity, and in such a suit complainant would have full opportunity to plead and prove either that the injury did not occur upon the navigable waters of the United States or that the relation of master and servant did not exist, and hence that the case lay outside the purview of the statute. As the question is one of the constitutional authority of the deputy commissioner as an administrative agency, the court is under no obligation to give weight to his proceedings pending the determination of that question. If the court finds that the facts existed which gave the deputy commissioner jurisdiction to pass upon the claim for compensation, the injunction will be denied in so far as these fundamental questions are concerned; if, on the contrary, the court is satisfied that the deputy commissioner had no jurisdiction of the proceedings before him, that determination will deprive them of their effectiveness for any purpose. We think that the essential independence of the exercise of the judicial power of the United States, in the enforcement of constitutional rights requires that the Federal court should determine such an issue upon its own record and the facts elicited before it. . . .

It cannot be regarded as an impairment of the intended efficiency of an administrative agency that it is confined to its proper sphere, but it may be observed that the instances which permit of a challenge to the application of the statute, upon the grounds we have stated, appear to be few. Out of the many thousands of cases which have been brought before the deputy commissioners throughout the country, a review by the courts has been sought in only a small number, and an inconsiderable proportion of these appear to have involved the question whether the injury occurred within the maritime jurisdiction or whether the relation of employment existed.

We are of the opinion that the District Court did not err in permitting a trial de novo on the issue of employment. . . .

[Judgment affirmed]

DISSENTING OPINION BY BRANDEIS, J.

[An injured worker] filed a claim against Benson under . . . the Longshoremen's and Harbor Workers' Compensation Act. . . . Benson's answer denied, among other things, that the relation of employer and employee existed between him and the claimant. The evidence introduced before the deputy commissioner, which occupies 78 pages of the printed record, was directed largely to that issue and was conflicting. The deputy commissioner found that the claimant was in Benson's employ at the time of the injury, and filed an order for compensation. . . . Benson brought this proceeding . . . to set aside the order. The district judge transferred the suit to the admiralty side of the court and held a trial de novo, refusing to consider upon any aspect of the case the record before the deputy commissioner. On the evidence introduced in court, he found that the relation of employer and employee did not exist, and entered a decree setting aside the compensation order. . . . The Circuit Court of Appeals affirmed the decree. . . . In my opinion, the decree should be reversed, because Congress did not authorize a trial de novo. . . .

The courts below held that the respondent was entitled to a trial de novo; that all the evidence introduced before the deputy commissioner should go for naught; and that respondent should have the privilege of presenting new, and even entirely different, evidence in the District Court. . . .

First. The initial question is one of construction of the Longshoremen's Act. The act does not in terms declare whether there may be a trial de novo either as to the issue whether the relation of employer and employee existed at the time of the injury, or as to any other issue, tried or triable, before the deputy commissioner. It provides . . . that "the deputy commissioner shall have full power and authority to hear and determine all questions in respect of" a claim; . . . that the compensation order made by the deputy commissioner "shall become effective" when filed in his office, and, "unless proceedings for the suspension or setting aside of such order are instituted as provided in [a] subdivision (b) of this section, shall become final . . ."; and . . . that, "If not in accordance with law, a compensation order may be suspended or set aside, in whole or in part, through injunction proceedings . . . instituted in the Federal district court. . . ."

The phrase . . . providing that the order may be set aside "if not in accordance with law" was adopted from the statutory provision, enacted by the same
Congress, for review by the Circuit Courts of Appeals of decisions of the Board
of Tax Appeals. This Court has settled that the phrase as used in the tax statute
means a review upon the record made before the Board. . . . The Compensation
Commission has consistently construed the Longshoremen's Act as providing
for finality of the deputy commissioner's findings on all questions of fact; and
care has been taken to provide for formal hearings appropriate to that intention.
. . . The lower federal courts, except in the case at bar, have uniformly construed
the act as denying a trial de novo of any issue determined by the deputy
commissioner; have held that, in respect to those issues, the review afforded
must be held upon the record made before the deputy commissioner; and that
the deputy commissioner's findings of fact must be accepted as conclusive if
supported by evidence, unless there was some irregularity in the proceeding
before him. Nearly all the state courts have construed the state workmen's
compensation laws, as limiting the judicial review to matters of law. Provisions
in other federal statutes, similar to those here in question, creating various
administrative tribunals, have likewise been treated as not conferring the right
to a judicial trial de novo.

The safeguards with which Congress has surrounded the proceedings before
the deputy commissioner would be without meaning if those proceedings were
to serve merely as an inquiry preliminary to a contest in the courts. Specific
provisions of the Longshoremen's Act make clear that it was the aim of Congress
to expedite the relief afforded. . . . Procedure of this character, instead of
expediting relief, would entail useless expense and delay if the proceedings
before the deputy commissioner were to be repeated in court, and the case tried
from the beginning, at the option of either party. The conclusion that Congress
did not so intend is confirmed by reference to the legislative history of the Act.
. . .

Second. Nothing in the statute warrants the construction that the right to a
trial de novo which Congress has concededly denied as to most issues of fact
determined by the deputy commissioner has been granted in respect to the issue
of the existence of the employer-employee relation. The language which is held
sufficient to foreclose the right to such a trial on some issues forecloses it as to
all. . . . Congress expressly declared its intention to put, for purposes of review,
all the issues of fact on the same basis, by conferring upon the deputy commissioner "full power to hear and determine all questions in respect of such claim,".
. . .

The suggestion that "such claim" may be construed to mean only a claim
within the purview of the Act seems to me without substance. Logically applied,
the suggestion would leave the deputy commissioner powerless to hear or determine any issue of asserted nonliability under the Act. For nonexistence of the
employer-employee relation is only one of many grounds of nonliability. Thus,
there is no liability if the injury was occasioned solely by the intoxication of the
employee; or if the injury was due to the willful intention of the employee to
injure or kill himself or another; or if it did not arise "out of or in the course

of employment"; or if the employer was not engaged in maritime employment in whole or in part; or if the injured person was the employee of a subcontractor who has secured payment of compensation; or if the proceeding is brought against the wrong person as employer; or if the disability or death is that of a master or a member of the crew of any vessel; or if it is that of a person engaged by the master to load or unload or repair any small vessel under eighteen tons net; or if it is that of an officer or employee of the United States or any agency thereof; or if it is that of an officer or employee of any state, or foreign government, or any political subdivision thereof; or if recovery for the disability or death through workmen's compensation proceedings may be validly provided by state law. And obviously there is no liability if there was in fact neither disability nor death. It is not reasonable to suppose that Congress intended to set up a fact-finding tribunal of first instance, shorn of power to find a portion of the facts required for any decision of the case; or that, in enacting legislation designed to withdraw from litigation the great bulk of maritime accidents, it contemplated a procedure whereby the same facts must be twice litigated before a longshoreman could be assured the benefits of compensation. . . .

. . . On bills in equity to set aside orders of a federal administrative board there is no trial de novo of issues of fact. . . .

Third. It is said that the provision for a trial *de novo* of the existence of the employer-employee relation should be read into the Act in order to avoid a serious constitutional doubt. It is true that where a statute is equally susceptible of two constructions, under one of which it is clearly valid and under the other of which it may be unconstitutional, the court will adopt the former construction. . . . But this Act is not equally susceptible to two constructions. The court may not, in order to avoid holding a statute unconstitutional, engraft upon it an exception or other provision. . . . Neither may it do so to avoid having to resolve a constitutional doubt. To hold that Congress conferred the right to a trial *de novo* on the issue of the employer-employee relation seems to me a remaking of the statute and not a construction of it.

Fourth. Trial de novo of the issue of the existence of the employer-employee relation is not required by the due process clause. That clause ordinarily does not even require that parties shall be permitted to have a judicial tribunal pass upon the weight of the evidence introduced before the administrative body. . . .

It is suggested that this exception is required as to issues of fact involving claims of constitutional right. . . . But even assuming it to be so, the conclusion does not follow that trial of the issue must therefore be upon a record made in the district court. That the function of collecting evidence may be committed to an administrative tribunal is settled by a host of cases, and supported by persuasive analogies, none of which justify a distinction between issues of constitutional right and any others. . . . The holding that the difference between the procedure prescribed by the Longshoremen's Act and these historic methods of hearing evidence transcends the limits of congressional power when applied to the issue of the existence of a relation of employment, as distinguished from that of the circumstances of an injury or the existence of a relation of dependency, seems to me without foundation in reality. Certainly there is no difference to the litigant. . . .

Fifth. Trial de novo of the existence of the employer-employee relation is not required by the Judiciary Article of the Constitution. The mere fact that the act deals only with injuries arising on navigable waters, and that independently of legislation such injuries can be redressed only in courts of admiralty, obviously does not preclude Congress from denying a trial de novo. For the Court holds that it is compatible with the grant of power under Article III to deny a trial de novo as to most of the facts upon which rest the allowance of a claim and the amount of compensation. Its holding that the Constitution requires a trial de novo of the issue of the employer-employee relation is based on the relation which that fact bears to the statutory scheme propounded by Congress, and to the constitutional authority under which the Act was passed. The argument is that existence of the relation of employer and employee is, as a matter of substantive law, indispensable to the application of the statute, because the power of Congress to enact the legislation turns upon its existence; and that whenever the question of constitutional power depends upon an issue of fact that issue must, as a matter of procedure, be determinable independently upon evidence freshly introduced in a court. Neither proposition seems to me well founded. . . .

Sixth. Even if the constitutional power of Congress to provide compensation is limited to cases in which the employer-employee relation exists, I see no basis for a contention that the denial of the right to a trial de novo upon the issue of employment is in any manner subversive of the independence of the federal judicial power. Nothing in the Constitution, or in any prior decision of this Court to which attention has been called, lends support to the doctrine that a judicial finding of any fact involved in any civil proceeding to enforce a pecuniary liability may not be made upon evidence introduced before a properly constituted administrative tribunal, or that a determination so made may not be deemed an independent judicial determination. Congress has repeatedly exercised authority to confer upon the tribunals which it creates, be they administrative bodies or courts of limited jurisdiction, the power to receive evidence concerning the facts upon which the exercise of federal power must be predicated, and to determine whether those facts exist. The power of Congress to provide by legislation for liability under certain circumstances subsumes the power to provide for the determination of the existence of those circumstances. It does not depend upon the absolute existence in reality of any fact.

It is true that, so far as [an injured employee] is concerned, proof of the existence of the employer-employee relation is essential to recovery under the act. But under the definition laid down in *Noble v Union River Logging R. Co.,* 147 US 165 (1893), that fact is not jurisdictional. It is quasijurisdictional. The existence of a relation of employment is a question going to the applicability of the substantive law, not to the jurisdiction of the tribunal. Jurisdiction is the power to adjudicate between the parties concerning the subject matter. . . . Obviously, the deputy commissioner had not only the power but the duty to determine whether the employer-employee relation existed. When a duly constituted tribunal has jurisdiction of the parties and of the subject matter, that jurisdiction is not impaired by errors, however grave, in applying the substantive law. . . . This is true of tribunals of special as well as of general jurisdiction. It is true of administrative, as well as of judicial, tribunals. . . .

Eighth. No good reason is suggested why all the evidence which Benson presented to the district court in this case could not have been presented before the deputy commissioner; nor why he should have been permitted to try his case provisionally before the administrative tribunal, and then to retry it in the district court upon additional evidence theretofore withheld. To permit him to do so violates the salutary principle that administrative remedies must first be exhausted before resorting to the court, imposes unnecessary and burdensome expense upon the other party and cripples the effective administration of the Act. Under the prevailing practice, by which the judicial review has been confined to questions of law, the proceedings before the deputy commissioners have proved for the most part noncontroversial; and relatively few cases have reached the courts. To permit a contest de novo in the district court of an issue tried, or triable, before the deputy commissioner will, I fear, gravely hamper the effective administration of the Act. The prestige of the deputy commissioner will necessarily be lessened by the opportunity of relitigating facts in the courts. The number of controverted cases may be largely increased. Persistence in controversy will be encouraged. And since the advantage of prolonged litigation lies with the party able to bear heavy expenses, the purpose of the act will be in part defeated.

(b) Credibility of witnesses

NATIONAL LABOR RELATIONS BOARD v PITTSBURGH STEAMSHIP CO.

337 US 656 (1949)

The National Labor Relations Board ordered an employer to cease and desist from specified unfair labor practices. The court of appeals refused to enforce this order on the ground that it was invalidated by the prejudice of the board's trial examiner, as shown by the fact that he believed the witnesses of the board and disbelieved the employer's witnesses.

OPINION BY RUTLEDGE, J.

. . . We are constrained to reject the court's conclusion that an objective finder of fact would not resolve all factual conflicts arising in a legal proceeding in favor of one litigant. The ordinary law suit . . . normally depends for its resolution on which version of the facts in dispute is accepted by the trier of fact. . . . In the determination of litigated facts, the testimony of one who has been found unreliable as to one issue may properly be accorded little weight as to the next. Accordingly, total rejection of an opposed view cannot of itself impugn the integrity or competence of a trier of fact. . . . "The fact . . . that Examiner and Board uniformly credited the Board's witnesses and as uniformly discredited those of the respondent, though the Board's witnesses were few and the respondent's witnesses were many, would not furnish a basis for a finding by us that such a bias or partiality existed and therefore the hearings were unfair. . . ."

. . . Indeed, careful scrutiny of the record belies the view that the trial examiner did in fact believe all union testimony or that he even believed the union version of every disputed factual issue. Rather, the printed transcript suggests thoughtful and evaluating discrimination of the facts.

[Judgment reversed]

(c) Substantiation of findings of fact

The rule is that the appellate court will accept the administrator's findings of fact when supported by the record. What is the record? When the appeal is taken directly from the decision of the administrator to the court, the record will, of course, be the proceedings before the administrator. In some instances, there are two steps or phases to the administrative action: (1) an examiner or auditor makes an initial determination, and (2) a board or commission acts upon that determination. When an appeal is taken in such a case from the board or commission to a court, the record which the court examines is not merely the record of the proceedings before the board or commission but also includes the report of the examiner or auditor. The reviewing court must then determine if this expanded record, as a whole, supports the administrative findings, rather than merely examining the record to see if it contains evidence, which if believed, would support those findings.

UNIVERSAL CAMERA CORPORATION v NATIONAL LABOR RELATIONS BOARD

340 US 474 (1951)

The National Labor Relations Board found that the Universal Camera Corporation had committed an unfair labor practice in dismissing an employee for having testified against it in proceedings before the board. The corporation appealed to the court of appeals, claiming that there was not "substantial evidence" in the record to support the finding of the board.

OPINION BY FRANKFURTER, J.

The Wagner Act provided: "The findings of the Board as to the facts, if supported by evidence, shall be conclusive.". . . This Court read "evidence" to mean "substantial evidence," . . . and we said that "Substantial evidence . . .

means such relevant evidence as a reasonable mind might accept as adequate to support a conclusion." . . . Accordingly, it "must do more than create a suspicion of the existence of the fact to be established, . . . it must be enough to justify, if the trial were to a jury, a refusal to direct a verdict when the conclusion sought to be drawn from it is one of fact for the jury." . . .

. . . The phrasing of this Court's process of review readily lent itself to the notion that it was enough that the evidence supporting the Board's result was "substantial" when considered by itself. . . . By imperceptible steps regard for the fact-finding function of the Board led to the assumption that the requirements of the Wagner Act were met when the reviewing court could find in the record evidence which, when viewed in isolation, substantiated the Board's findings. . . . This is not to say that every member of this Court was consciously guided by this view or that the Court ever explicitly avowed this practice as doctrine. What matters is that the belief justifiably arose that the Court had so construed the obligation to review.

Criticism of so contracted a reviewing power reinforced dissatisfaction felt in various quarters with the Board's administration of the Wagner Act in the years preceding the war. . . . [In 1947 the Wagner Act was amended by the Taft-Hartley Act.] . . . We hold that the standard of proof specifically required of the Labor Board by the Taft-Hartley Act is the same as that to be exacted by courts reviewing every administrative action subject to the Administrative Procedure Act.

Whether or not it was ever permissible for courts to determine the substantiality of evidence supporting a Labor Board decision merely on the basis of evidence which in and of itself justified it, without taking into account contradictory evidence or evidence from which conflicting inferences could be drawn, the new legislation definitively precludes such a theory of review and bars its practice. The substantiality of evidence must take into account whatever in the record fairly detracts from its weight. . . .

To be sure, the requirement for canvassing "the whole record" in order to ascertain substantiality does not furnish a calculus of value by which a reviewing court can assess the evidence. Nor was it intended to negative the function of the Labor Board as one of those agencies presumably equipped or informed by experience to deal with a specialized field of knowledge, whose findings within that field carry the authority of an expertness which courts do not possess and therefore must respect. Nor does it mean that even as to matters not requiring expertise a court may displace the Board's choice between two fairly conflicting views, even though the court would justifiably have made a different choice had the matter been before it *de novo*. Congress has merely made it clear that a reviewing court is not barred from setting aside a Board decision when it cannot conscientiously find that the evidence supporting that decision is substantial, when viewed in the light that the record in its entirety furnishes, including the body of evidence opposed to the Board's view.

We conclude, therefore, that the Administrative Procedure Act and the Taft-Hartley Act direct that courts must now assume more responsibility for the reasonableness and fairness of Labor Board decisions than some courts have shown in the past. Reviewing courts must be influenced by a feeling that they are not to abdicate the conventional judicial function. Congress has imposed on them responsibility for assuring that the Board keeps within reasonable grounds. That responsibility is not less real because it is limited to enforcing the requirement that evidence appear substantial when viewed, on the record as a whole, by courts invested with the authority and enjoying the prestige of the Courts of Appeals. The Board's findings are entitled to respect; but they must nonetheless be set aside when the record before a Court of Appeals clearly precludes the Board's decision from being justified by a fair estimate of the worth of the testimony of witnesses or its informed judgment on matters within its special competence or both. . . .

Our power to review the correctness of application of the present standard ought seldom to be called into action. Whether on the record as a whole there is substantial evidence to support agency findings is a question which Congress has placed in the keeping of the Courts of Appeals. This Court will intervene only in what ought to be the rare instance when the standard appears to have been misapprehended or grossly misapplied. . . .

The decision of the Court of Appeals is assailed on [the] ground . . . that the court erred in holding that it was barred from taking into account the report of the examiner on questions of fact insofar as that report was rejected by the Board. . . .

The Court of Appeals deemed itself bound by the Board's rejection of the examiner's findings because the court considered these findings not "as unassailable as a master's." . . . They are not. Section 10(c) of the Labor Management Relations Act provides that "If upon the preponderance of the testimony taken the Board shall be of the opinion that any person named in the complaint has engaged in or is engaging in any such unfair labor practice, then the Board shall state its findings of fact. . . ." . . . The responsibility for decision thus placed on the Board is wholly inconsistent with the notion that it has power to reverse an examiner's findings only when they are "clearly erroneous." . . .

We are aware that to give the examiner's findings less finality than a master's and yet entitle them to consideration in striking the account, is to introduce another and an unruly factor into the judgmatical process of review. But we ought not to fashion an exclusionary rule merely to reduce the number of imponderables to be considered by reviewing courts.

The Taft-Hartley Act provides that "The findings of the Board with respect to questions of fact if supported by substantial evidence on the record considered as a whole shall be conclusive." . . . Surely an examiner's report is as much a part of the record as the complaint or the testimony. According to the Administrative Procedure Act, "All decisions (including initial, recommended, or tentative decisions) shall become a part of the record. . . ." We found that this Act's provision for judicial review has the same meaning as that in the Taft-Hartley Act. The similarity of the two statutes in language and purpose also requires that the definition of "record" found in the Administrative Procedure Act be construed to be applicable as well to the term "record" as used in the Taft-Hartley Act.

It is therefore difficult to escape the conclusion that the plain language of the statutes directs a reviewing court to determine the substantiality of evidence on the record including the examiner's report. . . . Nothing suggests that reviewing courts should not give to the examiner's report such probative force as it intrinsically commands. To the contrary, § 11 of the Administrative Procedure Act contains detailed provisions designed to maintain high standards of independence and competence in examiners. Section 10(c) of the Labor Management Relations Act requires that examiners "shall issue . . . a proposed report, together with a recommended order." Both statutes thus evince a purpose to increase the importance of the role of examiners in the administrative process. High standards of public administration counsel that we attribute to the Labor Board's examiners both due regard for the responsibility which Congress imposes on them and the competence to discharge it. . . .

We do not require that the examiner's findings be given more weight than in reason and in the light of judicial experience they deserve. The "substantial evidence" standard is not modified in any way when the Board and its examiner disagree. We intend only to recognize that evidence supporting a conclusion may be less substantial when an impartial, experienced examiner who has observed the witnesses and lived with the case has drawn conclusions different from the Board's than when he has reached the same conclusion. The findings of the examiner are to be considered along with the consistency and inherent probability of testimony. The significance of his report, of course, depends largely on the importance of credibility in the particular case. To give it this significance does not seem to us materially more difficult than to heed the other factors which in sum determine whether evidence is "substantial." . . .

We therefore remand the cause to the Court of Appeals. On reconsideration of the record it should accord the findings of the trial examiner the relevance that they reasonably command in answering the comprehensive question whether the evidence supporting the Board's order is substantial. But the court need not limit its reexamination of the case to the effect of that report on its decision. We leave it free to grant or deny enforcement as it thinks the principles expressed in this opinion dictate.

[Action remanded]

§ 23:7. REVIEW OF ENFORCEMENT METHOD

Under earlier regulatory systems, no discretion was vested in the administrator as to the enforcement method to be followed. Under those statutes the administrative course of action was defined. As an example, the health officer with authority to kill diseased cattle had only to determine whether the cattle were or were not diseased. If the health officer determined that they were, the administrative duty to have them destroyed was clear.

Under modern regulations, which more frequently include a pattern of control as well as prohibition or destruction of the subject matter regulated, the administrator is frequently given a degree of discretion or latitude in selecting an appropriate method of enforcing or in carrying out determinations. The general attitude of the modern court is that, so long as the administrator keeps within the confines of the statute creating the administrator, the courts will not interfere with the choice of a particular method of enforcement decided upon by the administrator. The fact that the court might consider that a less or more drastic method of enforcement would be preferable is not sufficient to justify interference with the administrative determination.

(a) Dissolution of holding company

AMERICAN POWER AND LIGHT CO. v SECURITIES AND EXCHANGE COMMISSION

329 US 90 (1946)

Under the authority of the Securities and Exchange Act, the Securities and Exchange Commission directed the dissolution of a holding company that it found to serve no useful economic purpose. The objection was made that the policy of the Act could be carried out without going to the extreme of ordering the dissolution of the holding company.

OPINION BY MURPHY, J.

. . . [The] evidence is more than enough to support the finding that American and Electric are but paper companies without legitimate function and purpose. They serve merely as a mechanism by which Bond and Share maintains a pyramided structure containing the seeds of all the attendant evils condemned by the Act. It was reasonable, therefore, for the Commission to conclude that American and Electric are undue and unnecessary complexities in the Bond and Share system and that their existence unfairly and inequitably distributes voting power among the security holders of the system.

The major objection raised by American and Electric relates to the Commission's choice of dissolution as "necessary to insure" that the evils would be corrected and the standard of [the Act] . . . effectuated. Emphasis is placed upon alternative plans which are less drastic in nature and which allegedly would meet the statutory standards.

It is a fundamental principle, however, that where Congress has intrusted an administrative agency with the responsibility of selecting the means of achieving the statutory policy "the relation of remedy to policy is peculiarily a matter for administrative competence.". . . In dealing with the complex problem of adjusting holding company systems in accordance with the legislative standards, the Commission here has accumulated experience and knowledge which no court can hope to attain. Its judgment is entitled to the greatest weight. While recognizing that the Commission's discretion must square with its responsibility, only if the remedy chosen is unwarranted in law or is without justification in fact should a court attempt to intervene in the matter. Neither ground of intervention is present in this instance.

Dissolution of a holding company or a subholding company plainly is contemplated by [the Act] . . . as a possible remedy. . . .

Nor can we say that the Commission's choice of dissolution with respect to American and Electric is so lacking in reasonableness as to constitute an abuse of its discretion. The Commission chose dissolution because it felt such action is calculated to correct the situation most effectively and quickly. . . .

Without attempting to invade the domain of the Commission's discretion, we can readily perceive a factual basis underlying the choice of dissolution in this instance. The Commission reasonably could conclude from the record that American and Electric performed no justifiable function; they are unnecessary complexities enabling Bond and Share to perpetuate its pyramided system. The actual and potential evils resulting from their continued existence may well be said to outweigh any other claimed advantages, especially since many of the latter seem impossible of attainment due to the unsound financial structure of the companies. . . .

We are unimpressed, moreover, by the claim that dissolution is so drastic a remedy as to be unreasonable. Elimination of useless holding companies may be carried out by fair and equitable methods so as to destroy nothing of real value. American and Electric, the Commission found, are little more than a set of books and a portfolio of securities. And we cannot say that the Commission was without basis for its belief that dissolution under these circumstances would harm no one. It may well have considered the fact brought out in the argument before us that "so far as Bond and Share and the public security holders are concerned, dissolution would mean little more than the receipt of securities of the operating companies in lieu of their present shares in American and Electric. Any number of benefits might thereafter accrue to these security holders. Their equities in the Bond and Share system would be materially strengthened by the removal of the useless and costly subholding companies and their voting power would tend to be more in proportion to their investment. The financial weaknesses of the various companies remaining in the system would be easier to correct, with numerous benefits to the consumers and the general public as well as the investors. . . ." These factors [support] the Commission's conclusion that "the dissolution of these companies which . . . never served any useful purpose but have been a medium of much harm will be . . . beneficial to the public interest and . . . investors and consumers. . . ."

In view of the rational basis for the Commission's choice, the fact that other solutions might have been selected becomes immaterial. The Commission is the body which has the statutory duty of considering the possible solutions and choosing that which it considers most appropriate to the effectuation of the policies of the act. Our review is limited solely to testing the propriety of the remedy so chosen from the standpoint of the Constitution and the statute. We would be impinging upon the Commission's rightful discretion were we to consider the various alternatives in the hope of finding one that we consider more appropriate. Since the remedy chosen by the Commission in this instance is legally and factually sustainable, it matters not that American and Electric believe that alternative orders should have been entered. It is likewise irrelevant that they feel that Bond and Share is the principal offender against the statutory standards and that the Commission should merely have required Bond and Share to divest itself of its interests in American and Electric. . . .

[Judgment for SEC]

(b) Scope of administrative discretion as to enforcement

While an appellate court will not interfere with the administrator's exercise of discretion in choosing a particular permissible enforcement method, the administrative action will be reversed if the court concludes that the administrator has gone beyond the scope of the administrator's authority in imposing a particular method or remedy. In such a case, it is not a question of the discretion of the administrator, but of the lack of authority to have acted in the particular manner in question. If the court disagrees with the administrator as to the latter's scope of authority, it will reverse the administrative action as a matter of law. The court exercises a freer hand in reviewing questions of law, as will be discussed in § 23:9.

REPUBLIC STEEL CORP. v NATIONAL LABOR RELATIONS BOARD
311 US 7 (1940)

The National Labor Relations Board ordered the reinstatement of employees improperly discharged by the employer and payment to them of back pay for the period since their improper discharge. The board directed that there be deducted from such back pay the amounts received by the employees from government relief and that such deduction be paid to the government. The authority to direct this deduction was challenged.

OPINION BY HUGHES, C. J.

. . . The National Labor Relations Board, finding that the Republic Steel Corporation had engaged in unfair labor practices in violation of § 8(1), 8(2) and 8(3) of the National Labor Relations Act, ordered the company to desist from these practices, to withdraw recognition from a labor organization found to be dominated by the company, and to reinstate certain employees, with back pay, found to have been discriminatorily discharged or denied reinstatement. The Board, in providing for back pay, directed the company to deduct from the payments to the reinstated employees the amounts they had received for work performed upon "work relief projects" and to pay over such amounts to the appropriate governmental agencies. . . .

The amounts earned by the employees before reinstatement were directed to be deducted from their back pay manifestly because, having already been received, these amounts were not needed to make the employees whole. That principle would apply whether the employees had earned the amounts in public or private employment. Further, there is no question that the amounts paid by the governmental agencies were for services actually performed. Presumably these agencies, and through them the public, received the benefit of services reasonably worth the amounts paid. There is no finding to the contrary.

The Board urges that the work relief program was designed to meet the exigency of large-scale unemployment produced by the depression; that projects had been selected, not with a single eye to costs or usefulness, but with a view to providing the greatest amount of employment in order to serve the needs of unemployed workers in various communities; in short, that the Work Projects Administration has been conducted as a means of dealing with the relief problem. Hence it is contended that the Board could properly conclude that the unfair labor practices of the company had occasioned losses to the Government financing the work relief projects.

The payments to the Federal, State, County, or other governments concerned are thus conceived as being required for the purpose of redressing, not an injury to the employees, but an injury to the public,— an injury thought to be not the less sustained although here the respective governments have received the benefit of the services performed. So conceived, these required payments are in the nature of penalties imposed by law upon the employer,—the Board acting as the legislative agency in providing that sort of sanction by reason of public interest. . . . The question is,—Has Congress conferred the power upon the Board to impose such requirements?

We think that the theory advanced by the Board proceeds upon a misconception of the National Labor Relations Act. The Act is essentially remedial. It does not carry a penal program declaring the described unfair labor practices to be crimes. The Act does not prescribe penalties or fines in vindication of public rights or provide indemnity against community losses as distinguished from the protection and compensation of employees. Had Congress been intent upon such a program, we cannot doubt that Congress would have expressed its intent and would itself have defined its retributive scheme.

The remedial purposes of the Act are quite clear. It is aimed, as the Act says (§ 1) at encouraging the practice and procedure of collective bargaining and at protecting the exercise by workers of full freedom of association, of self-organization and of negotiating the terms and conditions of their employment or other mutual aid or protection through their freely chosen representatives. This right of the employees is safeguarded through the authority conferred upon the Board to require the employer to desist from the unfair labor practices described and to leave the employees free to organize and choose their representatives. They are thus protected from coercion and interference in the formation of labor organizations and from discriminatory discharge. Whether the Act has been violated by the employer—whether there has been an unfair labor practice—is a matter for the board to determine upon evidence. When it does so determine the Board can require the employer to disestablish organizations created in violation of the Act; it can direct the employer to bargain with those who appear to be the chosen representatives of the employees and it can require that such employees as have been discharged in violation of the Act be reinstated with back pay. All these measures relate to the protection of the employees and the redress of their grievances, not to the redress of any supposed public injury after the employees have been made secure in their right of collective bargaining and have been made whole.

As the sole basis for the claim of authority to go further and to demand payments to governments, the Board relies on the language of § 10(c) which provides that if upon evidence the Board finds that the person against whom the complaint is lodged has engaged in an unfair labor practice, the Board shall issue an order—"requiring such person to cease and desist from such unfair labor practice, and to take such affirmative action, including reinstatement of employees with or without back pay, as will effectuate the policies of this Act."

This language should be construed in harmony with the spirit and remedial purposes of the Act. We do not think that Congress intended to vest in the Board a virtually unlimited discretion to devise punitive measures, and thus to prescribe penalties or fines which the Board may think would effectuate the policies of the Act. We have said that "this authority to order affirmative action does not go so far as to confer a punitive jurisdiction enabling the Board to inflict upon the employer any penalty it may choose because he is engaged in unfair labor practices even though the Board be of the opinion that the policies of the Act might be effectuated by such an order." We have said that the power to command affirmative action is remedial, not punitive. . . . We adhere to that construction.

In that view, it is not enough to justify the Board's requirements to say that they would have the effect of deterring persons from violating the Act. That argument proves too much, for if such a deterrent effect is sufficient to sustain an order of the Board, it would be free to set up any system of penalties which it would deem adequate to that end. . . .

In truth, the reasons assigned by the Board for the requirement in question—reasons which relate to the nature and purpose of work relief projects and to the practice and aims of the Works Project Administration—indicate that its order is not directed to the appropriate effectuating of the policies of the National Labor Relations Act, but to the effectuating of a distinct and broader policy with respect to unemployment. The Board has made its requirement in an apparent effort to provide adjustments between private employment and public work relief, and to carry out supposed policies in relation to the latter. That is not the function of the Board. It has not been assigned a role in relation to losses conceived to have been sustained by communities or governments in connection with work relief projects. The function of the Board in this case was to assure to petitioner's employees the right of collective bargaining through their representatives without interference by petitioner and to make good to the employees what they had lost through the discriminatory discharge.

We hold that the additional provision requiring the payments to governmental agencies was beyond the Board's authority. . . .

[Judgment for NLRB as to reinstatement and award of back pay; judgment against NLRB as to deduction of any amount from such pay]

---

§ 23:8. MISCELLANEOUS LIMITATIONS ON APPELLATE REVIEW

The most important principles that protect the administrative determination from reversal have already been stated in this chapter. In addition, an administrative appeal may be unsuccessful because the action of the administrator appealed from is legislative rather than judicial in character, because it relates to foreign affairs, or because it relates to a governmental privilege. In such cases, the courts are reluctant to set aside the action of the administrator.

§ 23:9. QUESTIONS OF LAW

When the question which is raised on appeal is a question of law, the appellate court will reverse the administrative determination if it disagrees with the conclusion reached by the administrator. This is the only area in which the court does not restrict itself in its examination of what the administrator has done. If it does not agree with the administrator, it overrules the administrative action.

(a) Wages for purpose of statute

SOCIAL SECURITY BOARD v NIEROTKO

327 US 358 (1946)

The National Labor Relations Board may order the reinstatement of an improperly discharged employee and direct that the employer pay the employee the back pay lost during the period of wrongful discharge. The benefits obtained under another statute, the Social Security Act, are affected by the amount of wages received by an employee. In this case, the question arose whether the back pay awarded by the National Labor Relations Board should be regarded as "wages" for the purpose of the Social Security Act, and whether the employee should be regarded as having been employed during the period from the date of wrongful discharge until reinstatement under the order of the board.

OPINION BY REED, J.

. . . The respondent, Joseph Nierotko, was found by the National Labor Relations Board to have been wrongfully discharged for union activity by his employer, the Ford Motor Company, and was reinstated by that Board in his employment with directions for "back pay" for the period February 2, 1937, to September 25, 1939. The "back pay" was paid by the employer on July 18, 1941. Thereafter Nierotko requested the Social Security Board to credit him in the sum of the "back pay" on his Old-Age and Survivor's Insurance account with the Board. In conformity with its minute of formal general action of March 27, 1942, the Board refused to credit Nierotko's "back pay" as wages. . . .

Wages are the basis for the administration of federal old-age benefits. . . . Only those who earn wages are eligible for benefits. The periods of time during which wages were earned are important and may be crucial on eligibility under either the original act or the Amendments of 1939. . . . The benefits are financed by payments from employees and employers which are calculated on wages. The Act defines "wages" for Old-Age benefits as follows:

"Sec. 210. When used in this title—

"(a) The term 'wages' means all remuneration for employment, including the cash value of all remuneration paid in any medium other than cash, . . ."

Employment is defined thus: "(b) The term 'employment' means any service, of whatever nature, performed within the United States by an employee for his employer, except—."

The tax titles of the Social Security Act have identical definitions of wages and employment. An employee under the Social Security Act is not specifically defined but the individual to whom the Act's benefits are to be paid is one receiving "wages" for "employment" in accordance with § 210(c) and employment is service by an "employee" to an "employer." Obviously a sharply defined line between payments to employees which are wages and which are not is essential to proper administration.

Under the National Labor Relations Act an employee is described as "any individual whose work has ceased . . . because of any unfair labor practice." . . . The enforcement provisions of this Act under which Nierotko received his "back pay" allow the Labor Board to reinstate "employees with or without back pay." § 10(c). The purpose of the "back pay" allowance is to effectuate the policies of the Labor Act for the preservation of industrial peace.

The purpose of the federal old-age benefits of the Social Security Act is to provide funds through contributions by employer and employee for the decent support of elderly workmen who have ceased to labor. Eligibility for these benefits and their amount depends upon the total wages which the employee has received and the periods in which wages were paid. While the legislative history of the Social Security Act and its amendments or the language of the enactments themselves do not specifically deal with whether or not "back pay" under the Labor Act is to be treated as wages under the Social Security Act, we think it plain that an individual, who is an employee under the Labor Act and who receives "back pay" for a period of time during which he was wrongfully separated from his job, is entitled to have that award of back pay treated as wages under the Social Security Act definitions which define wages as "remuneration for employment" and employment as "any service . . . performed . . . by an employee for his employer."

Surely the "back pay" is "remuneration." Under Section 10(c) of the Labor Act, the Labor Board acts for the public to vindicate the prohibitions of the Labor Act against unfair labor practices . . . and to protect the right of employees to self-organization which is declared by Section 7. It is also true that in requiring reparation to the employee through "back pay" that reparation is based upon the loss of wages which the employee has suffered from the employer's wrong. "Back pay" is not a fine or penalty imposed upon the employer by the Board. Reinstatement and "back pay" are for the "protection of the employees and the redress of their grievances" to make them "whole." . . . A worker is not given "back pay" by the Board equal to what he would have earned with the employer but for the unlawful discharge but is given that sum less any net earnings during the time between discharge and reinstatement.

Since Nierotko remained an employee under the definition of the Labor Act, although his employer had attempted to terminate the relationship, he had "employment" under that Act and we need further only consider whether under the Social Security Act its definition of employment, as "any service . . . performed by an employee for his employer," covers what Nierotko did for the Ford Motor Company. The petitioner urges that Nierotko did not perform any service. It points out that Congress in considering the Social Security Act thought of benefits as related to "wages earned" for "work done." We are unable, however, to follow the Social Security Board in such a limited circumscription of the word "service." The very words "any service . . . performed . . . for his employer," with the purpose of the Social Security Act in mind import breadth of coverage. They admonish us against holding that "service" can be only productive activity. We think that "service" as used by Congress in this definitive phrase means not only work actually done but the entire employer-employee relationship for which compensation is paid to the employee by the employer.

An argument against the interpretation which we give to "service performed" is the contrary ruling of the governmental agencies which are charged with the administration of the Social Security Act. Their competence and experience in this field command us to reflect before we decide contrary to their conclusion. The first administrative determination was apparently made in 1939 by an Office Decision of the Bureau of Internal Revenue on the problem of whether "back pay" under a Labor Board order was wages subject to tax under Titles VIII and IX of the Social Security Act which the Bureau collects. The back pay was held not to be subject as wages to the tax because no service was performed, the employer had tried to terminate the employment relationship and the allowance of back pay was discretionary with the Labor Board. . . . This position is maintained by the Social Security Board by minute of March 27, 1942. It is followed by the National Labor Relations Board which at one time approved the retention by the employer of the tax on the employees' back pay for transmission to the Treasury Department as a tax on wages and later reversed its position on the authority of the Office Decision to which reference has just been made. . . .

The Office Decision seems to us unsound. . . . there is nothing . . . which supports the idea that the "back pay" award differs from other pay. . . .

But it is urged by petitioner that the administrative construction on the question of whether "back pay" is to be treated as wages should lead us to follow the agencies' determination. There is a suggestion that the administrative decision should be treated as conclusive. . . .

The Social Security Board and the Treasury were compelled to decide, administratively, whether or not to treat "back pay" as wages and their expert judgment is entitled, as we have said, to great weight. . . . however, . . . such decisions are only conclusive as to properly supported findings of fact. . . . Administrative determinations must have a basis in law and must be within the granted authority. Administration, when it interprets a statute so as to make it apply to particular circumstances, acts as a delegate to the legislative power. Congress might have declared that "back pay" awards under the Labor Act should or should not be treated as wages. Congress might have delegated to the Social Security Board to determine what compensation paid by employers to employees should be treated as wages. Except as such interpretive power may be included in the agencies' administrative functions, Congress did neither. An agency may not finally decide the limits of its statutory power. That is a judicial function. Congress used a well understood word—"wages"—to indicate the receipts which were to govern taxes and benefits under the Social Security Act. There may be borderline payments to employees on which courts would follow administrative determination as to whether such payments were or were not wages under the act.

We conclude, however, that the Board's interpretation of this statute to exclude back pay goes beyond the boundaries of administrative routine and the statutory limits. This is a ruling which excludes from the ambit of the Social Security Act payments which we think were included by Congress. It is beyond the permissible limits of administrative interpretation.

Petitioner further questions the validity of the decision of the circuit court of appeals on the ground that it must be inferred from the opinion that the "back pay" must be allocated as wages by the Board to the "calendar quarters" of the year in which the money would have been earned, if the employee had not been wrongfully discharged. . . .

. . . We have no doubt that it should be allocated to the periods when the regular wages were not paid as usual. Admittedly there are accounting difficulties which the Board will be called upon to solve but we do not believe they are insuperable.

[Judgment for Nierotko]

§ 23:10. CONCLUSION

The practical result of the limitations discussed in this chapter is that, unless the administrative determination is based on a clear-cut question of law, there is very little chance that the appellate court will reverse the administrative decision when an appeal is taken. If the administrator has failed to follow the procedure prescribed by the statute and this departure is of a serious character, the administrator will be reversed. It is, however, most unlikely that such a breach of procedure will occur after an administrative agency has been functioning for a reasonable period of time. Once the agency has enough experience to proceed by the proper pattern stated in the statute, the limitations described in this chapter come into play to give the administrative determination virtual immunity from judicial reversal.[3]

From the standpoint of the person in business and the citizen, the limitations discussed in this chapter underscore the importance of taking administrative action seriously. It is not a dress rehearsal but, for practical purposes, may be the only day in court that will be of any value to the person who is affected thereby. This further emphasizes the importance of the intelligence and integrity of administrators. They are, in effect, the "government." The better they are, the more likely that America will achieve its goals and its dreams.

Questions for Discussion

1. Why is a complainant required to exhaust all administrative remedies before appealing to a court for aid?

2. When the plant of a particular enterprise is inspected to see if it is safe for workers, can it object that other plants which are more unsafe are not being inspected?

3. Will a court reverse the administrative action if the court, upon examination of all the evidence, concludes that the administrator believed the wrong witnesses?

4. Will a court reverse the administrator because of an error of law when the error was reasonable?

5. Can you reconcile the *Moog* case with the concept of equality before the law?

6. Was there any evidence of agency bias against the Moog industry?

7. The extent of judicial review varies inversely with the extent of the discretion exercised by the administrator. Appraise this statement.

8. Compare the appellate review of findings of fact made by an administrator and those made by a jury.

---

[3]The precision of the classification made by the sections of this chapter is obscured to some extent by the fact that, in some instances, facts have been regarded as "jurisdictional" or as "constitutional," or questions have been regarded as "mixed questions of law and facts." As a practical matter, however, these variations do not affect the great bulk of appeals from administrative decisions.

9. The *S* holding company is ordered dissolved by the Federal Trade Commission. It appeals on the ground that this is a harsh remedy and shows that other remedies are available and are not as harsh. Will the reviewing court reverse the Federal Trade Commission?

10. The appropriate environmental protection agency imposes a large penalty on the *X* company factory for polluting the environment. Neighboring factories think that this action is wrong and that they may be next. They therefore file an appeal from the decision of the agency. Can they do so?

11. Why does not the Court hold that the determination of the administrator is subject to review on the basis that the administrator has believed all the witnesses of one party and disbelieved all the opposing witnesses?

12. Does the Court in the *Nierotko* case consider whether the administrator's interpretation of the statute was reasonable?

13. When an appeal is taken from the administrator to a court, should the court hear the case all over from the beginning? What are the advantages and disadvantages of such a trial de novo?

14. What are the arguments for and against: (a) Finality of administrative determinations.   (b) Complete review of administrative determinations.

15. A federal statute provides that when a contract between the government and a contractor provides for the determination of a dispute by a federal department head or agency, the decision "shall be final and conclusive unless the same is fraudulent or capricious or arbitrary or so grossly erroneous as necessarily to imply bad faith, or is not supported by substantial evidence." Bianchi contracted with the government to build a water tunnel. The contract contained a standard provision for additional compensation in the event of "changed conditions." The contractor claimed that conditions discovered after the work was begun constituted "changed conditions" and claimed additional compensation. In accord with a provision of the contract, he submitted this claim first to the contracting officer and then to the Board of Claims and Appeals of the Corps of Engineers. Both rejected his claim. Six years thereafter Bianchi sued in the Court of Claims, claiming that he was entitled to additional compensation and that he was not bound by the decision of the contracting officer and of the Board of Claims because their decisions were "capricious or arbitrary or so grossly erroneous as necessarily to imply bad faith, or were not supported by substantial evidence." In this proceeding, a substantial amount of new evidence was heard and a decision made in favor of the contractor. The United States appealed. Decide. [*United States v Bianchi,* 373 US 709 (1963)]

16. What is meant by the "fourth estate" in American constitutional law?

17. To what extent is the Court influenced in *Crowell v Benson* by a fear of bureaucracy?

18. Why does the Federal Administrative Procedure Act provide that administrators subject to the Act must include in their decisions "a statement of . . . findings and conclusions, as well as the reasons or basis therefor, upon all the material issues of fact, law, or discretion presented on the record"?

19. The Federal Trade Extension Act provides that if the Secretary of the United States Treasury finds that an "article is being imported into the United States in such quantities or under such circumstances as to threaten to impair national security," the President of the United States is authorized to "take such action, and for such time, as he deems necessary to adjust the imports of [the] article . . . so that the imports will not threaten to impair the national security." The treasurer reported to the president that national security was endangered by American imports of foreign crude oil. Acting under the statute, the president imposed a license fee, or tax, on every barrel of oil imported. Suit was brought to declare that the president had no authority to impose a license fee but could only impose a quota on the quantity imported. Was the president's action valid? [*FEA v Algonquin SNG, Inc.,* 426 US 548 (1976)]

20. A number of motor freight carriers applied to the Interstate Commerce Commission for permission to carry freight between certain specified points. This application was opposed by the existing carriers serving that area. The Interstate Commerce Commission granted the application and issued the applicant carriers a certificate of convenience and necessity authorizing them to carry freight as requested. The objectants appealed to the Supreme Court. They claimed that this additional service was not required by the public convenience and that it would be harmful to them. Decide. [*Bowman Transportation, Inc., v Arkansas-Best Freight System, Inc.,* 419 US 281 (1974)]

Appendix: Constitution of the United States

WE THE PEOPLE of the United States, in Order to form a more perfect Union, establish Justice, insure domestic Tranquility, provide for the common defence, promote the general Welfare, and secure the Blessings of Liberty to ourselves and our Posterity, do ordain and establish this CONSTITUTION for the United States of America.

ARTICLE I

Section. 1. All legislative Powers herein granted shall be vested in a Congress of the United States, which shall consist of a Senate and House of Representatives.

Section. 2. (1) The House of Representatives shall be composed of Members chosen every second Year by the People of the several States, and the Electors in each State shall have the Qualifications requisite for Electors of the most numerous Branch of the State Legislature.

(2) No Person shall be a representative who shall not have attained to the Age of twenty-five Years and been seven Years a Citizen of the United States, and who shall not, when elected, be an Inhabitant of that State in which he shall be chosen.

(3) Representatives and direct Taxes shall be apportioned among the several States which may be included within this Union, according to their respective Numbers, which shall be determined by adding to the whole Number of free Persons, including those bound to Service for a Term of Years, and excluding

Indians not taxed, three fifths of all other Persons. The actual Enumeration shall be made within three Years after the first Meeting of the Congress of the United States, and within every subsequent Term of ten Years, in such Manner as they shall by Law direct. The Number of Representatives shall not exceed one for every thirty Thousand, but each State shall have at Least one Representative; and until such enumeration shall be made, the State of New Hampshire shall be entitled to chuse three, Massachusetts eight, Rhode-Island and Providence Plantations one, Connecticut five, New-York six, New Jersey four, Pennsylvania eight, Delaware one, Maryland six, Virginia ten, North Carolina five, South Carolina five, and Georgia three.

(4) When vacancies happen in the Representation from any State, the Executive Authority thereof shall issue Writs of Election to fill such Vacancies.

(5) The House of Representatives shall chuse their Speaker and other Officers; and shall have the sole Power of Impeachment.

Section. 3. (1) The Senate of the United States shall be composed of two Senators from each State, chosen by the Legislature thereof, for six Years; and each Senator shall have one Vote.

(2) Immediately after they shall be assembled in Consequence of the first Election, they shall be divided as equally as may be into three Classes. The Seats of the Senators of the first Class shall be vacated at the Expiration of the second year, of the second Class at the Expiration of the fourth Year, and of the third Class at the Expiration of the sixth Year, so that one-third may be chosen every second Year; and if Vacancies happen by Resignation, or otherwise, during the Recess of the Legislature of any State, the Executive thereof may make temporary Appointments until the next Meeting of the Legislature, which shall then fill such Vacancies.

(3) No Person shall be a Senator who shall not have attained to the Age of thirty Years, and been nine Years a Citizen of the United States, and who shall not, when elected, be an Inhabitant of that State for which he shall be chosen.

(4) The Vice President of the United States shall be President of the Senate, but shall have no Vote, unless they be equally divided.

(5) The Senate shall chuse their other Officers, and also a President pro tempore, in the Absence of the Vice President, or when he shall exercise the Office of President of the United States.

(6) The Senate shall have the sole Power to try all Impeachments. When sitting for that Purpose, they shall be an Oath or Affirmation. When the President of the United States is tried, the Chief Justice shall preside: And no Person shall be convicted without the Concurrence of two thirds of the Members present.

(7) Judgment in Cases of Impeachment shall not extend further than to removal from office, and disqualification to hold and enjoy any Office of honor, Trust or Profit under the United States: but the Party convicted shall nevertheless be liable and subject to Indictment, Trial, Judgment and Punishment, according to Law.

Section. 4. (1) The Times, Places and Manner of holding Elections for Senators and Representatives, shall be prescribed in each State by the Legislature thereof; but the Congress may at any time by Law make or alter such Regulations, except as to the places of chusing Senators.

(2) The Congress shall assemble at least once in every Year, and such Meeting shall be on the first Monday in December, unless they shall by Law appoint a different Day.

Section. 5. (1) Each House shall be the Judge of the Elections, Returns, and Qualifications of its own Members, and a Majority of each shall constitute a Quorum to do Business; but a smaller Number may adjourn from day to day, and may be authorized to compel the Attendance of absent Members, in such Manner, and under such Penalties as each House may provide.

(3) Each House may determine the Rules of its Proceedings, punish its Members for disorderly Behavior, and, with the Concurrence of two thirds, expel a Member.

(3) Each House shall keep a Journal of its Proceedings, and from time to time publish the same, excepting such Parts as may in their Judgment require Secrecy; and the Yeas and Nays of the Members of either House on any question shall, at the Desire of one fifth of those present, be entered on the Journal.

(4) Neither House, during the Session of Congress, shall, without the Consent of the other, adjourn for more than three days, nor to any other Place than that in which the two Houses shall be sitting.

Section. 6. (1) The Senators and Representatives shall receive a Compensation for their Services, to be ascertained by Law, and paid out of the Treasury of the United States. They shall in all Cases, except Treason, Felony and Breach of the Peace, be privileged from Arrest during their Attendance at the Session of their respective Houses, and in going to and returning from the same; and for any Speech or Debate in either House, they shall not be questioned in any other Place.

(2) No Senator or Representative shall, during the Time for which he was elected, be appointed to any civil Office under the Authority of the United States, which shall have been created, or the Emoluments whereof shall have been encreased during such time; and no Person holding any Office under the United States, shall be a Member of either House during his Continuance in Office.

Section. 7. (1) All bills for raising Revenue shall originate in the House of Representatives; but the Senate may propose or concur with Amendments as on other Bills.

(2) Every Bill which shall have passed the House of Representatives and the Senate, shall, before it become a Law, be presented to the President of the United States; If he approve he shall sign it, but if not he shall return it, with his Objections to that House in which it shall have originated, who shall enter the Objections at large on their Journal, and proceed to reconsider it. If after such Reconsideration two thirds of that House shall agree to pass the Bill, it shall be

sent, together with the Objections, to the other House, by which it shall likewise be reconsidered, and if approved by two thirds of that House, it shall become a Law. But in all such Cases the Votes of both Houses shall be determined by Yeas and Nays, and the Names of the Persons voting for and against the Bill shall be entered on the Journal of each House respectively. If any Bill shall not be returned by the President within ten Days (Sundays excepted) after it shall have been presented to him, the Same shall be a Law, in like Manner as if he had signed it, unless the Congress by their Adjournment prevent its Return, in which Case it shall not be a Law.

(3) Every Order, Resolution, or Vote to which the Concurrence of the Senate and House of Representatives may be necessary (except on a question of Adjournment) shall be presented to the President of the United States; and before the Same shall take Effect, shall be approved by him, or being disapproved by him, shall be repassed by two thirds of the Senate and House of Representatives, according to the Rules and Limitations prescribed in the Case of a Bill.

Section. 8. (1) The Congress shall have Power To lay and collect Taxes, Duties, Imposts and Excises, to pay the Debts and provide for the common Defence and general Welfare of the United States; but all Duties, Imposts and Excises shall be uniform throughout the United States;

(2) To borrow Money on the credit of the United States;

(3) To regulate Commerce with foreign Nations, and among the several States, and with the Indian Tribes;

(4) To establish an uniform Rule of Naturalization, and uniform Laws on the subject of Bankruptcies throughout the United States;

(5) To coin Money, regulate the Value thereof, and of foreign Coin, and fix the Standard of Weights and Measures;

(6) To provide for the Punishment of counterfeiting the Securities and current Coin of the United States;

(7) To establish Post Offices and post Roads;

(8) To promote the Progress of Science and useful Arts, by securing for limited Times to Authors and Inventors the exclusive Right to their respective Writings and Discoveries;

(9) To constitute Tribunals inferior to the supreme Court;

(10) To define and punish Piracies and Felonies committed on the high Seas, and Offenses against the Law of Nations;

(11) To declare War, grant Letters of Marque and Reprisal, and make Rules concerning Captures on Land and Water;

(12) To raise and support Armies, but no Appropriation of Money to that Use shall be for a longer Term than two Years;

(13) To provide and maintain a Navy;

(14) To make Rules for the Government and Regulation of the land and naval Forces;

(15) To provide for calling forth the Militia to execute the Laws of the Union, suppress Insurrections and repel Invasions;

(16) To provide for organizing, arming, and disciplining, the Militia, and for

governing such Part of them as may be employed in the Service of the United States, reserving to the States respectively, the Appointment of the Officers, and the Authority of training the Militia according to the discipline prescribed by Congress;

(17) To exercise exclusive Legislation in all Cases whatsoever, over such District (not exceeding ten Miles square) as may, by Cession of particular States, and the Acceptance of Congress, become the Seat of the Government of the United States, and to exercise like Authority over all Places purchased by the consent of the Legislature of the State in which the Same shall be, for the Erection of Forts, Magazines, Arsenals, dock-Yards, and other needful Buildings;—And

(18) To make all Laws which shall be necessary and proper for carrying into Execution the foregoing Powers, and all other Powers vested by this Constitution in the Government of the United States, or in any Department or Officer thereof.

Section. 9. (1) The Migration or Importation of such Persons as any of the States now existing shall think proper to admit, shall not be prohibited by the Congress prior to the Year one thousand eight hundred and eight, but a Tax or duty may be imposed on such Importation, not exceeding ten dollars for each Person.

(2) The Privilege of the Writ of Habeas Corpus shall not be suspended, unless when in Cases of Rebellion or Invasion the public Safety may require it.

(3) No Bill of Attainder or expost facto Law shall be passed.

(4) No Capitation, or other direct, tax shall be laid, unless in Proportion to the Census or Enumeration herein before directed to be taken.

(5) No Tax or Duty shall be laid on Articles exported from any State.

(6) No Preference shall be given by any Regulation of Commerce or Revenue to the Ports of one State over those of another: nor shall Vessels bound to, or from, one State, be obliged to enter, clear, or pay Duties in another.

(7) No Money shall be drawn from the Treasury, but in Consequence of Appropriations made by Law; and a regular Statement and Account of the Receipts and Expenditures of all public Money shall be published from time to time.

(8) No Title of Nobility shall be granted by the United States: And no Person holding any Office of Profit or Trust under them, shall, without the Consent of the Congress, accept of any present, Emolument, Office, or Title, of any kind whatever, from any King, Prince, or foreign State.

Section. 10. (1) No State shall enter into any Treaty, Alliance, or Confederation; grant Letters of Marque and Reprisal; coin Money; emit Bills of Credit; make any Thing but gold and silver coin a Tender in Payment of Debts; pass any Bill of Attainder, expost facto Law, or Law impairing the Obligation of Contracts, or grant any Title of Nobility.

(2) No State shall, without the Consent of the Congress, lay any Imposts or Duties on Imports or Exports, except what may be absolutely necessary for executing its inspection Laws: and the net Produce of all Duties and Imposts,

laid by any State on Imports or Exports, shall be for the Use of the Treasury of the United States; and all such Laws shall be subject to the Revision and Controul of the Congress.

(3) No State shall, without the Consent of Congress, lay any Duty of Tonnage, keep Troops, or Ships of War in time of Peace, enter into any Agreement or Compact with another State, or with a foreign Power, or engage in War, unless actually invaded, or in such imminent Danger as will not admit of delay.

ARTICLE II

Section. 1. (1) The executive Power shall be vested in a President of the United States of America. He shall hold his Office during the Term of four Years, and, together with the Vice President, chosen for the same Term, be elected, as follows:

(2) Each State shall appoint, in such Manner as the Legislature thereof may direct, a Number of Electors, equal to the whole Number of Senators and Representatives to which the State may be entitled in the Congress: but no Senator or Representative, or Person holding an Office of Trust or Profit under the United States, shall be appointed an Elector.

The electors shall meet in their respective States, and vote by ballot for two Persons, of whom one at least shall not be an Inhabitant of the same State with themselves. And they shall make a List of all the Persons voted for, and of the Number of Votes for each; which List they shall sign and certify, and transmit sealed to the Seat of the Government of the United States, directed to the President of the Senate. The President of the Senate shall, in the Presence of the Senate and House of Representatives, open all the Certificates, and the Votes shall then be counted. The Person having the greatest Number of Votes shall be the President, if such Number be a Majority of the whole Number of Electors appointed; and if there be more than one who have such Majority, and have an equal Number of Votes, then the House of Representatives shall immediately chuse by Ballot one of them for President; and if no Person have a Majority, then from the five highest on the List the said House shall in like Manner chuse the President. But in chusing the President, the Votes shall be taken by States, the Representation from each State having one Vote; A quorum for this Purpose shall consist of a Member or Members from two-thirds of the States, and a Majority of all the States shall be necessary to a Choice. In every Case, after the Choice of the President, the Person having the greatest Number of Votes of the Electors shall be the Vice President. But if there should remain two or more who have equal Votes, the Senate shall chuse from them by Ballot the Vice President.

(3) The Congress may determine the Time of chusing the Electors, and the Day on which they shall give their Votes; which Day shall be the same throughout the United States.

(4) No Person except a natural born Citizen, or a Citizen of the United States, at the time of the Adoption of this Constitution, shall be eligible to the Office of President; neither shall any Person be eligible to that Office who shall not

have attained to the Age of thirty-five Years, and been fourteen Years a Resident within the United States.

(5) In Case of the Removal of the President from Office, or of his Death, Resignation, or Inability to discharge the Powers and Duties of the said Office, the same shall devolve on the Vice President, and the Congress may by Law provide for the Case of Removal, Death, Resignation, or Inability, both of the President and Vice President, declaring what Officer shall then act as President, and such Officer shall act accordingly, until the Disability be removed, or a President shall be elected.

(6) The President shall, at stated Times, receive for his Services, a Compensation, which shall neither be encreased nor diminished during the Period or which he shall have been elected, and he shall not receive within that Period any other Emolument from the United States, or any of them.

(7) Before he enter on the Execution of his Office, he shall take the following Oath or Affirmation:—"I do solemnly swear (or affirm) that I will faithfully execute the Office of President of the United States, and will to the best of my Ability, preserve, protect and defend the Constitution of the United States."

Section. 2. (1) The President shall be Commander in Chief of the Army and Navy of the United States, and of the Militia of the several States, when called into the actual Service of the United States; he may require the Opinion, in writing, of the principal Officer in each of the executive Departments, upon any Subject relating to the Duties of their respective Offices, and he shall have Power to grant Reprieves and Pardons for Offenses against the United States, except in Cases of Impeachment.

(2) He shall have Power, by and with the Advice and Consent of the Senate, to make Treaties, provided two thirds of the Senators present concur; and he shall nominate, and by and with the Advice and Consent of the Senate, shall appoint Ambassadors, other public Ministers and Consuls, Judges of the supreme Court, and all other Officers of the United States, whose Appointments are not herein otherwise provided for, and which shall be established by Law: but the Congress may by Law vest the Appointment of such inferior Officers, as they think proper, in the President alone, in the Courts of Law, or in the Heads of Departments.

(3) The President shall have Power to fill up all Vacancies that may happen during the Recess of the Senate, by granting Commissions which shall expire at the End of their next Session.

Section. 3. He shall from time to time give to the Congress Information of the State of the Union, and recommend to their Consideration such Measures as he shall judge necessary and expedient; he may, on extraordinary Occasions, convene both Houses, or either of them, and in Case of Disagreement between them, with Respect to the Time of Adjournment, he may adjourn them to such Time as he shall think proper; he shall receive Ambassadors and other public Ministers; he shall take Care that the Laws be faithfully executed, and shall Commission all the Officers of the United States.

Section. 4. The President, Vice President and all civil Officers of the United States, shall be removed from Office on Impeachment for, and Conviction of, Treason, Bribery, or other high Crimes and Misdemeanors.

ARTICLE III

Section. 1. The judicial Power of the United States, shall be vested in one supreme Court, and in such inferior Courts as the Congress may from time to time ordain and establish. The Judges, both of the supreme and inferior Courts, shall hold their Offices during good Behaviour, and shall, at stated Times, receive for their Services, a Compensation, which shall not be diminished during their Continuance in Office.

Section. 2. (1) The judicial Power shall extend to all Cases, in Law and Equity, arising under this Constitution, the Laws of the United States, and Treaties made, or which shall be made, under their Authority;—to all Cases affecting Ambassadors, other public Ministers and Consuls;—to all Cases of admiralty and maritime Jurisdiction;—to Controversies to which the United States shall be a Party;—to Controversies between two or more States;—between a State and Citizens of another State;—between citizens of different States,—between citizens of the same State claiming Lands under Grants of different States, and between a State, or the Citizens thereof, and foreign States, Citizens or Subjects.

(2) In all Cases affecting Ambassadors, other public Ministers and Consuls, and those in which a State shall be Party, the supreme Court shall have original Jurisdiction. In all the other Cases before mentioned, the supreme Court shall have appellate Jurisdiction, both as to Law and Fact, with such Exceptions, and under such Regulations as the Congress shall make.

(3) The Trial of all Crimes, except in Cases of Impeachment, shall be by Jury; and such Trial shall be held in the State where the said Crimes shall have been committed; but when not committed within any State, the Trial shall be at such Place or Places as the Congress may by Law have directed.

Section. 3. (1) Treason against the United States, shall consist only in levying War against them, or in adhering to their Enemies, giving them Aid and Comfort. No Person shall be convicted of Treason unless on the Testimony of two Witnesses to the same over Act, or on Confession in open Court.

(2) The Congress shall have Power to declare the Punishment of Treason, but no Attainder of Treason shall work Corruption of Blood, or Forfeiture except during the Life of the Person attainted.

ARTICLE IV

Section. 1. Full Faith and Credit shall be given in each State to the publict Acts, Records, and Judicial Proceedings of every other State. And the Congress may by general Laws prescribe the Manner in which such Acts, Records and Proceedings shall be proved, and the Effect thereof.

Section. 2. (1) The Citizens of each State shall be entitled to all Privileges and Immunities of Citizens in the several States.

(2) A person charged in any State with Treason, Felony, or other Crime, who shall flee from Justice, and be found in another State, shall on Demand of the executive Authority of the State from which he fled, be delivered up to be removed to the State having Jurisdiction of the Crime.

(3) No Person held to Service or Labour in one State, under the Laws thereof, escaping into another, shall, in Consequence of any Law or Regulation therein, be discharged from such Service or Labour, but shall be delivered up on Claim of the Party to whom such Service or Labour may be due.

Section. 3. (1) New States may be admitted by the Congress into this Union; but no new State shall be formed or erected within the Jurisdiction of any other State; nor any State be formed by the Junction of two or more States, or Parts of States, without the Consent of the Legislatures of the States concerned as well as of the Congress.

(2) The Congress shall have Power to dispose of and make all needful Rules and Regulations respecting the Territory or other Property belonging to the United States; and nothing in this Constitution shall be so construed as to Prejudice any Claims of the United States, or of any particular State.

Section. 4. The United States shall guarantee to every State in this Union a Republican Form of Government, and shall protect each of them against Invasion; and on Application of the Legislature, or of the Executive (when the Legislature cannot be convened) against domestic Violence.

ARTICLE V

The Congress, whenever two thirds of both Houses shall deem it necessary, shall propose Amendments to this Constitution, or, on the Application of the Legislatures of two thirds of the several States, shall call a Convention for proposing Amendments, which, in either Case, shall be valid to all Intents and Purposes, as Part of this Constitution, when ratified by the Legislatures of three fourths of the several States, or by Conventions in three fourths thereof, as the one or the other Mode of Ratification may be proposed by the Congress; Provided that no Amendment which may be made prior to the Year One thousand eight hundred and eight shall in any Manner affect the first and fourth Clauses in the Ninth Section of the first Article; and that no State, without its Consent, shall be deprived of its equal Suffrage in the Senate.

ARTICLE VI

(1) All Debts contracted and Engagements entered into, before the Adoption of this Constitution, shall be as valid against the United States under this Constitution, as under the Confederation.

(2) This Constitution, and the Laws of the United States which shall be made in Pursuance thereof; and all Treaties made, or which shall be made, under the Authority of the United States, shall be the supreme Law of the Land; and

the Judges in every State shall be bound thereby, any Thing in the Constitution or Laws of any State to the Contrary notwithstanding.

(3) The Senators and Representatives before mentioned, and the Members of the several State Legislatures, and all executive and judicial Officers, both of the United States and of the several States, shall be bound by Oath or Affirmation, to support this Constitution; but no religious Test shall ever be required as a Qualification to any Office or public Trust under the United States.

ARTICLE VII

The Ratification of the Conventions of nine States, shall be sufficient for the Establishment of this Constitution between the States so ratifying the Same.

Articles in Addition to, and Amendment of, the Constitution of the United States of America, Proposed by Congress, and Ratified by the Legislatures of the Several States Pursuant to the Fifth Article of the Original Constitution

[ARTICLE I]

Congress shall make no law respecting an establishment of religion, or prohibiting the free exercise thereof; or abridging the freedom of speech, or of the press; or the right of the people peaceably to assemble, and to petition the Government for a redress of grievances.

[ARTICLE II]

A well regulated Militia, being necessary to the security of a free State, the right of the people to keep and bear Arms, shall not be infringed.

[ARTICLE III]

No Soldier shall, in time of peace be quartered in any house, without the consent of the Owner, nor in time of war, but in a manner to be prescribed by law.

[ARTICLE IV]

The right of the people to be secure in their persons, houses, papers, and effects, against unreasonable searches and seizures, shall not be violated, and no Warrants shall issue, but upon probable cause, supported by Oath or affirmation, and particularly describing the place to be searched, and the persons or things to be seized.

[ARTICLE V]

No person shall be held to answer for a capital, or otherwise infamous crime, unless on a presentment or indictment of a Grand Jury, except in cases arising in the land or naval forces, or in the Militia, when in actual service in time of War or public danger; nor shall any person be subject for the same offense to be twice put in jeopardy of life or limb; nor shall be compelled in any Criminal Case to be a witness against himself, nor be deprived of life, liberty, or property, without due process of law; nor shall private property be taken for public use, without just compensation.

[ARTICLE VI]

In all criminal prosecutions, the accused shall enjoy the right to a speedy and public trial, by an impartial jury of the State and district wherein the crime shall have been committed, which district shall have been previously ascertained by law, and to be informed of the nature and cause of the accusation; to be confronted with the witnesses against him; to have compulsory process for obtaining Witnesses in his favor, and to have the Assistance of Counsel for his defence.

[ARTICLE VII]

In suits at common law, where the value in controversy shall exceed twenty dollars, the right of trial by jury shall be preserved, and no fact tried by a jury shall be otherwise reexamined in any Court of the United States, than according to the rules of the common law.

[ARTICLE VIII]

Excessive bail shall not be required, nor excessive fines imposed, nor cruel and unusual punishments inflicted.

[ARTICLE IX]

The enumeration in the Constitution, of certain rights, shall not be construed to deny or disparage others retained by the people.

[ARTICLE X]

The powers not delegated to the United States by the Constitution, nor prohibited by it to the States, are reserved to the States respectively, or to the people.

[ARTICLE XI]

The Judicial power of the United States shall not be construed to extend to any suit in law or equity, commenced or prosecuted against one of the United States by Citizens of another State or by Citizens or Subjects of any Foreign State.

[ARTICLE XII]

The Electors shall meet in their respective states, and vote by ballot for President and Vice-President, one of whom, at least, shall not be an inhabitant of the same state with themselves; they shall name in their ballots the person voted for as President, and in distinct ballots the person voted for as Vice-President, and they shall make distinct lists of all persons voted for as President, and of all persons voted for as Vice-President, and of the number of votes for each, which lists they shall sign and certify, and transmit sealed to the seat of the government of the United States, directed to the President of the Senate;— The President of the Senate shall, in the presence of the Senate and House of Representatives, open all the certificates and the votes shall then be counted;— The person having the greatest number of votes for President, shall be the President, if such number be a majority of the whole number of Electors appointed; and if no person have such majority, then from the persons having the highest numbers not exceeding three on the list of those voted for as President, the House of Representatives shall choose immediately, by ballot, the President. But in choosing the President, the votes shall be taken by states, the representation from each state having one vote; a quorum for this purpose shall consist of a member or members from two-thirds of the states, and a majority of all the states shall be necessary to a choice. And if the House of Representatives shall not choose a President whenever the right of choice shall devolve upon them, before the fourth day of March next following, then the Vice-President shall act as President, as in the case of the death or other constitutional disability of the President. The person having the greatest number of votes as Vice-President, shall be the Vice-President, if such number be a majority of the whole number of Electors appointed, and if no person have a majority, then from the two highest numbers on the list, the Senate shall choose the Vice-President; a quorum for the purpose shall consist of two-thirds of the whole number of Senators, and a majority of the whole number shall be necessary for a choice. But no person constitutionally ineligible to the office of President shall be eligible to that of Vice-President of the United States.

[ARTICLE XIII]

Section 1. Neither slavery nor involuntary servitude, except as a punishment for crime whereof the party shall have been duly convicted, shall exist within the United States, or any place subject to their jurisdiction.

Section 2. Congress shall have power to enforce this article by appropriate legislation.

[ARTICLE XIV]

Section 1. All persons born or naturalized in the United States, and subject to the jurisdiction thereof, are citizens of the United States and of the State wherein they reside. No State shall make or enforce any law which shall abridge the privileges or immunities of citizens of the United States; nor shall any State deprive any person of life, liberty, or property, without due process of law; nor deny to any person within its jurisdiction the equal protection of the laws.

Section 2. Representatives shall be apportioned among the several States according to their respective numbers, counting the whole number of persons in each State, excluding Indians not taxed. But when the right to vote at any election for the choice of electors for President and Vice President of the United States, Representatives in Congress, the Executive and Judicial officers of a State, or the members of the Legislature thereof, is denied to any of the male inhabitants of such State, being twenty-one years of age, and citizens of the United States, or in any way abridged, except for participation in rebellion, or other crime, the basis of representation therein shall be reduced in the proportion which the number of such male citizens shall bear to the whole number of male citizens twenty-one years of age in such State.

Section 3. No person shall be a Senator or Representative in Congress, or elector of President and Vice President, or hold any office, civil or military, under the United States, or under any State, who, having previously taken an oath, as a member of Congress, or as an officer of the United States, or as a member of any State legislature, or as an executive or judicial officer of any State, to support the Constitution of the United States, shall have engaged in insurrection or rebellion against the same, or given aid or comfort to the enemies thereof, But Congress may by a vote of two-thirds of each House, remove such disability.

Section 4. The validity of the public debt of the United States, authorized by law, including debts incurred for payment of pensions and bounties for services in suppressing insurrection or rebellion, shall not be questioned. But neither the United States nor any State shall assume or pay any debt or obligation incurred in aid of insurrection or rebellion against the United States, or any claim for the loss or emancipation of any slave; but all such debts, obligations and claims shall be held illegal and void.

Section 5. The Congress shall have power to enforce, by appropriate legislation, the provisions of this article.

[ARTICLE XV]

Section 1. The right of citizens of the United States to vote shall not be denied or abridged by the United States or by any State on account of race, color, or previous condition of servitude.

Section 2. The Congress shall have power to enforce this article by appropriate legislation.

[ARTICLE XVI]

The Congress shall have power to lay and collect taxes on incomes, from whatever source derived, without apportionment among the several states, and without regard to any census or enumeration.

[ARTICLE XVII]

The Senate of the United States shall be composed of two Senators from each state, elected by the people thereof, for six years; and each Senator shall have one vote. The electors in each state shall have the qualifications requisite for electors of the most numerous branch of the state legislatures.

When vacancies happen in the representation of any state in the Senate, the executive authority of such state shall issue writs of election to fill such vacancies: Provided, that the legislature of any state may empower the executive thereof to make temporary appointment until the people fill the vacancies by election as the legislature may direct.

This amendment shall not be so construed as to affect the election or term of any Senator chosen before it becomes valid as part of the Constitution.

[ARTICLE XVIII]

Section 1. After one year from the ratification of this article the manufacture, sale, or transportation of intoxicating liquors within, the importation thereof into, or the exportation thereof from the United States and all territory subject to the jurisdiction thereof for beverage purposes is hereby prohibited.

Section 2. The Congress and the several States shall have concurrent power to enforce this article by appropriate legislation.

Section 3. This article shall be inoperative unless it shall have been ratified as an amendment to the Constitution by the legislatures of the several States, as provided in the Constitution, within seven years from the date of the submission hereof to the States by the Congress.

[ARTICLE XIX]

The right of citizens of the United States to vote shall not be denied or abridged by the United States or by any State on account of sex.

Congress shall have power to enforce this article by appropriate legislation.

[AMENDMENT XX]

Section 1. The terms of the President and Vice President shall end at noon on the 20th day of January, and the terms of Senators and Representatives at noon on the 3d day of January, of the years in which such terms would have ended if this article had not been ratified; and the terms of their successors shall then begin.

Section 2. The Congress shall assemble at least once in every year, and such meeting shall begin at noon on the 3d day of January, unless they shall be law appoint a different day.

Section 3. If, at the time fixed for the beginning of the term of the President, the President elect shall have died, the Vice President elect shall become President. If a President shall not have been chosen before the time fixed for the beginning of his term, or if the President elect shall have failed to qualify, then the Vice President elect shall act as President until a President shall have qualified; and the Congress may by law provide for the case wherein neither a

President elect nor a Vice President elect shall have qualified, declaring who shall then act as President, or the manner in which one who is to act shall be selected, and such person shall act accordingly until a President or Vice President shall have qualified.

Section 4. The Congress may by law provide for the case of the death of any of the persons from whom the House of Representatives may choose a President whenever the right of choice shall have devolved upon them, and for the case of the death of any of the persons from whom the Senate may choose a Vice President whenever the right of choice shall have devolved upon them.

Section 5. Sections 1 and 2 shall take effect on the 15th day of October following the ratification of this article.

Section 6. This article shall be inoperative unless it shall have been ratified as an amendment to the Constitution by the legislatures of three-fourths of the several States within seven years from the date of its submission.

[AMENDMENT XXI]

Section 1. The eighteenth article of amendment to the Constitution of the United States is hereby repealed.

Section 2. The transportation or importation into any State, Territory, or possession of the United States for delivery or use therein of intoxicating liquors, in violation of the laws thereof, is hereby prohibited.

Section 3. This article shall be inoperative unless it shall have been ratified as an amendment to the Constitution by conventions in the several States, as provided in the Constitution, within seven years from the date of the submission hereof to the States by the Congress.

[AMENDMENT XXII]

Section 1. No person shall be elected to the office of the President more than twice, and no person who has held the office of President, or acted as President, for more than two years of a term to which some other person was elected President shall be elected to the office of the President more than once. But this Article shall not apply to any person holding the office of President when this Article was proposed by the Congress, and shall not prevent any person who may be holding the office of President, or acting as President, during the term within which this Article becomes operative from holding the office of President, or acting as President during the remainder of such term.

Section 2. This article shall be inoperative unless it shall have been ratified as an amendment to the Constitution by the legislatures of three-fourths of the several States within seven years from the date of its submission to the States by the Congress

[AMENDMENT XXIII]

Section 1. The District constituting the seat of Government of the United States shall appoint in such manner as the Congress may direct:

A number of electors of President and Vice President equal to the whole number of Senators and Representatives in Congress to which the District would be entitled if it were a State, but in no event more than the least populous State; they shall be in addition to those appointed by the States, but they shall be considered, for the purposes of the election of President and Vice President, to be electors appointed by a State; and they shall meet in the District and perform such duties as provided by the twelfth article of amendment.

Section 2. The Congress shall have power to enforce this article by appropriate legislation.

[AMENDMENT XXIV]

Section 1. The right of citizens of the United States to vote in any primary or other election for President or Vice President, for electors for President or Vice President, or for Senator or Representative in Congress, shall not be denied or abridged by the United States or any State by reason of failure to pay any poll tax or other tax.

Section 2. The Congress shall have power to enforce this article by appropriate legislation.

[AMENDMENT XXV]

Section 1. In case of the removal of the President from office or of his death or resignation, the Vice President shall become President.

Section 2. Whenever there is a vacancy in the office of the Vice President, the President shall nominate a Vice President who shall take office upon confirmation by a majority vote of both Houses of Congress.

Section 3. Whenever the President transmits to the President pro tempore of the Senate and the Speaker of the House of Representatives his written declaration that he is unable to discharge the powers and duties of his office, and until he transmits to them a written declaration to the contrary, such powers and duties shall be discharged by the Vice President as Acting President.

Section 4. Whenever the Vice President and a majority of either the principal officers of the executive departments or of such other body as Congress may by law provide, transmit to the President pro tempore of the Senate and the Speaker of the House of Representatives their written declaration that the President is unable to discharge the powers and duties of his office, the Vice President shall immediately assume the powers and duties of the office as Acting President.

Thereafter, when the President transmits to the President pro tempore of the Senate and the Speaker of the House of Representatives his written declaration that no inability exists, he shall resume the powers and duties of his office unless the Vice President and a majority of either the principal officers of the executive department or of such other body as Congress may by law provide, transmit within four days to the President pro tempore of the Senate and the Speaker of the House of Representatives their written declaration that the President is unable to discharge the powers and duties of his office. Thereupon Congress shall decide the issue, assembling within forty-eight hours for that purpose if not in session. If the Congress, within twenty-one days after receipt of the latter written declaration, or, if Congress is not in session, within twenty-one days after Congress is required to assemble, determines by two-thirds vote of both Houses that the President is unable to discharge the powers and duties of his office, the Vice President shall continue to discharge the same as Acting President; otherwise, the President shall resume the powers and duties of his office.

[AMENDMENT XXVI]

Section 1. The right of citizens of the United States, who are eighteen years of age or older, to vote shall not be denied or abridged by the United States or by any State on account of age.

Section 2. The Congress shall have power to enforce this article by appropriate legislation.

Proposed Amendment
[Equal Rights For Men and Women]

ARTICLE—

Section 1. Equality of rights under the law shall not be denied or abridged by the United States or by any State on account of sex.

Section 2. The Congress shall have the power to enforce, by appropriate legislation, the provisions of this article.

Section 3. This amendment shall take effect two years after the date of ratification.

SUBJECT INDEX

A

Administration: details of, 297–298; expert, 298; flexibility of, 298–299; localized, 299. *See also* Rule-making authority

Administrative action: discrimination by, 72–73; publicity and, 312–313; review of. *See* Review of administrative action

Administrative agencies, powers of new constitution exercised by, 3

Administrative determination, enforcement of, 354–357

Administrative discretion, and enforcement, 388–391

Administrative evidence, 348–350; weight of, 350–354

Administrative functions, decentralization of, 295

Administrative investigation: Antitrust Civil Process Act, 322; compliance with court order, 325–327; constitutional limitations on, 327–329; for enforcement, 325–327; federal agencies empowered to procure documents, 320; grant of authority, 323–325; inspection of premises, 327–328; power to investigate, 316–322; production of papers, 320–322, 328–329; for rule making, 323–325; subpoena power, 317–320

Administrative law, 294

Administrative procedure: abolition of railroad grade crossings, 334–335; absence of jury trial, 343–346; administrator as judge, 341–343; basis for decision, 347–348; delegation of judicial power, 333; nature of hearing, 340–348; necessity of notice and hearing, 333–337; pattern of, 331–333; railroad rate determination, 335–337; and rent control, 338–339; time for hearing, 338–339

Administrative Procedure Act, and rule making, 300–301

Administrator, 295; cooperation with producers, 311–312; creating without prescribing policy, 309–310; discretion of, 364–372; federal, 349–350; as judge, 341–343; legislative power of, 295–296; technology and authority of, 296

Advertising, and state regulation, 128–129

Aftermarket, 171–173

Agricultural Adjustment Act of 1933, 210

Agricultural Adjustment Act of 1938, 211–214, 217

Agricultural Marketing Agreement Act of 1937, 227, 311

Agriculture, power to regulate, 209

Aliens, protection from discrimination, 86–89

Alimony, and protection from sex discrimination, 92–94

Amendment of the Constitution, 26–27; by judicial interpretation, 27–28

Antitrust Civil Process Act, 322

Antitrust Improvement Act of 1976, 147, 175n

Antitrust regulation: Antitrust Improvement Act of 1976, 147; area of application of, 148–155; Capper-Volstead Act, 161; Clayton Act of 1914, 147, 163–164; conspiracy to monopolize local markets, 152–155; corporate ownership of property, 167–175; cross licensing, 186–188; dissolution of holding companies, 173–175; exceptions to, 164–165; franchise restrictions, 188–190; horizontal market allocation, 190–193; labor unions and, 162–164; mergers, 175–181; Newspaper Preservation Act of 1970, 161; Norris-LaGuardia Act, 163–164; patents, 186–188; *per se* violation, 160; and price fixing, 193; production, 150–152; and purchase by customer of stock of supplier, 168–170; and purchase by customer of supplier's assets, 170–173; and rule of reason, 155–160; Sherman Antitrust Act, 146–147; statutory and judicial exemptions to, 161–164; stock and director control, 185–186; transportation, 148–149; tying contracts, 183–185; tying of unrelated enterprises, 184–185; Webb-Pomerene Act of 1918, 161

Appellate review, limitations on, 391

Article V, 26–27

Articles of Confederation, 5

Atomic Energy Control Act of 1946, 285

B

Bank, national, incorporation of, 24–25

Basing-point pricing system, 200–201

Bedrock view of Constitution, 21, 22–24

Bigness, and regulation of enterprise structure, 167

Bill of Rights, 62–63, 75–76

Bonds: federal gold, devaluation of, 240–241; private gold, devaluation of, 246–248; state, 51–53

Borrowing power, 239–241

Business, regulation of, 4: comparison of national, state, and local, 13–14; police power, 7

C

Capper-Volstead Act, 161

Child-labor-made goods, embargo on, 116–118

Civil Aeronautics Board, 294

69–71; due process as guarantee of, 43–44; guarantee by law, 62–63; improper classification, 66–71; moral standards and culture patterns, 66–69; tax law exemption, 64; traffic regulation exemption, 65–66

Equal protection clause, 63, 79–80, 90–91; and First Amendment, 69–71

Evidence, administrative, 348–350

Exports: crop standard maintenance, 141–143; state barriers, 141–143

F

Fair Labor Standards Act, 118–120

Farm products: regulation of marketing, 214–215; regulation of price, 214–215; standards of, 214–215

Federal Administrative Procedure Act, 349–350, 361–362, 365

Federal Aeronautics Act (FAA), 9–11

Federal Agricultural Adjustment Act, 130

Federal Aviation Act of 1958, 9–11

Federal Communications Act of 1934, 128, 296

Federal Communications Commission, 129, 294

Federal Fair Labor Standards Act, 226

Federal Food Stamp Act, 66

Federal Labor Management Relations Act of 1947, 114

Federal law, as contrasted to state law, 9

Federal Maritime Commission, 294

Federal Narcotics Act, 238–239

Federal power: over production, 114–115; as prohibiting state regulation, 123–126; and state monopoly of navigation, 124; supremacy in foreign affairs, 253–255

Federal Power Commission, 227, 294

Federal preemption: economic matters, 11–13; physical matters, 9–11; of state powers, 8

Federal Register, 313

Federal Register Act, 313

Federal regulation: antitrust. *See* Antitrust regulation; supremacy of, 125–126

Federal Rent Control Act, 252–253

Federal Social Security Act, 64, 233–234, 242–243

Federal supremacy, over state powers, 7–8

Federal Trade Commission, 294, 312, 320, 325–327

Federal Trade Commission Act, 320

Fifth Amendment, 63

First Amendment, and equal protection clause, 69–71

Foreign affairs power, 253–255

Fourteenth Amendment, 63, 71–72

Franchise restrictions, 188–190

Freedom of contract, due process as guarantee of, 37–40

G

Gold bonds: federal, devaluation of, 240–241; private, devaluation of, 246–248

Government: increase of powers of, 3; strong, as result of new constitution, 2

Government ownership of business: acquisition of existing enterprise, 285–288; background, 274–276; constitutionality of, 278–283; intergovernmental relations, 288–291

H

Hamilton, Alexander, 251

Hearing, in administrative procedure, 338–348

Hearsay statements, weight of in administrative hearing, 350–354

Holding companies, dissolution of, 173–175, 307–308, 386–388

Horizontal market allocation, 190–193

Horizontal or vertical integration, 175

Horizontal price fixing, 200

Human rights: marriage, 78–80; as protected by new constitution, 3; protection from sex discrimination, 91–94; protection from wealth and poverty discrimination, 89–91; protection of, 75–78; protection of parental control, 83–86; protection of privacy, 78–83; protection of stranger from discrimination, 83–86; zoning, 80–83

Human rights-property rights classification, erosion of, 94–96

I

Imports: local price control of, 136–138; reciprocity requirement, 138–141; state barriers, 138–141

Inalienable right, 75

Individual right, guarantees of, 30–31

Intergovernmental relations, 288–291

Interstate commerce, 101, 227–228; code of competition for bituminous coal industry, 106–107; code of competition for industry, 104–106; crossing a state line, 103–107; embargo on child-labor-made goods, 116–118; Fair Labor Standards Act, 118–120; manufacturing, 103–104; power to prohibit, 115–120; state regulation as burden on, 129–134

Interstate Commerce Act, 310, 323–325

Interstate Commerce Commission, 226, 294, 309–310, 323–325

Investigation, administrative. *See* Administrative investigation